"I thought I had never seen so flat and muddy a place:
no trees, no hills, no boundaries of any kind.
This lack of boundaries, physical and mental . . .
opened up a whole new world for me."

—ISABEL BEVIER

visiting the University of Illinois in 1900

NO

URBANA AND CHICAGO

BOUNDARIES

UNIVERSITY

OF ILLINOIS

VIGNETTES

Edited by Lillian Hoddeson

PREFACE BY RICHARD H. HERMAN

UNIVERSITY OF ILLINOIS PRESS

Library of Congress Cataloging-in-Publication Data

No boundaries : University of Illinois vignettes /
edited by Lillian Hoddeson.
p.   cm.
Includes bibliographical references and index.
ISBN 0-252-02957-7 (cloth : alk. paper)
ISBN 0-252-07203-0 (pbk. : alk. paper)
1. University of Illinois at Urbana-Champaign.
I. Hoddeson, Lillian.
LD2381.N6   2004
378.773'66—dc22   2003026803

CONTENTS

PREFACE

Richard H. Herman

In American higher education, the University of Illinois at Urbana-Champaign has for a long time been one of the institutions that everybody knows something about. Illinois is widely recognized as a place of excellence, innovation, and tradition. It played a central role in defining the public research university throughout the twentieth century, and developments at Illinois were attracting a lot of attention as the twenty-first century drew near. This is why, when I was approached about the possibility of becoming provost at Illinois, I listened carefully and with great interest. The more I learned, the more excited and honored I became at the chance to become a part of so distinguished an institution.

When I arrived on campus in 1998, I brought with me a newcomer's curiosity to learn all that I could about the university. It did not take me long to figure out that there was an ethos here that was different from that of other public universities with which I was familiar. Over time, I naturally heard lots of stories about notable faculty members, past and present. The stories were sometimes funny, sometimes moving, sometimes amazing, and always humbling. I began to notice some common threads interwoven among these stories, connecting the past to the present, threads that helped me begin to understand how Illinois was able to rise to such heights.

The story of this institution is, in fact, the story of the remarkable people who fashioned it across the generations, across so many fields of learning, and who continue to remake it in new ways. It is a story worth telling, and that's why I asked Lillian Hoddeson to undertake this project. Professor Hoddeson had recently coauthored a brilliant study of the life of John Bardeen, one of Illinois's most renowned scientists in recent years, and she seemed ideally suited to the task. She agreed that the project was worthwhile, not only as a social and intellectual history of one institution told through the experiences and achievements of a few faculty members but also, and more important, as a way of revealing how knowledge is produced and how great public universities come to be. I am indebted to her and to the authors she recruited to the task of producing a unique work.

This volume is not a history of the University of Illinois, although it presents something of the university's history. Nor is it a paean to all of the exceptional faculty who have been drawn to Illinois, although in its pages you will meet a number of these faculty members. Instead, this volume tells three different stories that blur together.

The essays in this volume tell the stories of remarkable individuals, all of whom came to play leading roles in their fields and make contributions of lasting importance. Reading them, we learn about the many motivations that drive such people, about what led them to make their careers at Illinois, about the challenges they faced, and about what they accomplished. Some of these people are well known; others, less so. They exemplify, in different ways, the rare joining of determination, ability, commitment to excellence, and, sometimes, genius that marks the academy at its best. In reading about the twenty-one people profiled here, one cannot fail to notice how, at its highest levels, excellence attracts excellence. Again and again, you will meet people of extraordinary ability, students and faculty, who came to Illinois for the chance to work with colleagues who were themselves extraordinary.

Inescapably, these essays also tell the story of how a great university comes to be. The story is appropriately and best told in personal terms, for a university is a magnificently human institution. One of the qualities that marks the people described in the essays is vision. From presidents of the university to deans to builders of departments to exceptional faculty members—the real story of the university is found in how these visions overlap each other, complement each other, and sometimes collide with each other to shape an institution. You may also be struck, as I was, by how often and in how many different ways this institution was willing to take risks at critical junctures—investing in new ideas, new directions, new fields whose promise was by no means certain. This courage and willingness to support innovation emerges through the stories as a fundamental characteristic of the institution, one that I hope continues in the present day.

Finally, taken together, these individual stories show how in every generation a uniquely American idea—the land-grant, public university—has provided the compass for guiding Illinois. From its beginnings in the Civil War era through the high aspirations built in the early twentieth century to its rise to prominence in the postwar era, the university has been shaped in profound ways by the land-grant commitments: to offer the very best education to each generation, to engage the most vexing problems of the day, to uplift the possibilities of the future, and to be a vital part of the society it serves. There is a nobility of purpose here and a legacy to be preserved and built upon. It is a privilege to be a part of such an undertaking.

> I take it first of all, then, that this institution is to be and to become in an ever truer sense, a university. . . . [This] has been settled by the ever-increasing purpose of the great mass of the people of this State, the plain people of the farm and the mill, of the country, the village and the city to build here a monument which will be to them and their children an honor and a glory forever, an evidence which all the world can see and understand of their corporate appreciation of the things of the spirit.
>
> Edmund Janes James
> Inaugural address as president
> of the University of Illinois
> October 1905

ACKNOWLEDGMENTS

I would like to express heartfelt thanks to Melissa Rohde for her many hours of thoughtful work preparing the manuscript of this book for publication. I am also grateful for the imaginative and useful suggestions offered by members of the advisory committee appointed by Richard Herman to oversee this project: Nina Baym, Maynard Brichford, Richard Burkhardt, Laura Greene, Edwin Goldwasser, William Greenough, Tina Gunsalus, Masumi Iriye, William Maher, and Winton Solberg.

Lillian Hoddeson

LILLIAN HODDESON

Work, Place, and Workplaces at the University of Illinois

This is a book about people whose work shaped, and was shaped by, the University of Illinois. Written by scholars in different fields, the stories range over twenty disciplines and extend over the entire history of the university since its inception in 1867. They illustrate the power of Thomas Jefferson's notion of the American public university, and how one outstanding public university achieved greatness.

Unfortunately, much relevant material could not be included. To keep the volume to manageable proportions, its coverage had to be restricted to individuals who are no longer living.[1] A fuller account of the early years of the university can be found in Winton S. Solberg's history of the University of Illinois from 1867 to 1904.[2]

This book is also a kind of environmental history in that it deals with the role of "place" in a university's production of knowledge, culture, and well-educated people. The term *place* is used here in its broadest possible sense, to refer to social and cultural contexts as well as to geographical ones. Place also includes community and connections with other places, for the prominence of the work done in a place derives from its ability to propagate and influence people and institutions beyond its borders.

Again and again, these vignettes highlight encounters between people, or between people and nonhuman actors (for instance, materials, technologies). These encounters infused the life of the university with meanings that have come to express the identity of the place—its intangible "spirit," or *genius loci*.[3]

In a number of the stories, geography or climate is prominently featured. For example, Illinois rivers, lakes, and prairie were important in the ecological work of Stephen A. Forbes and in the landscape architecture of Florence Bell Robinson and Stanley Hart White. Climate was crucial to the architectural design work of Nathan M. Clifford Ricker, the civil engineering of Nathan M. Newmark, and the home economics of Isabel Bevier.

Community plays an important role in every story. Julian Simon moved from the Department of Advertising to Business Administration and Economics to gain support for his controversial ideas about economics, and eventually population economics. John Bardeen came to the University of Illinois to find physics colleagues eager for him to work on superconductivity. The photosynthesis research of Robert Emerson and Eugene Rabinowitch relied on the collaboration and collegiality they established in their shared laboratory. The Illinois art community joined in celebration at the contemporary art festivals held at the University of Illinois through the middle of the twentieth century. And William Warfield was attracted to the supportive environment he experienced in the university's voice department; he then devoted himself to cultivating that context to nurture voice students.

The role of connection between different fields, and between the university and distant fields, is illustrated in many of the chapters. Lejaren Hiller's work bridged musical composition, computer science, and chemistry; Robert C. Zuppke's football coaching brought performance and psychology to sports. Connections to distant fields were crucial in the literary studies of Stuart Pratt Sherman and J. Kerker Quinn, in Oscar Lewis's studies of poverty in Mexico, in Nathan M. Newmark's consulting on the design of the Latino-American Tower in Mexico City, and in Ralph Early Grim's geological consulting work in Africa. Grim coordinated a sizable brick-manufacturing industry from his base in the Department of Geology, with samples flown to Urbana from Africa for testing in his laboratory. Charles Osgood's study of semantic differentials relied on research in Finland, Japan, Croatia, Thailand, and other countries. Political connection was central to the work of chemist Roger Adams, who forged links between science at the University of Illinois and policy in a variety of national and international spheres. In the development of digital computers, connections were crucial between researchers at Illinois and scientists (for example, John von Neumann) at other institutions.

The university's library allowed scholars to reach distant intellectual fields. Katharine L. Sharp and subsequent university librarians worked to build a strong library. Then, in precious library collections, classicist William Abbott Oldfather made contact with ancient civilizations. In rare special collections, the historian James G. Randall accessed little known details about the Civil War and the career of Abraham Lincoln.

While the chapters of this book work together to speak to the larger theme of place and the production of knowledge and culture at a particular public university, each chapter was written to stand alone. As a collection the essays suggest the variety of ways that place can influence a university's production of knowledge, culture, and educated people. One powerful way to model the complex relationships involved is by studying the networks through which materials entering the university are transformed by its faculty, staff, and students, before passing out again beyond the university's boundaries. William Cronon's book, *Nature's Metropolis: Chicago and the Great West*, illustrates this approach. As Cronon explains, the city of Chicago, centrally located between East Coast centers and the American West, became a great city, because of its ability to process goods that flowed through the city's factories, warehouses, and other institutions. Tangible goods, such as grain, lumber, and meat, as well as intangible goods, like ideas, images, and information, even propaganda, were transformed as they passed through, before being shipped out.[4]

Just as the people of Chicago transformed goods they directed through the city, the people of the University of Illinois re-formed materials, knowledge, and students that passed through its laboratories, offices, and classrooms, producing new cultural products. For example, J. Kerker Quinn gathered literary essays into a magazine, *Accent*, that influenced a generation of intellectuals. Robert C. Zuppke turned student football players into competitive athletes. Lejaren Hiller transformed computers into music composition machines. Such actions were influenced by community relationships, political environments, and the many connections between the university and other institutions that complicated the encounters featured in the chapters that follow.[5]

The chapters are arranged in four parts, roughly chronologically. The first part, *The University Place*, focuses on two backbones of the university—its buildings and its library. Paul Kruty's opening chapter about

Nathan Clifford Ricker tells of the establishment of the university's school of architecture and of Ricker's designs for several early buildings (including Altgeld Hall, the Natural History Building, Harker Hall, and the Mechanical Engineering Building). Donald Krummel's treatment in chapter 2 of the establishment of the university's world-class library focuses on the pioneering work of librarian Katharine L. Sharp, who founded the library school in 1897, and her successors, Phineas L. Windsor and Robert B. Downs, who built up its collections and brought national prominence to the university's library.

Part II, *Academics and Athletics*, deals with the inception of academic programs and of the athletic program devoted to football. Paula A. Treichler's chapter 3 on Isabel Bevier tells how this remarkable woman promoted the cause of higher education for women while she boldly reconceptualized the traditional woman's field of home economics as a scientific field. In chapter 4, Richard W. Burkhardt Jr. and Daniel W. Schneider tell how Stephen A. Forbes drew on his Illinois surroundings to found ecology, a new field concerned not only with scientific knowledge but with social issues such as conservation and pollution. Winton U. Solberg tells in chapter 5 how William Abbott Oldfather made the classics relevant to the lives of his students. In chapter 6, Bruce Michelson addresses the questions of how and why Stuart Pratt Sherman and J. Kerker Quinn were able, in their different periods, to transplant East Coast literary criticism and journalism to the midwestern prairie. Chapter 7, by Robert W. Johannsen, tells how some of the university's early historians, including Evarts B. Green and especially James G. Randall, drew on the Civil War and the career of Abraham Lincoln to bring the university's program in history to national prominence.

The local landscape of Illinois figures in chapter 8, by Natalie Alpert (edited by Dianne Harris) and Gary Kesler, who recount how Florence Bell Robinson and Stanley Hart White established the research and teaching programs of the university's leading Department of Landscape Architecture. Forging political connections between the scientific research at the University of Illinois and science policy on the state and world levels is a central thesis of Ronald E. Doel's chapter 9 about the policy work of chemist Roger Adams and of Adams's graduate student Wallace Brode. In chapter 10, William J. Hall tells how Nathan M. Newmark, an expert in the impact of shock on structures, developed at Illinois a world-class civil engineering program of international reach. We change gears in chapter 11 and look at the emergence of football at the University of Illinois; Maynard Brichford tells how Robert C. Zuppke succeeded in creating a leading team by approaching college football coaching as a performing art.

Part III, *The Postwar Rise to Prominence*, carries the story of the University of Illinois forward into the period following World War II, when numerous departments and institutes in the fields of science, engineering, business, and the social sciences achieved international stature and the University of Illinois assumed its place among the great American institutions of higher learning. Community, connection, and physical place are, again, common themes in this part of the book. Chapter 12, by Govindjee, illustrates the power of collaboration and a supportive community in scientific work in telling of the pioneering work of Robert Emerson and Eugene Rabinowitch on photosynthesis. In chapter 13, Susan M. Rigdon discusses the painstaking anthropological studies of poverty conducted by Oscar Lewis (often with his wife Ruth Maslow Lewis) in various communities in Mexico, Spain, India, Puerto Rico, Cuba, and elsewhere. In chapter 14, William F. Brewer tells of the enormous impact of Charles Osgood, not only in the field of psychology, in which he made leading contributions to the psychology of meaning and linguistics, but through his talent for building new interdisciplinary units on campus, including the Institute of Communications Research.

In chapter 15, Sylvian R. Ray explains how and why the University of Illinois was home to several pioneering digital computers in the ILLIAC family. In recounting, in chapter 16, how John Bardeen came to his two Nobel Prize winning achievements in physics, I call attention to aspects of the settings that supported (or did not support) these works. In chapter 17, Rita J. Simon draws on her late husband Julian Simon's writings to lay out the odyssey of his search for a context that would support his unconventional studies of population economics. In the final chapter of this section, 18, Albert V. Carozzi recalls the adventures in Africa that he shared with clay mineralogist Ralph Early Grim during their geological consulting in the Ivory Coast, adding to our emerging story of the connectedness and influence of the University of Illinois on distant fields.

Part IV, *Fine Arts*, opens with James Bohn's chapter 19 on Lejaren Hiller, who broke new ground by employing the university's unique resources in digital computing to devise a revolutionary way of composing music. In chapter 20, Muriel Scheinman tells how the university helped bring the visual arts of central Illinois to worldwide attention by transforming a collection of individual pieces of art into a series of exciting contemporary art festivals in the 1950s, 1960s and 1970s. The closing chapter, by Ollie Watts Davis, explains how and why William Warfield, internationally known for his memorable role in *Porgy and Bess* and for singing "Ol' Man River" in *Showboat*, shaped the university's voice program into a home that nurtured students of every race and creed, and helped some of them become leading artistic performers.

While these chapters are primarily intended as interesting reading about important work done at the University of Illinois, the collection can help us begin to understand how a great university—or any place—influences the cultural creations it engenders.

ACKNOWLEDGMENT

I am grateful to Everett J. Carter who, as a research assistant in 2001, contributed his careful research and important insights on "place" to this introductory essay.

NOTES

1. The decisions about whose stories to include in this volume were guided by an advisory committee composed of Nina Baym, Maynard Brichford, Richard Burkhardt, Laura Greene, Edwin Goldwasser, William Greenough, Tina Gunsalus, Richard Herman (ex officio), Lillian Hoddeson, Masumi Iriye, William Maher, and Winton Solberg.
2. Winton U. Solberg, *The University of Illinois, 1867–1894: An Intellectual and Cultural History* (Urbana: University of Illinois Press, 1968), and *The University of Illinois, 1894–1904: The Shaping of the University* (Urbana: University of Illinois Press, 2000).
3. William E. Leuchtenburg, *American Places: Encounters with History* (Oxford: Oxford University Press, 2000), see especially, xvii. There exists an extensive interdisciplinary literature about place. A few examples include Marc Verhoeven, *An Archaeological Ethnography of a Neolithic Community: Space, Place and Social Relations in the Burnt Village at Tell Sabi Abyad, Syria* (Istanbul: Nederlands Historisch-Archaeologisch Instituut, 1999); Frances Downing, *Remembrance and the Design of Place* (College Station: Texas A&M University Press, 2000); Leonard Lutwack, *The Role of Place in Literature* (Syracuse: Syracuse University Press, 1984); Michel Foucault, "Of Other Spaces," *Diacritics* (Spring 1986): 22–27; and Michael Keith and Steven Pike, eds., *Place and the Politics of Identity* (London: Routledge, 1993).
4. William Cronon, *Nature's Metropolis: Chicago and the Great West,* (New York: W.W. Norton, 1991).
5. One example of such an attempt is Adi Ophir and Steven Shapin, "The Place of Knowledge: A Methodological Survey," Science in Context 4, no. 1 (1991): 3–21.

PART I

THE
UNIVERSITY
PLACE

PAUL KRUTY

CHAPTER 1

Nathan Clifford Ricker:

Establishing Architecture at

the University of Illinois

In 1922, when Dr. Nathan Clifford Ricker was feted with a convocation in his honor, he could look back on almost fifty years of service to the University of Illinois. He taught there from 1872 until 1917, chairing the Department of Architecture between 1873 and 1910 and serving as dean of the College of Engineering from 1878 to 1905. Not only did he create a department and a curriculum that influenced generations of American architects, but he shaped the physical form of the university in its first half century, as did no other single person.

Not until early in 1867 did Ricker travel west to Illinois, from New England, to visit an uncle who lived in La Harpe, in Hancock County, near the Mississippi River at Nauvoo. Ricker had been born in 1843 on a farm near Acton, a tiny community in Maine on the New Hampshire border. In 1856 the family moved to nearby Springvale, where Clifford's father built a mill in which the young man worked long hours. But the ambitious youngster longed for a liberal education. Supplementing his local schooling with a self-appointed regimen in mathematics and Latin, he was by his eighteenth

3

birthday in a position to replace a country schoolteacher and, with his supplemental income, buy more textbooks in the sciences and humanities. When he turned twenty-one, Ricker took a job making piano cases, apparently reveling in the application of practical skill while he continued along his personal path of learning. In 1867, after joining his uncle at La Harpe, Ricker took up making wagons in a blacksmith's shop in which he bought a half interest.

The events that brought Ricker to study architecture in America's heartland have attained a kind of legendary status at Illinois. They began late in 1869, when Ricker encountered a student of the new Illinois Industrial University, which had recently been established in Urbana. When the student extolled his first semester's experience, Ricker decided that this serendipitous event signaled his own professional calling. The transplanted Yankee sold his business for $750 and set off across the state of Illinois for Champaign County. He arrived there on January 2, 1870, during the semester break of the second season of instruction at the fledgling university.

Public institutions of higher education had taken form slowly following Thomas Jefferson's concept of a public university for each state—a concept exemplified by Jefferson's architectural masterpiece, the University of Virginia, which opened in the mid-1820s. In fact, the Northwest Ordinance of 1789 had established that two townships (i.e., two land parcels each measuring six by six miles) be set aside in every state for public university level education. In Illinois this did not begin to materialize until 1862, when Congress passed the College Land Grant Act, popularly known as the Morrill Act, after its proponent, Justin S. Morrill. Under the terms of the act, states were awarded the profits from the sale of selected public lands to be used to build schools of higher learning.

The Illinois Industrial University began offering classes in 1868, after the selection of a site located between the villages of Urbana and Champaign. They were held in a building at Wright Street and University Avenue, constructed in 1861 for the Champaign and Urbana Institute, an institution that soon become defunct. (The building was demolished in 1881.) The new university was intended to provide a technical and practical education. A board of trustees appointed in 1867 was charged with managing the new university so as "to teach, in the most thorough manner, such branches of learning as are related to agriculture and the mechanic arts, and military tactics, without excluding other scientific and classical studies." The charter further stipulated that "no student shall at any time be allowed to remain in or about the university in idleness, or without full mental or industrial occupation." No fear of any of those from the new candidate. Young Ricker was ready to devote himself, both mentally and industrially, to completing his education.

What had particularly intrigued Ricker in the circular that his friend from La Harpe had brought by was a description of the new university's program in architectural design. The idea of offering college instruction in architecture was exceedingly novel. Architects in America were taught by other architects, not by instructors at institutions of higher learning. The first architectural curriculum in the country had only recently been established, in 1868, at the Massachusetts Institute of Technology (MIT), another new land-grant college. The Illinois curriculum in architecture was the nation's second such program.

When Ricker requested more information about the new architectural program at Illinois, he discovered that he was the first student to inquire about that offering. He was placed in a program of mathematics, German, and drawing, the latter administered by James W. Bellangee, a Chicago architect. When Bellangee left at the end of the 1870–71 school year, he was replaced by another Chicago architect, the Swedish-born Harold Hansen, who had studied in Berlin at the famous Prussian school, the Bauakademie. Ricker found Hansen a stimulating mentor, and he responded well to the practical, if rigorous, course of instruction based on the German model.

Through exemption by examination for several courses, and by sheer hard work, Ricker would have been eligible to graduate in June 1872 had his studies not been interrupted in October 1871 by an assignment from his unit of the Illinois National Guard: he was asked to help restore order in Chicago after the Great Fire. He further delayed his graduation by working for an architect in Chicago during the spring and summer of 1872.

On returning for the fall 1872 semester, Ricker discovered that Hansen, who also had gone to Chicago to help rebuild the city, had decided to remain there. Ricker and three newer students in the program found themselves in a difficult position until President John Milton Gregory allowed Ricker to oversee his own education—to create courses, study the material, and administer exams to himself and his three colleagues! On March 12, 1873, Ricker was granted a graduation certificate. Because MIT's commencement for its first class of architecture students was not held until June 1873, Ricker was the first graduate of any architectural program in the United States.

President Gregory had additional plans for Ricker. He offered to send the thirty-year-old to Berlin to study at the Bauakademie during the remainder of the spring and for the following summer, on the condition that Ricker would return in the fall and take control of the Illinois university's

Nathan Ricker (*center*) and his first class of students, fall 1873.

architecture program. Ricker agreed. And so Illinois's first architecture graduate became the guiding force in creating the school's curriculum. By late March, Ricker was on his way to Europe, where he made visits to England, Belgium, and France. Study in Berlin was followed by a European tour to the Vienna Exposition of 1873, where Ricker was particularly impressed with a demonstration of the Russian system of incorporating "shop" practice into design studies. Ricker's vision for the new Illinois program in architecture drew on his travels and studies abroad, as well as on his personal mastery of the critical literature and his innately pragmatic and persevering approach to life itself.

Ricker's perspective developed over the next few years. He came to believe that an architect should, first and foremost, be a safe and economical builder, and, second, a capable businessman. Lastly, he should be a designer of pleasing forms. In 1899 Ricker explained his pedagogical goal in *Inland Architect* magazine as creating builders of "good architecture," which he explained, "must largely consist of good and honest construction, obtaining the best results possible for the means available for the purpose, employing all improvements in the system of construction and materials, and in the protection of the life and health of inmates of the buildings." Regarding the relative importance of aesthetics in design, he noted, "The highest perfection of style is demanded by comparatively few buildings."

Ricker worked to create a course of study that would promote this point of view. Because of the individual nature of his instruction, Ricker could find no suitable textbooks for many of his courses. He solved the problem by making "blueprint" copies of his notes to be distributed to students. These eventually amounted to more than 2,000 pages. An outline of the school's curriculum published in 1887 reveals how Ricker's particular emphases were put into practice. Students took classes during their first year in mathematics and structural forces (a course called "graphic statics"—the visual representation of forces—which was Ricker's favorite teaching method of structure); study of materials in the second year; chemistry, physics, and architectural history the third year; and architectural design only in the fourth year. The students' final assignment was to combine every aspect of the profession, from initial conception to construction documents, in a single project. Clearly, the entire method was derived from Ricker's personal values and his exposure to the Germanic principles, as taught by Hansen and espoused at the Bauakademie. Ricker's method was diametrically opposed to the more popular French system being taught in Paris at the Ecole-des-Beaux-arts, with its emphasis on design, representation, and rendering, a system followed at MIT and the majority of new American architecture schools created in succeeding decades.

In 1871, the university had commissioned the architect John Mills Van Osdel, Chicago's first important designer, to create a new building that was to house Ricker's new program. But it was not yet ready in the fall of 1873 when the program started. Not until early 1874 was the new University Hall, a large classical structure with elements of the fashionable "Second Empire" style, ready for occupancy. (University Hall would be demolished in 1938 and replaced in 1941 by the Illini Union.)

Ricker had to realize his program within the dilapidated halls of the Champaign and Urbana Institute, but after only one semester in the old Institute building, Ricker and the six students of his first class, the Class of '77, moved into University Hall. They occupied the third floor of the northeast tower. The program remained here for twenty years, even while Architecture and Engineering periodically expanded into more and more space. Among the students of the next class, that of '78, was Mary L. Page, who became the first woman to be awarded an architecture degree in the United States. Henry Bacon, who later designed the Lincoln Memorial in Washington, D.C., attended classes in Ricker's department in 1884–85.

No sooner did Ricker start teaching than he began helping with the university's physical plant, serving as consultant, occasional designer, and general factotum. In 1878, the year the university became known as the University of Illinois, Ricker designed the first of five campus buildings. The Chemistry Building (now Harker Hall) was created as a complement to Van Osdel's University Hall. After a hiatus during the 1880s, Ricker provided four more designs in the 1890s: the Drill Hall (Armory—Kenny Gym Annex) in 1890; Natural History, immediately east of University Hall, in 1892; Mechanical Engineering ("Aeronautical B") in 1895, the only Ricker building to be demolished; and the Library Building, "Altgeld Hall" (now the Mathematics Library), built west of University Hall in 1895–97. Ricker was able to incorporate the creation of Altgeld Hall into his teaching. Not only did his students produce presentation drawings for the various versions of the building presented to the trustees, but the actual working drawings for the final version were produced as a class project.

Ricker's life became entwined with that of the growing university. In 1875 he married Mary Carter Steele (Class of '75) of Galesburg, Illinois. Their only child, Ethel, was born in 1883. In 1890 the family moved into a handsome shingled house designed by Ricker at 612 W. Green Street. The building was lovingly restored in 1999 by Urbana-Champaign's Preservation and Conservation Association. Growing up in a college town, Ethel attended the University Academy and stayed to earn a professional degree in architecture in 1904. After Mary Ricker's death in 1910, Ethel remained with her father in the Green Street house until his death in 1924.

By 1893 the university was ready to accede to Ricker's urgent requests for a new building for the College of Engineering. This proposal was even bolder than is immediately evident. When Engineering Hall opened in the fall of 1894, it was the first building in the country to be dedicated solely to engineering. The proposed site faced the existing buildings that were picturesquely grouped along the south side of Green Street—University Hall and Ricker's Chemistry and Natural History buildings. The design was to be selected by invited competition. The invitations were sent only to the most promising practitioners among the five dozen graduates of Ricker's program. Just as President Gregory was able to trust Ricker with the completion of his own education, so now the university adopted Ricker's belief that the very best architects available for the kind of building he wanted were to be found among his own students.

Ricker wanted a structure that would include the latest developments in building technologies (including lighting, ventilation, and heating), and he would make these elements as freely visible and understandable as was practically possible. (One hundred years later, Ralph Johnson [Class of '71], the designing architect of the Chicago firm of Perkins & Will, was given a similar charge in creating the Department of Architecture's fifth home, Temple Hoyne Buell Hall.) The competition guidelines called for a substantial building with only minimal decoration and, perhaps recalling the cramped quarters in University Hall, with no freestanding towers.

Sixteen alumni submitted designs. The first prize was awarded on June 9, 1893, to George W. Bullard (Class of '82), who had established a practice in Tacoma, Washington. Following Ricker's guidelines, Bullard's design placed the Department of Architecture on the top floor, its four studios lit by enormous skylights above the exposed trusses. Engineering Hall was completed in a single year; its cornerstone was laid on December 13, 1893. Classes were using the building in the fall semester of 1894. The official dedication took place on November 15, 1894. Architecture remained on the fourth floor of Engineering Hall until January 1928, when it was separated from the College of Engineering to become part of the new College of Fine and Applied Arts in Charles Platt's building created for "Architecture and Kindred Subjects."

In the fall of 1894, Ricker moved into a building that had everything he had hoped for—design studios, seminar rooms, a lecture hall, photographic and blueprint rooms, a museum, and a library. In addition to 300 plaster casts of sculpture and architectural fragments, the museum held numerous scale models of different structural systems and examples of various building materials. Among the thousands of blueprints in the collection available to students was a complete set of structural drawings of the buildings of the 1892 World's Columbian Exposition, given to the school by Ricker's friend, the engineer Edward Shankland. Typically, Ricker brought important structural engineers, including Shankland, William Sooy Smith, and Louis Sullivan's partner Dankmar Adler, rather than famous architects, to deliver major lectures at the school. Architects were not slighted, however; records indicate that such nationally and internationally significant Chicago architects as Sullivan, Frank Lloyd Wright, Walter Burley Griffin, George W. Maher, and Irving K. Pond were among the guests of the department.

The great glory of the new building was its architectural library. Ricker had felt the need for appropriate texts since his first teaching semesters. His reverence for the printed word dated back to his earliest desire to expand his own understanding of the world through books. At first he used his own salary to pay for important publications; later he dedicated a substantial part of his budget to this goal. As the years went by, it became increasingly clear how unusual the collection had become under his guidance. In 1917 the library was officially named after him. Today the Ricker Library of Architecture and Art is a nationally known repository of important and rare nineteenth-century material.

At the same time that Ricker argued for the importance of having technical, historical, and theoretical information available in the library for his students, he realized that foreign languages might prove a barrier for many of them. In 1880 he translated the first of more than thirty French and German books into English—an undertaking that extended over the next forty years. The majority of his translations appeared within a few years of the works' original publication. Thus, Illinois students were reading Rudolph Redtenbacher's 1883 classic *Architektonik der Modernen Baukunst* in Ricker's 1884 translation as *The Architectonics of Modern Architecture: an aid in the solution of architectural problems* before most American architects had ever heard of it. Ricker admired the French architect E. E. Viollet-le-Duc's emphasis on structural analysis in understanding architectural design and its history. Viollet's twenty *Discourses* had been translated into English shortly after their publication in 1872; however, his encyclopedic *Dictionary of Medieval Architecture* remained unavailable in English. Ricker translated many entries from this work through the years and set about completing his translation of the entire text after his retirement. When completed in 1919, the eleven volumes of typed pages contained the first English translation of this seminal work of medieval scholarship. In 1902 one of Ricker's many translations became available nationally in published form. The second (1898) edition of *Moderne Architektur* by the Austrian modern architect and pedagogue Otto Wagner was published by Rogers and Manson of Boston as *Modern Architecture*, following its serial appearance in *Brickbuilder* magazine in 1901.

Ricker's own research involved the improvement of roof trusses. His lectures on the use of graphic statics in understanding such forms led to the publication in 1885 of his first book, *Elementary Graphical Statics and Construction of Trussed Roofs*. It was followed in 1912 and 1913 with two books, his *Treatise on Design and Construction of Roofs and Simplified Formulas* and *Tables for Floors, Joists and Beams; Roofs, Rafters, and Purlins*. By joining his practical inclinations with his scholarly ambition, Ricker the carpenter, piano maker, and blacksmith had been re-created as doctor, dean, and professor.

Ricker's five buildings and Bullard's Engineering Hall, substantial as they were, were not the extent of Ricker's influence on the campus infrastructure. During the expansive years just after the turn of the nineteenth century and following the precedent of Engineering Hall, Ricker's former students regularly returned to campus as architects of new buildings. Thus, Joseph C. Llewelyn (among Ricker's first students in the Class of '77), returned from a flourishing practice in Chicago in 1899 as architect of the

College of Agriculture building (Davenport Hall), while Nelson S. Spencer (Class of '82) designed the new chemistry building (Noyes Hall), which opened in 1902. Spencer also designed the wood shop, formerly at Springfield and Burrill, in 1901. In 1906 Clarence Blackall (also from the original Class of '77), a well-known Boston architect who had created a campus plan in 1905, provided a fitting southern termination to the emerging main quad with his auditorium (now Follinger), modeled after the ancient Roman Pantheon and Thomas Jefferson's library at the University of Virginia. By this time buildings had begun to appear that were not by Ricker or his students, including McKim, Mead and White's Women's Building, as well as a group by the Illinois state architect, William Carbys Zimmerman, including Lincoln Hall and the administration building. Yet Ricker's influence continued in the form of James M. White (Class of '90), Ricker's right-hand man during his later years, who served not only as architect of Smith Music Hall and a number of additions to existing buildings, including Altgeld Hall, but who also was campus supervising architect for the eastern designer, Charles Platt, during the comprehensive expansion plan of the 1920s.

Having set the standards for a professional architectural education in America, Ricker was greatly concerned about raising the general level of professional competence in architecture. He joined forces with Dankmar Adler to promote a state law to license architects. On June 3, 1897, after numerous attempts made over many years, the Fortieth General Assembly of the State of Illinois passed into law "[a] bill for an act to provide for the licensing of architects, and regulating the practice of architecture as a profession" to become effective on January 1, 1898. Illinois had become the first state in the nation to require licenses for its architects, and thus had led the way to what would eventually become a standard part of an architect's career, much like that other nineteenth-century novelty for architects, so dear to Ricker, the completion of a university degree. The first article of the new bill called for "the appointment of a State Board of Examiners, to be composed of a faculty member from the University of Illinois, and four Illinois architects with experience of at least ten years." Ricker was immediately appointed to the first board, convened in the fall of 1897. Not only was he on the faculty of the university, he was certainly the reason that such a stipulation had been added to the bill. Ricker also served as board president from 1899 to 1916.

In its annual reports, the Illinois board evaluated the effects of the licensing law and its various clauses. For Ricker, the law was a personal vindication of his life's work to establish what was perhaps the country's most thorough and rigorous course of architectural education. In 1901 he proudly reported, "The Board has had every opportunity to see the beneficent results of the establishment of the School of Architecture at the University of Illinois, which was one of the earliest, and the forerunner in making architecture a part of university education, an example that has been followed by many other states." As Ricker's main teaching focus at Illinois had always been on structure and technology, so the Illinois law stressed these aspects in assessing professional competency.

Among the many successful architects who had attended the University of Illinois by the World War I were a surprising number of the major players in Chicago's modern movement, the famous prairie school. These included three of Frank Lloyd Wright's most trusted draftsmen: Walter Burley Griffin (Class of '99), William Drummond (Class of '98-'99), and Harry F. Robinson (Class of '06). But the father of the prairie school and Wright's own teacher, Louis Sullivan, benefited as well, employing William L. Steele (Class of '96) and Parker Berry (Class of '07-'08) after their studies at Illinois. A dozen peripheral players in America's first architectural attempt at modernism were schooled at the drafting tables of Illinois' land-grant campus. Spurred by Sullivan's antiacademic rhetoric (he was schooled at MIT and the Ecole des Beaux-arts in Paris), many of these architects routinely denied that their education at the university had taught them anything useful, yet they all carried the knowledge of practical things that made their later creative work possible.

By 1900 design at the school began to move in the direction of a modified Beaux-Arts method involving competitions, program analysis, and stylistic suitability. Because Ricker stressed a scientific and rational approach to architecture, these Beaux-Arts methods continued to be subordinate in the overall education of students to the intense examination of structure and materials. While classicism was the expected language in which architectural thoughts would be expressed, style was not the primary emphasis of the program of instruction. This point of view profoundly shaped the prairie school students' approach to architecture, perhaps more than they themselves realized. It provided them with an approach to design and construction that allowed them later to cast off what they considered the thin veneer of the historical design styles and reveal what they could argue was a modern, rational kind of architecture, stressing the practicality of their plans and an economic use of materials. Such an argument echoed Ricker's fundamental beliefs.

In 1912 when Walter Burley Griffin won the international competition for the design of "Canberra," the proposed new capital city of Australia, *American Contractor* reported that his success as an Illinois graduate

Portrait of
Nathan Ricker,
ca. 1910.

"serves naturally to call attention to this school and its remarkable growth and services to the country." The magazine reporter pondered such a turn of events. "If anyone had picked out thirty years ago the most unfavorable place in the United States for the location of a course in architecture, no one would have made a mistake in putting it upon the banks of the Boneyard stream in the city of Urbana, in Illinois, far removed from any specimens of architecture that were worthy of study, with no collections worth visiting within a thousand miles."

How, then, had this unexpected development transpired? The reporter felt the answer lay with one person: Professor Nathan Clifford Ricker. "Summer and winter, rain or shine, in storm and quiet, he has persistently hammered away to lay broad and deep the foundations of the school and rear its superstructure high until it has become one of the four greatest schools of architecture in the new world, and has an attendance during the present year exceeding that of any other school of architecture in this hemisphere. It has become a source of inspiration in every county in the commonwealth, and the traces of its influence are to be seen in the buildings going up throughout this state." Praising Ricker's efforts on behalf of the licensing law, the reporter continued: "He has done much to set standards and elevate the general level of the profession," and, hoping to catch the ear of Springfield legislators, he concluded, "The school has certainly made good and justified in every respect the expenditures which the state has made for its support." Indeed those "expenditures" allowed Nathan

Clifford Ricker to alter the course of architectural education, to elevate the standards of architectural practice, giving form to his alma mater's campus, and to guide successive generations of young people toward the creation of America's built environment.

SELECTED REFERENCES

Allen, Lynn Monical. "Nathan Clifford Ricker and His Students: A Legacy in Architectural Education." Master's thesis, Western Illinois University, 1971.

Alofsin, Anthony. "Tempering the Ecole: Nathan Ricker at the University of Illinois, Lanford Warren at Harvard, and their Followers." In *The History of History in American Schools of Architecture*, ed. Gwendolyn Wright and Janet Parks, 73–88. New York: Temple Hoyne Buell Center for the Study of American Architecture, 1990.

Baker, Ira O. "Makers of the University, VI: Nathan Clifford Ricker." *Alumni Quarterly* 6 (April 1912): 97–101.

Bannister, Turpin C. "Pioneering in Architectural Education: Recalling the First Collegiate Graduate in Architecture in the U.S.A.: Nathan Clifford Ricker." *Journal of the American Institute of Architects* 20 (July–August 1953): 3–8, 76–81.

Charney, Wayne M., and John W. Stamper. "Nathan Clifford Ricker and the Beginning of Architectural Education at Illinois." *Illinois Historical Journal* 74 (1986): 257–66.

"Distinguished Graduates from Architectural School." *American Contractor* 33 (July 13, 1912).

Geraniotis, Roula. "The University of Illinois and German Architectural Education." *Journal of Architectural Education* 38 (Summer 1985): 15–21.

Kruty, Paul. "A New Look at the Beginnings of the Illinois Architects Licensing Law." *Illinois Historical Journal* 90 (Autumn 1997): 154–72.

———. "Walter Burley Griffin and the University of Illinois." *Reflections* 9 (1993): 32–43.

Laing, Alan K. *Nathan Clifford Ricker, 1843–1924: Pioneer in American Architectural Education*. Champaign, Ill.: Building Research Council, 1973.

Newcomb, Rexford. "Doctor Nathan Clifford Ricker: A Pioneer in Architectural Education in America." *Western Architect* 31 (June 1922): 78–79.

O'Donnell, Thomas E. "The Ricker Manuscript Translations, I–IV." *Pencil Points* 1 (November 1926): 665–67; 8 (March 1927): 156–62; 8 (May 1927): 286–92; 8 (August 1927): 477–82.

Quinn, Chris. "Nathan C. Ricker at the University of Illinois." *Humanities Collections* 1 (2001): 47–75.

———. "Nathan Clifford Ricker: Translator and Educator." *Arris* 11 (2000): 40–54.

Ricker, Nathan Clifford. "Teaching Style in Architecture." *Inland Architect* 33 (July 1899): 46.

———. "The Story of a Life." 1922, manuscript, archives, University of Illinois at Urbana-Champaign.

DONALD KRUMMEL

CHAPTER 2

Katharine L. Sharp and the Creation

of the University Library

One of the treasures of the University of Illinois is its library, of worldwide fame and uncommon strength. The whole university community depends on it. Many faculty settle in Champaign or Urbana because of the university's magnificent library, which clearly owes much to the hundreds who have worked in it over the years and to the dozens who have managed its units.

The character of the University Library was molded by four of its early head librarians—Katharine Lucinda Sharp, Phineas Lawrence Windsor, Robert B. Downs, and Hugh Atkinson. Each had a different, very creative, vision of what the library ought to be. Sharp's decade at Illinois (1897–1907) saw the collection triple in size, from 29,100 to 96,000 volumes. Her vision reflected the lessons of her mentor Melvil Dewey, as well as her own fierce efforts to see that vision realized.

Regent John Milton Gregory began the library, even before the Illinois Industrial University opened its doors to students in 1868. He stored 1,039 volumes in a room behind his office. Most were, reputedly, purchased with money out of his own pocket. Soon the collection needed to be moved over to a large room on the third floor of University Hall on Green Street. There, books were shelved against the wall with central reading tables—for young men on the east and young women on the west.

The library collection quickly outgrew its quarters. State funds were finally appropriated for the building called Library Hall, later renamed Altgeld Hall. (The librarian's responsibilities, incidentally, included handling student mail, which called for the branch post office that is still located in this building.) For the dedication of the new building, on June 8, 1897, university President Andrew S. Draper called in an old friend to deliver the main address, the redoubtable Melvil Dewey, now remembered for his decimal classification scheme. Dewey was the founder of the American Library Association and of the nation's first library school, the New York State Library School, then based in Albany, New York.

Now that the University Library had a new building, it needed a head librarian. Dewey no doubt sang the praises of his former student, Katharine Sharp, whose fledgling library school at the Armour Institute in Chicago was about to close. Draper listened and outbid the University of Wisconsin for the program. He lured Sharp to Urbana by offering her the responsibility for directing the library and heading up a new library school. Her title was "Professor of Library Economy." Thus began the first great period in the history of the library.

Sharp had been born in Elgin, Illinois, on May 21, 1865. Educated in the Chicago area, she worked there briefly before deciding to attend Dewey's library school in Albany in 1890. She completed the program in 1892. By October of the next year, she was back in Chicago and at the age of twenty-eight was in charge of the Comparative Library Exhibit for the 1893 World's Columbian Exposition. Dewey stood as a father figure behind this assignment, as he would in many later stages of Sharp's career.

Sharp described what she did at this fair in an essay in the *Library Journal*. For this comprehensive and extensive exhibit, a distinguished and representative committee chose 5,000 titles. The titles were catalogued using several systems, classified using two systems, and listed in a separate book. An array of library forms, furniture, and building plans were also on display. Here was an education not only for those who attended the fair but for Sharp, who gained invaluable experience in managing a large library. For her work, the Board of Lady Managers of the Exposition awarded her a special medal and diploma.

Sharp's experience at the World's Columbian Exposition led to her next assignment, to set up a school for the training of librarians at the newly established Armour Institute in Chicago. Dewey had argued for the Armour Institute school and endorsed Sharp's candidacy. In 1922, he recalled the event (with his notorious simplified spelling): "My old pastor F. W. Gonzales [i.e., Frank Gunsaulus, president of the Armour Institute], a member of the Boston Shakespeare Club of which I was president, came to Albany and said, 'In old Boston days yu fild my hed with certain dreams that ar now coming true. Armour Institute and I want the best man in America to start the library and library school and carry out yur ideas.' I replied 'The best man in America is a woman, and she is in the next room.'"

At the time, several other early library schools had been directed by women. But in her Chicago position, Sharp was the only woman to head both a library school and a library. On moving her program downstate, she became the head of a large and general academic library at a state university. Not until well into the 1960s were any other major American academic libraries headed by women.

An important word for Sharp was *professional*. In an 1898 essay, she defended her perceived need that a librarian have not only special training in the workings of a library but a broad liberal arts education—"a combined edition of the encyclopedia, the dictionary, the dictionary of phrase and fable, the universal history, the bibliographer's manual and general biography," and all that this implies in the way of training, idealism, competence, and seriousness of purpose. Students applying to her program faced a fearsome entrance examination. How many of us today can write a brief essay on France and Siam, or on the Massacre of St. Bartholomew, and identify George Meredith, Maarten Maartens, or F. Marion Crawford?

Sharp's concern for systematic library procedures carried over into her courses while her library school curriculum reflected library activities. This close relationship between the library and library school benefited both, implementing rational procedures and yielding the theory of the library profession. The catalogue achieved consistency. Accessions and shelf lists were prepared so that for the first time the library knew exactly what it had and where it was located in its collection. The needs of readers were attended to in cataloguing, accessions, and management policy. The courses offered to Sharp's students were taught by librarians who also worked in her library. Some of the early classics of the library profession in America were written by Sharp's faculty.

The gender implications are clear in Sharp's argument that with this rigorous program, "we are far from the danger predicted by a New York Senator that the University would next be turning out Bachelors of Hemstitching." The librarian is almost always referred to as "he" in Sharp's

1898 essay on "Librarianship as a Profession." The one exception is where Sharp speaks of a "trained librarian" as one who would not "keep her crocheting in the library because she has so much spare time." Yet the numbers of Sharp's graduates tell a different story. Of those who attended Sharp's programs at Armour and at Urbana, 349 were women and twelve were men. Sharp's era witnessed a rapid feminization of the librarian profession.

No small credit for this feminization was due to Melvil Dewey, who was, as usual, a wild card in the game. Earlier he had been forced to move his program from Columbia University to Albany, in part because his classes were made up largely of women. In the summer of 1905, during a post-conference trip of the American Library Association to Portland, Oregon, several leading women in the profession accused Dewey of sexual improprieties. He promptly resigned and was never again active in an organization that he had founded, or in the profession in which he had been so conspicuous a leader.

What was Sharp's relationship to her mentor? Over the years she grew even closer to Dewey and his family, but there is no suggestion of innuendo, or even of gossip, in the close community of librarians. Sharp's program at Illinois offers clear evidence of support for Dewey against the criticisms that his approach "smacks of arithmetic and commerce." The author of those criticisms, Mary Salome Cutler Fairchild, one of Sharp's teachers at Albany and also one of Sharp's closest friends, was soon dismissed by Dewey.

Sharp's mission extended outside her own library and into the world of libraries at large. In Chicago she had been active in the Chicago Library Club and in the Illinois State Library Association, for which she served as president after moving to the University of Illinois, and also became a leader in the American Library Association. She promoted the local public libraries in Champaign and Urbana through student assignments and through her personal involvement and support. In 1896 she studied "Libraries in Secondary Schools," with a survey of the legislation in twenty-two of the states and with a closely argued analysis of the problems. Two years later she wrote on "Instruction in Library Economy through University Extension Methods," anticipating by about a century some developments at the school she founded. Two years later she surveyed traveling libraries (most of them promoted by the Illinois Farmers' Institute) and libraries sponsored by Illinois women's clubs, with lists of titles and summaries of the practices. A famous outreach program of the Iowa Library Commission was set up by Alice Tyler, one of Sharp's students. On the campus, Sharp worked with Violet Jayne and Isabel Bevier in the newly established women's Department, whose executive committee Sharp chaired in 1904.

Imbued with an ideal of how a library ought to be run, Sharp worked at the task with uncontrolled energy. Dewey, among many others, often warned her to pace her activities, but the work took precedence. It was all the more difficult because of funding cutbacks and space shortages. Slowing the usual stream of staff resignations took a toll on Sharp's time and energy. (For instance, Margaret Mann, her distinguished cataloguer and later one of the most respected names in the American library world, was Sharp's house guest for an extensive time due to illness.) The new library building (later Altgeld Hall) was proving inadequate for readers, and the collections were growing so rapidly as to require a revamping of the staff and systems for processing them. The weaknesses in the intellectual systems of the library became all the more apparent and funding was never sufficient. Meanwhile the opportunities for service and outreach were endless.

Sharp's health had never been strong and it declined rapidly throughout her time at Illinois. In the spring of 1896, just before coming to Urbana, she had been ill for several weeks with typhoid fever. In March the next year she had to decline Dewey's invitation to lecture in Albany. Although by summer she was well enough to travel to a library conference in England, she needed to go back early and, before returning to Urbana, stopped off at Lake Placid in the Adirondack mountains to recuperate. The next year, Dewey admonished her, "You have magnificent possibilities of usefulness, but they are all contingent on your taking needed rest and husbanding your strength."

Sharp rested whenever she could, but her health continued to decline. In 1900 she made plans to go to another sanitarium in upstate New York over the summer. The summer of 1902 she again spent at Lake Placid, and she did not return until November. Although she appears to have been in good health during 1903 and 1904, the death of her father in April 1905 was devastating for her and for her health. She entered another sanitarium, in Battle Creek, Michigan, and spent the subsequent summer with the Deweys at Lake Placid. In January 1906 she planned another leave of several months and was in Chicago when a favorite younger brother suddenly died. She returned to Battle Creek for several weeks and later went to Lake Placid. She was back in Urbana as of May 1906, but on April 1, 1907, she submitted her resignation to President James, effective the next September.

Sharp had clearly been ill during much of her ten-year career at Illinois, yet her tenure saw the establishment of philosophies and practices that

Portrait of
Katharine Lucinda Sharp.

have distinguished the university's library ever since. Thanks to her work
and the support she cultivated among her students and with other libraries
in the state, the character of the University Library was to survive largely
intact over subsequent decades.

Sharp never returned to Illinois after her resignation, nor did she
remain active in the library world. She spent her last seven years with her
second family, that of Melvil and Annie Godfrey Dewey at Lake Placid in
upstate New York. And, almost in the style of Trilby, she helped to manage
her Svengali's far-flung programs. She was forty-nine at the time of her
tragic death on June 1, 1914, following an automobile accident.

There is yet another chapter to the story of Katharine Sharp. She kept
in touch with her students through a vast correspondence, and she saved
her letters to them, as did her assistant, Frances Simpson, who maintained
the correspondence for many years after Sharp's departure. Folders of letters for all but two of Sharp's 361 students, with some folders containing
dozens of letters, record the story of the growth of the library world in the
first decades of the twentieth century. A generation later, Robert B. Downs
helped one of his doctoral students, Laurel Grotzinger, uncover Sharp's
poignant story in a landmark dissertation. A generation after that, Elizabeth Cardman, another doctoral student, uncovered the evidence of
Sharp's closeness with her students, as recorded in Sharp's vast correspondence. For once on their own, Sharp's students could expect her loyal support, along with candid advice and motherly criticisms. In their letters to

Lorado Taft Memorial Plaque for Katharine Lucinda Sharp, dedicated 1922. The original is mounted in the north corridor of the University Library.

Sharp, her students shared their careers, describing financial plight, major illnesses, or unhappy work settings, along with their happy news as "crusaders," to use a favorite word in their letters.

Based largely on Sharp's correspondence, Cardman has traced the library careers of Sharp's graduates. A few dropped out of the profession, but many became leaders in it. The men were more likely to reach high administrative positions. The evidence is clear, however, that all entered the field more for love than for money. Homesickness was a common problem that Sharp and Simpson often addressed in their letters. But there were rewards as well. One student (Josie Houchens) bequeathed a handsome endowment to the library school for the support of her successors; others left local memorials. Still another (Miriam Carey) had this said of her—and it is no less true of Sharp: "She was one of that nucleus of remarkable women whom the turn of the century saw shaping the future of library affairs in the midwestern states. . . . To try to translate the remarkable spirit of this woman into phrases is futile, but there is a duty to the young to pass on the tradition. . . . Fortunate is that one [who can] have such traditions as part of his or her inheritance."

Sharp's successor was chosen two years later. Phineas L. Windsor, whose long tenure extended from 1909 to 1940, was, like Sharp, a native of Illinois. He was born in Chenoa on February 21, 1871. And also like Sharp, he had been educated and worked a few years in the Chicago area. Between 1897 and 1899, he too studied at Dewey's New York State Library School in

Albany. After brief assignments at the Library of Congress and the University of Texas, he came to Urbana charged with building the library that the venerable Edmund J. James, who had become university president in 1904, had in mind. To appreciate Windsor, one needs to look at what James asked him to do.

James's vision of the university reflected his own rigorous German academic background in which the emphasis was on offering a broad humanistic education in the service of the state. The library was clearly central to the institution, and James not only preached this, but saw that it happened. Sharp's commitment to library education may not always have reflected James's agenda, but if he and Sharp disagreed, it was largely over priorities. James wanted collections and to attract faculty and students more than he wanted the outreach and refinements of procedures that Dewey and Sharp preferred. Windsor long remembered one of James's early statements to the board of trustees: "The library is of value from various points of view. First of all, it saves time.... It provides the assistance which a scientific man needs ... It acts further to provide a stimulus to scientific work on the part of the members of an instructional staff.... I have had more people whom I have approached to consider positions at the University of Illinois turn down my proposition because of the lack of library facilities than for any other one reason."[1]

The philosophy of President James, both in general and as it referred to library matters, was to endure long after his administration ended in 1920. James had recruited a strong, library-minded faculty whose pride in the library would persist. Windsor's great challenge was to make creative use of this community in the cause of building a great collection for the library.

James had proposed to the trustees that the library include "at least a million books as rapidly as possible."[2] Windsor and his faculty quietly achieved an impressive growth of the collection to 1.5 million volumes, with research-level collections adding depth to the holdings in many areas. James had also recommended that the state spend $1 million for a new library building. The site of today's University Library had been agreed on as early as 1914, but at first Windsor had to settle on stacks additions, one built that year, another in 1918. The present building was finally dedicated in 1926. Several large seminar collections that had earlier been dispersed for lack of space in Altgeld Hall now came back to the new main library. They are still maintained there today, complemented by nearly two dozen collections across campus nearer to their readers.

The new building is itself a monument. Windsor's model (reflecting the Bibliothèque Ste.-Geneviève in Paris and the Boston Public Library) was essentially "transactional": the front for readers, the back for books, with a circulation desk in between for the transactions and space to the sides for library work. The space for readers was handsomely proportioned and impressively decorated. The book stacks are meant to be endlessly expandable (into the parking area in Champaign, someday perhaps over Sixth Street and across to threaten the armory).

Windsor was by nature sober and serious. The son of a Methodist minister, his sins were few; the best that his successor Robert Downs can recall were his "big black pipes and Tampa cigars," and that he "bought his first car about 1933, at age 62, and thereafter drove . . . at high rates of speed." Tall, lean, and with a distinctive goatee, he worked quietly but thoroughly. He held several positions of national prominence, and his work with the library school assured him a continuing procession of protégés. His reputation, however, was earned mainly for managing and adding to the research collections of the library of the University of Illinois.

In 1943, three years after Windsor's retirement, Robert Bingham Downs became university librarian. Born in the mountains of North Carolina on May 25, 1903, he attended the University of North Carolina, where he found a mentor and role model in a distant family member, Louis Round Wilson, one of the most respected librarians of his generation. After attending library school at Columbia University, Downs moved upward quickly, from Colby College, back to his alma mater, and then to New York University. By the time he came to Illinois he had established a reputation as a professional leader.

Under Windsor the library had become strong. Under Downs it became famous for being strong thanks to Downs's powerful involvement in the library world. As the president of the American Library Association in 1952–53, he was rumored to be a likely choice for the post of Librarian of Congress in 1953. That year he became the guiding spirit behind the Farmington Plan, which had been bringing foreign books into American libraries to foster America's involvement in the world at large.

Building on the faculty support that Windsor had created, Downs, over his twenty-seven-year incumbency, helped the library expand its collection to over four million volumes, making it the largest library of any state university and the third largest academic library in the United States, a position it still maintains. He considered primary source materials, especially in literature and science, most important. Antiquarian dealers came to respect his shrewdness, supporters his right-mindedness. The hard-driving Harris Francis Fletcher continued to build his preeminent Milton collection, but Downs also steered into the library the personal collection of Fletcher's great faculty rival, the Shakespeare scholar T. W. Baldwin. Thanks to Ernest Ingold, a San Francisco businessman and Illinois alumnus, Downs acquired rare Shakespeare folios and quartos. With the help of Gordon N. Ray, then provost of the university, the library acquired the personal papers of H. G. Wells and the archives of the London publishers Richard Bentley and Grant Richards. Downs's interests in folklore, first stimulated in North Carolina, helped line up the personal papers of Carl Sandburg. Through Downs's neighbor, the English professor and American folklorist John T. Flanagan, the library acquired the Franklin Meine collection of American humor. For Professor Philip Kolb (French), the library built its remarkable collection of Marcel Proust manuscripts. The library also claims much of the private collection of George White, as well as other rare geology books acquired on his advice. Through Ralph T. Fisher of the history department, the library developed its Slavic collections. The communications library as well as the burgeoning map collection became notable assets. Downs's championing of the cause of intellectual freedom during the McCarthy era was reflected in the Ewing C. Baskette and Merten J. Mandeville collections. Also part of the library are the extensive university archives, which now include the archives of the American Library Association and other library organizations.

Downs expected intense loyalty within the library, as he called on those with whom he worked. He in turn helped them, often through crucial career placements. He battled with the university administration for building additions and for acquisitions funds, which, with faculty backing, he often acquired. Notable weaknesses in his program included preservation and access; he would acquire collections and allow them to lay untreated and uncatalogued. Also, he often failed to place women in positions of major responsibility. (The rare exception was Helen Welch in acquisitions, his favorite area.) Nor was he all that keen to replace the tired old Dewey classification system. Yet despite his autocratic management style, the library worked.

Downs's foreign assignments after the war were frequent, varied, and important. The first involved planning the National Diet Library in Tokyo. Later projects took him to Mexico, Turkey, Afghanistan, Brazil, Puerto Rico, Colombia, Canada, Sweden, Australia and New Zealand, and the Soviet Union. Like the many books he authored, the assignments were often more extensive than intensive, but what they accomplished was important and timely. His surveys, mostly of collections but also of management, buildings, and cooperative programs, began with a survey of southern libraries in 1935. "With the exception of Maurice Tauber," Downs modestly proposed, "I have probably taken part in more surveys than any other American librarian."[3] His surveys of regional holdings began in the 1930s at Chapel Hill and extended to dozens of universities in the United States and abroad. Some were immensely important, among them the one that made the library at Purdue University more than a campus decoration. His vast bibliography, *American Library Resources* (1951; supplements in 1962, 1972, and 1981), is still invaluable in citing descriptions of the special strengths of the nation.

After the war, recognizing the needs for his profession, he was quick to institute a doctoral program at Illinois in 1948. Academic libraries, library resources, and historical topics were the focus of the doctoral dissertations he supervised. His support was invaluable in establishing the publications program (headed by *Library Trends* and the *Occasional Papers* series) and the Allerton Park conferences and Windsor Lectures, and in promoting the school at home and abroad.

Downs's 1985 essay, *Books in My Life*, written for the Center for the Book at the Library of Congress, expressed his faith in books as civilization. This faith led him in several imaginative directions. His synopsis of great writings, *Books that Changed the World* (1956), became a widely translated best-seller. This book, with its several sequels, reflected his faith in historical literature. His interest in folklore and humor led to *The Family Saga* (1958, with Mody Boatright and John Flanagan, his neighbor) and *The Bear Went Over the Mountain* (1964, 1971), as well as numerous brief articles and lectures.

Downs's most important writings are, arguably, those on intellectual freedom, which he championed during his incumbency as American Library Association president during the treacherous McCarthy era. Soon after "The Freedom to Read" statement was adopted in 1953, he received the landmark letter from President Eisenhower offering reassurances that "the libraries of America are and must ever remain the homes of free, inquiring minds." The battle for intellectual freedom was not over, however. A noteworthy conflict with James J. Kilpatrick in 1961 made it clear that Downs knew how complex the issues were.[4] His major statement was *The First Freedom* (1960), edited for the American Library Association. Downs was the moving spirit behind the great bibliographies on freedom of the press prepared by Ralph McCoy, one of his students. It is ironic that one of the manifestations of student unrest during the Vietnam War era should have led to the vandalizing of the library's main card catalogue.

Awesome in numbers, Downs's writings were impressive in their impact. The list in his festschrift runs to nearly 400 titles and stops in 1970; a final list may well be half again as large. The considerable redundancy in his writings reflects what was surely the great strength of his career, the fact that his many activities as administrator, consultant, national and international leader, spokesman, author, and personal friend were programmed to reinforce one another.

As an administrator and a consultant, Downs toyed with automation as a time-saver in the library. But in a day when few computer programs were successful, especially in large libraries, Downs came to oppose computers as enemies of books, partly because their cause was in the hands of salesmen who were not themselves passionate readers, and whom he therefore did not respect. He feared the simplistic attraction of nonhuman forces that might supplant both the act of reading and the political forces that were enlightened by reading.

Downs's successor was Lucien White. As White's career was cut short by his early death, a new direction for the library did not emerge until Hugh Atkinson was named White's successor in 1976. In contrast to Downs, who was reserved and dignified, to many even austere, Atkinson was exuberant, gregarious, and downright boisterous. He was famous on campus for his motorcycle, which he managed well in spite of his distinctive eye-patch. He wore his learning lightly, and engaged those he talked to with witty, often audacious, but always provocative repartee.

The philosophy of the library during Atkinson's tenure at Illinois, from 1976 to 1986, was a radical departure from that of the Downs era. Atkinson's objective was to rejuvenate what he saw as a stodgy institution. His program was widely (if not unanimously) seen as a useful corrective, although it is not easy to explain precisely what was corrected, or to describe the long-term impact of his program on the library or on the university. The genius of his program lay in the dialectic interplay between the components that Atkinson orchestrated. To the sum total he applied the term *holistic librarianship.* Few now can agree on what exactly this means, but there can be no doubt that it is a creative conception. Feelings ran high as the library came to life in a way that scandalized the no less passionate but always characteristically soft-spoken Downs.

Computerizing the catalogue, for instance, addressed a massive backlog in card filing. It was funded largely to offer wider access of the collections to the citizenry of the state of Illinois. This in turn called for a rudimentary networking system involving other libraries in Illinois, most of whom used different cataloguing and classification schemes. The acronym that Atkinson chose, LCS, originally designated a Library Computer System, but its main use was at first in circulation. The *C* was generally thought to stand for catalogue because in 1978 this was widely recognized as the first attempt at a comprehensive computerized catalogue for a major American research library.

Meanwhile, within the library the cataloging department itself was largely abolished, its activities and staff mostly transferred to departmental collections, where the decisions of acquisitions were also to be made. For this administrative decentralization, Atkinson's "holistic" vision may have been ambiguous, but it was also political, so as to further confuse and confound both his many supporters and his many detractors. For the colleges and departments in the university—already relatively autonomous in their land-grant setting—the long-range implications were clear. Budgetary constraints, along with concerns for the long-term strength of the university and its programs, argued that the administrative units, more than the individual faculty members, as in the Downs era, needed to involve themselves in deciding how much and what kind of a library they needed and wanted.

To provide better services (and no doubt also to encourage the units of the university to want to pay for it), campus delivery of library books to faculty offices was implemented. Within the library, participatory management was emphasized, within carefully managed constraints, to involve the librarians in committee work as never before. In order to be awarded tenure, meanwhile, faculty members were formally required to have a publication record. Research time was allowed for this, and sabbaticals awarded to what was now recognized as a "library faculty." So intricate a plan, brilliantly conceived in the interplay of its components, also depended on—as it promoted—a mixture of synergy and disequilibrium, both inside the library and in its workings within the university at large. Disruptive and energizing, the strategy challenged the library communities to make their systems work. Atkinson's early death left his goals less than fully realized, but his vision of an institution responsive to change will likely not be forgotten.

Libraries exist to encourage the creative efforts of their readers based on the burgeoning evidence of the past. For librarians themselves to be creative may seem self-contradictory, but it can be argued that Sharp's great contribution lay in her creative application of Dewey's theory to the practice of running the University Library and enriching its communities. The fact that most of them are still in place today is evidence of her importance. Windsor's genius lay in the way he quietly transformed and enhanced the collections. Downs built on what he was blessed with by studying its inner workings and expanding its importance. His greatest achievement—and probably the most difficult for a person born into parochial circumstances—lies in his promoting the cause of intellectual freedom. Atkinson's deconstruction of the library, and the brilliant rationalization of his juggling act, are the signs of a creative mind at its most creative. The preeminence of the University Library has been nurtured by these librarians' contrasting styles.

A NOTE ON SOURCES

This text has greatly benefited from Laurel Ann Grotzinger's dissertation, published as *The Power and the Dignity: Librarianship and Katharine Sharp* (New York: Scarecrow, 1966), and Elizabeth R. Cardman, "Interior Landscapes: Personal Perspectives on Professional Lives, The First Generation of Librarians at the Illinois Library School, 1893–1907" (Ph.D. dissertation, University of Illinois, 1996). For more on all four librarians, see the *Dictionary of American Library Biography* (Littleton, Colo.: Libraries Unlimited, 1978; first supplement 1990, second supplement 2003). My own general essay on the history of the library appears in the *Dictionary of Library Histories* (Chicago: Fitzroy-Dearborn, 2001), 2:833–35.

NOTES

1. The quotation is from a 1949 talk by Phineas Windsor, as transcribed in *Non Solus* 2 (1975): 35–44.
2. Ibid.
3. Robert Bingham Downs, *Perspectives on the Past: An Autobiography* (Metuchen, N.J.: Scarecrow, 1984), 72.
4. Much of this discussion is reprinted in ibid., 165–73.

PART II

ACADEMICS

AND

ATHLETICS

PAULA A. TREICHLER

CHAPTER 3

Isabel Bevier and

Home Economics

Isabel Bevier was nearly forty when she visited the University of Illinois in the spring of 1900 as a candidate for the new position of professor of household science. It was her first encounter with the prairie. "I thought I had never seen so flat and so muddy a place," she wrote later; "no trees, no hills, no boundaries of any kind." Once back in her faculty position at Lake Erie College, she recalled "the dead level of the landscape in the Twin Cities" and reflected wryly that if she did accept the position, she "certainly could not hope to look to the hills for inspiration." Yet the place had character, and as she considered all that she had seen and heard at Illinois, the landscape became for her a powerful metaphor for the institution she was about to join: its openness to new ideas, its support for coeducation, and its commitment to the land-grant mission that linked theory to practice, learning to labor, and science to the problems of the world where men and women live. The possibilities exhilarated her: "This lack of boundaries, physical and mental, the open-mindedness of the authorities and their

31

willingness to try experiments, indeed their desire to do so, opened up a whole new world for me."

On April 18, 1900, Bevier was appointed professor of household science at an annual salary of $1,500. Over the next two decades she developed a Department of Household Science that brought distinction to the University of Illinois and led the way for universities across the nation and abroad. Her insistence that science drive the curriculum emphasized her break with the "cooking and sewing school" tradition of women's education and domestic science; her high admissions standards and rigorous curriculum won the respect of colleagues and educators across the disciplinary spectrum. Equally influential was her vision of household science as an interdisciplinary enterprise that required social, economic, aesthetic, and technical knowledge, a vision that continues to inform the field today.

Bevier's legacy extends far beyond the portrait and building that bear her name at the University of Illinois. Even during her lifetime her influence was unquestionable. Alfred True, national director of the Office of Agricultural Experiment Stations (which had oversight for funded home economics research), said in 1910 that "if anyone should ask me to see a real college department of Home Economics, I should send him first to the University of Illinois." When Bevier left Illinois in 1921, her longtime colleague Dean Eugene Davenport spoke of the "real vision" required to build an outstanding academic program from nothing amid many obstacles and pressures: "it takes fortitude and strong will power to remain 'fixed in the midst of unfixedness.'" In 1933, Columbia University Professor of Chemistry Henry C. Sherman wrote that the "scientific esteem in which Home Economics is held in any comparable institution is closely proportional to the fidelity with which it has followed the standards set by Miss Bevier." Moreover, said Sherman, just as Louis Pasteur brought chemistry into medicine, Bevier brought chemistry into home economics. Like Pasteur, too, she knew what to do with an opportunity: "She saw, and she seized." Bevier's life and work hold special interest today, as feminist scholars of American women's history engage in a serious reevaluation of the home economics movement and the significance of its leading figures.[1]

By the time Bevier arrived at Illinois, she had served as professor of natural sciences at Pennsylvania College of Women in Pittsburgh; studied chemistry at a number of universities, including Case School of Applied Science, Western Reserve, and Harvard; and worked with such pioneering researchers as agricultural chemist and nutritionist Wilbur O. Atwater at Wesleyan and food and sanitation chemist Ellen H. Richards at MIT. When in 1898 she became professor of chemistry at Lake Erie College in

Painesville, Ohio, she was committed to studying the chemistry of food and to developing a science of the home. Yet she had begun her education with a very different plan. Born in 1860 to a noted line of French Huguenot and Dutch settlers and raised on a 200-acre farm outside Plymouth, Ohio, she graduated from Wooster College in 1885 and in 1888 obtained a master's degree from Wooster in Latin and German, with the expectation of teaching languages and marrying the medical student to whom she was engaged. The accidental drowning of her fiancé that same year dramatically changed the course of her life and work. At first she sought merely to be busy, but soon she was caught up in the early home economics movement. Within a decade, she was a respected scientist with a good job, journal publications in nutrition and the chemistry of food, and a deep investment in teaching and research.

Bevier thus brought strong credentials to the exciting but daunting responsibility of starting a new department at Illinois essentially from scratch. She also brought a mature educational vision. She had lost patience with women's colleges and the narrow approach to women's education that in her view characterized the classical institutions of the East. When she was offered the position at Illinois, she felt unequal to the task—her family farm seemed poor preparation for the "wide open spaces" and vast scale of things at the university—but "I did so want the opportunity! Life in women's colleges had always irked me, had always seemed to me an abnormal life if one lived in the college, as I always was expected to." Illinois "was a coeducational institution, and the ideas I had acquired needed a coeducational setting if I were to work them out in a plan for the liberal education of women."

She could not have come at a better time. Women had been admitted to the University of Illinois in 1870, only two years after it opened in 1868 as the Illinois Industrial University; Regent John Milton Gregory, for whom Gregory Hall is named, cast the deciding vote for coeducation, expressing even as he did so his reservations about this "innovation of doubtful wisdom." The land-grant movement was hospitable to the notion that women should be educated, and in time Gregory changed his mind, not least because he hired Louisa C. Allen in 1874 to teach domestic science and then fell in love with her. Allen, for whom Allen Hall is named, built up the program until 1880, when she left the university to marry Gregory, a widower.

Gregory's successor, Regent Selim Peabody (for whom Peabody Hall is named), declared the program "an experiment in darkness" and wasted no time abolishing it. Domestic Science was then an "extinct dep't" until its prior history was unearthed ten years later by Katharine L. Kinnard and

Charles H. Shamel, two Illinois graduates of 1890 who lobbied industriously for the restoration of household science at the university. Echoing the growing sentiments of women around the state, Kinnard wrote in 1891 to the *Farmer's Review* that "science is the hand maid of home culture no less than the hand maid of agriculture." Such trustees as Lucy Flower of Chicago were powerful allies for the cause of women's education, including household science. Other supporters of household science were Henry Dunlap, state senator for the university's district, and his formidable wife, Nora—who would later head the household science department of the Farmers' Institute (hereafter FIHSD, to avoid confusion with Bevier's university department).

What "science" was to mean for these various advocates of household science—indeed what "household science" was to mean—were questions Bevier would have to face, and these relationships with external constituencies would not always be harmonious. For now, however, the campus was home to a number of women faculty and bright young women students eager for education and opportunity. For them, as for Bevier, the university opened up a whole new world.

Bevier often spoke of the campus atmosphere in those early days: "It was literally buzzing with newness, new buildings, new courses, new members of the faculty; Miss Katharine L. Sharp and Miss Violet D. Jayne were already at their respective jobs in the library and as Dean of Women; and a spirit of adventure, open-mindedness and experimentation prevailed." Shortly before Bevier's arrival, Dean Jayne had undertaken a project that illustrates this spirit of adventure. Seeking to build a stronger sense of community and intellectual purpose among the women students, she worked with them to edit and produce a special issue of the student paper featuring reports from women in virtually all curricular areas—including medicine, pharmacy, and architecture. The contributors to the *Illini Women's Number* of March 11, 1898, expressed buoyant optimism that the union of "learning and labor" would benefit all women, not just those with professional goals. Thus the essay by a woman in architecture distinguished the career-oriented woman from the homemaker but envisioned science and learning as fundamental to both roles. There was also great faith in the land-grant spirit and its promised "lack of boundaries" for women: "The fact that there need be no discrimination of sex in science," wrote the women in medicine, "has been fully demonstrated." While such optimism would often be challenged in the decades ahead, the campus at the turn of the century was unquestionably a thrilling place to be.

On September 1, 1900, Bevier settled into two rooms at 802 West Illinois Street in Urbana and went to confer with her new colleagues, including President Andrew Draper, Vice President Thomas Burrill, Dean of Agriculture Eugene Davenport (Bevier's immediate superior, whose career at Illinois hers would closely parallel), and faculty in a number of departments. Her tasks for the new department were many and pressing: she needed a name, a curriculum, students, faculty, a laboratory, a budget, and a building.

The selection of the department's name was a task assigned to Bevier, Davenport, and Burrill. In her published history of the department, Bevier described their decision: "The three of us wanted science as the basis and the scientific approach to the subject, but it was Dean Davenport who said, 'I believe there will be some day a science of the household. Let's get ready for it and develop it.' So the child was named 'Household Science' and thus due warning was given that neither a cooking school nor a milliner's shop was being opened in the university." Nonetheless, Bevier noted that in the university's annals of 1900 her "new child" was called variously the Department of Domestic Science, the School of Household Science, and Household Economics. "This variety of names," she pointed out, "shows something of the confusion attending the work."

Despite any reservations Bevier herself may have had about her new undertaking at Illinois, she was already, in Dean Mumford's words, "a woman of decided opinions and the courage to express them." What we know about Bevier's character and personal qualities comes largely from the descriptions of her contemporaries, published biographical accounts, and whatever deductions we can make from her own writings. Physically, she was tall, with clear skin and striking blue eyes, and she dressed beautifully. "When she came out to the President's reception in an Alice blue taffeta and silver lace gown," remembered one student, "we were as proud of her beauty as had she belonged to us." Widely admired by her students, she regularly invited them to tea at her home (and expected them to come) and kept in touch with them after they graduated; though kind, she preferred to inspire students to achievement than to coddle them.

Commentaries by students, friends, colleagues, and journalists are remarkably consistent and consistently decorous. Called Bel, Belle, or "Lady Bevier" by her friends, she was formally addressed as "Doctor Bevier," "Professor Bevier," and, in keeping with prevailing academic custom, "Miss Bevier." Intelligent and articulate, confident and determined, she would be called charismatic today. An unswerving Presbyterian throughout her life, she was frank, with little tolerance for puffery. Her detractors said she was tactless, dominating, and heedless of the interests of others—but her detractors were few and largely those who, in a phrase she often used, "did not speak the same language." Both male and female, her kindred spirits understood that the land-grant university opened "another great door of opportunity . . . for human betterment, another chance . . . for men and women, hand in hand, to work at the world's problems."

Bevier was both brilliant and steady in advocating for her program and the larger enterprise of home economics. Her academic writing is consistent and economical, with specific passages appearing and reappearing in lectures, articles, and books. Serious and visionary, Bevier was also lively and fun-loving, and liked nothing better than a good laugh. At one point, fed up with the never-ending problems of renovating and maintaining her department's physical space, she remarked to her former mentor Ellen Richards, "If only we could get a few things fixed and have them stay fixed." She never forgot Richards's reply: "My child, the things that are fixed are dead." She was herself capable of turning a humorous phrase. Asked to sit for the fashionable New York City portrait artist Louis Betts, she at first resisted; then "I thought, well, here I am getting older and uglier every day. If it has to be done, the sooner it is over the better." After she retired from Illinois, she chaired the home economics department at UCLA for two years and spent a semester at the University of Arizona, a state she came to hold in low esteem. "There is one thing I am sure of," she wrote to a friend, "and that is that the end of the world is a long way off. The Lord has too much to do in Arizona yet."

In 1900, Bevier needed a curriculum. Her guiding principle was that household science would introduce the *home* into the education of women, for women everywhere are members of households. Given the basic elements of human homes and households—food, clothing, and shelter—Bevier started with shelter. The curriculum required 130 semester hours for graduation, of which most were to be taken in the liberal arts and sciences and about a fourth in household science. So along with chemistry, bacteriology, and English literature that semester was the first offering in household science: "Home Architecture and Sanitation."

In the second semester, Bevier moved on to food. (She would soon add courses in clothing and textiles, and would later add a fourth basic element: art.) But how to teach about food? She consulted her domestic science counterparts at other land-grant institutions: "They reported that some began with water, others with fire." These struck her as "cooking school" approaches, and she decided instead to begin with the scientific classification of foods into the categories she had studied in Atwater's laboratory: proteins, fats, and carbohydrates. Once this broad principle was in place, "cooking" seemed an altogether inadequate approach, and so the course was titled "Selection and Preparation of Food." Such decisions were to be the source of her growing fame as a university educator but a source of vexation to her critics outside the university, who were faintly suspicious of "science" and "arts" applied to the stuff of everyday life. One of these, a school superintendent with two daughters at the university, took her to task over the first-year courses. "Do you know, " he said, waving the catalogue at her, "that nowhere here can one find the word 'cooking'?" "No indeed," she agreed serenely, "for cooking is certainly not the only thing we do with food. Some food we freeze, some we dry, some we just wash and eat raw. We are interested in much more than cooking." Meanwhile, the liberal arts faculty were equally skeptical: "How much credit do you give for bread baking?" asked the dean of the College of Literature and Arts sarcastically. Though Bevier's department would in fact conduct important research on the chemistry of bread, she had little interest in baking for its own sake. She was gratified when the same dean requested two years later that her household science courses be listed in the college's new catalogue. For a "department looked on with suspicion," she wrote later, this was a considerable triumph. (The College of Literature and Arts was consolidated in 1913 into the College of Liberal Arts and Sciences.)

Bevier was able to hire some faculty of her own; most she enlisted (that is to say, scrounged) from other departments, usually calling upon male full professors like James M. White in architecture, A. W. Palmer and H. S. Grindley in chemistry, and Eugene Davenport in agriculture. Ellen Richards had told her to look up "that nice old man in engineering, Dean Ricker. He is the best of them all." Ricker's original six lectures were eventually expanded into "The History of Architecture," offered to household science students. Through this strategy, Bevier obtained an excellent and prestigious faculty at no cost, secured the interdisciplinarity she sought, and strengthened campus investment in the success of the household science program. Many of these faculty would speak up during times of trouble in the years to follow.

Of students, there was no shortage. Twenty were admitted the first year, forty the second, sixty the third, and eighty the fourth. Bevier could have admitted many more, but she was determined to form a program of "real college students" enrolled to obtain a baccalaureate degree as opposed to "special students"—part-time or continuing education enrollees typically admitted for specific courses by less strict criteria. Her high admissions

Lucy Alexander demonstrates the chemical meat thermometer to Dr. Mohler, Dr. Stanley, and Miss Bevier. Appalled at the amount of overcooked meat she encountered in the Midwest, Bevier was the first to advocate the use of a thermometer to cook meat.

standards soon became another source of grievance to some of the department's external supporters—for were not young men admitted to other agriculture departments under lower standards than the campus average, and what was Household Science that it could afford to be so snobbish? But Bevier stuck to her guns and was rewarded when a Carnegie Foundation report rated Household Science the only real academic department in the college.

Bevier and her faculty had no choice but to write their own textbooks. For the "Home Architecture and Sanitation" course, for example, Bevier developed a text that later evolved into her published book, *The House* (1906, 1911). Praised by the educator and philosopher John Dewey as no "mere record of the past—but 'indirect sociology,'" *The House* illustrates the close relationship for Bevier of theory, innovative technologies, and everyday practice. On page 151, for example, she argues that aesthetic respect for color and form constitutes a *moral* obligation; poor heat and ugly design are "morally reprehensible" and lower "the value of human life." On page 155 is an illustration of an ingenious table on rollers designed for use in the kitchen, while on the opposite page we learn that wallpaper can be cleaned with bread dough. The book's diverse metaphors underline Bevier's vision of the ideal household science graduate: as the trained nurse sustains the life of the patient, so the trained house manager sustains the life of the household. Elsewhere, explaining the importance of plumbing, heating, and electrical wiring in the home economics curriculum, she compares the mistress of the home to the leader of an orchestra who must understand all the various instruments to achieve a pleasing harmony.

Obtaining a building for Household Science was an adventure all its own. Temporarily housed on the fourth floor of the Natural History Building, the department soon moved into the new Agriculture Building, where it occupied the north wing over the dairy. The space contained a kitchen, an office, part of a chemistry lab, and two classrooms, and was stocked with a variety of illustrative materials (many, again, the product of gifted scrounging). Soon after the move, Bevier's faculty learned the trustees were on campus. "I suppose the women trustees will come here first," said one, assuming they would want to see this brand-new department in its new quarters. "I doubt it," Bevier replied. "They usually go to the cattle barns and don't have time to get here." Only over time did she develop a mutual language and understanding with the women trustees and come to think of them as her allies.

With its enrollment and activities expanding, the department needed new space almost at once. For many years, there had been efforts to construct a Woman's Building. Finally, in 1903, thanks once again to the efforts of Mrs. Dunlap, the state legislature appropriated $80,000 for the purpose and in 1905 (with an additional appropriation of $15,000), the Woman's Building became a reality. Dedicated on October 16, 1905, the new building was a handsome New England colonial of red brick and white stone designed by the New York architectural firm of McKim, Meade and White. As President Draper, to Bevier's sorrow, had left for a position in the East, Edmund James, now president, spoke at the dedication.

The name of the Woman's Building—with *woman* in the singular—was intended to give every individual woman on campus a sense of proprietorship and belonging. The household science department was housed in the north wing. Stocked with new laboratories and equipment, the space would also accommodate the annual school for housekeepers; this event, which had grown in five years from an attendance of thirty to 175, was held on campus each January in cooperation with the FIHSD. The central section of the building housed the Department of Physical Education and included a women's swimming pool and a gymnasium. The south wing served as social headquarters for women on campus, with the dean of women's office, lounges for students, and upper parlors for social events. Here women could go to retreat, as needed, from the strains of coeducation; men's access to the building was greatly restricted, despite their requests for wider use. This points to the important function of the Woman's Building as a kind of campus hospitality center, providing food, pleasant space, and spectacular dances. *Illio* yearbooks and other memorabilia, including enchanting dance cards, describe the arrival of guests under the graceful west side portico and commemorate the glamour and excitement of these evenings.

In 1909, the household science department also opened an experimental house near the Woman's Building, on the corner of Wright and Daniel streets in Champaign. Though such a laboratory for home economics teaching and research had been proposed on other campuses, the house at Illinois seems to have been the first to actually exist. By spending time there, even living in for short periods, students learned to divide up domestic floor space; figure out where to put the furnace, doors, and windows; apply paint and wallpaper; furnish rooms to achieve different aesthetic effects; and manage a household budget. The house contained an expensive kitchen and an inexpensive kitchen, as well as rooms furnished in both good and bad taste. The house attracted considerable media attention and sometimes as many as eighty visitors a day.

* * *

After a decade at Illinois, Bevier had achieved her original goals. Students, faculty, building, and curriculum were in place, and the department was held in high academic esteem from coast to coast. She decided to take a leave in 1910 to catch her breath and visit other schools and research programs around the country. In her absence, the growing friction between her and her critics outside the university came to a head. In her own writings, Bevier described the prolonged crisis in fairly restrained language: "Meanwhile the age-old conflict between the cooking and sewing school adherents and those who believed in the scientific method of approach to the teaching of HS had gone on in the Farmers' Institute circle." (Elsewhere Bevier called their work "haphazard, politically dominated.") An early grievance was that Bevier had hung a reproduction of Millet's painting *The Gleaners* in the Household Science reception room; some of the FIHSD ladies objected to this "foreign example" for they themselves did not approve of American women working in the fields. Another point of contention was the selection of a home advisor, usually a woman with some farm experience. When someone objected to the selection of a particular candidate without such experience, Bevier said, "I'm not so much interested in whether the young woman has lived on a farm or in town as I am whether or not she has *lived*. I think this woman has."

In 1908, Mrs. Dunlap had become president of the FIHSD. She grew increasingly infuriated with what she perceived as Bevier's high-handed manner and failure to consult regularly with the external benefactors of Household Science. Her grievances soon encompassed Bevier's insistence on university standards for entrance; her failure to provide instruction around the state in practical cooking, sewing, and nutrition; and her commitment to what Mrs. Dunlap considered scientific nonsense. (Mrs. Dunlap had lost several children and had come to attribute their deaths not to diphtheria, the doctors' explanation, but to nutritional deficiencies; this populist antagonism toward physicians and scientists may have exacerbated her hostility toward the university in general and Bevier in particular.) Things calmed down somewhat during Bevier's absence, but when Mrs. Dunlap learned that Bevier would be returning in the fall of 1911, she was enraged and called a special meeting of the FIHSD board at her home in Champaign. Earlier, they had demanded that Bevier accept the appointment of an external advisory committee made up of women from the FIHSD; if she agreed to this, Mrs. Dunlap and her supporters would in turn seek an additional appropriation for the university's household science activities. To this Bevier had replied tartly that she already had three distinguished deans and a university president to advise her and that was quite sufficient. Bevier later reflected that "possibly had I not been so busy developing the department, writing textbooks, speaking, etc and had had the patience and had taken the time to seek the favor of these women, the breach might have been avoided." But she did not have patience, and had known from the beginning that they would never speak the same language on the subject of household science.

At Mrs. Dunlap's special July board meeting, it was resolved to further investigate "the matter of cooperation with the Household Science Department in the university"; to go to the board of trustees to seek "a satisfactory adjustment"; and to withhold nominations for scholarships, cooperation on speakers for events, publicity for the housekeepers school, and so on until such "adjustment" was secured. Implicitly, the charges against Bevier's department were now also tied to the FIHSD's willingness to seek further state appropriations for household science.

The dispute, and particularly the matter of the appropriation, was of great concern to the university, or at any rate to Davenport, who continually worried about money and whose College of Agriculture depended so critically on good relationships with the farming constituency. He also believed that a good administrator should always be able to avoid such disputes, and had expressed his irritation with Bevier in a letter to President James in March: she "seems to regard criticism from outside the university as an unwarranted interference, quite opposite to the feeling in other departments of the College of Agriculture." Davenport was pleased with Susannah Usher, Bevier's replacement during her leave, who "has shown a remarkable faculty for getting on with people and situations." He recommended to the president that Bevier be asked to resign and that Household Sciences become a college separate from Agriculture. (At the same time, he strongly defended the university's autonomy in a long letter to the president of the Farmers' Institute, enumerating the negative consequences of the FIHSD's "extremely dangerous" course of action for long-term relationships between the university and "outside organizations.")

Bevier, meanwhile, was pondering what to do. She had been "warned by Dean Davenport if I refused this offer [of the external advisory council] I must do it at my own risk. I said, 'I take the risk.'" Despite Davenport's recommendation that she resign, she was confident in the support of her department and others at the university and felt strongly that an external group should not be given power over the actions of a respected professor. Nonetheless, she wrote, "Dean Davenport honestly felt that the good of the department would be served by my resignation." Finally, she consulted her old friend and mentor, former President Andrew Draper. "He said, 'If you leave now you can spend the rest of your life telling why you left the university of Illinois. Go back and tend strictly to your own business and I think you will be supported.'"

In his account of this crisis, historian Richard Gordon Moores attributes its resolution to the skillful behind-the-scenes maneuvering of Davenport, Burroughs, other friends-of-Agriculture, and the board of trustees. But women on and off campus also provided strong support for Bevier. It soon became clear that Davenport had urged her to resign without really investigating Mrs. Dunlap's charges or how representative they were. Not only were Bevier's university colleagues up in arms, outrage was spreading among many members of the FIHSD. Shortly after the special meeting in July one of the organization's former presidents received a letter reporting the actions against Bevier: "I am struck *dumb*," she wrote back, indicating that she would propose a resolution condemning the FIHSD's action. Her additional comment suggests that Mrs. Dunlap was actually rather isolated in her views and vehemence: "I think Nora (Mrs. Dunlap) will do less harm to the Uni[versity] now that she has come out openly against it than she used to. She will have so much rope she will hang herself. I don't know what she will talk about when she cannot find fault with the Uni." She then cosigned a letter to President James from herself and two other FIHSD presidents, together spanning the years 1898–1908, testifying to their high regard for Bevier. The view expressed by the current officers of the FIHSD, they wrote, "is so untrue and so unjust that we hasten to refute it." Throughout their years as officers, they testified, Miss Bevier had worked with them "earnestly and carefully and cheerfully. Her assistance was of inestimable value to the work of our organization." Once it was clear that, as Davenport later conceded, he had "greatly overestimated the strength of the opposition," the crisis appeared to be resolved and the close working relationship between Bevier and Davenport resumed, with its former respect and cordiality. Though Moores concedes that Davenport may have been "understandably upset" by Bevier's attitude, he by no means exonerates him. "The important point . . . is that Isabel Bevier was brought to the University of Illinois to develop a home economics curriculum of genuine college caliber and she had succeeded brilliantly. Making all due allowances for the harassment Davenport suffered from the [FIHSD] as a result of Miss Bevier's lack of tact, the fact remains that he sacrificed academic principle for political expediency in asking for her resignation."

In any case, the legislature appropriated funds for an addition to the Woman's Building in 1911, and Bevier's department could at last look forward to more space. Despite their need, they hated the new design, which threatened to spoil "our beautiful colonial architecture." Particularly irritating, Bevier told President James, was the addition of pillars to the front entrance, along the east side of the building. "For heaven's sake," said the president, "don't call them pillars. The state architect nearly had a fit with the trustees calling them pillars." Rather, he told her, they must be called "pylons." "Never anything better named," Bevier replied. "The whole addition is a pile-on."[2]

Ugly or not, Household Science got a new kitchen and dining room in the basement, a diet kitchen on the second floor, and a room for electrical equipment. Best of all, they got a cafeteria and a five-room practice apartment. President James had resisted Bevier's request for the apartment, which was to be built in otherwise wasted space. "You won't like it when you get it," he told her; "the windows will have to be in the corners because it is such a queer shape, and the space is altogether too small." She replied that if whole families in Chicago could live in apartments far smaller than this one, she believed the architects would be able to manage. Like the earlier experimental house (which had been shut down during Bevier's 1910–11 leave), the practice apartment constituted a laboratory for research and teaching with emphasis (in contrast to the cafeteria) on the problems of the private household. A student would typically spend a week cooking for a group of six, then the next week tackle some other phase of domestic life, including home care of the sick and public health concerns in the home. The opening of the new addition was celebrated informally on April 25, 1913, with luncheon in the new cafeteria served by the household science department to members of the University Senate.

The Smith-Lever Act of 1914, the "third leg of the three-legged stool" of agricultural education, research, and extension, formally clarified the relationship of the university to such nonprofessional organizations as the Farmers' Institute by instructing land-grant institutions to work cooperatively with the Department of Agriculture to extend teaching and research throughout the state. Extension agents and offices would henceforth be hired to translate new academic knowledge in agriculture and household science into information that could be put into practice statewide.[3] For this task the institutions would receive significant federal funding, and thus considerable financial independence from external lobbying organizations. Mamie Bunch, the first household science extension worker in Illinois, was a graduate of Bevier's department. The Smith-Hughes Act of 1917 provided additional federal funding to promote vocational training in home economics, agriculture, trades, and industry and to support the training of teachers in these subjects. In the wake of these two powerful mandates, Bevier proposed to change the name of her program, and in 1918 it officially became the Department of Home Economics. The change may have been pragmatic, but it also shifted the focus of the department's activities to those that had become most crucial during World War I.

When the United States entered the war in 1917, Bevier began to develop a range of domestic conservation efforts, training women throughout Illinois in a comprehensive program of thrift: home canning of vegetables and fruit, clothing renovation and cooking substitutions for rationed materials, home nursing, first aid. Serving as chair of the Department of Conservation of the Illinois women's committee of the Council of National Defense (as did home economics leaders at other land-grant institutions), she brought further national and international recognition to the university and to the field itself. Indeed, suggests Moores, it was during the war that "home economics came of age." As Bevier herself observed, "the people of the United States learned more of . . . home economics in one year of war time than they had learned in five years before."

Bevier was then called to Washington with other home economics practitioners to plan war work for the Department of Agriculture in cooperation with state extension services and other agencies. Thereafter she was appointed director of home economics for Illinois under the U.S. Food Administration. In October of that year, President Herbert Hoover asked that she be granted a leave of absence from the university to work with the Food Administration in Washington. Returning to campus in 1918, she chaired the Subcommittee on Food of the University War Committee. Many photographs in the *Illio* yearbooks of this period document the war activities of students, faculty, and the cooperative extension. Overall, the war made the nation aware of important connections beween food and health, and significant new research initiatives took shape in the postwar period. At the same time, the war had created new opportunities for women. Bevier energetically documented the roles that women trained in home economics could fill.

The war had also, however, brought much of the department's research and internal development to a halt. In her 1917 annual letter to alumnae, Bevier commented philosophically on this inevitable disruption: "I think the Department has seemed somewhat phlegmatic because we have neither thundered nor lightened, but we have done considerable in the way of getting word to the papers as to what to do with asparagus and rhubarb, and the Extension Division is to follow it up as other fruits and vegetables appear. The regulars are to publish meals and menus giving calorific value and actual meals eaten in the apartment or in the cafeteria."

Things gradually returned to normal, but by 1920 Bevier recognized that before long her department would once again have to find new space. Physically exhausted, unwilling to go through another building quest, and eager to do new things, Bevier submitted her resignation to Dean Davenport. At that point she was earning an annual salary of $4,000, of which one-fourth was paid from Smith-Lever funds. Davenport and Kinley persuaded her to stay on until August 1921, for which service Davenport obtained a raise to $4,500. In April 1922, the board of trustees conferred on her the title of professor emeritus.

After two decades at Illinois, she was urged by her department to sit for the portrait artist Louis Betts. Once she had decided to do so, she embarked on the two weeks of daily sittings in New York City with her typical zest and sent many entertaining accounts home to her friends of "having my picture made." Betts asked her, "I can paint the executive, the woman, or the scholar—Which shall it be?" and Bevier had promptly replied, "The woman." To the blue velvet gown Bevier brought with her to wear, Betts added a white lace shawl and, in order to create "a portrait of and for all times," removed jewelry and anything else that would date the work. Bevier reportedly found the final product pleasing and unpretentious. Presented to the university by the Department of Home Economics on May 21, 1921, the portrait generally evoked admiration. One friend wrote to Bevier that

Louis Betts's famous portrait of Isabel Bevier, dedicated on May 21, 1921. The painting was hung on the wall of the Green Parlour in the Woman's Building until it was moved to the newly built Bevier Hall where, with Lita Bane's portrait, it was rededicated in 1975.

"Nothing could be more lovely! All the nicest of you, the real you, right there before me!" Another reported that when visitors to campus saw the portrait, she was "continually forced to correct them by saying, 'No, not a foreign princess, but our Miss Bevier.'"

Whereas Bevier's public writing and correspondence communicate a firm, unflappable administrative style, her personal diaries sometimes record a less serene perspective on her department's administrative crises. In March 1918, for example, her cooperative spirit was sorely tried: "Had a great shock today. Summoned to the President's office and told that Woman's Bldg. was to be given to aviators. Trustees agree. Deed practically done. Secret talks only to Professor White and president."[4] The building crisis went on for two weeks. At first discouraged and determined to resign if the building were taken away, Bevier took heart when others joined her efforts. Her resistance led to a sharp exchange with the president, who called her threat to resign "a coward's trick." Later that afternoon the president stopped by her office and, finding her out, called her at home later: "Apologizes!!" she wrote in her diary. "Says matter not settled. Just wants to do what is wise." The following day she prepared to address the Administrative Council on the subject, accompanied by six other women faculty. But an inspector general representing the aviators appeared suddenly at her department. "His visit upsets Council meeting so we seven—dressed up and nowhere to go—[eat dinner on campus] in fighting mood."[5] After several attempts to reschedule her presentation and to have the president meet with the group of women faculty, she got a surprise phone call: "A brand new experience. Sat. the president had a sudden inspiration that I should speak before legislative Council. So one woman and seven men journeyed to Springfield," where they addressed the councils for both the Illinois House and Senate. Bevier's final administrative crisis at Illinois soon came to a happy conclusion. "A memorable day," she wrote on March 27, "perhaps a historic one because today two representatives of the College of Liberal Arts—Misses Kyle and Blaisdell—two of the Library school—Misses Simpson and Curtiss—two of my staff, Misses Bunch and Wheeler—went with me to the Trustee room to speak about the reasons why the Woman's Bldg should not be given over to the aviators. Speakers were so good. President so gracious. Came away much encouraged."

* * *

In a 1935 radio talk celebrating Bevier's seventy-fifth birthday, Margaret Whitlock lamented that no Boswell had existed to record and commemorate her Beverian outlook. Bevier's personal diaries, attesting to her occasional "fighting mood," begin to add such a dimension to the official record. *Co-ed*, a novel published in 1926 by Illinois alumna Olive Deane Hormel (Class of '16), further enriches our portrait of Bevier and the life of the campus. In *Co-Ed*, the coming-of-age novel meets roman à clef, and fabled faculty and administrators of the period appear, thinly disguised, in its cast of characters. These include Miss Bevier ("Miss Bovard"), Queen Lois Shepard in philosophy ("Miss Herder"), and Lorado Taft ("Leonardo Kraft"), sculptor of the Alma Mater statue. The novel was enthusiastically praised by David Kinley, the straitlaced university president, who called it a true picture of the institution. In fact, what he really liked was that *Co-Ed* helped supplant *Town and Gown*, an earlier novel about the university he disliked intensely.

Published in 1923, *Town and Gown* is a collection of linked stories by Lois Seyster Montross (Class of '19) and her husband, Lynn Montross. Fairly sophisticated and ironic in tone, the book was called "unwholesome" by some reviewers. *Town and Gown* is largely concerned with fraternity and sorority life; the "land-grant mission" appears only to be mocked (to be fair, most characters in the stories are unappealing though by no means uninteresting). In one story, two undergraduate students have sexual intercourse beside a tombstone in what is clearly Mount Hope Cemetery. For Kinley, this was bad enough. Much worse was that the couple had no apparent intent to marry. "Will do for the great universities of the mid-west," wrote one enthusiastic reviewer, "what F. Scott Fitzgerald did for Princeton." Exactly! Kinley wanted it banned.

Co-Ed, then, was a great relief. True, its protagonist Lucia Leigh is also a sorority girl, but she grows disenchanted with Greek life, sensing "something rotten at the core of things." Gradually she sees that the university's real significance lies in its intellectual resources, serious commitment to women's education, and land-grant philosophy. Other ideas and debates of the day play out in the novel. Bevier believed, for example, that home economics had the opportunity "to teach something of the beauty of life and the unity of life, to teach that there is an art in the well-ordered home and the well-ordered life: and that perhaps is the greatest thing that home economics has to do." Lucia's parents and their family home embody such a life. They are surrounded by books and music, art and beauty, and an equally well-ordered experimental farm. Their house, "Broadlands on the Sangamon," is "a long low house" at the end of a "pine and hawthorn bordered drive": "Wide-roofed and generous-windowed, it stood on the crest of a broad undulation, its level lines melting into the flowing contour of surrounding prairie, as authentic a part of the landscape as the broad-branching trees which sheltered it."[6] Lucia later learns that the house is celebrated in the landscape department, which proclaims it "a triumph of harmonious heterogeneity in the prairie tradition." Though such jargon is not at all Beverian, the house clearly represents her aesthetic taste, which ran toward the clean designs of William Morris and Frank Lloyd Wright: in her book *The House*, she urged homemakers to gather their pretentious, nonfunctional, and purely decorative possessions—their "rubbish"—and exchange them all "for one beautiful picture, or comfortable chair, or a table that will hold something and thus add simplicity and comfort to the house."

Though many inhabitants of Champaign-Urbana's "dead-level landscape" have sought in vain for such a house as Broadlands—set "on the crest of a broad undulation" indeed!—the novel is otherwise full of references and scenes that are familiar. In an early scene, Lucia tells two male undergraduates that she plans to go to Vassar. The quieter of the two, Phil Moore, says nothing, but the cheekier one asks, "So you're headed for that hennery on the Hudson, are you?" and recommends that she give "Old State" a try. Laughing that her aunt "turns pale" at the thought that she might go to a public university, Lucia is nonetheless impressed by the enthusiasm with which the young men talk about their campus. Its scale is immense and its buildings all appear to be architectural treasures— University Hall, Lincoln Hall, the Music Building. The Chemistry Building is "the biggest college building in the world, you know, given all to just one subject." And "the Armory. A whale of a shack. Gosh, you can see it for miles—and it's the biggest undivided floor space in the country under a single roof without visible supports. Something about the angle of the arch, you know." Lucia's father chimes in to praise "the whole state-university system with its great ideal of education for the people by the people." And the cradle of it all is Illinois, "a Farmer's Convention at Granville back in 1851." He and the young men praise the democratic leveling power of the public university. Its cross-fertilization across fields of study and student backgrounds constitutes "a mighty power against class insulation and intolerance." (While *Co-Ed* tackles class in many guises, it is disappointing on racial insulation and intolerance.) Such cross-fertilization across fields is illustrated when Lucia's friend in landscape design describes a brilliant classmate who's graduating in June, probably as valedictorian: "Stepping right into a good position in a big brick-works as soon as he graduates, but interested in a lot more than brick-laying. Has some ideas on the artistic possibilities of manufacture that I want him to talk over with Leonardo Kraft when he comes down to give his Sculpture Series."

Most interesting as far as Bevier herself is concerned is Lucia's visit to "Miss Bovard" in the Woman's Building to see the dining room and practice apartment, where she finds two of her friends living in for two weeks, learning to manage all the domestic arrangements that would be required of a woman in charge of a home. Such training, Miss Bovard tells Lucia, seeks "to instill ideas and real possession of skill into the making of a better home life, and to transform the housewife by virtue thereof from harassed drudge to intelligent director in the domestic demesne." As an earnest tribute to the midwestern land-grant university, *Co-Ed* was immensely appealing to President Kinley. Though in fact *Co-Ed* touches on just as many unsavory undergraduate doings as *Town and Gown*, including premarital sex, sexual harassment, abortion, kickbacks, drinking, and graft, it is redeemed by its unequivocal moral uplift. When Lucia and Phil walk together into the South Farms at sunset, the university president must have been particularly pleased.

Perhaps no episode epitomizes Bevier's own commitment to the well-ordered life as her encounter with breast cancer at the age of seventy-seven. In excellent health her whole life, she was at home in Urbana when she made the following diary entry: "As I was getting ready for bed, I, to my amazement discovered a little lump in my left breast. I realized what it might mean and went to bed a good deal disturbed."[7] Breast cancer at the time was by no means the acknowledged public reality it has become today (accounts of

Bevier's life do not mention it). There was no *Susan Love's Breast Book*, no self-help videos at libraries and drugstores, no prostheses and special bras in mail order catalogues, no proud one-breasted supermodels on magazine covers, no Internet support groups. Yet as Bevier's diary makes clear, she was neither ignorant nor silent about the lump and its implications. The following morning she showed the lump to her grandniece and companion, Mary Morrow, and asked Dr. Draper, her local physician, to come to her home. Her surprise at finding the lump was evidently echoed by Dr. Draper: "The lump seemed so small and so soft and I was so well I thot [*sic*] it must certainly be harmless and Dr. D. seemed to agree."[8] Yet he was unequivocal: the lump must come out. To her surprise, Bevier learned that he himself could do the procedure—presumably a biopsy—in Urbana. Despite the greater risk of publicity, she decided not to go to Chicago; staying at home would be "Easier for Mary and everybody."[9] The next day, a Sunday, she went to church, "feeling I might not go again for some time."

As she prepared for her hospital stay, she learned of close friends and colleagues who had faced the same ordeal. Lita Bane, her colleague, friend, and later biographer, "had had a lump removed from each breast at different times";[10] another woman, she learned, "had had 2 operations also, and ate supper after the first one!!"[11]

She prepared for her hospital stay with her customary care: "I got nightgowns, a coral dressing jacket. Got out the 'pull-overs' I owned and shawls ready for my bag." "Of course I dreaded the hospital," she added, "but felt it could not be malignant." Though Bevier's matter-of-fact account never uses the word *cancer,* she clearly understood that a positive biopsy would necessitate the removal of the breast. As a scientist, she wanted no part of the delicate convention in which such bad news was never directly communicated to the woman herself, and recorded on March 3 that Dr. Draper "had promised he would tell the truth whatever it was." On Friday, March 4, Lita took her to the hospital "under cover of darkness." Her plans were known only to the hospital and a few friends and colleagues who served throughout the experience (as they do for many academics) as her family. "Lita," she wrote, "unpacked my bag and did all she could to give me moral support. She left early evening. Nurses appeared. I was given a sleeping potion and slept well."[12]

At least some of Bevier's diary entries concerning the breast lump and surgery appear to have been composed in retrospect, with some information supplied by others and entered chronologically, probably after she had returned home. Thus Saturday, March 5, 1938: "The day I had dreaded began before 6 with a man to get blood for tests. Then a nurse shaved my breast and all about it. Fannie [Brooks] telephoned she would arrive at 7:40. By that time I was so drugged I knew very little." Bevier carefully related the surgery and its outcome: "Was back in my room the nurse said before 10 A.M. but I knew nothing until about 4. Then I knew from the look on Lita's face that it was malignant. She and Fannie had stood by. And they and the Dr. were so disappointed. Dr. D. said 'I took the left breast off.' That told the truth as promised. I had no appetite. Was given a drink of ice water which came right up then hot tea which did likewise. I felt as tho I had 3 big plasters of mud drying on me and I was uncomfortable all night. Felt so warm. In the A.M. orange juice really tasted good and I ate a little chicken at noon. Kathryn marvelled that I looked so well." Friends, students, and colleagues soon learned she was ill. By Tuesday "the word had gone out and flowers began to come in."[13] "Surely nobody ever had more reason to thank for her friends," she wrote some days later. "Betsey Ross came with wonderful glads. Mrs. Adams brot violets, and cards came every mail."[14] Meanwhile, she was recovering from the surgery. A few days later, "Dr. Draper came and took out the stitches and said the wound was healing wonderfully. I had little pain but so conscious of my breast and its loss. Was glad to have the bandage so much less. Had my first night alone and really was glad to be alone."

The diary does not make clear whether the nature of her illness was widely known. Certainly it was never reported in the newspaper, in professional correspondence, or in existing biographical accounts of her life and work. Nor do the diaries indicate the long-term outcome of the malignancy. Official accounts attribute her death four years later, on March 17, 1942, to arteriosclerotic heart disease "following a long illness." The local newspaper obituary reported that "Miss Bevier had been in failing health for some time and more recently had been receiving treatment in McKinley hospital."

Just as Bevier's scientific approach to the problems of the home emphasized theory and practice, her legacy is both theoretical and practical. Alongside the theoretical foundations of the field she developed are a number of significant technological innovations. Her interest in chemistry, for example, led her to originate the use of the chemical thermometer in the cooking of meat. Her determination that students grasp the chemical principles that produce good bread led her to design a "score card" to quantify the properties of bread for scientific research; it was then widely used to standardize judging in state and county baking competitions. As the graduate program began developing, one of her research faculty discovered precisely what makes jelly jell, a secret which, Bevier noted, "had been carefully guarded by commercial workers." The Demonstration Car for extension work, a converted Pullman, was fitted out with the latest in plumbing, electricity, and sanitation systems as well as modern conveniences, including a washing machine, mangle, cream separator, vacuum cleaner, and ice cream freezer. It toured the state with a male extension agent and a female extension agent (who, spending day after day together, were married in 1918).

Let me close with the opening verse of an anthem written by Regent John Gregory for the university's inaugural ceremonies in 1868 and set to music by Chicago composer George F. Root:

> O'er homes of the millions, o'er fields of rich toil,
> Thy science shall shine as the sun shines on soil,
> And Learning and Labor—fit head for fit hand—
> Shall crown with twin glories our broad prairie land.

Richard Gordon Moores chose *O'er Fields of Rich Toil* as the title for his history of the College of Agriculture at Illinois. The other half of the first line makes a fitting legacy for Isabel Bevier, who joined "Learning and Labor" and made science shine "o'er homes of the millions." A frequently quoted passage by Bevier herself offers her own tribute to the land-grant institution she came to love and the kind of learning and labor it enabled her to do: "In the early days of my own work, I very soon learned to distinguish whether the passing visitor, of whom there were many, belonged to the Land-grant College or to the traditional classical school, by the response which they made to my statement: 'We are working at the problems of the home from the scientific basis.' The man from the Land-grant College said: 'Yes, the home opens up a very interesting field for the application of science.' The man from the classical school looked at me a little questioningly and said: 'Yes, yes,—are we a little late for breakfast? Are the biscuits gone?' In other words, the former understood my language."

ACKNOWLEDGMENTS

I want to thank Himika Bhabhachandra, doctoral student in the School of Social Work, whose able research assistance on this project included the identification and copying of materials in the UIUC archives as well as transcription of Bevier's personal diaries. Alice Filmer, doctoral student in the Institute of Communications Research, secured additional resources from the home economics library. Thanks also to William Maher, Director of the UIUC archives, for his expert assistance and to Lillian Hoddeson for excellent editorial suggestions.

A NOTE ON SOURCES

Primary sources for this essay include the papers in the UIUC archives of Isabel Bevier, Eugene Davenport, Edmund James, and Charles Shamel. Bevier materials located for many years in the home economics library were moved in early 2003 to the new library of the College of Agricultural, Consumer and Environmental Sciences (ACES). Photocopies of Bevier's diaries are in the archives; the originals are in the ACES Library archives. The diary entries on breast cancer are in her 1935–40 papers, box 3. Photographs come primarily from the UIUC archives and from the author's collection of yearbooks, photographs, and memorabilia. Material and citations from Bevier come chiefly from "The History of Home Economics at University of Illinois, 1900–1921" (typewritten manuscript, home economics library, University of Illinois, 1935), fifty pages; "Recollections and Impressions of the Beginnings of the Department of Home Economics at the University of Illinois," *Journal of Home Economics* 32 (May 1940): 291–97 (this published paper shares many passages with Bevier's 1935 manuscript, but often not verbatim); *The House* (Chicago: American School of Home Economics, 1911); and numerous lectures, manuscripts, and published papers collected in the archives. Additional primary sources include Dorothy Day, *The Long Loneliness: The Autobiography of Dorothy Day* (New York: Harper, 1952); Olive Deane Hormel, *Co-Ed* (New York: Charles Scribner's Sons, 1926); and Lois Seyster Montross and Lynn Montross, *Town and Gown* (New York: George H. Doran, 1923).

Secondary sources include Lita Bane, *The Story of Isabel Bevier* (Peoria: University of Illinois Chapter of Phi Upsilon Omicron, 1955), which quotes extensively from Bevier's accounts of the history of home economics; Joan Jacobs Brumberg and Nancy Tomes, "Women in the Professions: A Research Agenda for American Historians," *Reviews in American History* 10 (1982): 275–96; Mary Loise Filbey, "Early History of the Deans of Women, University of Illinois, 1897–1923" (typescript, 1969), Filbey Family Papers, RS 41/20/38, University of Illinois at Urbana-Champaign archives; Margaret Goodyear, "Rededication of Portraits of Isabel Bevier and Lita Bane," School of Human Resources and Family Studies Alumni Meeting, October 18, 1975 typescript; original in 41/67/70 Home Economics Alumni Association History, University of Illinois at Urbana-Champaign archives; Karl Max Grisso, "David Kinley, 1861–1944: The Career of the Fifth President of the University of Illinois" (Ph.D. dissertation, University of Illinois at Urbana-Champaign, 1980); Richard Gordon Moores, *Fields of Rich Toil: The Development of the University of Illinois College of Agriculture* (Urbana: University of Illinois Press, 1970); Jessica Mudry, "Enumerating Food," paper presented at the annual meeting of the National Communication Association, New Orleans, November 2002; Allan Nevins, *Illinois* (New York: Oxford University Press, 1971); Rosalind Rosenberg, *Beyond Separate Spheres: Intellectual Roots of Modern Feminism* (New Haven: Yale University Press, 1982); Margaret Rossiter, *Women Scientists in America: Struggles and Strategies to 1940* (Baltimore: Johns Hopkins University Press, 1982); Sarah Stage and Virginia B. Vincenti, eds., *Rethinking Home Economics: Women and the History of a Profession* (Ithaca: Cornell University Press, 1997); Carl Stephens, "Manuscript History of the University of Illinois," RS 26/1/21, University of Illinois at Urbana-Champaign archives; Janice Smith, 1962; "Isabel Bevier, Pioneer in the Land-Grant Movement," *Home Economics Alumni Association History* (Fall 1962): 16–17; Winton U. Solberg, *The University of Illinois 1867–1894* (Urbana: University of Illinois Press, 1968) as well as Solberg's entry on Bevier in *Notable American Women*, ed. Edward T. James (Cambridge, Mass.: Belknap Press of Harvard University Press, 1971); Paula A. Treichler, "Alma Mater's Sorority: Women at the University of Illinois 1890–1925," in *For Alma Mater: Theory and Practice in Feminist Scholarship*, ed. Paula A. Treichler, Cheris Kramarae, and Beth Stafford (Urbana: University of Illinois Press, 1985), 5–61; Laurence R.

Veysey, *The Emergence of the American University* (Chicago: University of Chicago Press, 1965); and Margaret Whitlock, radio talk celebrating Isabel Bevier's seventy-fifth birthday, Homemakers' Hour, University of Illinois Radio Station, November 15, 1935, transcript in Bevier papers, University of Illinois at Urbana-Champaign archives.

A number of Web sites document the history of home economics. On the Smith-Lever Act, for example, see ‹www.reeusda.gov/1700/legis/s-l.htm›. On the University of Illinois extension, see ‹www.extension.uiuc.edu/about/history.html›. A conference rethinking the history of home economics was held at Cornell University in 1996; papers from the conference are collected in Sarah Stage and Virginia B. Vincenti, eds., *Rethinking Home Economics: Women and the History of a Profession* (Ithaca: Cornell University Press, 1997), and the Web site created for the conference includes the following URLs (for materials in the Cornell Rare Manuscript Collection): ‹www.rmc.library.cornell.edu/homeEc/masterlabel.html› and ‹www.rmc. library.cornell.edu/homeEc/bibliography.html›.

NOTES

1. Heeding Joan Jacobs Brumberg and Nancy Tomes's 1982 call for a new research agenda for the historical study of women in the professions, scholars at a conference at Cornell University in 1996 challenged three earlier assumptions about the founders of home economics: that they were reformist rather than revolutionary, that they acquiesced to the "separate spheres" division of labor, and that they accommodated rather than resisted the patriarchal structure of existing institutions (see the 1997 collection edited by Sarah Stage and Virginia B. Vincenti under "A Note on Sources").
2. Isabel Bevier, "The History of Home Economics at University of Illinois, 1900–1921" typewritten manuscript, home economics library, University of Illinois, 1935, 39.
3. The original extension model envisioned professional experts taking elite knowledge "down to the farms." Only in the last couple of decades have land-grant institutions begun to reconfigure the extension mission as interactive rather than authoritative, a collaboration of research findings and local knowledge.
4. Isabel Bevier diaries, March 13, 1918 entry, ACES library archives, University of Illinois at Urbana-Champaign.
5. Ibid., March 19, 1918 entry.
6. Olive Deane Hormel, *Co-Ed* (New York: Charles Scribner's Sons, 1926), 4.
7. Bevier diaries, February 23, 1938 entry.
8. Ibid., February 24, 1938 entry.
9. Ibid.
10. Ibid., February 28, 1938 entry.
11. Ibid., March 1, 1938 entry.
12. Ibid., March 4, 1938 entry.
13. Ibid., March 8, 1938 entry.
14. Ibid., March 11, 1938 entry.

RICHARD W. BURKHARDT JR.

AND DANIEL W. SCHNEIDER

CHAPTER 4

Stephen A. Forbes:

The Intricate Interrelations of Living Things

Today the term *ecology* has two very different meanings. On the one hand, it refers to environmental politics, as in the phrase "the ecology movement." In this sense, it encompasses political efforts to conserve biodiversity, control pollution, and curb global warming. *Ecology* also refers to the scientific study of organisms and their relationships to their physical environment and each other. The work of Stephen Alfred Forbes (1844–1930), one of the founders of American ecology, embraced both these meanings. To fashion his career, Forbes drew on his immediate surroundings. The rivers, lakes, prairies, and farms of Illinois, his home state, offered the natural settings for his ecological concepts, while the University of Illinois provided the institutional base for his activities as scientist and public servant.

Forbes was forty in 1884 when he accepted a professorship at Illinois Industrial University, soon to be renamed the University of Illinois. His starting salary was $3,000—50 percent higher than that of any other full professor. He had spent the last decade and a half practicing medicine, teaching, and studying plants and animals in Illinois. He had come to hold "a conviction of the general beneficence of Nature, a profound respect for the natural order, a belief that the part of wisdom is essentially that of practical conservatism in dealing with the system of things by which we are surrounded." In addressing ecological questions he characteristically recommended "conservative action" and "exhaustive inquiry" (i.e., more science).[1]

Forbes was born May 29, 1844, in Stephenson County, Illinois, to a pioneering family of Scotch and Dutch descent. His father, Isaac Forbes, and his uncle, Stephen Van Rensselear Forbes, first visited Illinois fifteen years earlier as part of a surveying party. Stephen V. R. Forbes settled in the Chicago area in 1830 and became Chicago's first schoolteacher. Later he was elected Cook County's first sheriff. Isaac Forbes brought his family from New York in 1836 to settle near Freeport, Illinois, where he hoped to make a living as a farmer.

Life on the prairie proved hard. When Isaac succumbed to pneumonia in 1854, he left behind his widow, Agnes, two married daughters, and three other children: Henry (age twenty-one), Stephen (ten), and Nettie (nine). Henry, who took charge of the family and saw to the education of Stephen and Nettie, was impressed by Stephen's scholarly aptitudes.

In 1860, Henry sent Stephen to Beloit Academy for college preparatory classes. But with the coming of the Civil War, Stephen was able to spend only one term at Beloit. He enlisted as a soldier in the Seventh Illinois Cavalry Regiment. Four years later, he was one of those fortunate enough to be able to look back on his war involvement as a positive, character-building experience. He emerged from the war uninjured, with the rank of captain and full of confidence in his own abilities. What he now needed was to identify a vocation that suited his talents.

Over the course of the next several years he successively studied medicine at Rush Medical College, tried strawberry farming in Carbondale, practiced medicine as an apprentice-physician, taught in a small country school, and served as a school principal. In this period he also became fascinated with botany. It may have been the medicinal value of plants that led him to study plants in the first place, but he soon found himself attracted to other features as well. He became an ardent collector, taking notes on the habitats and geographical distribution of his specimens, the times of year that different species bloomed, and so forth. These observations formed the basis for his first scientific paper, which appeared in 1870 in the *American Entomologist and Botanist*.

This paper gained Forbes attention from naturalists around the country. In particular, it impressed George Vasey, the editor of *American Entomologist and Botanist*. Vasey was at the time deputy curator of the Museum of Natural History at Illinois State Normal University, serving in that capacity while the museum's curator and founder, Major John Wesley Powell, was off exploring the Rocky Mountains. In the spring of 1871 Forbes enrolled at Normal as a special student. Once there, he had the chance to become better acquainted with Vasey and with the Museum of Natural History. The following year, Vasey left the university to become director of the U.S. National Herbarium and Powell officially resigned from the museum's curatorship. Forbes, then twenty-eight, was chosen to fill the vacancy.

Forbes was already adept as a field naturalist. His formal scientific training was at this point minimal, but his capacity for self-education was great, and his organizational talents made him well-suited to improve the museum's natural history collections. Furthermore, thanks to his omnivorous reading habits and his command of foreign languages, he had a good sense of current developments in natural history. He paid close attention, for example, when in 1873 the country's most distinguished zoologist, Louis Agassiz of Harvard, established a summer school for young naturalists on Penikese Island in Buzzards Bay, off Massachusetts's southeast coast. There, at the Anderson School of Natural History, Agassiz urged his students to "study Nature, not books," and turned their attention to the myriad marine forms around them. Two years later, Forbes instituted a summer school in central Illinois for fifty young student naturalists. They studied specimens shipped in from as far away as the Zoological Station at Naples, Italy, and they also did fieldwork on the Illinois prairie.

Forbes's scientific career began at a time when natural history was being transformed in several directions. In the first place, there was a move to infuse *life* into a subject that had become too closely associated with dead and dusty specimens. Second, there was an effort to bring the rigorous techniques of the laboratory to bear upon the study of living things. Third, theoretically inclined naturalists found themselves facing the great subject of organic evolution that Darwin had recently laid out in his revolutionary masterpiece of 1859, *On the Origin of Species by Means of Natural Selection*. Forbes would make important contributions to natural history on each of these fronts.

Forbes was one of the first American naturalists to embrace Darwin's ideas of struggle for existence and natural selection. He used Darwin's interpretive framework to make sense of the ecological relationships he studied. Not all of his contemporaries greeted Darwin's theorizing so enthusiastically. Indeed, the American response to Darwin corresponds rather closely with Max Planck's famous observation: "a new scientific truth does not triumph by convincing its opponents and making them see the light, but rather because its opponents eventually die, and a new generation grows up that is familiar with it." Agassiz was adamantly opposed to Darwin's idea of species change. Up to his death in 1873 at the age of sixty-six, the dean of American zoology remained convinced that Darwin's theory was fundamentally wrong. In contrast, the next generation of naturalists, including many of Agassiz's own students, concluded that Darwin's general idea of organic evolution was most probably correct. Only a few of the naturalists of this generation, however, were inclined to think that natural selection was the primary means by which organic change takes place.

Forbes made Darwin's idea of natural selection central to his own thinking about the balance of nature. In 1880, in his first paper of a primarily theoretical nature, he observed: "For the purposes of this inquiry I shall assume as established laws of life, the reality of the struggle for existence, the appearance of variations, and the frequent inheritance of such as conduce to the good of the individual and the species—in short, the evolution of species and higher groups under the influence of natural selection."[2]

Darwin, whose own vision of ecology was shaped by his encounter with the Brazilian rain forest, had spoken about ecological relationships in the *Origin of Species*, albeit not by that name. (The word *Oekologie* was first coined in 1866 by the German zoologist Ernst Haeckel.) In the concluding paragraph of his book, Darwin wrote: "It is interesting to contemplate an entangled bank, clothed with many plants of many kinds, with birds singing on the bushes, with various insects flitting about, and with worms crawling through the damp earth, and to reflect that these elaborately constructed forms, so different from each other, and dependent on each other in so complex a manner, have all been produced by laws acting around us."

Forbes was inclined to contemplate the balance of nature in the more utilitarian contexts of Illinois agriculture and "fish culture." There is nothing surprising about this utilitarian dimension of Forbes's thinking. Given his position at the State Natural History Museum, he was eager to make the value of natural history visible to the state. In turn, various organizations were keen to use natural historical knowledge for their own purposes and for the public good. In 1875, urged by the Illinois State Horticultural Society, Forbes launched a quantitative study of the food habits of different birds. The society wanted to know whether birds were on balance beneficial or detrimental when it came to the regulation of insect pests. In the same period, Forbes undertook a study of the food habits of Illinois fish.

Forbes also engaged in institution building. Wishing to do more than simply assemble specimens in a museum, he lobbied educators and legislators to establish an Illinois State Laboratory of Natural History for the advancement and diffusion of scientific knowledge. The Illinois General Assembly approved Forbes's plan in May 1877. And in 1880, when he published his comprehensive, quantitative analyses of the food habits of the most important birds and fish of Illinois, he was able to do so in the institution's new journal, the *Bulletin of the Illinois State Laboratory of Natural History*.

"Food relations," as Forbes explained to his readers, offered a superb entry into the study of the relations of living things. Or, as he put it, "It is through the food relation that animals touch each other and the surrounding world at the greatest number of points, here they crowd upon each other the most closely, at this point the struggle for existence becomes sharpest and most deadly; and, finally, it is through the food relation almost entirely that animals are brought in contact with the material interests of man. Both for the student of science and for the economist, therefore, we find this subject of peculiar interest and value. It includes many of the most important relations of a species, and may properly be made the nucleus about which all the facts of its natural history are gathered."[3]

The economic questions Forbes addressed in studying birds were very similar to those he addressed in studying fish. With birds the issue was the relation of bird life to agricultural crops. Farmers knew of course that birds eat insects, but they also knew that some insects serve to control other insects. What remained uncertain was whether particular species of birds were on the whole beneficial or detrimental when it came to the control of insect pests. If they ate too many helpful insects, this could counterbalance whatever good the birds did in eating the insects that were a problem.

When it came to matters of fish culture, questions of nature's balance were again crucial. If one wanted to increase the numbers of a particularly desirable fish species, Forbes explained, it was not necessarily a good idea simply to stock a stream with another species upon which the desired species normally preyed. If the prey fish consumed too many of the tiny organisms that the young of the desired fish required in the early stages of their existence, this could actually reduce, instead of increase, the numbers of the fish one wanted to promote.

But how was one to study what a bird or a fish ate? Neither experiments in the laboratory nor careful field observations promised to be reliable approaches to the problem. Lab experiments were likely to prove too artificial; field observations would inevitably be incomplete. The more promising method, Forbes decided, was to study the stomach contents of many different specimens, juveniles as well as adults. He based his 1880 report on "The Food of Birds" on his examination of the stomach contents of some 1,500 birds representing eighty different species. He described the theoretical significance of his bird studies as follows: "Since the struggle for existence is chiefly a struggle for subsistence, a careful comparative account of the food of various competing species and genera, at different places and seasons and at all ages of the individual, such as had not heretofore been made for any class of animals, cannot fail to throw much light upon the details, causes and effects of this struggle."[4]

But it was not just theory that interested him in this report. He was also able to draw specific conclusions about the relative helpfulness or harmfulness of different bird species with respect to the interests of farmers and fruit growers. He found the robin and the thrush to be valuable, on balance. The case of the catbird, on the other hand, was more problematic. The catbird consumed beneficial and injurious insects in roughly equal amounts, but it also damaged fruits. Forbes, however, proved in no hurry to support a war on catbirds. He told his readers that those who sought to disturb the balance of nature for a "prospective good" ran the risk of creating some "greater evil." He likewise concluded his early fish studies with the observation: "Only harm can come from an imperfect balance of the forces of organic nature, whether the excess be upon one side or the other."[5]

Forbes's interest in pursuing pure science for purposes that were ultimately practical was nicely displayed in his attention to "disturbances" in the balance of nature. Studying how disturbances affected the "Natural system," he explained, was an excellent way of gaining a better understanding of how human activities also disrupted that system. For the farmer, the most destructive insects were those that oscillated dramatically in their numbers. Crickets and common grasshoppers caused relatively little if any damage, but the Colorado grasshopper, the chinch-bug, and the army worm had become the farmer's dreaded enemies. Humans needed to keep these oscillating species in check and see to it that other species remained stationary in their numbers. The best way to do this, Forbes maintained, was to "study the methods by which Nature reduces these disturbances, and learn how to second her efforts to our own best advantage."[6]

In 1882 Forbes was appointed state entomologist of Illinois. Two years later, Indiana University awarded him a Ph.D. in recognition of his scientific work. In 1884 Forbes was also invited to join the faculty at Illinois Industrial University. Instead of resigning from his previous positions as state entomologist and director of the State Laboratory of Natural History,

Stephen A. Forbes,
from the 1880s.

the forty-year-old naturalist continued to pursue the intricate interrelationships of living, bringing both positions with him to Urbana.

Forbes is best known among ecologists for his groundbreaking paper, "The Lake as a Microcosm," in which, based on studies of the food of fishes, Forbes advanced the notion of ecological *communities*.[7] Community, one of the central concepts of ecology today, extended ecology's focus from the interactions of organisms with the physical environment to the interactions of organisms with each other. Lakes provided the ideal environment for Forbes's study of these interactions. He called a lake "a little world within itself—a microcosm within which all the elemental forces are at work and the play of life goes on in full." This microcosm consisted of a community of interests, a "complete and independent equilibrium of organic life and activity."

Fieldwork is a distinguishing feature of ecological science. In the late nineteenth century, ecology began to differentiate itself from the more established biological disciplines such as botany and zoology by studying the adaptations of organisms to environmental conditions—and to each other. As ecologists went out into nature, they selected particular locations for detailed scientific observation and analysis. Often new to these sites themselves, they relied on local people to provide not only manual labor but also knowledge of the animals, plants, and habitats of the area. As they became connected to particular biological habitats, ecologists also became connected to the people, culture, and politics of the locales they studied.

Once Forbes embarked on his work on the Illinois River floodplain, his science became intertwined with the human conflicts on the river. His efforts helped establish the science of ecology as an enterprise fundamentally related to human concerns of environmental politics and transformation. At ecologists' study sites, scientific research goals and local cultures of resource use came to be intimately interrelated.

In the period when ecology was becoming a science, local Illinoisians were fighting intense battles over the new science's object of study. In 1887, when Forbes first presented his paper on "The Lake as a Microcosm" to a small scientific society in the town of Peoria on the Illinois River, he spoke about the ecology of "fluviatile" lakes "situated in the river bottoms and connected with the adjacent streams by periodical overflows." Such lakes were of great interest to the local populace. That same year, less than thirty miles downstream, a battle brewed as members of the Peoria elite began placing "No Trespassing" signs on several thousand acres of the same types of lakes that Forbes was studying. Local residents who had been hunting and fishing in these lakes for decades shot down the signs in protest. Poaching fish, ducks, and muskrat, they in effect claimed the land and resources as their own. The battles over the Illinois River floodplain escalated over the next several decades. Forbes and his colleagues had begun their systematic investigation of the Illinois River and its floodplain at the precise moment when the ecosystem became the focus of a struggle over rights to lands and waters.

As early as 1876, Forbes had worked with local fishermen on the Illinois, Ohio, and Mississippi rivers while investigating the food habits of fish. He had been both repelled and intrigued by the fishermen. He was initially taken aback by their customs and living conditions. On a collecting trip to the Kentucky bottomlands in 1879, he wrote to his wife: "I am working alone on an indescribably dirty table . . . in the genuine Kentucky farm house—built up on stilts apparently to afford shelter for the pigs under it. . . . The boards of the floors are all loose and slip and rattle under our feet, and whatever is dropped falls through to the pigs." However, as he continued to work with the locals, he developed empathy with them: "I succeed quite to my own admiration," he told his wife, "in affiliating with these bottom-landers. We work and talk together with a mutual confidence quite touching."[8]

Over the following decades, local fishermen played a crucial role in the scientific studies conducted by Forbes and his colleagues on the Illinois River. In 1894, Forbes established the Illinois Biological Station on the Illinois River near Havana. Havana had the largest fishery on the river, accounting for over 20 percent of the entire river's catch in 1896. In 1908, Havana's catch alone represented 10 percent of the entire freshwater fishery in the United States. With the establishment of the Havana station, Forbes put in place a series of fixed sampling sites that linked his work not only to a particular habitat, but to a particular community, with its culture and its politics. The field station connected the university directly with the concerns of local people.

"Bottom-landers"—fishermen, hunters, and boatmen—were central players in the scientific enterprise of the station. They worked as field assistants, guiding survey scientists in unfamiliar locations. They also helped the scientists as laborers, rowing boats and collecting fish in their seines, trammel nets, and fish traps. In the course of many decades of experience on the Illinois River they had adapted their gear to the special conditions of the river and its floodplain. They used a variety of nets and fish traps. Their boats were designed to navigate with heavy loads of fish on the often shallow and weed-choked backwaters. The scientists soon adopted many of the techniques of the local fishermen.

But the locals offered more than manual labor. They provided knowledge about the natural history of the fish and how to catch them. Forbes filled his reports with commentary on the habits of the fish that he learned of in talking with fishermen. His research frequently confirmed local knowledge and he developed a trust in his informants. One of the Havana Station's first employees was a local fisherman, Miles Newberry. Newberry had already worked on the river for eighteen years. He proceeded to put his skills to work for Forbes, constructing and repairing nets, fixing the boats and engines, serving as a river guide, helping to sample, and serving as an unofficial liaison to other fishermen on the river. He also provided specific advice on particular research projects, recommending the sampling scheme that was then used for research on the distribution, migration, breeding habits, and food of the Illinois River fishes.

Besides profiting from the knowledge of men like Newberry, Forbes's understanding of the river was informed by the political struggles over resource use in which the local fishermen were then involved. Prior to 1880, the floodplain had been treated as a commons. Up and down the river, people harvested the fish, hunted waterfowl, grazed their livestock on floodplain grasses, cut timber, and collected pecans. Beginning in the 1880s, wealthy sportsmen began buying up the floodplain and restricting access to these once-public areas. Independent commercial fishermen protested these changes through trespass, poaching, and legal challenge. As these protests increased, hunting clubs and other land owners gave up on preserving flooded areas for the pleasure of private duck hunting, and began looking for a new kind of profit. They converted their holdings to cropland

Fishermen's blockade of the Spring Lake Levee and Drainage District. Fishermen had blocked a dredge creating the district and were accused of blowing a hole in the already completed section of the levee shown here.

by building levees and draining the enclosed lakes and wetlands. In response to the loss of these waters, fishermen increased their protests, culminating to the success, in 1908, of about fifty armed fishermen who blocked a dredge from completing an agricultural levee that would drain an important fishing lake. As a Chicago newspaper described it, "a state of armed siege exi[s]ts in some sections, with bloodshed almost sure to ensue at once unless quick and drastic action is taken by the state authorities. Feeling runs high all along the river for a hundred miles and more. Power boats are bristling arsenals hidden in caves, lagoons, sloughs and bayous. Skulking forms creep over the embankment to watch the movement of armed guards employed by private hunting and fishing clubs and the land exploiting companies. On these men's faces is the grim determination to protect their public fishing grounds against the encroachments of Indiana and Cincinnati millionaires, and do it with powder and ball if it becomes necessary."[9]

For their part, Forbes and his co-workers quickly recognized the threat to the fishery that drainage represented. By 1910, as the pace of levee construction quickened and its harm to the fishery became apparent, survey scientists repeated their warnings against drainage. "Nothing can be more dangerous to the continued productiveness of these waters than a shutting of the river into its main channel and the drainage of the bottom-land lakes for agricultural purposes," declared Forbes to the American Fisheries Society. By 1910, two-fifths of the floodplain had already been drained, and "in the face of the gigantic interests—agricultural, industrial, commercial, and political—which are now mustering along its course," Forbes worried that the remainder of the floodplain would be destroyed and the fishery permanently decimated.[10]

The impending loss of the floodplain suggested new research questions and experiments to Forbes. His research began to focus on a new problem: how to develop ways to protect the fishery of the river from drainage. This was both an ecological and a political problem. "Since 1910," Forbes wrote, "we have given all our work a turn towards the fisheries interest." He thought it would be exceedingly difficult to fight the "gigantic interests" threatening the floodplain; backwater lakes would be drained as long as drainage remained the most profitable use of the land. In an attempt to reverse the cost-benefit analysis, Forbes encouraged research to make the fishery more economically valuable, so that it could compete with agriculture.[11]

Forbes's research priorities had political implications. Recreational and commercial fisheries' interests were in conflict during this period. Research on rotational use of the floodplain and use of carp was directed toward preserving the health of the "wild fishery" rather than developing methods of fish culture. Forbes worked to protect the floodplain lakes from drainage and preserve the ability of the river and floodplain to produce fish without augmentation from hatcheries. While hatcheries were primarily developed for increasing sport-fish production, the goal of preserving the wild fishery of the Illinois River supported the political interests of the commercial fishermen, because it emphasized the protection of the habitat—the floodplain lakes that produced the wild fishes that commercial fishermen targeted.

In addition to concerns with the overall productivity of the river, conflict on the river centered on access, whether fishermen would have the right to fish on the privatized floodplain. This denial of access affected researchers as well, and helped to move the survey into taking a direct political role in the struggle. Thus, the conflict on the river did more than simply influence the direction and priorities of scientific research. It drew the ecologists directly into the political battles. As privatization expanded, the survey could no longer get access to important study sites, and the scientists found themselves to be political allies of the fishermen in much more direct ways. Further, as the conflict over access propelled agriculturalists and speculators to levee the bottomlands, the very lakes the biologists were studying were destroyed.

The political interests of the fishermen and the survey coalesced in the struggle to prevent Thompson Lake, the largest lake on the Illinois floodplain, from being drained. The lake was controlled by the Thompson Lake Rod and Gun Club, which began to put up no trespassing signs and hired wardens to prevent locals from fishing and hunting in the lake, as they had done for decades. Local fishermen and hunters fought back, continuing to hunt and fish on the lake without permission. The club responded by going to court for injunctions against the commercial fishermen. Forbes, who had worked with some of the very fishermen being arrested for trespassing, recognized the interests of both fishermen and scientists, and recommended to the newly established Rivers and Lakes Commission that "the reservation of the most valuable feeding grounds and breeding grounds of fishes might well be undertaken by whatever legal process is necessary and possible."[12]

As pressure increased from both poachers and the state to establish public rights to Thompson Lake, the Thompson Lake Club gave up maintaining a hunting and fishing reserve, and reorganized itself into a levee district in order to drain Thompson Lake for agriculture. The affected fishermen, recognizing the permanent threat to the fishery that drainage represented, purposely went out on Thompson Lake in 1913, in defiance of the injunction and intending to be arrested, in order to test the ownership of the lake in the courts. Among them was Miles Newberry. This former survey employee, whom Forbes described as having "served the station very efficiently from the beginning," broke the law in order to challenge the right of the gun club to drain Thompson Lake. The fishermen argued that "Thompson Lake is a public body of water owned by the State of Illinois." When the club sued them, the State of Illinois joined the case on the fishermen's behalf.[13]

Thompson Lake thus became a test case for the state to assert ownership and control on the Illinois River floodplain in the interests of conservation. The case eventually reached the Illinois Supreme Court. University scientists and local fishermen together testified to save Thompson Lake from being drained. Their efforts notwithstanding, the case was decided in 1917 in favor of the Thompson Lake Club. In 1922 Thompson Lake was drained and converted to agriculture.

Just as Forbes's notion of the lake as a microcosm reflected a more extended view of ecological relationships, his participation in the fight for

Thompson Lake can be seen as representative of a broad pattern of activities that characterized his whole career. These activities included other work on the Illinois River, ranging from problems of fish conservation to the issue of the extent to which sewage from Chicago was polluting the river. They also included his efforts to bring ecological perspectives on the farmer's need to control insect pests. Clearly the kind of field natural history Forbes promoted was not that of an asocial individual shunning civilization and seeking solitary communion with nature. Throughout his career he interacted productively with farmers and fishermen, life scientists and legislators, in developing and applying the concepts of the emerging science of ecology.

Forbes was an energetic man. As Ernest Forbes noted of his father: "While at the height of his powers his course through the natural history building could be traced by the slamming of doors behind him. The attitude of command, attained during his extensive military service, was habitual, and he expected action on the part of his subordinates."[14] Stephen Forbes served as director of the Illinois State Laboratory of Natural History from 1877 to 1917 and then chief of that institution's successor, the State Natural History Survey, from 1917 until 1930 (the year of his death). He also served from 1888 to 1905 as dean of the College of Science at the University of Illinois.

Forbes found outlets for his energies not only in administrative service but in many forms of exercise. He particularly liked bicycling, which he insisted added years to his life. He also turned his hand to golf, but he never became very proficient at it. Although he had the distinction of serving as first president of the university golf club, he surely would have swapped whatever satisfaction that position gave him for the joy of scoring a hole-in-one (see, in this regard, chapter 16 on John Bardeen).

Like others of his generation, Forbes grew up before the invention of the automobile, and the experience of driving a car came relatively late in life. As a driver he became "locally famous," as his son Ernest later put it, "for a long series of minor mishaps." Ernest attributed these mishaps only in part to his father's lessened physical adaptability as an older man. Another contributing factor, he recognized, was his father's disposition to concentrate his entire attention on whatever he was thinking about at the time, which often was not the road in front of him.[15]

Forbes remains most famous for thinking about the intricate interrelations of living things. He maintained that even in the case of one species preying upon another, there is a "community of interest" between the two of them. It seemed to him that an ultimate "beneficence" characterizes the general laws of organic nature. Out of "fierce and continuous" competition, he explained, arises an equilibrium that "actually accomplishes for all the parties involved the greatest good which the circumstances will at all permit." He concluded his paper on "The Lake as a Microcosm" by asking: "If the system of life is such that a harmonious balance of conflicting interests has been reached where every element is either hostile or indifferent to every other, may we not trust much to the outcome where, as in human affairs, the spontaneous adjustments of nature are aided by intelligent effort, by sympathy, and by self-sacrifice?"[16]

Forbes always viewed humans as an integral part of the natural environment. What remains to be seen is whether humans in the twenty-first century can act with the intelligence, sympathy, and self-sacrifice that Forbes recognized is necessary for being part of a healthy, balanced ecosystem.

NOTES

1. Stephen A. Forbes, "On Some Interactions of Organisms," *Bulletin of the Illinois State Laboratory of Natural History* 1, no. 3 (1880): 3–17, 15, 17. For an extended biography of Forbes, see Robert A. Croker, *Stephen Forbes and the Rise of American Ecology* (Washington: Smithsonian Institution Press, 2001).
2. Forbes, "On Some Interactions of Organisms," 5.
3. Forbes, "The Food of Fishes," *Bulletin of the Illinois State Laboratory of Natural History* 1, no. 3 (1880): 18–65, 19.
4. Forbes, "The Food of Birds," *Bulletin of the Illinois State Laboratory of Natural History* 1, no. 3 (1880): 80–148, 82.
5. Ibid., 85; and "On the Food of Young Fishes," *Bulletin of the Illinois State Laboratory of Natural History* 1, no. 3 (1880): 66–79, 77.
6. Forbes, "On Some Interactions of Organisms," 15.
7. Forbes, "The Lake as a Microcosm," *Illinois Natural History Survey Bulletin* 15 (1925): 537–50. Reprinted from Forbes's 1887 address to the Science Association of Peoria.
8. Daniel W. Schneider, "Local Knowledge, Environmental Politics, and the Founding of Ecology in the United States: Stephen Forbes and 'The Lake as a Microcosm' (1887)," *Isis* 91 (2000): 681–705, 690.
9. Daniel W. Schneider, "Enclosing the Floodplain: Resource Conflict on the Illinois River, 1880–1920," *Environmental History* (1996) 1:70–96, 83.
10. Schneider, "Local Knowledge."
11. Ibid.
12. Ibid., 698.
13. Ibid.
14. Ernest Browning Forbes, "Stephen Alfred Forbes: His Ancestry, Education and Character," in *In Memoriam, Stephen Alfred Forbes, 1844–1930* (1930), 5–15, Forbes papers, University of Illinois archives.
15. Ibid.
16. Forbes, "The Lake as a Microcosm."

CHAPTER 5

William Abbott Oldfather:

Making the Classics Relevant

to Modern Life

William Abbott Oldfather (1880–1945), a classical scholar who earned an international reputation, spent most of his academic career at the University of Illinois. A stimulating teacher, he was at his best directing graduate students and pursuing his own research. He published many valuable technical studies and a few popular works, but he was primarily devoted to making the classics relevant to modern life. Oldfather scorned those classicists who devoted themselves to remote antiquarian specialization and those whose conservative or reactionary views rendered them incapable of comprehending the meaning of classical culture. Fearless and opinionated, Oldfather expressed himself vigorously and often vituperatively. He was a powerful influence in the life of his university, as well as in the world of scholarship and the affairs of the nation.[1]

Born in Persia on October 23, 1880, Oldfather was ten when he "emigrated" to America. His family heritage and life in Asia shaped his character and his career. He was intimately familiar with an ancient culture and a foreign language. Nurtured by parents who were Presbyterian missionaries, he was indelibly stamped by the evangelistic fervor of the mission field. Old-father's paternal great-great-grandfather, Friedrich Altvater, had fled Germany in 1770 to seek greater religious freedom in America. Friedrich and his family settled in Pennsylvania, and his son Henry removed to south-western Ohio and changed the family name to Oldfather.

Henry's grandson, Jeremiah M. Oldfather (William's father), was born in 1841 near Lewisburg, Ohio. After attending Heidelberg College and Miami University and serving with an Ohio regiment in the Civil War, Jeremiah graduated from Miami University in 1869 and then went to Lane Theological Seminary in Cincinnati, a Presbyterian institution. On graduating in 1872, he was ordained in the ministry and married Felicia Narcissa Rice (1848–1941), who was born in Covington, Indiana.[2] Jeremiah and Felicia then sailed for Persia under auspices of the Presbyterian Board of Foreign Missions, arriving on October 29, 1872, in Oroomiah (now Urmia), a city of 40,000 in the Azerbaijan area, 600 miles northwest of Teheran. Oroomiah was located in the midst of a great plain, bordered by Turkey and Iraq to the west and southwest and what was then Russian-controlled Armenia to the north.[3] In this region, the Presbyterian mission aimed at reclaiming the Nestorian Christians to orthodox Christianity. They wanted to help them build a native church to be used to convert Jews and "Mussulmans." The work was evangelistic and educational.

By the time William arrived (the third of four children born in Persia), Oroomiah was a thriving Christian district in a Muslim land. The whole community was "a moral, Sabbath-keeping, and religious one." But "life there was harsh, not without dangers for Christian missionaries. The people were unfriendly and the missionaries led lonely, isolated lives."[4] William probably was educated by his father and, lacking social contact with peers other than siblings, he likely spent most of his time reading.

In 1886 Jeremiah was transferred to the mission station at Tabriz, which had a population of 150,000. He had charge of the city church. "The fruits of evangelization among Moslems are very great," he reported, but "one great need of this work is a more efficient force of active, zealous, warm-hearted evangelists to put the leaven into all Moslem measures."[5] The Presbyterian mission stations at Oroomiah and Tabriz were seen as strategic points for the great campaign of evangelization on the broad field of western Asia. The churches of the Nestorians and Armenians had been preserved as "the buried seed that is to spring up under the power of the pure Gospel, and thus to form the basis for the wider work for Jews and Moslems."[6]

Young Bill heard what the missionaries reported. Central Asia had been neglected by the Church of Christ, the Tartar and Iranian hordes had repeatedly run over Christendom, and it was vain to expect the sway of a Christian civilization until the millions of those vast regions had been brought under the scepter of the King of Peace. In all likelihood Oldfather saw himself as an outsider with a duty to spread light to the unenlightened.

In 1890 Jeremiah and Felicia returned to the United States to further the education of their children. The family settled in southern Indiana on the campus of Hanover College. In 1893 William entered the Preparatory Department of Hanover, and two years later became a freshman in the college. Hanover offered both classical and scientific courses of study. They differed very little. Of the twenty-six entering freshmen, Oldfather and fifteen others chose the classical course. He was the top scholar in both his freshman and sophomore years. As a junior he won two cash prizes, one for an essay on missions, the other for superior excellence in original oratory. As a senior he gave an address, "Is Science Necessarily Opposed to Religion?" He excelled at tennis and retained a lifelong interest in sport. In 1899 Oldfather received a B.A. and was awarded First Honor.[7] He then served for a year as principal and a teacher in the high school in Charleston, Indiana, and in 1900 he entered Harvard College, one of 388 members of the senior class, to study classical philology.

Under English influence, the classics had been at the core of the American college curriculum since the founding of Harvard. They were an adornment for gentlemen and clergymen and a means of instilling mental discipline. Teachers of classics were drill masters, not scholars. In the mid-nineteenth century, however, Germany became the model for classical scholarship in America. At the time the German universities were considered the best in the world, and aspiring American classicists went to Germany to earn a doctorate because England did not then offer a Ph.D. and America had not yet developed its own graduate schools. The wave of *Teutonomania* began when George M. Lane, Basil L. Gildersleeve, and William W. Goodwin earned doctorates in classical philology at the University of Göttingen in 1851, 1853, and 1855, respectively. Although the tide began to recede in the 1890s, Germany remained the model for American classical scholars until the outbreak of war in 1914.[8]

During Oldfather's time at Harvard, nine of the eleven members of the classics faculty had German doctorates or had studied in Germany. Oldfather received honorable mention in Final Honors and graduated in 1901 with a B.A. In the fall, he entered the Graduate School to study classical philology, earning an M.A. in June 1902. In September, after marrying Margaret Agnes Giboney, a graduate of Hanover in the Class of '98, he returned to Harvard for another year of graduate study.[9]

Oldfather began his academic career in 1903 at Northwestern University, in a department headed by John Adams Scott. He taught Greek and Latin, and became proficient in German. In 1906 he left for the Ludwig-Maximilians-University in Munich, where he studied Greek, Latin, ancient history, and archaeology under Robert Pöhlmann and other scholars who imbued Oldfather with an approach to classical culture that remained his ideal. "Oldfather's study at Munich was the critical formative experience of his life," Michael Armstrong writes. "There he learned exact German scholarly and historical method, and he also encountered German socialism. He was converted to both and retained all his life an ideal of precise and intensive scholarship, a view of antiquity as a cultural and historical whole, and an active commitment to social responsibility."[10] Oldfather's dissertation, suggested by Herbert W. Smyth of Harvard and directed by Otto Crusius, treated the topography, history, and culture of Locris, a region of ancient Greece. In 1908 he received took his Ph.D. summa cum laude.

It may be fair to conclude that Oldfather's study in Germany was the *second* critical formative experience in his life, his Persian experience being the first. His encounter with "German socialism" was largely an encounter with the communism and socialism of antiquity as depicted by the historian Pöhlmann. But many Germans then viewed socialism with great favor.

After Munich Oldfather returned to Northwestern, but not for long. In 1904 Northwestern University's president, Edmund J. James, became president of the University of Illinois. James was determined to build up classics at Illinois. He tried to recruit the best professors available within his resources, and he had Oldfather in mind for a position.

As of 1904 the classics department had not yet gained a decent footing. In 1891 Charles M. Moss, who had a Ph.D. from Syracuse, was appointed professor of Greek, and Herbert J. Barton, whose highest degree was an M.A. from Dartmouth, was named professor of Latin. In 1901 Kenneth P. R. Neville became an instructor in both departments. But the classics had little appeal to students in a decidedly utilitarian university.

On June 2, 1905, the board of trustees combined Greek and Latin into a Department of Classics and authorized the appointment of a full professor as head and of another assistant professor. James and Evarts B. Greene, dean of the College of Literature and Arts, then began a search for a person to head the department. For four years they negotiated with many of the leading classical scholars in the country about the position. Among those considered were Clifford H. Moore and Edward K. Rand of Harvard, and Edward B. Clapp and Henry W. Prescott of the University of California. In August Greene interviewed Arthur S. Pease, who like Oldfather and

William A. Oldfather as a student at the University of Munich, 1906–7.

many classical scholars of his generation was the son of a clergyman. Pease had taken three degrees at Harvard (A.B., 1902, summa cum laude; A.M., 1903; Ph.D., 1905). Greene offered an appointment as an associate at $1,500, but Pease, who was getting $1,800 from Harvard and Radcliffe, declined.[11] Negotiations with Rand, Moore, and Prescott also failed.

To staff the department, on January 15, 1909, the trustees appointed Pease as an assistant professor beginning on February 1. James then invited Oldfather to consider a position as an associate professor at Illinois. Oldfather was tempted by the higher rank, the greater salary, and the prospect of being at an institution headed by James. But he was reluctant to leave his friends and the proximity of library facilities in Chicago. He indicated that it would alter the case if the university would provide $300 to $500 a year for him to purchase books for his work.

Letters of recommendation helped decide the matter. The Harvard classicists were divided but favorable. Smyth described Oldfather as a man of "ability and promise," but "not the equal of Dr. Pease." Crusius wrote that Oldfather was "the most thoroughly trained and best informed student" he had had in recent years. Oldfather knew how to combine the strictly philological with the mythical and historical and had a fine understanding of archaeology. Dean J. B. Clark of Northwestern wrote that Oldfather would fill a first-class professorship and "fill it full." David Kinley, dean of the Graduate School, wrote that Oldfather "will not be among the classical scholars of greatest reputation, [but] his work will always command the respect of his colleagues." Both Barton and Moss recommended Oldfather, and Pease favored the appointment.[12]

On June 21 James met Oldfather in Chicago. They discussed terms and James offered him the job. Oldfather accepted. He came as an associate professor of classics, ranking after the two classics professors but above Pease, at a salary of $2,750. The classical work was to be organized with Barton as chair and Oldfather as secretary. Oldfather was to offer instruction in Greek and Latin, Greek and Roman history, and as soon as possible archaeology and Oriental languages and history. Moreover Oldfather could count on $1,000 during the next two years for books for the library within his own special interests, in addition to the allowance to the department. James also told Oldfather that hiring him would not interfere with the continued search for a man with a national reputation to head the classics department.[13] Accordingly, Oldfather informed James that Ferdinand F. C. Lehmann-Haupt at Berlin and Thaddeus Zielinski at St. Petersburg were both looking for opportunities in America. If James could get them, every scholar of classical antiquity would know that the University of Illinois was on the map.[14]

Oldfather's introduction to the classics department was not entirely smooth. He taught both Greek and Latin courses for advanced undergraduates and graduate students and offered one or more graduate-level courses in both Greek and Latin. From 1909 to 1911, as Oldfather noted, Barton discriminated against him by keeping his classes small, taking the ablest students for himself, and inviting both Pease and Canter to address the Classical Club before inviting Oldfather. And Oldfather was not properly consulted by the classics department when the history department hired a professor of ancient history.[15]

Oldfather's abilities were nevertheless recognized beyond his own department. In 1911, David Kinley invited Oldfather to become a member of the executive faculty of the Graduate School. In 1912–13 Oldfather and Pease introduced "Bibliography and Criticism," a seminar repeated annually, and Oldfather introduced a course in the history of Greece. In 1918–19 he introduced a course in Roman history.

On July 20, 1915, Oldfather received notice of his appointment as professor of Greek. Viewing the promotion as a restriction of his activity (as associate professor of classics), he asked about the reason for the change. Barton replied that he knew nothing about it; he was quite certain that no restriction was intended. Oldfather then questioned his college dean, who thought that there was no intent to restrict Oldfather's activity. The dean queried the president, who said that there was no significance to the change. Oldfather wondered if he should put the question to James. The dean advised him to say nothing. But the minutes of the trustees, published *after* these conversations, record that on July 14 Oldfather was promoted to professor of classics (not Greek). Apparently Barton listed "professor of Greek" when he submitted promotion papers and Oldfather's queries prompted James to change the official record before it was published.[16]

By 1915 Oldfather was the dominant person in the classics department. Committed to collective scholarship, as practiced in Germany, he inspired the formation of the Illinois Greek Club, which included faculty members from several departments. With the outbreak of war Oldfather turned his attention to military affairs. He and his colleague Harold V. Canter studied how the defeat of Varus in 9 C.E. led the emperor Augustus to create a buffer state on the northern frontier to defend the Roman Empire. *The Defeat of Varus and the German Frontier Policy of Augustus* was published in 1915. In 1916–17 Oldfather offered a course on the decline of ancient civilization, a topic that intrigued him. In 1917 Oldfather and others began to examine Greek military writers. Oldfather bore the brunt of the labor in producing *Aeneas Tacticus, Asclepiodotus, Onasander.*

The American declaration of war against Germany on April 6, 1917, made conditions problematic for anyone considered less than superpatriotic. Oldfather was known as a Germanophile and as sympathetic with socialism. In October 1917, Queen Lois Shepherd, an instructor of philosophy with a Ph.D. from the University of Illinois in 1913, refused the request of a colleague to subscribe to Liberty bonds. "No! Not if I had a million dollars," she allegedly responded. A few other faculty members also refused to buy Liberty bonds, and on October 31, William H. Kerrick, an agent of the Department of Justice, came from Peoria to investigate. He summoned Shepherd and two other faculty members to Urbana City Hall that evening. Flanked by Charles M. Webber, the Urbana postmaster, and Mary E. Busey, a university trustee, Kerrick inquired into their conduct. When Shepherd refused to answer Kerrick's questions, he called her "a damned rotten, vile, socialist, anarchist." A faculty member at the hearing hastened to get Oldfather, who hurried to City Hall to defend a young woman from unfair questions. Kerrick did not charge Oldfather with disloyalty, but said there would have been no trouble had not he and others intruded on the meeting.[17]

The next day the *Champaign Daily News* reported that eight faculty members had been called for questioning; some were said to be liberal Socialists and others of German descent. An investigation was long overdue, said the

Champaign Daily Gazette; six professors under suspicion for disloyalty had been spreading their beliefs on campus. Oldfather was not one of the six.

A local conflict quickly became a national cause célèbre. Although President James supported the American war effort, he had a German Ph.D. and a German wife and admired German culture. If he defended his faculty vigorously his own patriotism might be questioned, but if he dismissed the affair he would invite harsh criticism. Steering between Scylla and Charybdis, on November 9 James asked Oldfather to see him. He suggested that Oldfather write him a letter signed by Shepherd and the others accused of disloyalty in which they declared their loyalty. Shepherd, Oldfather, and three other faculty members signed the letter, but demanded that if formal charges of disloyalty were made they be allowed to defend themselves.

The board of trustees appointed a special committee to investigate. On November 27 it held a hearing that lasted from 8:45 A.M. to midnight. Webber and Kerrick vaguely charged five individuals with disloyalty, while Busey declared that none of the faculty had proved their loyalty at the inquiry. Shepherd explained her pacifism and professed to support the Allied cause.

Oldfather testified that he had maintained a position of neutrality prior to the war but had often argued that the Allied powers were guilty of just as many atrocities as the Germans. He had tried to correct the impression that he was pro-German, but the committee had heard only from those prejudiced against him. He had never spoken on behalf of Germany.

The report of the special committee concluded that there was no disloyalty at the university while also warning that faculty members were obliged to be "above the suspicion of disloyalty." With some reservations about the loyalty of Shepherd, the board concluded that the others were the victims of rumor and their own indiscreet behavior. Thus the affair was put to rest: no one had been dismissed and public opinion had been appeased.

By 1920 all the faculty members involved in the disloyalty incident except Oldfather had left the university. "Although others have been forced to leave the University," he reportedly explained, "I lie for the men who run it, now, so I'm allowed to stay." Oldfather may well have said this. He once declared that educational authorities tolerated display liberals in order to maintain the pretense of freedom of expression and that he was glad enough to be one of these shop window specimens.[18]

The following February Oldfather went to Washington, D.C., where he served until August 1918 in an editorial research and administrative capacity in the Division of Civil and Educational Cooperation of the Committee on Public Information. His duties were chiefly concerned with the preparation, distribution, and publicity of the committee's pamphlet publications.

After the armistice a nationalistic opposition to the influence of German classical scholarship on America became virulent. It was led by Paul Shorey of the University of Chicago and John Adams Scott of Northwestern. Their attack "cut off American classics from its German roots and stifled, perhaps forever, the development of significant research in classical philology in the United States."[19]

Despite this backlash, Oldfather remained true to his scholarly heritage. He published in Germany, reviewed German books, and promoted cooperation with German scholars on the great *Thesaurus Linguae Latina*, one of the largest international undertakings in classics. When Gilbert Norwood, professor of Greek at University College, Cardiff, declared in 1923 that the German spirit had "in large measure sterilized scholarship in America," Oldfather replied that to disparage scholarly works as "static, sterile, Byzantine" was to display ignorance of sound scholarship or to value but lightly the passion for truth. Oldfather's "moderated, reasoned reply," William M. Calder III writes, "was annihilating."[20]

By 1920 James had transformed the University of Illinois into a great American university, and between the wars Oldfather was at the height of his powers. In 1926 he became head of the department, which gave him a free hand within the university to develop the classics. Oldfather stressed the humanistic values with which it was the classicists' task to deal. These values were embedded in the aesthetic, literary, philosophical, and linguistic aspects of ancient Greek and Roman culture extending over a millennium and a half in human history. Oldfather was a convincing spokesman for those humanistic values which, in his view, alone justified the existence of the classics.

A forceful personality with engaging humor, Oldfather imbued his classes with the relevance of the classics for modern life. In 1923–24 he introduced a course on Greek athletics, open to all except freshmen. The course became very popular. A former student remembered "this stalwart man, with his back-thrown head, penetrating eyes, swinging stride, and growling laugh. In the lecture room he stood resting both hands on a lectern. One hand came into play occasionally for a controlled but vigorous hammering home of points. The strong voice . . . [with] words that were as lively and colorful as they were powerful, gripped the hearers with intellectual excitement. Here was a teacher, a master of knowledge, a man of forthright opinions, which he believed in stating clearly and emphatically." To the students he was "the lion of the campus."[21] Privately they called him "*der Herr.*"

Yet Oldfather regarded lecturing as a "terrible bore." He broke into "a heavy nervous perspiration" whenever he met a class for the first time. He went through the motions merely because he had to earn a living, endeavoring to do as good a job as he knew how. He really only enjoyed his own independent studies, which were almost never connected with any course he offered, and talking, one on one, about an interesting problem.[22]

Oldfather excelled as a director of graduate students. As the other titans passed from the scene he became the leader in classics in this country. Gildersleeve of Johns Hopkins, who had directed seventy-six dissertations, retired from teaching in 1915. Shorey, who had headed the classics department at Chicago since 1896, where he directed fifty-seven dissertations, retired in 1927. Oldfather's department was now the leading center for classical studies in America. He trained his students in the exacting methods of German classical scholarship, creating the "Oldfather School." Oldfather directed forty-six dissertations, including twelve by women.[23] One of his distinguished students was Kenneth M. Abbott, who earned his doctorate in 1934, married Oldfather's daughter Helen that same year, and was a professor of classics at Ohio State from 1934 to 1976. Another distinguished student, Richmond A. Lattimore, also received his Ph.D. in 1934. A poet and Greek scholar, who was for years a faculty member at Bryn Mawr and is chiefly known for his verse translations of Homer, Hesiod, and other Greek poets, Lattimore memorialized his mentor as "a Wilamowitz seen as Buffalo Bill," a "Jupiter of the seminar benign/with poets nuns and Baptists sitting at your feet."[24]

Oldfather was primarily a research scholar, but he had no patience for narrow specialists. "The more 'research' which I attempt to do," he wrote, "the more I feel doubt about its relative importance in the total scheme of cultural values. Treated as beautiful, stimulating, and meaningful for life and joy, Greek literature, thought, and fine art are of transcendent value; but treated as mere materials for scientific research, and by that I mean linguistics, and grammatical statistics, studies of drain-pipes, shoestrings, door knobs, locations, trivial forms of social and political organization, and all the rest of the tripe and garbage that are dignified by the term 'research,' they seem hardly more important than mineralogy, or comparative anatomy, or even educational statistics—than which what can be more banal? . . . When our subject ceases to mean something important for our daily living, then it will go, and it ought to go, the way of all flesh."[25]

Greco-Roman civilization was for Oldfather the fountain spring of our own culture, and knowing it prepared us for the great social struggles of our own day. In the depth of the Great Depression he wrote that he was liberal in his political and social thought and in favor of considerable experimentation with present economic matters, adding that "the past of two such really great cultures as those of Greece and Rome is only beginning to demonstrate its chief utility to the builders of a new society." At the time he was preparing the manuscript of a series of semi-popular lectures on causes that had been proposed for the decline of civilization in the classical world.[26]

"Even though we are moving toward a socialized economy," he wrote in 1937, "we must nevertheless insist upon an aristocracy of culture." He was cheerful enough to believe that it would be easier for culture to maintain its true position of leadership if the invidious distinctions of accumulated but unearned wealth were markedly reduced.[27]

Oldfather was assisted in his research by a small corps of graduate students, research assistants, and typists. Although his publications were mostly of a technical sort, he indulged in one or two semi-popular works—for example, an appreciation of the artist in Cicero, the function of the authors of Roman comedy in loosening up the Latin language and making it simple and pliable enough for such men as Cicero and Horace in the next age, and the German frontier policy of Augustus.

Oldfather impressed colleagues by the encyclopedic range of his knowledge, "which had probably never been equaled among American classical scholars," and by the scientific thoroughness that characterized everything he did. When he popularized he did not lower his scientific and scholarly standards. Not counting his more popular papers and many reviews, his scholarly writings consisted mainly of eleven substantial volumes (some written in collaboration with others), and some 480 articles and short notes of a scientific character scattered among many different journals, encyclopedias, and volumes of miscellanies.[28]

These writings dealt with antiquities, archaeology, bibliography, criticism, etymology, geography, grammar, inscriptions, lexicography, literary history, mythology, paleography, papyri, political and social history, text history, and topography. His translating and editing included, with a coauthor, a collection of the fables of Aesop in Latin verse accompanied by a fourteenth-century French translation, *Epictetus: The Discourses as Reported by Arrian*, translations of the jurist Samuel Pufendorf's *Elementa Jurisprudentiae Universalis* (2 vols., 1931), and, with his brother Charles as coauthor, Pufendorf's *De Jure Naturae et Gentium* (2 vols., 1934). He produced an erudite and almost exhaustive bibliography of Epictetus and edited a series of *Studies in the Text Tradition of St. Jerome's Vitae Patrum* (1943) by his former students. With collaborators and considerable labor Oldfather compiled and edited *indices verborum* to Seneca, Apuleius, and Cicero—indispensable reference works for generations to come. Oldfather contributed about 700 pages on Locris and about 200 other articles to the *Real-Encyclopädie der Classischen Altertumswissenschaft*, the fundamental and authoritative encyclopedia of modern classical studies. These service articles, succinctly written and packed with information of an objective character, are typical of his scholarly method.[29]

Oldfather was a prominent, constructive, and influential member of the University of Illinois faculty. He served on many important university committees and on the board of editors of *University Studies in Language and Literature*. In 1924 he became curator of the Museum of Classical Art and Archaeology. He presided over the creation of a superb classics library. He and University Librarian Phineas L. Windsor were the only two faculty members who served from 1911 to 1932 on committees that drafted the University Statutes, which gave the faculty a voice in the governance of the institution.

Oldfather's voice carried weight within the university, and he felt no need to pull his punches. In 1944, writing to W. W. Wilson, the chairman of the faculty advisory committee on the selection of a new university president, Oldfather denounced his friend, Coleman R. Griffith, an educational psychologist who was trying to play the role of "king maker," and he excoriated as a danger to the integrity of the university those (i.e., Griffith) who professed to be "conversant with the very latest Revelations from On High about Education" that emanated from "the Pundits of Teachers College" at Columbia University in New York City.[30]

Oldfather was active in many professional societies, including the American Council of Learned Societies, the Archeological Institute of America, and the American Philological Association (president, 1937–38). He served for years on the Managing Committee of the American School of Classical Studies at Athens and became familiar with the state of the classics in America by teaching in other universities. He was visiting professor of the classics and of ancient history during seven summer sessions at Chicago, Columbia (twice), UCLA, Colorado (twice), and Stanford. In 1934 he held the Sather Professorship of Classical Literature at the University of California, "the most honorific of all annual Classical professorships anywhere in the world." As the Sather Professor he gave eight public lectures at Berkeley on "The Decline of Culture within the Roman Empire."[31]

William A. Oldfather as a
faculty member, ca. 1930.

During the first semester of 1937–38 Oldfather was visiting professor at the American School of Classical Studies in Athens, and during the second semester he was visiting professor at Columbia University.

Always critical and admittedly of a slightly irascible disposition, Oldfather once wrote that "a man of any liberal sentiments among the classical scholars of this country is very much of a white crow."[32] In 1937, after his Sather appointment, he wrote William H. Alexander, a classicist who was about to take a job at Berkeley, "You will find there, I fear, an extremely conservative, not to say even reactionary Republican atmosphere regarding social questions, but I trust you will enjoy the opportunity of shaking them up a bit—they certainly need it. Just how men who know first hand how the great personalities of Classical Culture really were can themselves so complacently maintain the attitude of *stare decisis* has always been difficult for me to understand. It is like freezing a waterfall and then protesting that is what it always was."[33]

As a visiting professor at Columbia in the spring semester of 1938 Oldfather had the impression that it might be part of his duties to make an informal report to some university officer on the Department of Classics. He did not wish to do so, and Columbia officials excused him from the task. Nevertheless, he prepared an aide-mémoire for possible use in making an oral presentation. The document begins with an unsparingly critical evaluation of each departmental member that puts leaven into the Columbia lump with evangelical fervor. Of LaRue Van Hook, he writes, "once competent . . . a distinctly 2nd rate man." He describes Wilbert L. Carr as "breezy and energetic; talks pedagese and probably thinks it too." He depicts Gilbert A. Highet as "brash, wise-cracking, garrulous, full of endless funny stories told in a smart-alec fashion . . . not of professional caliber." Of Clinton W. Keyes he writes, "shrewd but timid New England Yankee, . . . a fair second rate man." The agent of Truth then issues a strong indictment of the department that ends, "In other words, it is rigid, timid, defeatist, feeble, pedantic, provincial, unproductive, and generally old-maidish."[34]

The gadfly of the campus whose self-appointed mission was to spread light to those in darkness, Oldfather declared that at least 80 percent of a newly established literary journal on the campus—*Accent*—was "just plain bilge." Although we live amid a "rising tide of relatively amiable barbarism, that doesn't really require us to submerge ourselves to it any sooner than we have to anyway." He rated "[James] Joyce and [Gertrude] Stein along with Picasso, Van Gogh, Cézanne and similar degenerates, as being just so much garbage that ought to be shipped to a reducing plant."[35] A lifelong Presbyterian, in 1930 Oldfather spoke at the university YMCA on the topic, "Is Religion Essential to Every Adequate Philosophy of Living?" After defining the terms and rebutting materialism, Oldfather said that for him religion was "reliance upon God for the achievement of good among men." Religion could secure for man three things that were good: tranquility and peace of mind, an abundant life, and joy, or happiness with a flair of gusto.[36]

Despite his cultural conservatism, in politico-economic matters Oldfather was decidedly liberal. During the Great Depression he lashed out at "the stupid and wicked system of capitalistic imperialism" that kept vast masses of Americans unemployed, and not only the ranks of unskilled labor but also "the educated and artistic proletariat." That all these victims of "an outrageous and unnecessary social organization" continued to suffer without effective protest was the most amazing of all the mysteries that he had encountered.[37]

In 1938 in his presidential address to the combined meeting of the American Philological Association and the Archaeological Institute of America Oldfather returned to a subject that always intrigued him. Speaking on "Some Ancient Thought on Progress and Decadence," he suggested a parallel between the economic and social ills that led to the destruction of ancient society and those that threatened contemporary civilization. He issued an implied warning to nations struggling with the Great Depression to give heed to the experience of the Greeks and Romans. Amplifying his remarks, the *New York Times* reported, Oldfather said that "a gross maldistribution of wealth and consequently of political and social power was the factor chiefly responsible for the destruction of Greek and Roman civilization." Other newspapers picked up the story, *Science Service* sent out a version of it to over 300 magazines, and Oldfather received considerable fan mail. But it was "frightful" the way he lost caste with fellow classicists by saying anything that the "public prints" found interesting.[38]

During the interwar years of totalitarianism and growing domestic tensions, Oldfather participated in efforts to defend the weak and create a better world. He was an active member of the American Association of University Professors, the American Civil Liberties Union, the American Friends of Greece, the American Committee for Democracy and Intellectual Freedom, the Committee to Defend America by Aiding the Allies, the American League against War and Fascism, the American Friends of Spanish Democracy, the League for Industrial Democracy, and the Tom Mooney Defense Committee.

Yet he could not shed his reputation as a Germanophile. In 1936 a faculty wife sent him a "Dear Bill" note: "Here you are [she enclosed a news clipping], you and your buddy Hitler and the Spanish fascist gang. Much idea you and your outfit have of the meaning of democracy." A month later she wrote again, saying that Oldfather had been taught at his papa's knee that the only perfect people in the world were the Germans, especially Gentile Germans. "How can there be progress toward a world order, toward a *union for social justice*, when each generation lisps the hatred, provincialisms, egotisms of past generations?" He merely filed away such criticisms.[39]

Endowed with indefatigable vigor, Oldfather loved physical activity. He was for years both a top tennis player and a golfer in the university. He loved trees and was extremely fond of out-of-door sports, walking in mountainous areas, camping, and canoeing. He led The Saturday Hike, faculty men who drove out every Saturday afternoon to the Salt Fork near Urbana, where they played softball, built a fire, cooked a supper, and sang.

Working hard and living strenuously, Oldfather strained both his mind and body. By late summer of 1942, at the age of sixty-two, he admitted to being extremely tired. He asked friends and former students if they would be willing to complete some of his projects under joint authorship. One of these was *Classica Americana*, a venture begun in 1934 and designed to record the titles of all books and articles published in America by scholars of any nationality or published abroad by Americans from 1639.

During the summer of 1943 Oldfather was ill and unable to work. His contract to teach summer school was canceled after four weeks of the session. He was under the care of a local doctor for several weeks, and in September returned to duty despite his doctor's advice. But he was unable to carry on and was given a leave of absence for six months. About the middle of September he entered the Neuropsychiatric Hospital of the University of Illinois in Chicago. His illness was diagnosed as something in the nature of nervous exhaustion. Recovery was slow. On December 21 he returned home, "rested, recovered, and ready" for his academic duties. He slept better than he had for several years and hoped to be able to hold the ground gained.[40]

He resumed work only to face some sharp new challenges. The nation was at war, and the classicists in the prestigious private universities along the Atlantic seaboard were not sympathetic with the German tradition represented by Oldfather.

On May 7, 1945, the European war ended, and twenty days later Oldfather was dead. He was canoeing on the Salt Fork, near Homer, Illinois, that afternoon, when he deliberately shot his canoe, as he had often done, over an abandoned mill-dam. The other man in the canoe, who went over the dam with him, swam to the shore, while Oldfather, grasping his canoe, shouted bravely to the rest of the party on the river-bank. They saw an undertow catch him and draw him down; they did not recover his body until midnight.

Oldfather's reputation as an admirer of German culture gave rise to the rumor that his death was an act of despair over the defeat of Germany. No reasonable person could believe this. He was loyal to every part of his heritage. He made the Illinois classics department a center for the study of classical antiquity and brought great distinction to the university. A fearless and outspoken humanist, Oldfather devoted his career to making the classics relevant to modern life.

NOTES

1. Oldfather is the subject of a considerable literature. The William A. Oldfather Papers, 1904–1945, 7.6 cubic feet, Record Series 15/6/20, in the University of Illinois archives, has materials for a full life. Recent brief biographies include John Buckler, "William Abbott Oldfather," in *Classical Scholarship: A Biographical Encyclopedia*, ed. Ward W. Briggs and William M. Calder III (New York: Garland, 1990), 346–52; and Michael Armstrong, "Oldfather, William Abbott," *American National Biography* 16 (2000): 670–71.

2. *The Miami Student* (April 1892), 140. Bob Schmidt, archivist of Miami University, kindly furnished this information. Henry's granddaughter, Helen Oldfather, married August K. Reischauer. They went to Japan as Presbyterian missionaries and remained there thirty-six years. Their son, Edwin Oldfather Reischauer, became a leading American scholar of the Far East, a Harvard professor, and from 1961 to 1966 U.S. ambassador to Japan. Joan Adams, the granddaughter of Henry's other granddaughter, married Walter Mondale, former vice president of the United States.

3. The account of the Oldfathers' experience in Persia is drawn from *Annual Report[s] of the Board of Foreign Missions of the Presbyterian Church in the United States of America*, 1873 to 1890, published in New York.

4. *Forty-fourth Annual Report* (1881), 44–45; *Forty-fifth Annual Report* (1882), 50–51 (first quotation); Edwin O. Reischauer, *My Life between Japan and America* (New York: Harper and Row, 1986), 14 (second quotation).

5. *Forty-ninth Annual Report* (1886), 86.

6. *Fifty-third Annual Report* (1890), 163–64.

7. These details are drawn from various Hanover College catalogues and from Frank S. Baker, *More Glimpses of Hanover's Past, 1827–1988* (Hanover College, 1988), 101.

8. For the context of scholarship in the classics, see William M. Calder III, "William Abbott Oldfather and the Preservation of German Influence in American Classics, 1919–1933," in *Altertumswissenschaft in den 20er Jahren Neue Fragen und Impulse*, ed. Hellmut Flashar (Stuttgart: Franz Steiner Verlag, 1995), 403–21; idem, "Classical Scholarship in the United States: An Introductory Essay," in *Biographical Dictionary of North American Classicists*, ed. Ward W. Briggs Jr. (Westport, Conn.: Greenwood, 1994), xxvi–xxix; and Michael Armstrong, "A German Scholar and Socialist in Illinois: The Career of William Abbott Oldfather," *Classical Journal* 88 (1993): 235–53.

9. Herbert Weir Smyth, "The Classics, 1867–1929," in *The Development of Harvard University since the Inauguration of President Eliot, 1869–1929*, ed. Samuel Eliot Morison (Cambridge, Mass.: Harvard University Press, 1930), 37–52.

10. Armstrong, "Oldfather, William Abbott," in *American National Biography* 16:670–71.

11. James to Greene, July 8, 1907, Greene to James, August 5, 1907, 2/5/6, B:6, F:Evarts B. Greene; RS 2/5/15, Arthur S. Pease Appointment File.

12. Smyth to Greene, May 19, 1909; Crusius to the dean of the College of Literature and Arts, June 1, 1909; Clark to Charles M. Moss, April 26, 1909; Kinley to Greene, May 31, 1909, Greene to James, May 29, June 7, 1909, 2/5/15, William A. Oldfather File.

13. *25th Report* (1910), 169; Oldfather to James, June 25, July 1, 1909; James to Oldfather, July 2, 1909, 2/5/15, William A. Oldfather File.

14. Oldfather to James, July 21, 1909, 2/5/15, William A. Oldfather File. Oldfather's information on the two European worthies was from Crusius of Munich.

15. Oldfather, Note Cards, 15/6/20, B:4, F:Oldfather, William A. 1906, 1909–12.

16. Oldfather, "Memorandum," July 21, 1915, 15/6/20, B:4, F:Oldfather, William A. 1913–20; *28th Report* (1916), 773.

17. "University of Illinois Faculty Disloyalty Investigation, Special Committee, Board of Trustees, November 27, 1917, 2/5/3, B:152, F:Disloyalty, Faculty (a transcript of the events and newspaper reports). See also Bruce Tap, "Suppression of Dissent: Academic Freedom at the University of Illinois during the World War I Era," *Illinois Historical Journal* 85 (Spring 1992): 2–22.

18. The statement about lying is quoted by Robert A. Feer, "Academic Freedom at State Universities: The University of Illinois, 1867–1950" (undergraduate thesis, Harvard College, 1950), 79. For the statement attributed to Oldfather Feer cited an interview on February 11, 1950, with a former University of Illinois faculty member and another on March 4, 1950, with a former University of Illinois graduate student who was on the Harvard faculty in 1950. On "display liberals," see Oldfather to W. H. Alexander, May 25, 1937, 15/6/20, B:1, F:A.General 1934–38.

19. Paul Shorey, "Fifty Years of Classical Studies in America," *Transactions and Proceedings of the American Philological Association* 50 (1919): 33–62; E. Christian Kopff, "Scott,

John Adams," in Briggs, *Biographical Dictionary of North American Classicists*, 572 (the quotation).

20. Gilbert Norwood, "Modern Classical Scholarship," *The Living Age*, 319 (December 15, 1923): 520–25; W. A. Oldfather, "Review of Eduard Norden, *Die Germanische Urgeschichte in Tacitus Germania*," *Classical Journal*, 19 (April 1924): 460–61; Calder, "William Abbott Oldfather and the Preservation of German Influence in American Classics 1919–1933," 409–10, 416.

21. [C. A. Forbes], "William Abbott Oldfather," *Classical Journal* 41 (1945): 9.

22. Oldfather to H. W. Anderson, December 7, 1937, 15/6/20, B:1, F:A. General 1934–38.

23. Suzanne N. Griffiths, "Doctoral Dissertations Completed at the University of Illinois under William Abbott Oldfather," *Classical Journal*, 74 (December 1978–January 1979): 149–53.

24. Richmond Lattimore, "Memory of a Scholar," *New Republic*, 145 (November 13, 1961): 13. A framed copy of the tribute and an oil portrait of Oldfather hang in the classics library at the University of Illinois. L. R. Lind paid poetic tribute to "William Abbott Oldfather" in *An Epitaph Years After* (East Lansing: Bennett & Kitchel, 1990), 15.

25. Oldfather to L. R. Lind, April 5, 1939, 15/6/20, B:4, F:L. R. Lind Correspondence 1930–49.

26. Oldfather to Ruth Campbell, April 21, 1936, 15/6/20, B:1, F:A. General 1934–38. Years earlier Oldfather had offered an economic interpretation of Greco-Roman history in "Social Conditions and Theories in the Graeco-Roman World," *Progressive Journal of Education* 2 (September–December 1909).

27. Oldfather to W. H. Alexander, May 11, 1937, 15/6/20, B:1, F:A. General 1934–38.

28. H. E. Cunningham, C. R. Griffith, and Ben E. Perry, "Memorial," 26/1/20, B:13, F:Senate Necrology.

29. Michael Armstrong, comp., "Bibliography: The Publications of William Abbott Oldfather," does not include Oldfather's contributions to Pauly-Wissowa. Ben E. Perry (a classicist) and two other colleagues, "Memorial," 25/1/20, B:13, F:Senate Necrology (the quotation).

30. Oldfather to W. W. Wilson, January 10, 1944, 7/1/2, Graduate College Dean's Office Administrative Correspondence, B:2, F:Faculty Advisory Committee on Selection of a New President.

31. Sterling Dow, *Fifty Years of Sathers: The Sather Professorship of Classical Literature in the University of California, Berkeley, 1913/4–1963/64* (Berkeley: University of California Press, 1965), 1 (the quotation), 62.

32. Oldfather to W. H. Alexander, May 25, 1937, 15/6/20, B:1, F:A. General 1934–38.

33. Oldfather to W. H. Alexander, May 3, 1938, 15/6/20, B:1, F:A. General 1934–38. On Berkeley, see Joseph Fontenrose, *Classics at Berkeley: The First Century, 1869–1970* (Berkeley: Department of Classics History Fund, 1982), a charming memoir.

34. Oldfather's document is in 15/6/20, B:2, F:Columbia University, 1937–38. For the text and an analysis, see William M. Calder III, "*Nuda Veritas*: William Abbott Oldfather on Classics at Columbia," *Studies in Honor of Miroslav Marcovich: Illinois Classical Studies* 18 (1943): 359–78.

35. Oldfather to R. L. Lind, December 13, 1940, 15/6/20, B:4, F:L. R. Lind Correspondence.

36. W. A. Oldfather, *Is Religion Essential to Every Adequate Philosophy of Living?* (Published by the Young Men's Christian Association, University of Illinois: 1930). In 1934 Oldfather gave the same lecture at Berkeley. The YMCA at the University of California published it.

37. Oldfather to Ferdinand Alexander, July 28, 1938, 15/6/20, B:1, F:A. General 1934–38.

38. Oldfather, "Some Ancient Thought on Progress and Decadence," *Proceedings of the American Philological Association* 69 (1938): xxvi; *New York Times*, December 29, 1938, 12; Oldfather to Carl Stephens, January 20, 1939, 15/6/20, B:5, F:Stephens, Carl.

39. The first note is dated January 9, 1936; the second, February 9, 1936. Both are signed "E.T.B." Oldfather made the B read "B(erdahl)." 15/6/20, B:1, F:B 1934–39. Evelyn Berdahl was the wife of Clarence A. Berdahl, a political science professor and loyal member of The Saturday Hike.

40. The relevant documents are in 2/5/15, William A. Oldfather File; see also Oldfather to Francis J. Gerty, December 30, 1943, 15/6/20, B:2, F:G 1940–45.

BRUCE MICHELSON

CHAPTER 6

American Literature in the Cornfields:

Stuart Pratt Sherman and J. Kerker Quinn

In the city of Urbana, at the place where Goodwin Street meets Nevada Street and where the Stuart Pratt Sherman family home once marked an edge of a sparsely built University of Illinois campus, a wide concrete ramp now slopes down to a brace of dumpsters. Just east of this void, one can see the recently built four-storied brick headquarters of the school of music, which gratefully received J. Kerker Quinn's massive collection of classical LPs when a coronary killed him suddenly in 1969. Out on the street now, when the weather is warm and construction teams take a break, you can sometimes hear young sopranos or instrumental quartets practicing. But walk twenty paces north of the former Sherman yard and you reach the portal of a soft-core rave joint, where our weekend evenings rattle and hum with the latest in alternative rock. Loiter where the Sherman front porch must have been, and enjoy the predicament that both of these Illinois professors helped bring on: conscientious first-rate classicism just over there; massive subwoofers in angst at your back.

This rambunctious heartland American culture, which Stuart Sherman championed for more than fifteen years at Illinois (1907–24), and which J. Kerker Quinn served quietly in a career that lasted thirty (to 1969), has inundated them both with noisy ramifications of what they wanted. The young campus they helped put on the American literary map has sprawled and devoured the don's house; tides of books by others, developing subjects that Sherman pioneered, have swept into obscurity the knee-high popular stack he had authored when a canoe accident and a heart attack caught him in icy Lake Michigan waters in the summer of 1926, only two years after the Shermans sold this house and moved out East, to be national arbiters of taste in New York City.

Quinn's legacy was *Accent*, or more precisely the spate of high-quality literary magazines that followed its lead, and the many fine authors that Quinn had helped make famous by the time he shut down *Accent* in what should have been the middle of his Illinois teaching career. In all dimensions but reputation, *Accent* was a consummate "little magazine," *his* little magazine, with a mission so modest as to be downright radical in an age of dreary and barren radical posturing. Quinn's dangerous quest was to publish the best new writing, regardless of coterie, region, or political stripe. When Quinn retired *Accent* in the winter of 1961, over the protests of friends and his fellow editors, it was already being crowded out by better-funded imitations at other schools. Thirty years after, there are shelves of good imprints that owe their existence to his daring.

From this place—an outback in the view of literary New Yorkers and Bostonians—Sherman made himself a national star. He wrote readable books with titles that can stun now for their simplicity, directness, presumption. He wrote essay collections called *Americans and The Genius of America*, and *On Contemporary Literature*, and *Men of Letters of the British Isles*. He turned out editions of Shakespeare plays and *Treasure Island* and story collections for high school students. He wrote much of *The Cambridge History of English Literature*—and after his death, volumes with his name on the spine were still coming out: *The Main Stream* and *The Emotional Discovery of America*. He was the only faculty member in the history of the university to inspire a two-volume "life and letters," a monumental work befitting an Emerson or a William James.[1] By the time he was thirty, Sherman had turned out over 150 publications—verse, short stories, political pamphlets, barrages of literary reviews. Getting his start in the pages of *The Nation* and the *New York Evening Post*, he continued to write elegant, contentious articles for wide-circulation journals. Ten years into his career, he risked a long and noisy public quarrel with H. L. Mencken, a gifted, indefatigable opponent and the most venomous literary and editorial showboat since the later years of Mark Twain. A full professor of English at Illinois when he was twenty-six, and chair of his rapidly growing department at thirty-four, Sherman wrote for the entire country as a cultural pundit, championing a New England tradition that others (especially Mencken) regarded as stodgy and narrowly regional; but he also spoke out for new voices from the American heartland. When he finally left Illinois to become literary editor of the *New York Herald Tribune*, that move was seen as a coup—for the newspaper and the metropolis together.

Eighty years after Sherman's glory days, even graduate students in American literature give you blank looks at the mention of his name. No surprise there: American literature, American studies, cultural studies— these conversations, which Sherman helped create at the opening of his century have swelled into disciplines within disciplines, turning inward, wrangling over their own methodology. Challenges that seemed imperative to Sherman, like discerning and describing the national character and the real or the best American cultural landscape, are seen by today's cautious careerists as too tricky to risk.

When Quinn died in 1969, with his teacher-boots on, collapsing in the hallway by the English Building's airy decrepit Room 259, he bequeathed those shelves of phonograph records and much of his personal fortune, memories of one ground-breaking magazine, and piles of correspondence with some of the best American writers of mid-twentieth century, much of which remains unpublished. And that was about it. A confirmed bachelor, remembered as dapper and courtly by his friends,[2] Quinn left no immediate family behind. And his 1950s-era ranch house on Mumford Drive in Urbana, where with notable style and expense he had entertained gaggles of friends, has drifted back into the blur of mid-market suburban real estate. Publishing little of his own work, and making no splash in other realms of academic life, he never broke above the rank of associate professor. As a teacher he wasn't showy; as a colleague he was known as a good citizen—which in academic parlance means that he was neither a leader nor a pest.

If we want to see the legacy of these two Illinois teachers, we must look at the lineaments of the national culture that both of them envisioned, promoted, and tried to express. The marks they made remain clearly upon its face. Each in his own way shook up the country a little, rearranged its thinking about itself. For about a decade in that house on West Nevada Street, and up at their roughneck summer hideout on the Michigan shore,

Sherman and his wife Ruth pondered and turned down a succession of attractive offers from glamorous schools back in the ancestral neighborhood—for Ruth Bartlett Sherman, daughter of a professor at Williams College, where Sherman had been an undergraduate, was also of the New England academic tribe. As for Quinn: by 1952, when the Illinois campus finally began thinking seriously about supporting *Accent* with actual cash, and bringing it thereby under what Professor and Chairman Gordon Ray called the "auspices" of the English department, the magazine had already built a reputation and audience that Quinn, as its founder, proprietor, and driving force, could have taken with him easily to another good college or university, had he wanted to move away.

So why did these literary men choose to do what they did, and do it at the University of Illinois?

In 1907, when Sherman and Ruth came to Illinois after one year at Northwestern, the arbiters of American culture were still solidly in the East, chiefly nestled into midtown Manhattan, or along Beacon Street in Boston and Massachusetts Avenue in Cambridge. Sherman knew that, and from the inside: though a small farm town in Iowa was his birthplace, Sherman was a New Englander in blood and training. His father, something of a family renegade, had come out to the prairies to escape a two-century accumulation of Connecticut Valley ancestors: parsons and pious homesteaders who had scattered their farms and bones over that neighborhood since the times of Cromwell. The father, John Sherman, had fled west to try something new, and eventually fled farther, to the California deserts, to stave off the lurking tuberculosis that killed him when Stuart was ten. After a few months of kicking around with another family in an Arizona gold-seekers' camp, Stuart was shipped back to his mother, who had now settled in with relatives in the Berkshires. A big, outdoors-loving athletic star student at Williams, Stuart blazed through doctoral work at Harvard and toyed with the idea of staying in Cambridge, for mighty Harvard had floated the possibility of an instructorship, a chance to snuggle into the cultural Heart of Light, amid the consoling ghosts of Emerson, Longfellow, William James, and the Lowells, in a seductive (and possibly stifling) long New England literary autumn.

If we insist on unromantic reasons why Sherman came to the Urbana flatlands instead, we can follow the money. Eager for bright young instructors for his new English department, the Illinois dean of men, Thomas Arkle Clark, was a good scout for talent. He had been courting Sherman since his undergraduate days at Williams. Illinois had been the first school to offer Sherman a teaching position. When Sherman came on the market after his one-year instructorship at Northwestern and cramped rented rooms in Evanston, the offer from downstate looked much better: a rank of associate, a salary 50 percent higher in a town where dollars went farther than they did on the North Shore—and a chance to create a nationally recognized program almost from scratch.

In those days, Illinois had about 4,000 enrolled students, about the size of Harvard or Yale at that time. But Illinois had ambitions, and cash flow and public support to make them come true—a place where vigorous people could shape an academic culture rather than pay homage to traditions and Great Questions ponderously "settled." When Sherman arrived, the English department had only four full professors, and everybody on the staff pitched in with the undergraduate teaching. Even Dean Clark was covering composition sections that required two four-page essays and one eight-page theme for him to grade every week. (Administrative life must have been simpler back then.) The English roster was lean: only one associate professor; three other tenure-track faculty. There were also fewer than two dozen associates, assistants, and instructors who taught on short contracts for low pay.

Twelve years later, the campus and the department had grown like a pampered kitten. Three new colleges had been founded, including a Liberal Arts and Sciences home for Sherman and his new cohorts; the university press was up and running; the student population and the inventory of buildings had more than doubled; the English department staff now topped sixty. And while he was writing up a storm, Sherman was in the thick of this development. As department chair in the early 1920s, he hired or backed the hiring of talented women onto the full-time faculty, and gifted Jewish scholars who were still being spurned by the Ivies. In building this staff he moved toward a kind of diversity that was right for Illinois undergraduates, students coming down from Chicago or in from the farms, students with names and pedigrees that many Boston dons of the time would have flinched to see in the yearbooks. Somehow Sherman also taught regularly—but not often the American authors he wrote so much about.

In academe, American literature and culture were still dubious enterprises. The first college anthology on the subject was not published until 1919, and even graduate work in English letters, other than hard-core philology and linguistics, was an idea of very recent vintage. So Sherman's regular assignments were Shakespeare, Renaissance drama, and upper-division courses in nineteenth-century British writers. Emerson, Mark Twain, Whitman, Wharton, Sandburg, and modern British and Irish writ-

Stuart Pratt Sherman
with poet and playwright
Percy Mackaye, 1921.

ers like Wells, Lawrence, Synge, Arnold Bennett, George Moore—all this was new territory; and the scrupulous attention that Sherman gave them, in poised, measured, general, accessible essays, helped bring intellectual dignity for these authors and a wide audience as well for this Illinois don.

Unfortunately, however, it was the controversy with H. L. Mencken, sage of Baltimore and national gadfly, that brightened the limelight around Sherman and created a role for him that is remembered better than his hard work to advance and dignify American literature. Between 1914 and 1917, as America moved toward war with Germany, Mencken, as a nationally syndicated columnist, went through a disgraceful patch of his career, crowing about German ethnic superiority, celebrating the failure of British and French counter-offensives, dodging and rationalizing reports of Central Powers atrocities, shrugging off the torpedoing of the *Lusitania*—and drubbing American culture and its "booboisie" for crudeness and stodgy "puritanism." Vintage Mencken from 1917: "the only domestic art this huge and opulent empire knows is in the hands of Mexican greasers; its only native music it owes to the despised Negro; its only genuine public is permitted to die up an alley like a stray dog."[3] "We detect certain curious qualities in every Slav simply because he is more given than we are to revealing the qualities that are in all of us. Introspection and self-revelation are his habit; he carries the study of man and fate to a point that seems morbid to westerners; he is forever gabbling about what he finds in his own soul."[4] And as literary critic, on Theodore Dreiser: "Once, seeking an analogy, I called him the Hindenburg of the novel. If it holds, then 'The Genius' is his Poland. The field of action bears the aspect, at the end, of a hostile province meticulously brought under the yoke, with every road and lane explored to its beginning, and every crossroads laboriously taken, inventoried and policed. Here is the very negation of Gallic lightness and intuition, and other forms of impressionism as well."[5]

Before the Great War began, this might have been merely pesky and provocative; but as one "hostile province" after another was "policed" with burned libraries and mass executions of civilians, as cathedral towns were shelled and phosgene gas was fired into Allied trenches, the *Deutschland Über Alles* theme of Mencken's "Free Lance" columns in the *Baltimore Sun* became obscene,[6] and had to be answered by somebody with intellectual weight. With nothing to gain, Stuart Sherman took on the job.

Latter-day Menckenites haven't forgiven him, and have no qualms about hurling Mencken-ish vituperation at a long-dead adversary: "hatchet man," "grumpy, pinch-faced professor," "prime blackguard," propagator of "wartime prejudice," and "calculated vengeance"—review the Mencken side of the Mencken-Sherman controversy, and you wade through language like this.[7] It is grossly misleading, for Sherman's responses to Mencken almost never lost their cool. In a way, that was their strength: the elegance and measure in Sherman's championing of American values underscored Mencken's vulgarity. And the theme that Sherman advanced as America entered the war hardly seems markedly unjingoistic for that moment. We were about to put hundreds of thousands of American troops onto a battlefield that had already killed millions. If with divided loyalties you are living in the United States, then decide what you are, and open up to the nation that gave you and your family refuge from oppression and poverty. From a U.S. government pamphlet that Sherman authored early in 1918 called "American and Allied Ideals," we read:

> there has been instituted an anti-American campaign of a more insidious character, conducted mainly in the English language and ostensibly by American citizens. Among its leaders are editors of magazines, poets, novelists, critics, brewers, and professors in the universities. The program of these men is about as follows: attack England; praise Germany; attack everything in America that is due to English influence; praise everything in America that is due to German influence. Accordingly they sneer at the ideals and professions of democratic government; they sneer at the Pilgrim Fathers and all the Puritans who since the seventeenth century have constituted the moral backbone of the nation; they set themselves against every movement of moral reform; they sneer at all the humanitarian movements associated

with Christianity; they sneer at the works of American literature which we recognize as classical. In short they keep up a continuous cannonade against every revered American tradition, against every established political ideal, against every accepted article of our public and private morality; against everything admirable in our social aspirations, against everything characteristic of the common sense of thee American people. On the other hand, they celebrate the biological-political ideals of Prussian statecraft, the biological immoralism of Nietzsche, and the literature of Berlin and Vienna, especially that nastiest part of it which they are certain will offend what they scoffingly call the Puritanical sensibilities of Americans.

This is about as hot as Sherman got, in the rising heat of the war's last years. In other publications, where Sherman attacks Mencken by name, the tone is more affable, wittier.

But what of all that now? Pamphlets and essays and ephemeral columns back and forth in newspapers—the austere rejoinder to wartime rhetoric is the silence in graveyards along the Albert-Bapaume road, or the untended German burial grounds farther north, or in the cathedral naves where small marble plaques remember "One Million Dead of the British empire." From so long after, the Mencken-Sherman war looks counterfeit, two grown men with typewriters, men too old for combat, striking postures like wrestlers safe in a scripted match. War takes a toll on judgment and prose. The public was mostly on Sherman's side, and Mencken endured a brief eclipse—but like any thick-skinned professional irritant he was back before long, and in the euphoria after the armistice both men turned to other subjects.

Nonetheless, the Illinois cornfields were central to their conflict, and they helped Sherman. It would have been tidier for Mencken if the counter-strike had come from a Boston neighborhood, associated with that "Puritan" culture Mencken had been decrying for years. Sherman would have been easier to classify and write off, a resentful survivor of a faded New England regime. By writing from out here, Sherman opened a second front: resistance from the Heartland, from a school attended by people from that mongrel new society and unfettered culture that Mencken at times was calling for. In the debate about what we are, the moment was important. And with an Urbana address, Sherman was stronger.

Even so, a deep concern had been broached in that controversy, and that subject was central in Sherman's thinking after the war: What would constitute the voice and the art of this "opulent empire," now the greatest economic and military power in the world? Where would taste be shaped or refereed? How would this polyglot America of German and Slavic and African and Mexican ancestry converse with itself with intensity about what it means to be human? This is the subject both antagonists returned to. With more books and essays and the passing of years, Sherman's own literary values changed, so much so that some detractors would accuse him of inconsistency. But Sherman was writing of America in a time of cultural change, and before assumptions took root that a critic had to ride the same ideological bicycle through all professional years and stages of personal growth. Eventually Sherman even published kind things about Dreiser, and the totalitarian Carlyle, and the naturalistic Sherwood Anderson, and the wayward Swinburne, and many other writers that few in 1914 could have predicted he would come to respect. And he stayed at Illinois, though his fame and his pile of publications guaranteed him entrée in cosmopolitan centers.

What was he thinking? Perhaps we can glimpse it in a 1911 letter to his longtime friend Carl Van Doren, whose upbringing and career track at the time was necessarily running opposite to Sherman's. A local boy, raised downstate, Van Doren was seeking his fortune in the big Eastern cities. Sherman was urging him to come home and join in building the culture of Illinois: "Here you are in the great heart of the country. Here is the place to feel the pulse of *real* people beat. Here is the place to study and create real American literature! Please read over what Lowell and a younger poet whose name escapes me have said about the native clay of this section, and its adaptability to the formation of great men." About the Heartland, Sherman was preaching to the choir, if not to the converted, for Van Doren, who ultimately stayed "out East," knew more about the prairies than Sherman did. A couple of years later, in another essay for *The Nation*, Sherman laid out the cause and mission of the public university, showing fervor and eloquence that few Big Ten presidents have come near since. The land-grant campuses, he said, would "dignify the entire range of human conduct by discovering for all the people and by making prevail from the lowest to the loftiest the right and the excellent form of every activity. They resent with justice the . . . notion that the consecrated search for light is a monopoly in the possession of the old New England colleges. . . . You have preserved your idealism in glass jars; we have not lost ours by putting it to work in the bread of life. Immersed though we seem to be, we are Platonists no less than you, pursuing through the things that lie nearest to us the divine idea, and we shall pass in due time from the love of sensuous to the love of supersensual beauty."

In 1936, when J. Kerker Quinn arrived at the University of Illinois as a graduate assistant in his mid-twenties with a Peoria upbringing, a bache-

lor's degree in English literature from Bradley, and a few months of experience editing a magazine on that campus, the Depression lay deep on the
Midwest; money was scarce in Urbana. Sherman was long gone, and his
buoyancy about the glorious future of this place seemed like rhetoric from
another age. Sherman had created a stir when he rolled in; Quinn was an
anonymous newcomer, chasing a master's degree and teaching low-level
courses to pay his way. But at the age of twenty-five, Quinn had an uncommon sense of where the big holes were in American literary publishing and
what the culture needed to find new directions and a burst of creative
energy. Financial hard times had killed a lot of imprints, and politics had
soured some of the major outlets. The high-prestige and quality journals
and literary reviews of 1940, when *Accent* was launched, make a very short
list: there was *The Southern Review* and *Decision* and *The Kenyon Review*,
which survived at the pleasure of cash-strapped campuses, and *The Partisan Review*, which was rocked with internal insurrections and at one point
had to pass the hat for subscriber donations in order to head off a shutdown.

Quinn wanted to create a new magazine that would step in boldly—
which meant, in his view, keeping clear of any too-close affiliation with any
academic department or campus. He preferred lean freedom to fat "auspices." The Illinois English department eventually gave him a workroom
on the second floor of the building, and not much else. When *Accent*
started, neither Quinn nor any of the other editors had the prestige to back
up a request for money from the campus or anywhere else. So the *Accent*
group scrounged dollars on their own, battled to cut costs, and pitched in
with the menial office work to conserve cash. When the price of decent
paper skyrocketed and subscribers backed off as the war came on, several
of the other major imprints suspended publication, widening the gap that
Quinn wanted his lean *Accent* to fill. "If they cannot hold on," he wrote,
"how can *Accent* hope to?"

Because they were planned from the start to operate at a huge deficit,
whereas *Accent* was not. *The Southern Review* contained 200 pages an issue,
printed beautifully on the best paper; the editors received a salary, and the
contributors were paid well. *The Kenyon Review*, subsidized by Kenyon
College, cost the school a reported $2,500 annually. *Accent*, on the other
hand, was planned to break even; it did so during its first year. It was not
so fat, not so well printed; its editors received no salary, its contributors little remuneration. The whole problem of readjustment was, therefore, not
so forbidding.

In this 1942 pitch-letter to the College of Liberal Arts and Sciences for
some kind of subvention, however, Quinn writes uneasily about the risks

Portrait of
J. Kerker Quinn.

of affiliating more closely with the campus: "While *Accent* was an independent magazine, the editors chose the best of the manuscripts submitted, without particular caution about offending readers who object to the frankness in literature. Though many stories and poems were rejected partly because they seemed too objectionable on moral grounds, we are aware that occasionally something we printed was disliked by a portion of our audience. We realize that, if *Accent* were to be officially associated with the University, a stricter censorship by the editors would be necessary. We guarantee that the greatest discretion would be employed by the editors."

Quinn was over a barrel, losing money as well as staff, for several of the editors were then heading off to war service. With cash problems of his own to worry about, Dean Hillebrand turned the request down. Nonetheless, *Accent* found money elsewhere to get by, and nearly ten years passed before a spurt of postwar inflation and competition from flush new journals sent Quinn and English department head Gordon Ray back to the campus wells. What was odd and powerful about *Accent*, in its twenty-year run under Quinn's proprietorship between the first issue in September 1940 and the last one in 1960, was that it favored poetry and fiction and lots of it, and avoided entanglements and posturing that had turned other promising reviews and "little magazines" into coterie publications or forgettable outlets for one political faction or another. *Accent* was light on manifestos and interventions. At the back of the first issue there was only this—a little evangelical perhaps, but wonderfully brief, and also right about the circumstances into which this little magazine was launched:

> The editors of *Accent* hope to build a magazine which discerning readers will welcome as a representative collection of the best creative and critical writing of our time, carefully balancing the work of established authors with that of comparative unknowns. By avoiding a biased viewpoint and rejecting the stereotyped and the trivial and the unintelligible, they will try to make the contents of each issue significant, varied, and readable.
>
> America has need and room for such a magazine. Look down the list of today's periodicals—the few that are open to the serious creative writer either allow articles on current events to dwarf the space left for him or else specialize in poetry or short stories or criticism to the exclusion of other fields. *Accent* has no first-rate parallel in aim and scope at this time.

In the opening years, Quinn and his fellow editors, a fluid staff that included, at various times, Charles Shattuck, W. R. Moses, George Scouffas, Dan Curley, and other lights of the creative writing program, worked the mail service and the telephones hard, wooing many of the "name" writers of the 1930s and 1940s to send in their work and give *Accent* the credibility and cachet to go forward with its aspirations. But the established authors were only part of the mix: the idea was to publish quality work by knowns and unknowns alike, and to present as many new voices as familiar ones. Each issue, therefore, was meant to be a paella of tastes, and a reader could settle in with certified names and styles and perspectives, launch into unknown sensibilities and imaginative territory, and "read around" in short journeys between a coalesced today and a disheveled tomorrow. *Accent* was always lean, navigable in a single evening. It was an exciting unpretentious experience in finding out, from a nonsectarian literary perspective, what was up. The list of established and future stars who appeared in its pages spells out Quinn's success, as an advocate and editor, a young man without reputation building an imprint from scratch. A sampling: Dylan Thomas, Wallace Stevens, Conrad Aiken, Richard Wilbur, Willliam Gass, Erskine Caldwell, Anne Sexton, David Daiches, Sylvia Plath, John Dos Passos, James T. Farrell, Howard Nemerov, Dwight MacDonald, e e cummings, R. P. Blackmur, Catherine Anne Porter, Austin Warren, Walter Van Tilburg Clark.

Run your eye over this list and you may notice a brusque disregard for region, or for membership in this or that "movement" valorized somewhere else. *Accent* readers recognized that "southern" writers were teaching on good salaries up in Minnesota, that "agrarians" had put down roots

in the anomalous soil of New Haven and New York, that New England pas-
toralists were plying their trade wherever the honoraria and the teaching
jobs required them to go. Part of the pleasure in these old issues lies in their
open-handed catholicity, this innocent or profound assumption that good
writing and good readers need to find each other across those illusory
boundaries that organize doctoral dissertations but really nothing else, and
that the arts in America might be better off if such categories and contentious descriptions are left behind.

As an editorial achievement, this was amazing—enough to make *Accent*
a leader to be chased and overtaken by other magazines with more money
and fresher and steadier personnel. That happened fast in the 1950s, and
Quinn's January 1961 letter to Dean Robert Rogers, calling it quits for
Accent, cites an array of better-paying alternatives that the best American
authors now could court: "As twenty years have passed, the whole literary
situation has changed radically. America is flooded with magazines which
are solidly financed—some handsomely subsidized by colleges (*Minnesota
Review* and *Massachusetts Review*, for example, both of which just started
last fall), some 'angled' by men of means (like *Paris Review* and *Hudson
Review*), and some sponsored by book firms (*Evergreen Review, Anchor
Review, New World Writing*, etc.) marketed wherever paper-back books are
on display, and consequently circulated very widely. I would estimate that
there are as many as fifty literary magazines now operating under responsible editorship. Perhaps twenty of them can remunerate contributors far
more liberally than anyone dreamed in 1940."

From the months before that, the correspondence files tell a tale of
slackening conviction and energy, an evaporating sense of the effort as
something special. Complaining letters accumulated: What happened to
the poems I sent you six months or a year ago? Where is my payment, or
my complimentary handful of copies? Why haven't we heard from you?
Life in the writing programs grew complicated; an old guard aged and
drifted away. In some ways it's gratifying that *Accent* didn't linger for years
as just another undernourished blossom of artsy discourse in a choked
garden. It was created for a specific moment, and its founder and editor
had the genius and grace to know when that moment had passed. Never
chasing fame himself, J. Kerker Quinn nonetheless shares something basic
and important with Stuart Pratt Sherman, who, as the bard said of
Beowulf, was "eager for fame." They didn't snuggle into trends but tried to
create something new—new voices, with a vigorous disregard for the pars-
ing of literature into hierarchies and sets. They understood what our tur-
bulent culture needed, and ignoring what others elsewhere had ordained

those needs to be, they brought the University of Illinois powerfully into important conversations.

NOTES

1. Jacob Zeitlin and Homer Woodbridge, *Life and Letters of Stuart P. Sherman* (New York: Farrar & Rinehart, 1929) is a source for many of the biographical facts in this essay. I am grateful also to the staff and resources of the University of Illinois archives for information about the Illinois campus, its curricula, and its faculty in the opening years of the twentieth century. Another concise, vigorous summary of Sherman's career and cultural importance is Arthur J. Carr, "Another 'Most Famous Graduate'?" *Williams Alumni Review* (Summer 1986): 27–30. I thank my college and friend Leon Waldoff for unearthing this essay, and for guiding me into the Sherman materials at the great University of Illinois library.

2. While there is no biography of J. Kerker Quinn, Jefferson Hendricks's unpublished dissertation, "'Accent,' 1940–1960: The History of a Little Magazine" (University of Illinois, 1990) includes important information about Quinn's early life and career at Illinois. The personnel files of the University of Illinois Department of English have also been helpful, as have several colleagues and friends who have shared with me memories of Quinn, especially A. Lynn Altenbernd, Paul Friedman, and Audrey Hodgins.

3. Henry Louis Mencken, *A Book of Prefaces* (New York: Octagon Books, 1977), 101.

4. Ibid., 14.

5. Ibid., 80

6. For Baltimoreans, Mencken's strutting can be understood as airing a local grudge: a German American boy from a downtown rowhouse, jabbing at pious Anglicans and Presbyterians who ran the city from protected neighborhoods and country clubs along North Charles Street. There is a picture from that time of Mencken and some pals dressed as rabble and peering through the iron-barred gate of the highly restricted Baltimore Country Club—from the outside. It speaks volumes. But Mencken had a national audience.

7. For hagiographic accounts of Mencken's life and professional controversies, see Carl Bode, *Mencken* (Carbondale: Southern Illinois University Press, 1969), and William Manchester, *Disturber of the Peace: The Life of H. L. Mencken* (Amherst: University of Massachusetts Press, 1986). The "Free Lance" articles for the *Baltimore Sun* have never been collected, perhaps for good reason. For a selection, see Bode, *The Young Mencken; The Best of His Work* (New York: Dial Press, 1973).

ROBERT W. JOHANNSEN

CHAPTER 7

Lincoln, the Civil War,

and Professor James G. Randall

In the historical memory of Illinois, the Civil War is inseparable from the martyred President Lincoln, who symbolized the moral underpinnings of democracy's struggle for survival. These two elements, Lincoln and the Civil War, would exert a strong influence on the way Illinoisans perceived their past and in the way history would be taught at the University of Illinois.

This university, it might be said, had its beginnings during the Civil War, when, in the summer of 1862, Congress passed and President Lincoln signed into law the Morrill Land Grant Act. Named for its sponsor, Vermont Senator Justin Morrill, the act was part of a package of domestic legislation that included the Pacific Railroad Act, the Homestead Act, and the Internal Revenue Act. This legislation, as one historian put it, helped "to change the course of national life" at a time when the country was fighting for that very life. The act provided grants of land to the states in support of higher education in "agriculture and the mechanic arts," fulfilling the dream of Illinois reformer Jonathan Baldwin Turner and the late Illinois

Senator Stephen A. Douglas (who died in 1861), both of whom had lobbied strenuously for the act's passage in the 1850s. Eventually, sixty-nine land-grant institutions of higher learning were established in whole or in part by the act.

Although the first class of students entered the new Illinois Industrial University (it would not become the University of Illinois until 1885) in March 1868, a year after the university was formally established, it was not until 1894 that the first full-time historian was appointed to the faculty. Evarts B. Greene, whose task it was to build a history department, typified the new professionalization of historical study in the 1890s. He held a Ph.D. degree (a prerequisite for professorial appointment) in American history from Harvard University, where he had studied under Albert Bushnell Hart. He was dedicated to the importance of original research in the study of the past. And he had studied for a year in Germany, at the University of Berlin. It was Greene who during the academic year 1902–3 first introduced a course on the Civil War into the history curriculum of the young University of Illinois.

Greene's new course, initially labeled American History, 1860–76, "with a concentration on the Civil War and Reconstruction," became in 1909 simply "The Civil War and Reconstruction." From that year, the centennial of Lincoln's birth, to the present, "The Civil War and Reconstuction" has remained one of the history department's mainstream offerings.

Lincoln became a subject for professional inquiry and research several years before, in 1900, when Daniel Kilham Dodge, a literary scholar in the English department, published the first scholarly monograph on Lincoln. Not only did Dodge's study of Lincoln's literary style reflect a new scholarly approach to the study of Lincoln, it also inaugurated a publication series based on original research that anticipated the later establishment of the University of Illinois Press in 1918.

In 1904, with the inauguration of Edmund J. James as its president, the university took a long step toward becoming the major research institution that it would later be. With a Ph.D. degree in economics from the University of Halle, where he had developed an admiration for German scholarship, James introduced a new era that emphasized extensive professional research in all fields, an expanded program of graduate teaching, and intellectual leadership in nation and state. He not only recruited a strong faculty, he sought also to create an atmosphere of creative scholarship on the campus, an environment that would support and encourage the research of the faculty. Crucial to achieving this end was his appointment of Phineas L.

Windsor, a "librarian of genius," whose mission was to build a first-class research library that would take its place among the great libraries of the world.

In January 1909, the Illinois state legislature appropriated $250,000 for the construction of a building that would house the university's humanities departments, including History and English. Greene, who at that time was dean of the College of Literature and Arts, proposed that the building be named for Lincoln, and that it be a memorial to the Great Emancipator in the centennial year of his birth. James agreed. "We have a special love for him here in this institution," for he was "of our very household." Moreover, "he is ours in a special sense for what he did for this and similar institutions . . . [as well as for] what he did for humanity." Construction began in 1910 and the first classes were held in the building in the fall of 1911. Lincoln Hall was dedicated on February 12, 1913.

Greene also suggested that "in some appropriate way the name of Lincoln and his writings be recognized in the main entrance." A bronze bust of Lincoln and a bronze plaque containing the Gettysburg Address, the latter commemorating the fiftieth anniversary of the battle and of Lincoln's address, were placed in the entrance hall. In addition, ten terra cotta panels, each depicting an episode in Lincoln's life between 1830 and 1865, and ten quotations from Lincoln's works, were added to the building's facade. Lincoln's memory "will abide with us," noted President James. "The beautiful structure across the way [Lincoln Hall] is named in his honor and ranks among the important monuments of this country to his memory."

This was the world that attracted James G. Randall, first in 1918 when he taught in the summer session at Illinois, and then, in 1920, when he confessed that a teaching position at Illinois appealed to him very much.

Born in 1881 in Indianapolis, Randall early in life chose a scholarly academic track. After graduating from Butler College in 1903, he selected the University of Chicago for his graduate work. In 1904, shortly after Randall completed the work for his master's degree, Professor Andrew C. McLaughlin came to Chicago, leaving his post at the University of Michigan. McLaughlin had won renown as a constitutional historian of the United States, for his book, *The Confederation and the Constitution, 1783–1789*, and succeeded J. Franklin Jameson as chairman of the history department at Chicago. Randall completed his doctoral work under McLaughlin's direction, and in 1911 was awarded his Ph.D.

Randall's doctoral dissertation, "The Confiscation of Property during the Civil War," was an exercise in the constitutional history of the Civil War. It has been described as a model monograph for its day. Two segments were published in the *American Historical Review*, "Some Legal Aspects of the Confiscation Acts of the Civil War" in October 1912 and "Captured and Abandoned Property During the Civil War" in October 1913.

In 1912, Randall secured an academic teaching position at Roanoke College, Virginia, where he remained until 1918. One high priority for Randall in these years was to complete his first book. McLaughlin advised Randall to direct his research toward a book-length expansion of his dissertation, to be called *The Constitutional Problems of the Civil War*. The work was aided in 1916 when Randall was awarded a year-long Harrison Research Fellowship for study at the University of Pennsylvania.

America's entry into World War I provided both insight and analogy to Randall's research on the wartime challenges of the Civil War, for example, his cogent analysis, "Democracy and War," in *The History Teacher's Magazine* in December 1917, and "The Newspaper Problem in its Bearing upon Military Secrecy during the Civil War" in *American Historical Review* in January 1918.

Impressed by the breadth of Randall's research, Evarts Greene recommended his appointment to the 1918 summer session staff at the University of Illinois. He taught the undergraduate survey in American history from 1783 to 1861 and a course in recent American history for both undergraduate and graduate students. In addition, Greene suggested he teach a graduate seminar based on his research. Randall supplied the details: "SEMINAR ON WAR PROBLEMS. War experience in the United States will be examined with special reference to the Civil War, and comparisons with present problems will be studied. Consideration will be given to such matters as the draft, punishment of treasonable activities, seizure of property, control of news, etc. Some attention will be given to economic and financial conditions."

This was the first time Randall taught a Civil War course at Illinois. Its description revealed strands of interpretation that would characterize his later work, for example, the centrality of the Civil War in American history and its influence on the American experience. His comparative approach pitted the wartime problems of the Civil War against the "present problems" of the United States in world conflict, and the impact of "economic and financial conditions" on political and governmental policy. Also of importance, if not mentioned explicitly, were the programs of the two presidents Randall most admired, Abraham Lincoln and Woodrow Wilson. His treatment of them in this course anticipated his later study in "Lincoln's Task and Wilson's" in *South Atlantic Quarterly* in October 1930 and "Lincoln's Peace and Wilson's" in *South Atlantic Quarterly* in July 1943.

Randall's teaching at Illinois during the summer of 1918 marked him, according to Greene, as "one of the most promising of our younger scholars." Still, a more permanent academic position at a large institution eluded him. He found a position in Wilson's wartime administration as a member of the U.S. Shipping Board. The post sharpened his perception of war's problems, as evidenced in "War Tasks and Accomplishments of the Shipping Board" in *The Historical Outlook* of June 1919. Following the end of the war, he was able to land a one-year appointment at Richmond College, but it was not renewed.

By early September 1920, the year that President James resigned his post, Randall was on the verge of accepting an offer to serve as historian of the Air Service in the War Department, when he learned of an opening at Illinois. Arthur C. Cole, who had taught the Civil War course for several years and whose highly acclaimed volume in the Illinois Centennial History Series, *The Era of the Civil War, 1848–1870*, had been published in 1919, was leaving for a position at Ohio State University. Randall expressed his interest in the position, and on September 14 the board of trustees of the university appointed him as an assistant professor of history.

Randall joined a thirteen-member department, small but outstanding in quality. Three (including Randall) were assistant professors. It was the beginning of a lifelong association. "At last," John David Smith has observed, "he had found a school with the library resources and academic environment necessary to support his research." Randall quickly earned national renown, as he rose through the academic ranks to full professor by 1930, and eventually served as president of three professional organizations, the Mississippi Valley Historical Association (1939), the Illinois State Historical Society (1945), and the American Historical Association (1952).

Randall's teaching program focused on his Civil War and Reconstruction course and his research seminar for graduate students. In both, Abraham Lincoln played a critical role against the backdrop of civil conflict. In addition, Randall offered the department's graduate course, "Historiography and Historical Method" (or what he called "the technic of historical investigation"), and, on a less regular basis, "The United States in the Great War," "The Constitutional History of the United States," and "The History of the South."

From the beginning, Randall developed a warm relationship with his students; he was sympathetic and supportive yet exacting, holding them to the same rigid standards of scholarship that he held for himself. He directed twenty-six Ph.D.s, many of whom became distinguished historians in their own right. His students passed on to their own students not only Randall's scholarly standards, but also his appreciation for Lincoln and the Civil War as serious subjects for scholarly inquiry.

Randall's first book, *Constitutional Problems Under Lincoln*, appeared in 1926. Reviewers were quick to recognize it as the first book to deal exclusively and comprehensively with the subject. Two points they noted were central to his treatment: the importance of the Civil War "as the first great test of a modern democracy" and the increasing importance and significance of Lincoln. Randall concluded that no president "carried the power of proclamation and executive order (independently of Congress) so far as did Lincoln." His unprecedented exercise of arbitrary power, however, was offset by his "humane sympathy, his humor, his lawyerlike caution, his common sense, his fairness toward opponents, [and] his willingness to take the people into his confidence."

Encouraged by the favorable reception of his book, Randall began work on an ambitious history of the United States, in which constitutional questions would be viewed in connection with "social factors." To clarify his interpretation, he presented a paper at the annual meeting of the American Historical Association in 1928 that was published in October 1929 as "The Interrelation of Social and Constitutional History" in *American Historical Review*.

Research on constitutional history, however, was set aside in 1929 when Allen Johnson, editor of the new *Dictionary of American Biography*, asked Randall to prepare the biography of Lincoln. An early biographer of Stephen A. Douglas, Johnson had been impressed by Randall's pioneering effort to view Lincoln objectively in the context of the Civil War in his *Constitutional Problems Under Lincoln*. Randall accepted the challenge. At 15,000 words it would be the longest article in the work. The result, after four years of painstaking research, revealed Lincoln as the complex figure that would characterize Randall's later work. Published in 1933, it has been termed one of the best introductions to Lincoln's life. For Randall's career, it was a significant turning point.

Randall became the first academically trained historian to apply the rigorous standards of historical scholarship to the study of Lincoln and the Civil War. As he surveyed the field of Lincoln studies, he found it severely wanting. Most of the writing about Lincoln, he wrote, "has been by authors who are not historians." No adequate life of Lincoln exists "which fully embodies the results of historical techniques and critical historical research." Randall set out to rescue the sixteenth president from "the blundering of amateurs."

In 1934, Randall established his agenda when he addressed a joint meeting of the American Historical Association and the Mississippi Valley Historical

Portrait of
James G. Randall,
ca. 1937.

Association. In an expanded presentation that attracted nationwide attention, he asked, "Has the Lincoln Theme Been Exhausted?" His answer was "No." Although Lincoln has been the "most overworked subject in American history," there were "valuable projects still to be undertaken." Lincoln, moreover, was "everybody's subject," and the "hand of the amateur has rested heavily upon Lincoln studies." The problem was that not enough "trained specialists," by which he meant academic historians committed to the highest standards of scholarship, were active in the Lincoln field. Reviewing some of the "unfinished tasks and current problems of Lincoln scholarship," he observed that "an adequate, full-length biography" is still in the future. Randall's address was published in the *American Historical Review* in January 1936, and some 1,100 reprints were circulated throughout the country. As it turned out, Randall himself answered his call.

Meanwhile, as Randall was establishing his credentials as a Lincoln scholar, he was also completing a comprehensive history of the Civil War, a textbook written in 1930 at the invitation of Allan Nevins, on behalf of D. C. Heath's New History Series. Seven years later, in 1937, Randall's 959-page *Civil War and Reconstruction* was published. The first scholarly history of the war, it would become the standard text for decades to come. "Up to recent times," Randall observed, "the bulk of writing in the field has been superficial, traditionally narrow, and partisan." His intention was to provide a volume that would bring the "whole period of conflict and readjustment into a scholarly synthesis [that] distilled the findings of historical scholarship for the general reader." The Civil War, he believed, was America's great tragedy. While he was unprepared to deny that the war could have been avoided, he strongly rejected the view that it was inevitable. The "cautious historian," he felt, would record the event "without committing himself to a particular formula of determinism, or, indeed, to any hypothesis."

Randall continued his exploration of the war's causation in the years following the book's publication. In his 1940 presidential address before the Mississippi Valley Historical Association he suggested that the Civil War in its reality was a "needless war," and he held Lincoln's generation to account as "A Blundering Generation"—Lincoln's generation, but not Lincoln. Moderate, temperate, and far-seeing, Lincoln, as Randall saw him, viewed "the war more clearly and faced it more squarely" than did his generation. Still unsure, however, Randall urged that "the whole subject of war 'causation'" be given "more searching inquiry." In the *Mississippi Valley Historical Review* in June 1940, Randall called upon the "inquisitive historians" to "reexamine the human beings of that war generation with less thought of the 'splendor of battle flags' and with more of the sophisticated and unsentimental searchlight of reality."

Randall continued to urge historians to replace the romantic elements of the war with the war's realities, even as he was bringing his biography of Lincoln to its conclusion. "The more the war is restudied," he wrote, the less it becomes "a matter of yellow sashes and tassels, of swords and roses" and the more it becomes "the ghastly scourge that it was." Historical scholarship, Randall declared in the *Journal of Southern History* in November 1940, "moves forward by way of new research, unflagging inquisitiveness, and revisionist studies"—a prescription he applied to his study of Abraham Lincoln.

The first two volumes of his Lincoln biography, *Lincoln the President: Springfield to Gettysburg* (New York: Dodd, Mead), appeared in 1945. A third volume, *Lincoln the President: Midstream* (New York: Dodd, Mead), was published in 1952. A fourth volume appeared in 1955 following Randall's death, completed by Richard N. Current from Randall's drafts and notes.

The publication of the biography brought Randall instant acclaim among reviewers and the general reading public, as well as the coveted Bancroft and Loubat Prizes. Not only was the biography the work of a "recognized Lincoln authority," it was the "first extensive treatment of Lincoln by a professional historian." "Almost every page," wrote one reviewer, "bears evidence of exhaustive research" and the "careful evaluation of material." Another found in the biography Randall's familiar characteristics as an historian that merits quotation in full: "massive research in the sources and thorough mastery of monographic writing, careful sifting and weighing of evidence before conclusions are arrived at, skillful marshaling of the opinions of secondary writers on disputed points, and the courage to adopt new viewpoints at variance with old myths."

The third volume, *Midstream*, carried Randall's search for the real Lincoln through the year 1863, ending with the battle of Chattanooga. "No account of Lincoln," wrote one reviewer, "is richer in evidence of the man's tremendous moral stature." Randall was praised for his "brilliant workmanship" and for producing a "model of historical research, method, interpretation, and expression."

Midstream was the first major work to make use of the Robert Todd Lincoln Collection of Lincoln Papers, opened for research by the Library of Congress in 1947 with a ceremony in which Randall took part. The event and the significance of the collection were aptly described in an appendix to the volume. The rich holdings on the Lincoln theme housed in the University of Illinois Library, Randall further acknowledged, had been greatly enhanced by the donation of one of the great private collections of Lincoln material, that of Harlan Hoyt Horner. Finally, Randall noted the opportunity to use the photostats of the forthcoming edition of *The Collected Works of Abraham Lincoln*, whose publication in 1953 was made possible by the Abraham Lincoln Association.

In 1947, as a supplement to the biographical volumes, Randall published *Lincoln the Liberal Statesman* making available eight of Randall's articles, all but two of them previously published elsewhere. Appearing for the first time was the article that gave the book its title, in which Randall declared that "the liberal credo was the key to Lincoln's views of man and the state," or put another way, that Lincoln "is to be understood in terms of courageous and undaunted liberalism."

Randall retired from teaching in 1949. Within a short time he was elected to the highest position available to an historian, the presidency of the American Historical Association. Alas, he had little time to savor his achievement. In the summer of 1952, he learned that he was suffering from leukemia. He "set his house in order," finished the third volume of his Lincoln biography, completed eight chapters of the fourth volume, and drafted his presidential address. His illness kept him from attending the annual dinner of the association on December 29, 1952, and his presidential address was read by a colleague. Two months later, on February 20, 1953, Randall died.

From left to right, James G. Randall, James Monaghan, Carl Sandburg, and L. A. Warren at the opening of the Lincoln Papers in the Library of Congress Document Room on July 26, 1947.

Randall's address, "Historianship," was a valedictory to his profession. Historical study is at its best, he declared, "when its effect appears not in any rigid pattern but in standards of scholarship." The standards of historical study—among them clarity, objectivity, tolerance, discrimination, a sense of proportion, insistence upon freedom of thought, [and] caution as to conclusions—are, in turn, "of value for the understanding of human affairs." "Society," he insisted, "has need of the historian." For ideally, the historian is not limited "to his own province or to a narrow present. He has reasonableness, loyalty, conviction, appreciation of human values. He has a training that sharpens his perceptions. From tested evidence he strives to recreate a past episode, [and] he recognizes the many-sidedness of historical interpretation."

Randall left behind a powerful legacy for the study of Abraham Lincoln and the Civil War that future generations of scholars have built upon and expanded. His work broke new ground and stimulated a new scholarly interest in Lincoln and the Civil War; his writings remained the standard works in the field for decades to come. By fresh inquiry, Randall hoped to come nearer to a past reality, a process that was dubbed "revision," although he preferred "historical restoration." Thanks in part to his scholarship, the library of the University of Illinois became a rich depository for Lincoln research, while in the Department of History a tradition was born.

SELECTED REFERENCES

James G. Randall Papers, University of Illinois archives.

University of Illinois, *Annual Register*, 1918–21.

University of Illinois, *Transactions of the Board of Trustees*, 1920–21.

Langdon, William Chauncy. *Abraham Lincoln Today: A War-Time Tribute*. Urbana: University of Illinois, 1918.

Department of History, 1894–1954: Opportunities for Research and Graduate Study. Urbana: University of Illinois, 1954.

Book reviews, *American Historical Review, Mississippi Valley Historical Review, Journal of Southern History*.

Peterson, Merrill D. *Lincoln in American Memory*. New York: Oxford University Press, 1994.

Smith, John David. "James G. Randall," in Clyde N. Wilson, ed., *Twentieth-Century American Historians*, vol. 17: *Dictionary of Literary Biography*. Detroit: Gale Research Company, 1983.

Donald, David Herbert. "James Garfield Randall," *Dictionary of American Biography, 5th Supplement, 1951–1955*. New York: Charles Schribner's Sons, 1977.

Pratt, Harry E. "James Garfield Randall, 1881–1953." *Journal of the Illinois State Historical Society* 46 (Summer 1953): 119–128, with a bibliography of Randall's writings by Wayne C. Temple, 128–131.

"Recent Deaths" (obituary), *American Historical Review* 58 (July 1953): 1054.

NATALIE ALPERT

(EDITED BY DIANNE HARRIS)

AND GARY KESLER

CHAPTER 8

Florence Bell Robinson and

Stanley Hart White: Creating a Pioneering

School of Landscape Architecture

In the early years of the twentieth century, new professional opportunities opened for women, responding to their wish to pursue their own lives and their realization that education might make that possible. Training was offered in diverse fields, including medicine, law, and landscape architecture. Of these, landscape architecture was perhaps the most socially approved career for women.[1]

The emergence of early "female schools" of landscape architecture, such as the Lowthorpe school, the Cambridge school, and others, addressed the frustrations of women who were unable to attend the Harvard Graduate School of Design, the male citadel of the profession. Women who did not, or could not, attend eastern schools often enrolled at coeducational land-grant schools that had fewer gender restrictions. Yet prior to the 1970s the University of Illinois may have been the only coeducational American university to employ women in tenure-track faculty positions in landscape architecture.

From 1912 to 1920, even before women's suffrage, women interested in landscape architecture had begun to invade the classrooms of the University of Illinois, taking surveying courses and learning the names and characteristics of plants. They then tried, usually unsuccessfully, to gain entry into male-dominated professional offices. Among the women whom the University of Illinois hired as faculty in the area that became landscape architecture were May Elizabeth McAdams and Florence Bell Robinson, two pioneering teachers from the Midwest. Of the two, Robinson, who joined the faculty in 1926, had the more notable career. Her emphasis on the interdependence of building and planting design influenced many students throughout their careers.

By this time, instruction in landscape architecture at the University of Illinois had begun to achieve stability. One important reason was the hiring in 1922 of Stanley Hart White, a graduate of Cornell and Harvard, and Karl Lohmann, a graduate of the University of Pennsylvania. White, who taught at the University of Illinois from 1922 to 1959, is considered one of the most influential educators in the history of landscape architecture. Florence Bell Robinson worked with White, through most of his time at Illinois, to shape the instructional program in landscape architecture. Mutual respect and admiration characterized their relationship.

Florence Bell Robinson was born in Lapeer, Michigan, on November 1, 1885, the only child of Dr. and Mrs. William Robinson.[2] She graduated from Kalamazoo College in 1908 with a Ph.B. (bachelor of philosophy), and obtained a second Ph.B. by taking correspondence courses from the University of Chicago that same summer. Her education at Kalamazoo College was primarily in the sciences, with additional emphasis on literary subjects. She was gifted in languages, particularly French and German.

From 1908 to about 1926, she taught in Detroit area high schools, covering such subjects as physics, chemistry, botany, biology, physiography, and drafting. During this period, she also spent two years, 1913–15, working for a degree in architecture at the University of Michigan, from which she received a bachelor's degree in architecture and an M.L.D. (master of landscape design) in 1924. From 1916 to 1926, she maintained a private landscape architectural practice while teaching in various high schools. She worked briefly as an architectural draftsman for J. W. Case in Detroit.

According to friends and students, Robinson possessed a bold personal resolve, hidden behind a facade of reserve and professional distance. These characteristics enabled her to travel, with a woman companion or by herself, to remote areas of the world, including China, Japan, and Guatemala, to take a tour of western parks, and probably to visit other destinations for which we have no documented records. Her familiarity with the plant material of the South, and photographs of plants of that region, indicate that she traveled there as well.

Robinson was forty-one in 1926 when she accepted an appointment at the University of Illinois as an associate in landscape design. She was expected to teach plant material and planting design; this was the typical slot reserved for women in most Departments of Landscape Architecture. Schools established for the benefit of women, such as the Smith College Graduate School of Architecture and Landscape Architecture and the Cambridge School of Domestic Architecture and Landscape Architecture, granted degrees in both "domestic architecture" and landscape design to prepare their students for country estate work. The University of Illinois was unique in that its undergraduate curriculum included a heavy dose of city planning, opening students' eyes to different scales and types of design.

Robinson's extensive travels in Europe during the summer of 1928 with her colleague Betty McAdams expanded her interests in landscape architecture. Her tour of China and Japan in 1929, led by Professor Philip H. Elwood Jr. of Iowa State College, developed her knowledge of Chinese garden design and eventually led to her translation of an article, "The Imperial Palaces of Peking," by Gisbert Combaz, a French author.[3] In 1931, she led her own tour through China and Japan; her legacy of that trip has been preserved in a collection of 800 hand-tinted glass lantern slides, which she abandoned when she left Illinois.[4] This record of sites, people, and activities in China, Korea, and Japan has been an invaluable historical resource, not only for their landscape interest but for researchers in fields as diverse as sociology, anthropology, industry, and history. An interesting feature of the collection is the number of slides devoted to the daily lives and traditional occupations of ordinary people, including women and schoolchildren. Many of the slides depict places that were subsequently destroyed by earthquakes and military action; photographs of these sites cannot be found in China, Korea, or Japan.

Competition in the workplace had begun early in the century for women in landscape architecture. Successful designers from the University of Illinois include Annette Hoyt Flanders (class of 1918) and Florence Yoch (class of 1915). Flanders began her career in the New York office of Vitale, Brinckerhoff and Geiffert; in 1922 she opened her own office there. Florence Yoch became one of the leading designers of Hollywood estate gardens and film sets until 1972. But to achieve full academic standing

Florence Bell Robinson,
November 1945.

including tenure at a major university was relatively rare for women until the 1970s. In a time when the norm was still to hire women for limited periods (for example, as adjunct or visiting professors), Florence Bell Robinson broke the tenure barrier in coeducational schools of landscape architecture. She was hired as an assistant professor in 1929 and she achieved the rank of associate professor in 1946, after seventeen years of teaching. She finally achieved the rank of full professor in 1951 two years before she retired.

As opportunities for significant private practice were not available in Champaign-Urbana, Robinson took advantage of her magisterial knowledge of plants to advance her academic standing. An understanding of art, architecture, science, and engineering and an encyclopedic knowledge of plant materials were the fundaments of Robinson's scholarship and her academic career. In the truest of academic traditions, she began to publish extensively from the moment she arrived on campus. In addition to her books, Robinson wrote numerous authoritative articles with lists of hybridized plants arranged in orderly schemes that spelled out height, flower color, and season of bloom.[5] These included articles in *Landscape Architecture Magazine, House and Garden, Country Life*, and others that would also appeal to the general public.

Building on her years of teaching plant materials and design were a series of books, pamphlets, and a card file system, which surfaced in several forms according to student needs. The card index system, developed by Robinson to record the materials viewed on the weekly plant walks in the plant identification course, was made commercially available by 1932 as *Deciduous Trees, Deciduous Shrubs and Conifers* and was reissued periodically by the Garrard Press until only recently. The card index system was a favorite of her students and was carried forward for use in their professional careers after graduation from Illinois. The contents were summarized in a book, *Tabular Keys for the Identification of the Woody Plants* (1941), used in several Midwest schools as a plant material source book.

Robinson's first major book, *Planting Design*, was published by McGraw-Hill in 1940, and was widely assigned in universities, because it was one of the few available books on the subject at the time. It became the standard text in plant material courses throughout the United States and at universities in Australia, the Philippines, Russia, and England. The illustrations in *Planting Design* used corrective planting design to hide the faults of bad architecture. The suggested solution was to arrange the plant material in the form of a scalene triangle to lengthen the lines of the house. Although the examples were misconstrued and the illustrations date the book, they are useful as a record of housing types found throughout the Midwest. Robinson's report, "Landscape Planting for Airports," written for the University of Illinois Institute of Aviation as *Aeronautics Bulletin #2* (1948), provides an interesting example of the range of her scholarship. Robinson's final major publication was *Palette of Plants* (1950), a romantic and poetic list of plant "personalities." The book includes a discussion on cemetery design that made Robinson something of an expert on the topic. She was frequently invited to give talks to meetings of cemetery associations.

Robinson considered her books and articles her major professional contributions. In 1950, in response to an inquiry from the alumni secretary of Kalamazoo, she wrote: "As for my achievements, they are limited to my profession of Landscape Architecture. I have been too busy making good in my job here at the University of Illinois to give attention to outside affairs. Here I have reached the top rank 'full Professor' of which I am rightfully proud. And I can say without boasting that I have some worldwide fame, slight though it may be. I have written five textbooks in my subjects, all of which are being used in a number of schools having landscape courses, and two of which have gained considerable distributions outside school circles."[6]

As a teacher, Robinson developed rigorous courses in plant identification and planting design, which reflected her background in architecture and science. Her approach to design was based on the application of principles of composition derived from works of art, particularly paintings. A creative work, she maintained, must reflect unity and harmony and incorporate ideas of simplicity, balance, scale, sequence, and focalization while considering mass, texture, and color. Student reaction to her courses ranged from dread to appreciation for the concrete content and relationship to the world of student experience.

Outside the university, Robinson shared her encyclopedic knowledge with more than fifty-eight talks to garden clubs, men's clubs, and church groups. From 1940 to 1952, she designed approximately thirty small gardens. She also developed an interest in the design of large parks and school grounds, and especially, conservation, which continued as a major interest following her retirement. Her character was summarized by Hideo Sasaki, one of her students, and also one of the most distinguished landscape architects of the twentieth century: "Miss Robinson is one of those unappreciated teachers who have had a greater influence than acknowledged. She loved her work, and when a student expressed interest in plants, he could be showered with her generosity . . . Her book *Planting Design* is a classic . . . She was a pro through and through, and I admired her for it."[7]

Stanley Hart White was born on February 15, 1891, in Brooklyn, New York, the fourth of six children of Samuel T. and Jessie White. Later that year the family moved to Mt. Vernon, New York. Samuel White had risen from a "bundle boy" to president of the Horace Waters and Company piano manufacturing firm. Consequently, White grew up in a home well supplied with musical instruments and early in life developed a love for music.[8] White's mother was the daughter of William Hart, a prominent painter of the Hudson River school. The well-known writer E. B. White, Stanley's younger brother, later wrote that Stanley resembled Grandfather Hart, and "like his grandfather, he liked to draw and paint."

In 1912, White graduated from Cornell University with a B.S. in agriculture. He worked for Hydes Nursery on Long Island in the summer of 1912. That fall he entered Harvard and graduated with the master of landscape architecture degree in 1915. For several months, White worked for Fletcher Steele, John Nolan and Harris Reynolds. Early in 1916 he became the landscape architect for the Lake Placid Club. But his stay at Lake Placid was short, for later in 1916 he went to work for the Olmsted office in Brookline, Massachusetts, where he remained until 1920. An attempt at his own practice from 1920 to 1922 was, in his words, a "fizzle." His second-place submission in 1922 for the Rome Prize, he concluded, was his most cherished "fizzle."

That year he decided to make a career of teaching landscape architecture. During his tenure with the Olmsteds, and continuing for two more years, he had been "exposed to the teaching fever" at the Lowthorpe school. Thus when offered a teaching position at the University of Illinois in 1922, he accepted. He left Boston and began his career at Illinois as an assistant professor of landscape architecture.[9]

White was an inspiration to a generation of students. Using his knowledge of music, art, and philosophy, his methods were often viewed as unconventional and frequently humorous—intended to encourage students to think in fresh and creative ways. The emphasis was always on the idea, which he described as "something between magic and philosophy." Students were encouraged to take chances and trust their intuition. In his *Primer of Landscape Architecture*, White defines landscape architecture as "the superb handling of the land by the creative artist who engraves upon the face of nature those expressions of the culture we need to set the stage of our ordinary lives."

Perhaps the most significant record of his approach to the art and theory of landscape architecture are White's renowned "Ten Slides on the Teaching of Landscape Architecture." These images, beautifully illustrated in the mid-1950s using colored chalk and a blackboard in the basement of his house, present a resume of White's approach to teaching landscape design. The content of the slides illuminates White's fascination with design process. The "right" solution was one that enhanced the character of the site and form that fit the land. He demonstrated this relationship by making a fist to represent the site, and then embracing the fist with the palm of his other hand. The slides guide the reader sequentially through this process, and conclude with commentary on qualities of light, form, and materials. Each image is striking in composition, and as a set, they comprise a rich and provocative statement about the complexity of landscape and the art of landscape architecture.

White retired from full-time teaching in 1959, but he continued to be active as an observer, writer, and guest instructor for many years after. In 1972 at the annual meeting of the American Society of Landscape Architects (ASLA) in Philadelphia, the Council of Education presented White with its first commendation, citing his "long years of service, for his sensitivity and ability in producing graduates who have changed, moved, and expanded the profession of landscape architecture."[10]

Throughout his career, White worked to improve the quality of landscape architectural education across the nation. He was very active in the National Conference on Instruction in Landscape Architecture, NCILA

Stanley White,
ca. 1950s.

(now CELA, the Council of Educators in Landscape Architecture), from his early years to his retirement in 1959. White's most noteworthy contribution to improving instruction was perhaps the development and administration of the Landscape Exchange Problems. The Landscape Exchange, a series of nationwide design competitions offered to intermediate and advanced students in landscape architecture, began in 1924 as a result of recommendations of the NCILA meeting at the University of Michigan that year. The initial organizers were White and Professor W. R. Sears of Ohio State. The large number of participants indicates that it was an immensely popular program that played an important role in the development of a standardized educational system for landscape architects. White continued as secretary and director of the program from 1924 until 1953.

White's organizational efforts in the creation and operation of the Landscape Exchange led to other associations as well. In the summer of 1925, Ferrucio Vitale, then chair of the ASLA Committee on Education, asked White to become involved in the Lake Forest Graduate Institute of Architecture and Landscape Architecture. Supported by the ASLA and funded by the Foundation for Architecture and Landscape Architecture and the Garden Club of Lake Forest, the institute offered summer courses in postgraduate design study from 1926 to 1931. White served as director of the institute for those years. The institute closed in 1931, but the foundation continued to support graduate study through scholarships for travel. In 1950, the foundation transferred its assets to the University of Illinois, which still maintains the annual awarding of the Edward L. Ryerson Traveling Fellowship.

White was a prolific writer and commentator but few of his words were ever formally published. Included among his unpublished manuscripts are the *Primer of Landscape Architecture, Teaching of Landscape Architecture,* and his fifty-two-year collection of professional diaries—referred to by White as the "Commonplace Books"—which comprise an insightful collection of sketches, notes, and comments on the practice and teaching of landscape architecture.

To many, White was the ideal foil to Robinson's more traditional instructional style. Former students have described White as "zany" and a "bit of a clown." Hideo Sasaki described White as a "great designer and spellbinder" who had "much of an actor's personality . . . He not only understood literature, music, art—he could do all these things." Chuck Harris, a student of White's who went on to chair the landscape architecture program at Harvard, concluded, "It didn't matter what subject Stan was teaching, he was trying to affect students' lives. He was getting to you in a very personal way."[11] White's younger brother Elwyn, the well-known author E. B. White, commented on Stan's penchant for teaching: "Although eight years older than me, Stan latched onto me because he liked to have someone to instruct. He was a born teacher . . . Stan taught me to read when I was in kindergarten and I could read fairly fluently when I entered the first grade—an accomplishment my classmates found annoying . . . Hardly a day passes in my life without my performing some act that reminds me of something I learned from Stan . . . He imparted information as casually as a tree drops its leaves in the fall."[12] By his own admission, the art of teaching consumed Stanley White. To attendees at the National Conference of Instruction in Landscape Architecture in 1957, White commented on his career: "Everything I had done was, as far as the University's pay to me was concerned, simply a by-product of my fooling around with this amazing problem, the fascinating problem of how to teach."[13]

Robinson's style offered an important contrast to that of White, whose imaginative approach to design was difficult to communicate to some students. One of Robinson's former students, Dale Scherer, highlighted the contrast and complementarity of Robinson's teaching style with that of White:

> Of course, one can hardly talk of Florence Bell Robinson without bringing into the discussion Stanley White: between the two of them, I hardly know

Faculty in the Department of City Planning and Landscape Architecture, ca. early 1950s, *from left to right:* Irving L. Peterson, Florence Bell Robinson, Walter M. Keith, Otto G. Schaffer (chair), Stanley Hart White, and Karl B. Lohmann.

where to draw the line. They both complemented each other so completely that if you took away one, you would also lose the other. The two most gentle-ish souls in the world . . . I don't ever recall either of them raising their voices, but you knew when you displeased them . . . Florence Bell instilled such a love of plant material and that love was translated into design by Stan White. I suspect that there was never a design that I prepared that didn't during some phase of its development reflect the teachings of these dear people. She was demanding while Stan was suggestive and pleading. She accepted only excellence and would not tolerate mediocrity. Stan on the other hand, accepted what's the best you could do, and then show you how it could be improved if you really put your mind to it. He made you expand your abilities, while Florence Bell Robinson would only accept perfection. She developed the principles and rules, which, if followed, would guarantee that only a perfect design would be the result.[14]

White clearly influenced Robinson's scholarship. The strong emphasis on ecological factors in Robinson's *Planting Design* was ahead of its time and is probably a reflection of the views of her close colleague, Stanley White. Robinson and White were just two of the prominent names to emerge from the Department of Landscape Architecture at the University of Illinois, which will mark its centennial year in 2007, continuing its tradition as one of the top five landscape architecture programs in the nation.

ACKNOWLEDGMENTS

Note: The section of this chapter on Florence Bell Robinson is based on an essay written by Natalie Alpert in the decade before her death in 1997. Professor Alpert served on the faculty of the Department of Landscape Architecture from 1970 to 1991, where she taught courses in planting design and landscape history. She had an enduring interest in promoting the role of women in the profession of landscape architecture. I have remained true to the content of Alpert's essay, editing it to fit this volume's format. Dianne Harris, Associate Professor of Landscape Architecture.

NOTES

1. For more on the history of women and landscape architecture or gardening, see Dianne Harris, "Cultivating Power: The Language of Feminism in Women's Garden Literature, 1870–1920," *Landscape Journal* 13, no. 2 (Fall 1994): 113–23; and "Women as Gardeners," *Encyclopedia of Landscape and Garden History* (Chicago: Fitzroy Dearborn Publishers, 2001), 3:1447–50.
2. The information on Robinson's education, degrees, activities, and publications was obtained from the Alumni Association of Kalamazoo College, the Alumni Association of the University of Michigan, and the University of Illinois archives (records of the College of Fine and Applied Arts, especially the yearly "Record of Activities"). Robinson died August 13, 1973, in Hendersville, North Carolina.
3. University of Illinois archives, Florence Bell Robinson Papers.
4. "A Traveling Seminar in the Orient, 1931," from the Loeb Library of the Harvard Graduate School of Design: VF NAB 947. The lantern slides are being digitized for storage on compact disks.
5. See, for example, Florence Bell Robinson, "Good Herbaceous Peonies," *Landscape Architecture Magazine* (July 1927): 287–94; and "The Lilies of the Field," *House and Garden* (October 1928): 114–15.
6.. See Kalamazoo College Alumni Association records and correspondence for the "citation" from the Alumni Association awarded to Robinson in 1951.
7. Correspondence with Hideo Sasaki. Sasaki, who died in 1999, became the founding principal in his multinational corporate design firm of Sasaki Associates, who designed the master plan for the University of Illinois campus in Urbana-Champaign.
8. Peter Walker and M. Simo, *Invisible Gardens: The Search for Modernism in the American Landscape* (Cambridge, Mass.: MIT Press, 1994), chapter 7, "The Modernization of the Schools."
9. The "Commonplace Books," White's personal diaries in the University of Illinois archives.
10. ASLA citation presented by the Council on Education, June 28, 1972.
11. Interviews with former students and colleagues of White, 1983–85, including Hideo Sasaki, Charles Harris, Larry Walquist, Larry Zeulke, Walter Keith, Terry Harkness, and Stuart Dawson.
12. Dorothy Lorano Guth, ed., *Letters of E. B. White* (New York: Harper & Row, 1976), 6.
13. University of Illinois archives, Stanley White Papers
14. Correspondence with Lynn Harriss, Jack Swing, Eldridge Lovelace, Sarah Pattee, Roberta Wightman, Bob Scherer, Edith Antognoli, Robert O'Donnell, Hideo Sasaki, Ralph Ellifrit, Dona Caldwell, Theodore D. Walker.

RONALD E. DOEL

CHAPTER 9

Roger Adams:

Linking University Science with Policy

on the World Stage

For nearly thirty years, Roger Adams served as head of the Department of Chemistry at the University of Illinois, assuming that post in 1926. By the eve of World War II, his department was among the top in organic chemistry in America. Adams himself had made significant contributions to organic chemistry, the elucidation of chemical structures, and the synthesis of local anesthetics. He was widely regarded as one of America's most influential chemists. "The Chief," as Adams was known to his graduate students and colleagues, was forceful, enthusiastic, confident, and disciplined. Dominating the chemistry laboratories, he walked the corridors before midnight and on holidays.

Over the course of his career, Adams trained over 200 Ph.D. students and postdoctoral fellows. Their combined influence on the American chemical industry was substantial. Several of his students became prominent researchers in their own right, among them, Ernest H. Volwiler, president of the pharmaceutical giant Abbott Laboratories, and Wallace H. Carothers, the inventor of nylon. Adams successfully transformed his department from one focused on undergraduate teaching to one emphasizing research and graduate education, following the pattern of many elite public and private universities in early twentieth-century America. This was a key transition in the history of modern American science, one in which Adams was a notable sparkplug.

Adams was also influential in the world of industry. As a consultant to major chemical firms, including Du Pont, he forged strong links between the university and chemical industries that became exemplars of the relationship between academic scientists and industry in twentieth-century America. The relationship helped support the modern technological state. He used his understanding of the chemical and pharmaceutical markets to become a successful investor. As a chemist, scientist, and administrator, his reputation was national and he received numerous prestigious offers. He was asked to become the first director of the National Science Foundation (NSF) and was called both to the Massachusetts Institute of Technology (MIT) and to Harvard—posts he turned down in favor of remaining in firm command at Illinois.[1]

Adams made yet another critical contribution to twentieth-century science, one that few other scientists at the University of Illinois attempted as early and as forcefully. In a period when American science was coming into prominence in the international arena, Adams helped join science at the University of Illinois with policy on the state and world levels. American science had undergone a profound transformation during World War II, one in which relations between scientists and the state expanded dramatically. Scientists became key players in national defense efforts ranging from the large-scale production of penicillin to radar and the atomic bomb. As the United States emerged from World War II as the world's leading economic and military power, scientists took on unfamiliar new roles as advisors on foreign policy and as leaders of scientific intelligence-gathering. They were called on to develop science policies for the defeated Axis nations. Adams became an early leader in these efforts; his graduate student Wallace R. Brode later extended them to the newly formed Central Intelligence Agency (CIA) and to the Department of State.

Adams's story therefore illuminates some of the challenges that university scientists faced in maintaining their voice in public policy matters. The policies and plans that he helped put in place were honed from his long experience at Illinois. They reflected his views about the optimum ways to cultivate academic and industrial research. Among the other chemists who in this era also shaped the integration of science and foreign policy were Adams's friend James B. Conant, the chemist-turned-Harvard president who helped develop the atomic bomb and policies regarding its use, and William ("Bill") O. Baker, the president of Bell Labs who became a close advisor to U.S. presidents from Dwight Eisenhower to Ronald Reagan.[2]

THE EDUCATION OF ROGER ADAMS

Roger Adams was born in Boston on January 2, 1889. Grover Cleveland was ending his term as president and the U.S. population was just sixty-two million, much of it still east of the Mississippi River. A direct descendent of the uncle of President John Adams, Adams was raised in a south Boston family that remained comfortably middle-class. While there was no particular pressure or expectation for Adams to take up a career in science, he was among the statistically most likely to do so in early twentieth-century America: he was Protestant, born on the East Coast in a major urban area, and directly exposed to the traditions of higher education from an early age. He entered Harvard University in 1905, at age sixteen. Three years later he graduated and directly entered graduate school, where he studied chemistry under Theodore William Richards, whose accurate determination of atomic weights would gain him the Nobel Prize for Chemistry in 1914. In 1912, Adams submitted his Ph.D. dissertation, on experimental organic chemistry, to Harvard.

Adams's early career resembled that of other eminent American chemists of his generation. In 1913, he traveled to Germany, which was then the world leader in chemistry. There, on a year-long postdoctoral fellowship, he rubbed shoulders with leading organic chemists, studying with the eminent Otto Diels and then at the new Kaiser Wilhelm Institute in Dahlem with Richard M. Willstätter, who won a Nobel Prize in 1915. Called back by Harvard the next year to fill a pending vacancy, Adams became a research assistant, excelling at teaching and research. When called in 1916 by William A. Noyes to an assistant professorship in chemistry at Illinois, Adams sensed better opportunities there than waiting for a permanent opening at Harvard.

No sooner was Adams comfortably settled in Urbana, when World War I disrupted his career and set him on the path of science politics. In 1917 he left for Washington, D.C., with assignments at the National Research Council and the Chemical Warfare Service. Like other chemists drawn to national defense problems, Adams worked on war gases and the challenge of maintaining adequate supplies of key chemicals and anesthetics. Before he departed for Washington, he began dating Lucile Wheeler, a fellow New Englander who was teaching home economics at Illinois. Their marriage, which began in 1918, was a close one that produced one daughter.[3]

Adams's rise at Illinois mirrored the rapid growth of American chemistry into world prominence. When the onset of World War I cut American access to dyes, photographic chemicals, medicinals, and other critical chemicals produced in Germany, U.S. chemical industries began a dramatic expansion to satisfy domestic needs (a transition aided after 1919, when the U.S. government seized German chemical patents as war reparations). Chemical research and development was one of several engines that drove the growth of industrial research laboratories and their parent corporations, including General Electric, American Telephone & Telegraph, Kodak, and Du Pont, and stimulated America's rapid industrialization early in the twentieth century. At the same time, U.S. universities were amid a wide-ranging transition from centers of instruction to research institutions whose contributions to new knowledge would be valued as much (and indeed more) than undergraduate pedagogy. Adams sought to strengthen both trends.

As Adams rose through the ranks at Illinois, becoming the department's head in 1926, he worked to apply chemical research by its faculty to chemical industries. Adams also fought to bring the research ethic he absorbed at Harvard to fruition at Illinois. He successfully challenged a senior dean who told him that he and fellow faculty ought not attend a meeting of the American Chemical Society (ACS) and should instead meet their classes. He also secured ample research funds, which he used to buy new equipment to outfit laboratories and to hire graduate research assistants. Loathing the German institute model he had experienced at Dahlem (where research programs reflected the often authoritarian visions of eminent individual directors like Willstätter), Adams joined leading American educators in reinforcing the existing democratic departmental structure at Illinois. He believed that advances would best come from hiring young faculty who showed promise in a wide range of chemical specialties and approaches. By 1925 Adams wrote confidently to the editor of the *Harvard Alumni Bulletin* that chemical research facilities at Illinois equaled those at Harvard. Adams's department soon gained recognition as one of the discipline's strongest homes, and rose to become the strongest science department at Illinois. Indeed, his efforts helped place Illinois among the top five public research universities in the United States. His beliefs about the proper environments for scientific research also served as core principles when he was called on to help rebuild shattered German and Japanese scientific institutions at the end of World War II.[4]

The peak of Adams's career came in the 1930s. By 1929, at age forty, Adams had already been elected to the National Academy of Sciences

Roger Adams and Dean R. D. Carmichael with the electron supermicroscope, June 1941.

(NAS). In 1935 he served as president of the ACS, and helped to secure its finances, despite the deep setbacks of the Great Depression. By then he had trained nearly a hundred Ph.D. students, including Ernest H. Volwiler, Wallace H. Carothers, and Wendell M. Stanley, who later received the Nobel Prize for chemical research on viruses. His core research program, on reaction mechanisms, was at the cutting edge of organic chemistry. While the Great Depression hindered research (at Illinois as throughout the nation), chemical consulting opportunities remained and Adams secured funds for an extensive tour in 1936 of chemistry research programs in Switzerland and other European nations while a U.S. delegate to the Twelfth International Conference on Chemistry. Adams's abilities as an administrator and research leader were also becoming evident. More than 700 faculty members later selected him by ballot to become the new president of the University of Illinois. He received more votes than any other proposed candidate, but Adams wanted to stay in research and turned this offer down. Nonetheless he remained committed to government service, especially as growing European tensions in the late 1930s made U.S. involvement in World War II increasingly likely.[5]

Churning national politics almost derailed Adams's potential contributions to federal science policy. In mid-July 1940 Vannevar Bush, the MIT engineer who became the chief architect of the mobilization of U.S. science during World War II, sought to bring Adams to Washington to help lead the National Defense Research Committee (NDRC), the predecessor agency to the better-known wartime Office of Scientific Research and Development (OSRD). Aware that many regarded Adams as the leading organic chemist in America and that Conant, Adams's close friend and former Harvard colleague, strongly wanted him to lead U.S. efforts to develop new explosives and to create needed synthetic chemicals, Bush used authority granted to him by President Franklin D. Roosevelt to request security clearances for Adams and other proposed NDRC members. Army authorities gave approval for Adams, but Navy security officials announced that they would "never approve such an appointment," citing derogatory information gained from the FBI. Perplexed and annoyed, and determined to appoint Adams without delay, Bush pressed FBI director J. Edgar Hoover for an explanation.[6]

Hoover kept an impatient Bush cooling his heels while his agents reviewed their files on suspect American citizens. Bureau information on "Roger Adams" told a story based on partially digested information, shoddy cross-referencing, and ideological convictions about the correctness of various sides in armed conflicts then splintering Western Europe in the late 1930s. FBI field agents informed Hoover that Adams was a leading member of what it termed "Lincoln's Birthday Committee for the Advancement of Science," which an FBI informant considered "an apparent Communist-front organization." Bureau files also indicated that a "Professor Adams" had been arrested in radical raids during World War I. "Professor Adams" had also turned up as a contributing member of a suspect Japanese propaganda magazine from the 1920s.

What also caught the attention of Hoover's agents was new research that Adams had taken on in late 1938 concerning marijuana. Adams was extending his long-running pharmaceutical studies by seeking to identify the active pharmacological agent in this plant, a contribution to what was then a major chemical and medical challenge: to explain how marijuana actually affects the brain. Sensing an opportunity to secure results before competing laboratories in the United States and Britain could do so, Adams had obtained samples of the red oil extract of *Cannabis sativa* from the Treasury Department and sought to identify the structure of its compounds and the source of its biological activity. In 1939 this problem of marijuana became the central focus of Adams's research.

Marijuana use in the United States had been sharply restricted by the Marihuana Tax Act of 1937, the first federal effort to restrict sales of this narcotic. FBI agents ominously reported that Illinois's most prominent chemist had read a paper on "The Chemistry of Marihuana" to the NAS. This was not the only time that Adams's work with marijuana would gain public attention. In 1940 H. J. Anslinger, the U.S. commissioner of narcotics who backed Adams's research (and strongly supported the criminalization of marijuana), rebuked Adams for publicly referring to "the pleasant effects of the use of this drug." Too many young people were willing to "experience the effects," Anslinger wrote, adding, "In my opinion, this drug is bad for human consumption and should be painted so." Adams apologized and quickly revised an in-press draft, yet his interest in marijuana was troubling to FBI officials.[7]

Convinced that Adams was a security risk, Office of Naval Intelligence officials continued to rebuff Bush. But by early August, as more accurate information about Adams emerged, J. Edgar Hoover sensed that political pressure over pursuing the case might damage the bureau's reputation. While increasingly suspicious of the political loyalties and the internationalist worldview of scientists, which he found subversive, Hoover tersely advised War Department officials that there was "no indication" that "'Professor Adams' is identical with Professor Roger Adams, except with regard to the similarity in name." Not until the end of August 1940 was the matter cleared up, allowing Adams to join the NDRC formally.[8] With this clearance Adams could take charge of wartime U.S. chemistry programs, including a successful effort to develop synthetic rubber sources to replace natural supplies no longer available from the Far East.

As it turned out, the Adams case revealed a great deal about the dynamically changing political environment for American scientists on the eve of World War II. Adams was indeed involved in politics, though neither as a leftist nor as a communist sympathizer. Conservative in outlook and a passionate advocate of freedom of speech, Adams found himself sympathetic with a highly publicized national movement of scientists to decry the often sloppy use of "race" in American textbooks and the misappropriation of race biology in Nazi Germany. Organized by Franz Boas, the internationally prominent anthropologist, the Lincoln's Birthday Committee for Democracy and Intellectual Freedom (LBCDIF) of 1939 had garnered the support of thousands of academics, ranging from the conservative Robert A. Millikan of the California Institute of Technology to the outspokenly liberal Harlow Shapley of Harvard. At the University of Illinois, Adams was one of seven members of the NAS who took part in that day's nationally coordinated events. Though the LBCDIF was moderate in tone, its chief figures were left-of-center, and in the increasingly heated political atmosphere of late 1930s America conservative academics soon tarred the group with red-baiting labels. The charge that Adams was a member of a communist-front organization was hardly credible, but Hoover's FBI looked with hostility on groups that promoted racial integration and supported Franco's opponents in Spain. As the FBI's review handling of Adams's security clearance shows, government efforts to impose political loyalty in science did not begin in the Cold War, but even before the Japanese attacked Pearl Harbor in December 1941. Tensions between scientists and the state would shape the involvement of Adams and his colleagues in foreign policy issues throughout the Cold War.[9]

FOREIGN SCIENCE POLICY IN
THE POST-WORLD WAR II WORLD

As World War II ended, Adams was thinking a great deal about rebuilding the structure of international science. In May 1945, just after the Allied defeat of Nazi Germany, Adams wrote to Frank Jewett, the engineer-turned-president of Bell Telephone Laboratories, then serving as president of the NAS. He expressed concern that the Hearst newspapers were causing Americans to fear the Russians. He found that unfortunate. For years, Adams wrote, he had thought highly of Russian scientists and believed "the future of the world in general will depend to a very large extent on a mutual understanding between the Russians and ourselves." He proposed a plan to bring select Soviet scientists to the United States to meet their scientific colleagues as a way of rekindling scientific internationalism.

It was not the first time that Adams had sought to aid Russian scientists. In 1942, Adams became the local sponsor of the Champaign-Urbana chapter of Russian War Relief, Inc., an effort to support America's wartime ally. In the brief window of warm postwar relations with this fourth member of the Allied forces, a small number of Soviet scientists did indeed tour the United States, a plan solidly supported by many U.S. scientists. While this window swiftly closed with the start of Cold War in 1947, it illuminated a commitment to foreign exchange central to Adams's world outlook. It was one he had apparently nurtured since his postdoctoral year in Germany in 1913, when he had traveled on from Berlin to Sweden, Finland, and Russia.[10]

Before he could return to Illinois from his wartime responsibilities in Washington, Adams was given a new assignment: to lead a mission to advise the U.S. armed forces about the reconstitution of science in occupied

Germany. The need for such a mission, which had not been felt after World War I, reflected the importance accorded by 1945 to science and technology, now seen as a component of national security as well as a force for economic and industrial advance. Scientists and governmental leaders both recognized that the development of jet engines, guided missiles, penicillin, and radar, in addition to the singular impact of the atomic bomb, had made science an element in foreign policy as never before. In November 1945, when Adams reached Berlin, thirty-two years had passed since he had served as a postdoc under Diels and Willstätter and nearly a decade after his crisscrossing of Nazi Germany following the Twelfth International Chemistry Conference. His task was to advise U.S. General Lucius Clay, then U.S. military governor of Germany and later famous for directing the Berlin airlift of 1948–49, on appropriate policies for science and scientists in the American sector of Germany.

In the cold early winter of 1945–46, Adams attempted to work out his views on German science policy in the still-evolving postwar world. He was well aware that the classical formulation of science as a transnational "Republic of Letters" was over. But what would replace it? The U.S. Department of State's 1937 view that international science contributed to the "advancement and dissemination of knowledge and improved methods which carry the march of civilization forward" had been dealt a crippling blow in World War II as science became more intimately tied to national defense. Adams's immediate tasks included assessing the state of critical German scientific publications, universities, research institutes, and teaching programs. He also needed to assess, as did counterpart advisors in the French, British, and Soviet zones of Germany, who among German scientists, engineers, and technicians were Nazis and what denazification programs were effective and appropriate.

Adams soon became concerned that American denazification procedures were puritanical and ineffective. They were halting the resumption of teaching and research, antagonizing individuals likely to encourage democratization, and inspiring German scientists eager to be in the American sector to have second thoughts. All directors of the Kaiser Wilhelm Institutes and all top civil service appointees, Adams pointed out, were in the U.S. immediate arrest categories. Adams also led efforts to undermine support for the Morgenthau Plan, which called for the industrial disarmament and "pastoralization" of Germany and hence dissolution of its research and technological capacity. While recommending that all German military research be halted, Adams continued to argue that university and industrial research and teaching programs be resumed. How much Adams understood or appreciated the wartime atrocities committed by German biologists and medical researchers remains uncertain. He did not mention these issues in his homebound letters, which concentrated primarily on chemical concerns and family issues. But Adams was clearly convinced that science required special treatment in international relations and, like many American scientists, strongly opposed those who believed that international science, as part of culture, needed to be subsumed under U.S. foreign policy.[11]

Adams returned to Illinois in early 1946, again taking over the reins of the chemistry department. He did not remain there long before being called to head another foreign science mission. In the autumn of 1945, Karl T. Compton, the president of MIT and a leading wartime science administrator, led an intelligence-gathering mission to Japan at the request of General Douglas MacArthur. This mission, similar to the famous expedition to Germany, code-named ALSOS (whose member-scientists directly followed advancing Allied lines in an effort to discover German advances in atomic weapons and in other scientific fields) was intended to document Japanese progress in science and technology during the wartime years. Compton's mission failed to do all it had first intended, including a careful survey of science and technology accomplished in occupied regions of Asia, including Korea. But it did report at length on scientific progress in this powerful Axis nation, including the bacteriological warfare program led by Japanese Lieutenant General Shiro Ishii. Compton's mission also made clear that, no less than for Germany, science policy goals needed to be created for Japan's disrupted scientific institutions and universities. In June 1947, MacArthur, who as supreme commander for the Allied powers in Japan remained head of its provisional postwar government, requested a new mission to work out the place for Japanese science in that country's reconstruction. There was now "urgent need" for American scientists to evaluate plans "submitted by the Japanese scientific groups for the democratization of scientific research in Japan." Adams accepted an invitation from Jewett on behalf of the academy to devote the summer of 1947 to presiding over this mission.

In setting up the Japanese mission, Adams drew on political and military savvy gained from his months in Germany. Assembling a team of six scientists from diverse fields, including the plant physiologist William J. Robbins and the physicist and university president William V. Houston of Rice, Adams and his colleagues toured scientific facilities and research institutes across the Japanese isles. Likely the most memorable visit for him—it was the only one he mentioned by name in a draft report he

Roger Adams and M. K. Dennett in Japan, summer 1947. Adams led a scientific mission to Japan at the request of General Douglas MacArthur, supreme commander for the Allied Powers, to help determine the postwar structure of science on this island nation. The approach Adams recommended for Japanese scientists—disparaging the German institute model in favor of more democratized, egalitarian relationships among faculty—was one he had supported at Illinois.

prepared—was to the Ise-Shima region, where he toured the laboratory and lagoons of Kokichi Mikimoto (1858–1954), the first person to create cultured pearls. This accomplishment, Adams wrote, "stirs the envy of any progressive nation." But Adams seemed most moved by his perception that Japanese science had not evolved as far or as fast as the United States had, although similar progress seemed possible. Regarding Japanese science as a comparatively recent import from the West with little indigenous tradition, he argued that its heavy reliance on the autocratic German institute model was an impediment to democratization. Adams and his colleagues urged Japanese scientists to better integrate their research and teaching; he also specifically encouraged them to attend scientific conferences and to take on work in private industrial laboratories. "Apparently for reasons of prestige and freedom in the technical conduct of their work they prefer government or university positions," he observed, "just as the United States scientists did early in the history of organized industrial research in that country." For Adams, the model that would best decentralize Japanese science and aid its development along democratic lines was the one he had nurtured in Illinois. He returned for a second visit to Japan in 1948 as a member of a follow-up mission, gratified to discover that some of the programs he had recommended were coming to fruition.[12]

Adams's planned return to Japan in 1948 and the initiation of the federal loyalty program by President Harry S. Truman occasioned another security clearance review by the FBI. This time Springfield, Illinois FBI agents had more accurate intelligence on Adams: the bureau's November 1947 investigation now found him a "sound, able businessman" not known to associate with campus radicals and, like his wife, of the "highest calibre." Agents also reported that his daughter was "always a well-mannered girl" and that Adams was a "firm believer in the constitutional right of free speech." They also favorably reported that "his political and economic choices have always been on the conservative side" and his public comments were noted for "severely criticizing Communists." This report was characteristic of the FBI's little-nuanced views of what values were properly American. Adams (like many fellow chemists who shared his political views) was not adversely affected by FBI loyalty investigations in the early Cold War, and his 1942 support for Russian War Relief was not revisited, as it was for more liberal American physicists. Nevertheless, the pervasive climate of suspicion of scientists, particularly atomic physicists, in the wake of these investigations was a reminder of the U.S. government's greater control over scientists after 1940.

The 1948 FBI report was correct in one central respect: Adams was indeed deeply involved in business. Already by 1928 Adams had become a paid consultant to the chemical giant E. I. Du Pont de Nemours, a role he continued in the postwar period. While Adams also consulted with other chemical firms, including Abbott Laboratories, his involvement with Du Pont was the defining outside connection of his career. In 1950 department faculty wrote a lengthy skit poking fun at Illinois's relationship with Du Pont. The skit's conceit was a grand jury investigation of the charge that the Du Pont company "has dominated, subjugated, intimated, prostituted, and just plain raised hell with the University of Illinois Chemistry Department." Called to testify, "Adams" revealed the extent of his financial benefits from vitamin promotion and clever consulting. In the field of chemistry—intimately tied to industries like Du Pont that were critical to the national defense—science, national service, and foreign policy all retained a close association. Supporting American chemistry and the U.S. chemical industry remained important concerns for Adams. In 1958 Adams returned to Germany on behalf of Du Pont, seeking promising young German chemists who were then invited by Du Pont to present seminars on their work.[13]

The continued rapid growth of American chemistry and chemical engineering in the decades following World War II reflected the international dominance of U.S. chemistry and the burgeoning growth of the nation's economy. But chemistry was also closely linked with national security, and the discipline continued to be deeply shaped by Cold War concerns in the last decades of Adams's life.

FROM THE CIA TO THE DEPARTMENT OF STATE: THE FURTHER INFLUENCE OF ROGER ADAMS

Adams's influence on science policy extended to his graduate students and colleagues. Only five of his nearly 200 Ph.D. students directly entered government service. Nonetheless, his students and postdocs, whom Adams placed widely in academia and industry, had considerable influence on U.S. science policy. They absorbed the lessons Adams imparted about the value of strong and intimate contacts between academic chemistry and the chemical industry, the professional values of the discipline, and the need to balance open publication with trade secrecy.

One of Adams's graduate students may be singled out as particularly important in shaping international science policy. Wallace R. Brode carried the professional values he first absorbed at Illinois to the highest levels of government. Solemn, blunt, and gaunt, Brode at six-foot-three towered over most of his colleagues. On a career path that was unimaginable back when Adams came to Illinois 1916, Brode served during the 1940s and 1950s as a key official and advisor at the CIA, then the National Bureau of Standards (NBS), and finally the Department of State. Like the geophysicist Lloyd V. Berkner, best known for his role in planning the International Geophysical Year of 1957–58, Brode was one of a handful of scientist-statesmen who brokered new arrangements between science and the nonmilitary branches of government closely linked with Cold War national security aims.[14]

Brode began his graduate work at Illinois in the early 1920s, taking his Ph.D. under Adams in 1925 with a dissertation on the absorption spectra of organic compounds. After a research appointment at the NBS in Washington, D.C., and two years in Germany and in England as a Guggenheim fellow, Brode, acting on Adams's advice, secured a professorship at Ohio State University in 1928. While in Columbus, Brode authored the widely used textbook *Chemical Spectroscopy*. World War II then drew Brode into less familiar pathways of government service. He first worked on infrared plastic filters in Washington, then in 1944 became head of the Paris liaison office of OSRD. Soon afterward, he, like Adams, became a member of ALSOS. Immediately after the war Brode began developing plans for gathering foreign scientific intelligence while associate director of the Naval

Ordnance Test Station at Inyokern, California, the Navy's leading rocket research laboratory. His considerable experience with intelligence—and his outspoken disdain for military officers who regarded scientists merely as skilled assigned civilian laborers rather than as equals in developing national security policy—attracted the attention of Vannevar Bush. In 1947 Bush offered Brode the opportunity to create an office of scientific intelligence within the newly created CIA.

What advice Adams may have provided Brode about this offer is uncertain. Brode asked to meet with his former mentor before he considered resigning from Ohio State, aware that he had exhausted his maximum leave and thus faced a critical decision. No record of this encounter has survived. Ultimately Brode accepted Bush's offer. The challenge of setting up a functioning office of scientific intelligence was immense. Brode had limited authority to demand intelligence gleaned from military sources, particularly for atomic issues. Moreover, Brode had to work under a cloak of secrecy. While employed by the CIA he held a "blind" cover post as associate director of the NBS, second in command to the controversial director Edward U. Condon. Yet there were advantages in having a chemist lead the effort. "Being tight-lipped is the secret of being a good consultant," Adams's colleague Carl Marvel perceptively noted. More chemists worked for industry and consulting than did the members of any other scientific field. While atomic physics, chemical and biological warfare, earth sciences, and medical intelligence all remained high priorities, East Bloc chemistry and chemical industries were important early targets of scientific intelligence, as they provided insight into the Soviet Union's ability to manufacture critical weapons and goods. (One of the CIA's first secret scientific intelligence studies drew on the American Chemical Society's comprehensive *Chemical Abstracts*, reporting that Soviet chemical citations had dropped by more than 50 percent since 1941—a significant find, for it suggested how much Russian research was now secret and unreported in the open literature.) In the year Brode stayed at the CIA, he first borrowed from the highly centralized Scientific Intelligence Service created in Great Britain during World War II, arguing that his specialists needed to trace foreign scientific research and development "to the point of production." Soon, however, he sought to re-create a university model for scientific intelligence production within the CIA, arguing that such an environment was necessary for recruiting top-notch scientists.[15] Both concepts shared much with the practice of Adams's laboratory in Illinois.

Brode nevertheless failed to produce the flow of scientific intelligence desired by military planners and civilian advisors. In October 1948, dismayed by the lack of support he was receiving from the tepid first director of Central Intelligence, Admiral Roscoe Hillenkoetter, Brode resigned from the CIA. But he did not return to research. Instead he forged a career in government service. Through the late 1950s Brode served as associate director of the NBS, moving full-time into the post that served as his blind while he organized what became the Office of Scientific Intelligence. His time at the NBS was frustrating and difficult; he became an embattled participant in the battery additive AD-X2 controversy that temporarily cost Bureau Director Allen V. Astin his post in 1953 when the newly inaugurated Eisenhower administration stressed commercial values over scientific testing. But Brode kept his hand in international issues, writing on the international exchange of scientific information and gaining responsibility for foreign relations within the NBS. In time he came to occupy key positions in many leading national scientific organizations: editor of the *Journal of the Optical Society of America*, member of the board of advisors and later president of the ACS, and president of the American Association for the Advancement of Science (AAAS). When Brode became president-elect of the AAAS in 1957, Adams penned an appreciation of Brode in which he praised the expanding role of chemists and government scientists in the nation's premiere scientific bodies.[16]

Late in 1957, Brode became science advisor to the secretary of state, the highest and most visible governmental post he would occupy. Following the launch of *Sputnik* that October, Eisenhower administration officials redoubled their efforts to promote science and technology programs to other parts of the globe, recognizing that these fields were now highly visible surrogates for national power and prestige. The revival of a program of science attachés in U.S. embassies became one of Brode's highest priorities. The attaché program had begun in the early 1950s during the Truman administration but withered in the first Eisenhower administration, a victim of Republican budget-cutting but even more of conservative suspicions of scientific internationalism. To fill these posts, Brode turned particularly to major public universities, requesting senior faculty to commit to two-year rotating appointments. Among his first appointments was the University of Illinois organic chemist Ludwig Audrieth, discoverer of the first artificial sweetener, as science attaché to West Germany. These new service roles for scientists were by now familiar to Illinois administrators and their counterparts across the nation. But Illinois's involvement in science policy issues was particularly strong, revealing the willingness of its top administrators to support such new ventures. While formally remaining in Urbana, Adams had himself served as foreign secretary of the NAS and head of the Division of International Relations of the National Research Council from 1950 to 1954.

Brode was never one of Adams's favorite graduate students. Separated by differences in character and temperament, no warm letters passed between them, as had with other former graduate students, such as Carothers and Volwiler, Adams's first Ph.D. student. In photographs Brode appears stiff and formal, while Adams by contrast appears at ease and confident. Their personal letters also reflect these characteristics. Yet Adams remained vitally interested in international relations and was keenly aware of the significance of Brode's position. For Adams, Brode became a conduit for sharing his concerns about U.S. science abroad. In 1958, reflecting on his last trip to Germany, Adams wrote Brode that German colleagues now held low opinions of Fulbright students in chemistry. They "did not work and mostly traveled," his colleagues reported. Who was determining their selection? Adams growled. "They are certainly poor emissaries."[17]

By late 1959 Adams parted company with Brode over what policy the United States ought to pursue regarding scientific internationalism. Brode had come to believe that America was best served when scientists did not press for exceptions to immigration and foreign policy, even when official U.S. policies banning visits from members of "nonrecognized regimes," such as Communist China, made it difficult to host international scientific meetings in the United States. Foggy Bottom, declared Brode, would insist "that science must join with economics, culture, politics and other major national forces in the present age" to become integral factors in foreign policy. The Cold War, he insisted, meant that "'traditional freedom' of science on a world-wide basis is a thing of the past." In speeches he made as president of the AAAS and as the Priestley Medalist of the ACS, Brode expanded these ideas, arguing that the ACS, the world's largest scientific organization, could serve as the new international home for Western chemistry if East-West tensions caused the International Union for Pure and Applied Chemistry to collapse. Well before then, Brode's restricted conception of international scientific cooperation met strong opposition from the Manhattan Project veteran George Kistiakowsky, then President Eisenhower's science advisor, who placed the issue before the National Security Council for secret top-level policy discussions. But Brode had continued to insist that U.S. scientists needed to conform to the spirit of U.S. foreign policy, urging the government to reject a draft resolution by the NAS to endorse the political nondiscrimination statement issued by the International Council of Scientific Unions (ICSU), which affirmed the right of scientists "of any country or territory to adhere to or to associate with international scientific activity without regard to race, religion or political philosophy."[18]

Responding to a poll of members of the NAS Governing Board about the ICSU resolution, Adams made clear that he favored it. "I agree entirely with the sentiments expressed in the resolution and have no suggestions for changes," Adams noted. His view was consistent with that he had articulated in late 1945, while advising General Clay on the future of Germany: science was a distinct entity that could not be contained or confined within traditional foreign policy. Science needed to be treated differently than other aspects of international diplomacy. Yet chemists on the whole were less inclined than physicists or earth scientists to regard internationalism a top priority for their discipline. Chemists supported internationalism as a "general principle," as ACS Executive Secretary Alden H. Emery told an inquiring physicist in 1956, but had faced few of the political difficulties experienced by members of other fields. Chemistry was a laboratory science rather than a field science, the United States remained the undisputed leader in world chemistry at the time, and U.S. chemists had won the bulk of Nobel Prizes in chemistry since World War II. Brode's plans to limit international scientific contacts to achieve foreign policy goals gained only lukewarm support from American chemists, earned strong condemnation from leaders of other scientific fields, and ultimately cost him his post at the Department of State. Adams's politics and political inclinations better represented the chemical community in Cold War America. Though the two-time Nobel laureate Linus Pauling was perhaps the best known chemist in the United States at the time, this outspoken liberal activist was far from the political center of American chemists.

Yet in the 1960s Adams found himself increasingly outside the emerging consensus among American scientists about what role the United States ought play in the development of foreign science. He remained in close contact with colleagues around the world in retirement and continued to travel, including an extended trip to Latin America in 1962, at age seventy-three, to address the Argentine Chemical Society. But he remained convinced that merit, rather than political exigency, was the sole criterion in determining support for science. Like Bush, Conant, and other leaders of American science in the World War II era, Adams was an old-line conservative and intellectual elitist who never felt comfortable with the new Cold War order embraced by Berkner and Brode. In 1964 he gently scolded Harrison Brown, the California Institute of Technology geochemist and then foreign secretary of the NAS, over Brown's ambitious plans for international science. Adams objected to Brown's efforts to steer academy support to science in third world nations, arguing that the NAS needed to aid only pure research, leaving political issues to entities such as the Department of State. National prestige for Adams had no place in decisions to support science projects.[19] But this debate was chiefly won by physicists and earth scientists, who argued through the 1960s that promoting science as an aspect of foreign policy, including through such government efforts as the U.S. Agency for International Development, did constitute a proper role for science. In 1971, when Adams died at age eighty-two, social unrest, the Vietnam War, and heightened popular hostility toward science and technology had blurred the lines between science policy and foreign policy further still, a situation that has persisted into the early twenty-first century.

CONCLUSION

Adams was part of a generation of scientists that experienced great change in what it meant to do science. More than his predecessors, Adams came to wear many hats. He was a prominent member of his scientific community and a consultant to industry, roles long familiar to American scientists. He also became an advisor on national security and an advocate of national science policies for defeated Axis nations. These new professional roles for American scientists were novel and often difficult. Like other leaders of American science who became involved in foreign policy, Adams worked to balance the aims of the state and national security concerns with the international ambitions of scientists and his own efforts to maintain the competitive edge of his institution. His graduate student Wallace Brode experienced these conflicts even more profoundly by becoming involved in scientific intelligence and the U.S. Department of State. But Adams also faced significant challenges in his own right. His conviction that scientists could be public intellectuals and political activists, aiding social progress and democratization, clashed with the views of increasingly powerful national security agencies, including the FBI, which even by 1940 saw such political activism as a threat to the state. While Adams did not suffer the fate of more liberal U.S. scientists as the internal security state expanded at the start of the Cold War, the strong anticommunism campaign clearly limited the extent of public debate. Adams's most prominent political activity was already behind him by 1940.

Adams's career also illuminates a little-appreciated aspect of the history of higher education in America during the twentieth century. Past accounts have focused largely on research achievements among the large elite private universities. When the flagship state universities did figure in, it was often to compare their scientific productivity against the standards set by Harvard or Princeton or Stanford. But state universities, including land-grant schools such as Illinois, also had well-established service roles within their regions, and it is perhaps not surprising that the University of Illinois became a significant home for researchers who took on new professional roles in the postwar years. What Illinois helped to nurture came to have a global influence.

ACKNOWLEDGMENTS

I wish to acknowledge support from the Smithsonian Institution, NSF SBR-9511867, a research grant from the Chemical Heritage Foundation, and assistance from the University of Illinois Archives.

NOTES

1. James Hershberg, *James B. Conant: Harvard to Hiroshima and the Making of the Nuclear Age* (New York: Knopf, 1993), 563. The most comprehensive account of Adams's life is D. Stanley Tarbell and Ann Tracy Tarbell, *Roger Adams: Scientist and Statesman* (Washington, D.C.: American Chemical Society, 1981), but also helpful is *The Roger Adams Symposium: Papers Presented at a Symposium in Honor of Roger Adams at the University of Illinois September 3 and 4, 1954* (New York: Wiley, 1955).

2. Hershberg, *James B. Conant*, and James Bamford, *Body of Secrets: Anatomy of the Ultra-Secret National Security Agency from the Cold War Through the Dawn of a New Century* (New York: Doubleday, 2001), 357, 462. For the history of twentieth-century chemistry, see Mary Jo Nye, *Before Big Science: The Pursuit of Modern Chemistry and Physics, 1800–1940* (New York: Twayne, 1996), and W. H. Brock, *The Chemical Tree: A History of Chemistry* (New York: Norton, 2000).

3. Tarbell and Tarbell, *Roger Adams*, see especially 7, 17, 20.

4. These issues are addressed in Larry Owens, "Science in the U.S.—The Last Century," in *Science in the Twentieth Century,* ed. John Krige and Dominique Pestre (London: Harwood Academic Press, 1997), 821–38; Robert E. Kohler; "'The Ph.D. Machine': Building on the Collegiate Base," *Isis* 81 (1990): 638–62; Kathryn Steen, "USA v. The Chemical Foundation, Inc., 1923–1926," *Isis* 92, no. 1 (2001): 91–122; and Roger Geiger, *To Advance Knowledge: The Growth of American Research Universities, 1900–1940* (New York: Oxford University Press, 1986), 207–8; for Adams's role, see Tarbell and Tarbell, *Roger Adams*, 53.

5. Tarbell and Tarbell, *Roger Adams*, 170; on this 1944 faculty vote, see "Director, FBI Re. Rogers Adams," May 12, 1948, 3, FBI Subject File Roger Adams, File Number 77-HQ-10721, obtained by author's Freedom of Information Act Request (Adams FOIA).

6. Hershberg, *James B. Conant*, 128; "Memorandum for Mr. Clegg," July 15, 1940, Adams FOIA. The FBI's relation to American science is analyzed in Jessica Wang, *American Science in an Age of Anxiety: Scientists, Anticommunism, and the Cold War* (Chapel Hill: University of North Carolina Press, 1999), and Fred Jerome, *The Einstein File: J. Edgar Hoover's Secret War Against the World's Most Famous Scientist* (New York: St. Martin's Press, 2002).

7. Ernest H. Wolwiler, "Remarks at Symposium Honoring Roger Adams," in *The Roger Adams Symposium*, 2; Tarbell and Tarbell, *Roger Adams*, 128–9; "Memorandum re. Professor Roger Adams," July 16, 1940, Adams FOIA, Anslinger to Adams, June 25, 1940, Box 52, folder 'marihuana research,' Roger Adams papers, University of Illinois archives. The antimarijuana campaign is described in Richard J. Bonnie and Charles H. Whitebread II, *The Marijuana Conviction: A History of Marijuana Prohibition in the United States* (Charlottesville: University Press of Virginia, 1974).

8. Hoover to Brigadier General Sherman Miles, August 3, 1940 [personal and confidential, by special messenger] and A. Rosen, memorandum for [name deleted], August 29, 1940, both Adams FOIA.

9. The story of the Lincoln's Birthday Committee for Democracy and Intellectual Freedom (and red-baiting in American science more generally before World War II) is treated in Peter J. Kuznick's *Beyond the Laboratory: Scientists as Political Activists in 1930s America* (Chicago: University of Chicago Press, 1987), especially 184–94 and 195–212. Recent scholarship has established the sharp rise in government surveillance of U.S. scientists after the late 1930s; see Naomi Oreskes and Ronald Rainger, "Science and Security Before the Atomic Bomb: The Loyalty Case of Harald U. Sverdrup," *Studies in History and Philosophy of Modern Physics* 31B, no. 3 (2000): 309–69, and Gregg Herken, *Brotherhood of the Bomb: The Tangled Lives and Loyalties of Robert Oppenheimer, Ernest Lawrence, and Edward Teller* (New York: Henry Holt, 2002).

10. Quoted in Tarbell and Tarbell, *Roger Adams*, 146–47; Hoover to Hon. Sherman Adams, Assistant to the President, May 13, 1954, Adams FOIA. U.S.-Soviet scientific exchanges after World War II are examined in Ronald E. Doel and Robert McCutcheon, "Introduction [to special volume, 'Astronomy and the State in the U.S.S.R. and Russia,'] *Journal for History of Astronomy* 26, no. 4 (1995): 3–20, and Nikolai Krementsov, *Stalinist Science* (Princeton, N.J.: Princeton University Press, 1997).

11. Quoted from Assistant Secretary of State Wilbur J. Carr, "Report Upon the Participation of the United States in International Conferences, Congresses, Expositions, Fair, and Commissions," July 20, 1937, 25, folder "AG and Depts: State 1937," Division of Foreign Relations collection, National Academy of Sciences archive; Adams to H. C. Green, Department of Commerce, March 16, 1946, Box 58, folder "Memoranda from Rogers Adams," Adams. Historians have substantiated Adams's impressions of the harsh quality of U.S. denazification efforts; see Mitchell G. Ash, "Denazifying Scientists—and Science," in *Technology Transfer Out of Germany After 1945*, ed. Matthias Judt and Burghard Ciesla (Amsterdam: Harwood Academic Press, 1996), 61–80, and John Gimbel, *Science, Technology, and Reparations: Exploitation and Plunder in Postwar Germany* (Stanford, Calif.: Stanford University Press, 1990). Adams's views on science policy are evident in *German Scientific Research and Engineering from the Standpoint of International Security*, July 2, 1945, (T.I.D.C. Project 3): 10, Box 58, Adams. The ethics of Nazi scientific research has recently become the subject of intense historical scrutiny; see Ute Deichmann, *Flüchten, Mitmachen, Vergessen: Chemiker und Biochemiker in der NS-Zeit* (Weinheim: Wiley-VCH, 2001); Michael J. Neufeld, *The Rocket and the Reich: Peenemünde and the Coming of the Ballistic Missile Era* (New York: The Free Press, 1995); and Robert Proctor, *The Nazi War on Cancer* (Princeton, N.J.: Princeton University Press, 1999).

12. R. W. Home and Morris F. Low, "Postwar Scientific Intelligence Missions to Japan," *Isis* 84 (1993): 527–37; "urgent need" quoted in Robert S. Patterson, secretary of war, to Dr. Frank B. Jewett, June 17 1947, Box 5, Adams. "Stirs the envy" quoted in "Address by Dr. Roger Adams for the Scientific Advisory Group," n.d. [summer 1947], Box 59, folder "Science

Advisory Mission to Military Government in Japan" Adams, 2. He revised these statements in his final draft, omitting direct mention of Mikimoto and changing "stirs the envy" to the more neutral "arouses the admiration." Adams's ideas are developed in "Present Status of Research in Japan," no date [summer 1947], and "Recommendations Concerning General Reorganization of Scientific Administration in Japan," August 23, 1947, both Box 5, folder "Japan," Adams. The final quote of this paragraph comes from "Address by Dr. Roger Adams," above, 6.

13. FBI Report on Roger Adams, November 8, 1947, 2, file 116-1886, Adams FOIA; Wang, *American Science in an Age of Anxiety*, 333; and untitled "Skit," dated "circa 1950," Box 6, Adams.

14. Allan A. Needell, *Science, Cold War, and the American State: Lloyd V. Berkner and the Balance of Professional Ideals* (London: Harwood Academic Press, 2000), and Ronald E. Doel and Allan A. Needell, "Science, Scientists, and the CIA: Balancing International Ideals, National Needs, and Professional Opportunities," in *Eternal Vigilance?: Fifty Years of the CIA*, ed. Rhodri Jeffreys-Jones and Christopher Andrew (London: Frank Cass, 1997), 59–81.

15. Doel and Needell, "Science, Scientists, and the CIA"; Marvel quoted in Charles Price oral history interview, 1983, cited in *Carl S. Marvel Finding Aid*, 40, Chemical Heritage Foundation. "Abstracting Services as an Intelligence Tool for Assessing Soviet Chemical Research," Office of Scientific Intelligence Report 4/49, December 19, 1949, is in Box 257, folder PSB, Harry S. Truman Presidential Library.

16. Brode to Lloyd Berkner, November 5, 1949, Box 1, folder 1, Wallace R. Brode papers, Library of Congress. Astin was reinstated as director of the NBS after intense outcry from the American scientific community. In addition to an early draft in the Adams papers, see Roger Adams, "W.R. Brode, President Elect," *Science* 125, no. 3242 (February 15, 1957): 279–80.

17. Ronald E. Doel and Zuoyue Wang, "Science and Technology," in *Encyclopedia of American Foreign Policy*, ed. Alexander DeConde, Richard Dean Burns, and Fredrik Logevall (New York: Scribners, 2001), 443–59; Tarbell and Tarbell, *Roger Adams*, 189; Adams to Brode, September 23, 1958, Box 12, Adams papers.

18. Brode, "Covering Memo to Planning Board Re. Dr. Kistiakowsky's Paper on International Scientific Cooperation," Section 1, 2 and 3, Box 25, folder 2, Brode; see also Frank Greenaway, *Science International: A History of the International Council of Scientific Unions* (Cambridge: Cambridge University Press, 1996), 93–94. Brode's views ignited a larger national controversy when, in an interview with a the *New York Times* reporter in April 1960, he suggested winning the Cold War would require American scientists to concentrate on applied research and adopt Soviet-style planning; see John A. Osmundsen to Brode, Mary 18, 1960, Box 25, folder 2, Brode. On the ICSU resolution, see S. D. Cornell to members of the Governing Board of the National Academy of Sciences, November 13, 1959, Box 23, folder "National Academy of Sciences, 1953–67," Adams.

19. Quoted in Adams to S T[sic] Cornell, November 24, 1959, Box 23, folder "National Academy of Sciences, 1953–67," Adams papers, and Emery to Dr. W. E. Meyerhoff, January 4, 1956, Box 31, folder "Professional and Economic Status. Legislation: Immigrant and Nationality Act," American Chemical Society papers, Library of Congress; see also Arnold Thackray et al., *Chemistry in America, 1876–1976: Historical Indicators* (Dordrecht: D. Reidel, 1985), 160–62. On Adams's views after 1960, see Adams, "The Fifty Years of Chemistry in the United States, 1912–1962," no date [1962], Box 54, "Speeches, 1954–1959" folder, and Adams to Harrison Brown, May 4, 1962, Box 54, both Adams papers.

WILLIAM J. HALL

CHAPTER 10

Nathan M. Newmark:

A Model of Engineering Creativity

In the early 1950s, Nathan M. Newmark, one of the twentieth century's leading educators and engineers in civil engineering, asked a graduate student assistant who had expressed opinions about some research findings, "Where did you learn that?" "In a book," the student responded. Newmark, who would in 1956 be appointed head of the Department of Civil Engineering at the University of Illinois, replied: "If all you know is what is in a book, you are in great difficulty."

Over the course of his career, Newmark developed many simple yet powerful and widely used methods for analyzing complex structural components and assemblies under a variety of loading conditions, and for calculating the stresses and deformations in the soil beneath their foundations. He contributed to achieving a better understanding of the behavior of structural materials under various environments, including fatigue and brittle fracture, and of structures subjected to impact, periodic excitation, wave action, wind, blast, and earthquakes. He also developed techniques for designing and carrying out simple numerical procedures, initially using the slide rule, later mechanical calculators, and still later electronic computers. Newmark's contributions to the University of Illinois and the engineering profession were enormous. His unceasing devotion to research, his noteworthy and continuing contributions to the betterment of structural engineering practice, and his leadership in engineering education, teaching, and professional activities have had a profound influence on civil engineering worldwide.

EARLY LIFE

Newmark was born on September 22, 1910, in Plainfield, New Jersey. He was the oldest of Abraham S. and Mollie (Nathanson) Newmark's three children; the other two were Nathan's sisters, Isabelle and Vera. That Nathan was a boy was of great significance in the family, especially on his mother's side, for his mother was the oldest of seven sisters. His father, well read in Hebrew, Yiddish, and English, was quite a philosopher. The family subsisted mostly on his mother's work as a seamstress and her odd jobs for people done out of the house. Nate's father's work went from farming in Fayetteville, North Carolina, and Fair Lawn, New Jersey (near Paterson), to a grocery business after the farms failed.

Education was of prime importance in the Newmark household. A precocious child, Nate excelled in school, despite the family's many moves and his many changes of school. His kindergarten teacher recognized his special abilities, even then, and called him "Dr. Nate." In seventh grade, in Fayetteville, North Carolina, Nate won the "Observer Composition Contest," with an essay on "Why I Want to be a Farmer When I am Grown." Attending Eastside High School in Paterson, New Jersey, Nate graduated as valedictorian at the age of fifteen. Highly proficient in all his studies, he was also a voracious reader. He worked on the farm during his high school vacations and as a salesperson in a specialty food store on Saturdays. After Nate finished high school, the family moved back to Plainfield. His family relationships were close; the girls depended on Nate for help with their homework, games, and problems. In later years, Nate saw to it that his two sisters received a college education.

When Newmark received a scholarship to attend Rutgers University, he matriculated in chemistry. Nate's father, who maintained an interest in scientific farming, felt that his son should study agriculture, as Rutgers had an excellent school of agriculture. But the story has it that Nate's Uncle Julius Newmark, a Rutgers graduate who worked as a civil engineer for the New Jersey highway department, finally persuaded Nate's father to let his son major in civil engineering. In 1930, Nate graduated from Rutgers with Special and High Honors in Civil Engineering.

The reputation that Newmark developed as a civil engineering student is suggested by the passage that accompanies Newmark's picture in the Rutgers yearbook of 1930: "The sages on Mount Olympus were filled with grief and despair. Three of their number, Archimedes, Galileo, and Newton, had been sorely wounded by a dragon in the guise of a problem in mathematics. No one on Mount Olympus dared attack it. The wise men were assembled by order of Plato to decide what to do. Suddenly, in their midst a spirit from the earth appeared, enveloped in a cloud of smoke (this is a pipe dream). 'I'll solve your problem,' spake the spirit. 'Who are you?' shouted Leibnitz. Came the ready answer, 'Newmark of Rutgers.' Then Nate woke up."

THE UNIVERSITY OF ILLINOIS
AT URBANA-CHAMPAIGN

In 1930, following his graduation from the Rutgers school of civil engineering, Newmark accepted a fellowship from the civil engineering department at the University of Illinois. This was the first of a long succession of positions that Newmark held at the University of Illinois, a succession that would extend over half a century. According to Newmark, a Rutgers faculty member who was familiar with the College of Engineering at Illinois strongly urged him to do graduate work at the University of Illinois because of its reputation for having a strong faculty in civil engineering. Newmark took the advice. On August 6, 1932, during this period at Illinois, he married Anne Mae Cohen, then a secretary in the Department of Theoretical and Applied Mechanics.

As early as 1867, the trustees of the new Illinois Industrial University had identified the Department of Civil and Rural Engineering as an element of the College of Engineering. The department became operative in 1868 when the university opened its doors.[1] It later assimilated the Department of Municipal and Sanitary Engineering to form the Department of Civil Engineering. The list of distinguished faculty associated with this department over the years includes such nationally prominent professors as John S. Crandell and Carroll C. Wiley (in highways); James J. Doland (in hydraulics); Harold E. Babbitt (in municipal and sanitary engineering); Charles A. Ellis, Wilbur M. Wilson, Hardy Cross, and Thomas C. Shedd (in structures); Herald M. Westergaard (in mechanics), Arthur N. Talbot (in public health, reinforced concrete, and railroad engineering); Frank E.

Richart (in reinforced concrete); and Herbert F. Moore (in materials). These individuals were among the leading engineering educators of their time and worked on many of the important projects of their period. They were well known for their research because it was applicable to practice, and for their research reports and textbooks, which were used nationally and internationally.

As a case in point, one day about 1962, shortly after Newmark took over as head of the Department of Civil Engineering, Joseph Pettit, dean of engineering at Stanford University (and later president of the Georgia Institute of Technology), approached Newmark about coming to Stanford as head of civil engineering. I well recall that in the midst of these discussions, to my great surprise, Joe Pettitt appeared in my office and asked, " . . . what is it that makes the University of Illinois Civil Engineering Department have such a strong reputation?" I responded, "All schools have buildings and books, but we have been blessed from the beginning with an extremely qualified and well known faculty, as well as excellent staff and students." I pointed out that the wide use of textbooks authored by the faculty at the university, as well as their publications arising from research that was central to civil engineering practice, contributed both to the reputation and to the desire of talented individuals to be part of the University of Illinois.

A succinct statement about Newmark's activities in his early years at Illinois appears in a 1942 report. The report refers to Newmark's work as "outstanding" in the field of civil engineering and explains that he was appointed a research graduate assistant in the Engineering Experiment Station, where he worked for two years under Professor Wilbur M. Wilson (who ran the experimental work in Talbot Laboratory) and then for two more years under Professor Hardy Cross, continuing his studies under Wilson and Professor Herald Westergaard.

Newmark was awarded his doctorate in 1934, with a thesis titled "Interaction Between Rib and Superstructure in Concrete Arch Bridges." A large-scale model of the type of bridge he analyzed in his doctoral thesis was built in Talbot Laboratory for physical study under the guidance of Wilson and Richart. Newmark's acknowledgment in the thesis gives credit to Cross for supplying some unpublished leads for carrying out the analyses; the "star-loaded" final doctoral committee consisted of Cross as chair, Richart, Shedd, Westergaard, and Wilson. Because Newmark's work with all his three professors—Wilson, Cross, and Westergaard—was outstanding, Wilson recommended that a permanent position be created for him on the civil engineering staff of the Engineering Experiment Station. In his letter to support Newmark for this postdoctoral appointment, Westergaard wrote, "I believe that his appointment will be a contribution to the solution of the difficult problems of future distinction of the University. His intellectual capacity is rare, his personality attractive. He is among the few who can be rated as truly brilliant." Cross and Wilson echoed these accolades.

The Engineering Experiment Station had been established in 1903–5 to manage research activities for the college, especially those conducted in its many laboratories, and to handle publications reporting on the work. It was no accident that Newmark was supported with Experiment Station funds ("soft money" in today's definition), given that he was so active in research.

In the materials on Newmark preserved in the Grainger Engineering Library are copies of two reports by Newmark written in the 1930s. One was a brief report in July 1931 to the chief design engineer of the Bureau of Reclamation, Department of the Interior, on the topic of abutment movements in arch dams. (This report came from Plainfield, New Jersey, obviously while Newmark was home after his first year of graduate work.) The second report, a product of what Newmark referred to later as "my first consulting job" (interpreted by him as the first engineering task for which he received payment), was to the Bureau of Reclamation in 1933; it dealt with the effect of damping on seismic vibration response of the twin water intake towers for Boulder Dam.[2]

Appointed initially as a research assistant, Newmark rose to research assistant professor in 1941, and he was in 1943 appointed research professor of civil engineering with tenure, skipping the intermediate rank of associate professor. The "research" in the title indicated that his salary was paid from research (i.e., soft) funds and he was not on the tenure track. Interestingly, Newmark was granted tenure in 1943 under what must have been special circumstances. The precise reason for skipping the intermediate rank is not known, but one can surmise that his prodigious research efforts in many areas, and possibly his World War II efforts, figured in the decision.

Through Newmark's work at the university and nationally, and through his efforts to place faculty and alumni on key committees and boards, the department and university activities surrounding Newmark flourished. Although many of his activities were consultative in nature, whenever possible he would write journal papers for applications by others. Many of his consulting efforts led to major research projects in the department, including support for graduate students.

In 1956 Newmark was appointed head of the Department of Civil Engineering, a position he held until 1973, when he became professor of civil engineering and professor in the Center for Advanced Study (the latter largely honorary at this late stage of his career). In the years before he became the department head, Newmark had aggressively led the department's structural research program in Talbot Laboratory. When he took over the headship, he applied the same aggressive leadership and support to all units of the department. His efforts in this regard were greatly enhanced by the numerous outstanding and nationally known faculty in the department, many of whom over time became members of the prestigious National Academy of Engineering.

In the years during which Newmark served as the department's head (1956–73), John Haltiwanger was the associate head, handling undergraduate student matters. I was responsible for graduate student and research matters. Newmark granted us great latitude, both in our handling of administration and in our dispersing of funds. The three of us were in close communication; Newmark always passed on major matters. Recently Haltiwanger and I realized that under Newmark's leadership we were never once criticized for any of our actions. Newmark was willing not only to delegate responsibility but to grant authority to fulfill the responsibilities for operation that he had delegated. The reputation and stature of the department, which had been great almost since the department's founding, rose to new heights under Newmark's leadership.

It seems appropriate to describe some of the broad interests and involvement of Newmark in the engineering programs in which he made major contributions. His engineering contributions, although far-reaching, focused largely, but not solely, on areas denoted as dynamics, namely, effects of blast, shock, and earthquake on the response and performance of structures and buried systems. He chaired or served on dozens of national committees that provided direction for national efforts in these technical areas, including related educational activities.

Unbeknownst to many who knew Newmark, he and his many colleagues contributed importantly, especially in later years, in areas dealing with the properties and behavior of materials. Among the many examples that could be cited are projects on welding procedures for steel that aided structural strength, investigations into brittle fracture propagation and arrest in steel that contributed to the solution of the merchant (and naval) ship fracture problem, work in metal fatigue that enhanced the life of highway bridges, and investigations into properties of soil and rock as they influenced the basic understanding of whole new fields of practical research within structural dynamics and soil dynamics.

For Newmark's extensive service related to the military, he was awarded the President's Certificate of Merit in 1948. During World War II, he was a consultant to the National Defense Research Committee and the Office of Field Service of the Office of Scientific Research and Development headed by Vannevar Bush of MIT. Part of his national service time was spent in the Pacific war zone, but his activities are not in the public record. Later, in addition to serving on numerous Department of Defense boards and panels, he made crucial technical contributions to the development of the Minute Man and MX missile systems. In addition, he and his colleagues helped to develop procedures for design, analysis, and vulnerability assessments, and for military protective systems of all kinds, including structures, tunnels, and associated systems. He was a member of many influential committees affecting U.S. defenses, including the Gaither Committee in 1957, under President Dwight Eisenhower, which looked at strategic defense, as well as boards for the Office of the Chief of Engineers, the Air Force Space and Missiles System Organization, the Defense Atomic Support Agency, the Defense Intelligence Agency, and the Office of the Secretary of Defense.

Beginning in 1949, Newmark served as principal consultant on the seismic design of the forty-four-storied Latino Americana Tower in Mexico City, a highly seismic region of the world. At the time it was constructed in the early 1950s, the Latino Americana Tower was nearly twice the height of the tallest buildings then existing in Mexico City. Since the foundation of the building was to be located in the caldera, the region of the city located in the bowl of an ancient volcano, and had to rest on deep deposits of lacustrine clay, it was necessary to conserve weight as much as possible. Thus the height of the building and its weight limitation, plus its location in this seismically active region, made it imperative that detailed consideration be given to earthquake forces and deformations.

Newmark undertook the seismic analysis with the assistance of one of his graduate students, the late Emilio Rosenblueth, who took his doctorate in 1951. Special story displacement instruments were installed in the tower to measure story deformations when the building is subjected to high wind or earthquake loading. In 1957, one year following the completion of construction and occupancy of the building, a major earthquake shook the tower with close to the maximum ground motions for which it had been designed and constructed. To recognize the successful structural performance of the tower during the earthquake, a plaque was mounted on the building naming the individuals responsible for the design. In 1985

Nathan Newmark with the Latino Americana Tower, Mexico, D.F., in the background, following the 1957 Mexican earthquake where the building's perfomance was as designed.

a slightly larger earthquake occurred and the building successfully withstood that earthquake too, again demonstrating that the height of a soundly designed and constructed building need not be severely limited in active seismic regions.

Newmark also played a pivotal role in the development of computers at the University of Illinois (see chapter 15). The actual introduction of computers into government, industry, and educational institutions did not begin in a major way until after World War II. Illinois was a leader in both the building and use of computers. The three key leaders in the University of Illinois's endeavor formally began their efforts in 1947 when William Everitt was the head of the Department of Electrical Engineering, Newmark was head of Civil Engineering, and Louis Ridenour was dean of the Graduate College. Newmark headed a committee to develop the program at the University of Illinois.

In 1949, with a push from the U.S. Army Ballistic Research Laboratory at Aberdeen Proving Ground in Baltimore, the University of Illinois took on the construction (from scratch) of two identical computers: the ORDVAC, for the U.S. Army, and a duplicate of the ORDVAC, the ILLIAC, for the University of Illinois. The design of the computer logic was largely due to John von Neumann of Princeton University, a national figure in mathematics about whom Newmark told me several times, "He was by far the most brilliant man I ever met." Coming from Newmark that was quite an endorsement. Both computers were extremely reliable and heavily used. An indication of the computer group's reputation later appeared in *Computing Reviews*: "ILLIAC II, at its conception in the mid-1950s, represented, together with some other independent design projects of the same period, the spearhead and breakthrough into a new generation of machines." The subsequent ILLIAC machines that were designed and constructed at the University of Illinois led the way into parallel computing. Newmark was the first director of the Digital Computer Laboratory (1947–57), which over time evolved into the Department of Computer Science.

Newmark also worked on nuclear power plants. Beginning in 1964, he was a consultant to the U.S. Nuclear Regulatory Commission on how seismic analysis affects the design and construction of power plants for the nuclear power industry. All told, he had input into the design and review of more than seventy-five nuclear power plants and several research reactors. Many publications related to the seismic design of new and existing nuclear power plants and became a staple for the analysis, design, and evaluation of such plants and related industries around the world and are still in use today.

Newmark was selected to be the engineer overseeing both the governmental and corporate seismic design projects associated with the Trans-Alaska Pipeline (TAPS) during its design and construction. This major engineering project, with a pipeline traversing almost 800 miles (N-S) across Alaska, with a dozen pump stations, was accorded special seismic design attention because of the 1964 Alaskan earthquake centered between Anchorage and Valdez. This earthquake affected buildings and landforms, causing changes in elevation of as much as thirty feet in the general Prince William Sound region, including Anchorage, Alaska. The U.S. government and the State of Alaska joined to establish stringent stipulations covering the design and construction of the pipeline so as to protect the environment to the fullest extent possible.

It was a major stroke of good luck that the timing of the development of the seismic criteria for the TAPS caused it to fall into the formative stages of the Applied Technology Council effort. As such, not only did the seismic loading criteria employed in the TAPS design turn out to be "modern," even by today's standards, but equally (perhaps more) important, the design and construction employed high-quality materials and construction practices that were at the forefront of practice at the time, and were almost identical to that which would be employed today. This project was at the time of construction the most costly privately constructed project in the history of the world. Today it falls behind by that measure only one other project, the Channel Tunnel project connecting England and France. So far the pipeline has performed admirably.

From 1974 to 1978, Newmark held principal technical responsibility for the development of the Applied Technology Council's Recommended Tentative Seismic Design Provisions for Buildings (so-called ATC-003). These recommendations, developed with the coordinated efforts of more than eighty engineers, seismologists, and building code officials, were published in 1978; for the first time modern approaches to seismic design were put forward. In large part, they are still reflected in current National Earthquake Hazard Reduction Program provisions, as well as in current building codes and industrial practice, such as the design of the TAPS.

Newmark's university instruction over the years tended to center on analysis concepts, primarily on the applications of dynamics in analysis, design, and construction. His lectures usually consisted of technically concentrated theoretical presentations that required detailed study of one's notes afterward to comprehend the concepts. I remember one version of the following incident (a slightly different one was recalled by a colleague). A student asked, "Dr. Newmark, in the last lecture you used alpha for the variable for . . . but in this lecture you used alpha to stand for another variable . . . why?" Answer: "Over the years I find that if I use the same term for different variables, often a lot of stuff cancels out, and the equations are simpler!" (great laughter). Another example: "Dr. Newmark, in the last lecture you employed alpha for variable . . . , while in this lecture you are using omega for the same variable . . . why?" Answer: "Doing this keeps both you and me awake, otherwise it would be boring!"

At the University of Illinois, Newmark was the adviser or coadviser for ninety-three doctoral candidates, and he served in many important leadership capacities. He has the distinction of having held the longest appointment to date on the UIUC Campus Research Board, one of the organizations responsible for placing Illinois among the great research institutions of the world. Newmark's vision and foresight played no small role in the success of this effort.

Newmark also played a major role in many important technical activities of the major American engineering societies. He was an honorary member of most of them. Within the American Society of Civil Engineers (ASCE), he was a founding member of the Engineering Mechanics Division and won five major awards from this society; he was a prime mover in the development of the society's computer application activities. In 1975 Newmark's former students established in his honor the annual ASCE

Dr. Newmark in his office ca. 1973, pondering
which pile to search for a specific project activity.

Newmark Medal. He was also a founding member of the National Academy of Engineering in 1964 and he was elected to membership in the National Academy of Sciences in 1966. Throughout his entire career he was active as a leader and participant in National Research Council endeavors. In 1968 Newmark received the National Medal of Science from President Lyndon B. Johnson, and in 1969 he received the Washington Award— jointly awarded annually by the major engineering societies of the United States. In 1979 Newmark was presented the John Fritz Medal, an all-engineering society award, thereby joining the distinguished company of such former John Fritz medallists as George Westinghouse, Alexander Graham Bell, Thomas Alva Edison, George Goethals, Orville Wright, Guglicimo Marconi, and Herbert Hoover. He was accorded honorary doctoral degrees by four institutions.

Newmark authored more than 200 papers, books, and chapters. The complete collection of his formal publications resides in Grainger Engineering Library and Information Center at the University of Illinois.[3] He was coauthor, with John A. Blume and Leo Corning, of *Design of Multi-Story Reinforced Concrete Buildings for Earthquake Motion* and with Emilio Rosenblueth, a former student, of *Fundamentals of Earthquake Engineering*.[4] He authored or coauthored dozens of technical reports that were widely distributed nationally and internationally, many of great significance to the profession.

Newmark possessed an unusual ability to attract young people to the field of civil engineering. He was able to guide, but not direct, their thinking and inspire them with the confidence needed for undertaking new and varied tasks. He also insisted that they receive appropriate recognition for their accomplishments. Engineers, young and old, who came in contact with this man sensed the intellectual and educational challenge he offered them. His penetrating insight, his keen engineering judgment, and his genuine interest in people were a constant source of inspiration to all who had the privilege of working with him. It is no accident that there grew up around him one of the most active research centers in civil engineering in the country, or that the alumni of this group have assumed broad leadership in education, industry, and government throughout the world.

On retiring in 1976, Newmark achieved the rank of professor emeritus of civil engineering. The University of Illinois awarded him the honorary degree of doctor of science in 1978. The citation read, in part, "His influence on engineering education has been extensive. Graduate study in structural engineering today bears his indelible imprint as a result of the large group that he attracted to Illinois to work with him, and because of the more than ninety Ph.D.'s for whom Professor Newmark was advisor or co-advisor. His style, combining rigorous analysis with a sophisticated appeal to experience and intuitive leaps, while inimitable, has provided generations of graduate students with a model of engineering creativity at its best."

A few days before Newmark's death, he told me, "The things I will be remembered for were very, very simple." Simple, often, but invariably powerful and useful. Newmark passed away in Urbana, on January 25, 1981. On February 19, less than a month after his death, in commemoration of Newmark's contributions to the university, the board of trustees of the University of Illinois renamed the Civil Engineering Building the Nathan M. Newmark Civil Engineering Laboratory.

NOTES

1. For details, see I. O. Baker and E. E. King, *A History of The College of Engineering of the University of Illinois, 1868–1945* (Urbana, 1945), Part 1.
2. This report actually is a discussion of a Westergaard report. Westergaard was a principal consultant on the dam.
3. The following five publications are examples of the range of his contributions: "A Distribution Procedure for the Analysis of Slabs Continuous over Flexible Beams," *Illinois Engineering Experiment Station Bulletin* 304 (1938); "An Engineering Approach to Blast-resistant Design," *Transactions, ASCE* (1956); "Effects of Earthquakes on Dams and Embankments," Fifth Rankine Lecture, Institute of Civil Engineers, London, Geotech-

nique, 1965; with W. J. Hall, "Development of Criteria for Seismic Review of Selected Nuclear Power Plants," U.S. Nuclear Regulatory Commission, Report NUREG/CR-0098, 1978; with W. J. Hall, "Earthquake Spectra and Design," monograph, Earthquake Engineering Research Institute, 1982.

4. Nathan Newmark, John A. Blume, and Leo Corning, *Design of Multi-Story Reinforced Concrete Buildings for Earthquake Motion* (Chicago: Portland Cement Association, 1961); Nathan Newmark and Emilio Rosenblueth, *Fundamentals of Earthquake Engineering* (Englewood Cliffs, N.J.: Prentice-Hall, 1971).

MAYNARD BRICHFORD

CHAPTER 11

Robert C. Zuppke:

The Performing Art of Football Coaching

In the first half of the twentieth century, America was involved in two world wars, a major economic depression, the cultural assimilation of a substantial immigrant population, the rapid development of public land-grant universities, and a dramatic increase in interest in sports. A diverse nation of competing ethnic and religious groups regarded baseball, football, and basketball as distinctive activities for Americanization. Public participation and support for these three sports symbolized the emergence of a popular sports culture.

A significant interest in the performing arts arose on college campuses. With new technologies, students, alumni, and faculty watched motion pictures and listened to radios. Among the most festive and popular forms of mass entertainment were football games at the stadium. The performers were football heroes and the artists were the coaches who directed the annual productions. Walter Camp, John Heisman, Knute Rockne, Amos Stagg, Fielding Yost, and Bob Zuppke were better known and better paid than their academic colleagues. Among successful coaches, Bob Zuppke stood out as an artist on the athletic field, with the media, and at the easel.

When the century began, Robert C. Zuppke was a twenty-one-year-old student at Milwaukee Normal School. The son of Franz and Hermine Zuppke, he was born in Berlin on July 2, 1879. In 1881, the family settled on Milwaukee's south side. Zuppke attended public schools and West High School, excelling in drawing and mathematics. In 1898, he entered the Normal School, where he quarterbacked a football team that lost its three games. Graduating in 1901, he entered the University of Wisconsin as a junior in 1903. He took eleven history, three philosophy, and two psychology courses, and decorated meticulous notes with sketches of locomotives and young ladies. He did not make the football team, but was on the practice squad and attended games. He saw the varsity play against Chicago coached by Amos Stagg, and against Minnesota coached by Henry Williams. As a senior, he was a guard on a championship basketball team.

Graduating from Wisconsin on June 22, 1905, Zuppke spent a year as an artist in New York. In 1906, he secured a position as football coach and gymnasium director at the high school in Muskegon, Michigan, where he organized gymnasium classes into small competitive groups with distinctive names and supervised twenty-two basketball teams. He coached swimming, track, and basketball and taught two history classes. Students were impressed by a teacher who compared Roman armies with football teams. He painted and swam at the beach, but football was "all he would talk or think about." He was a drillmaster, who experimented with punt formations and "flea flicker" lateral passes. In four years, the team had a 28–4 record and defeated Saginaw for the state championship.

In 1910, Oak Park High School in west suburban Chicago hired Zuppke for $2,000 to coach five teams and teach five history and three gymnasium classes. He reorganized gymnasium work and supervised physical education for 355 boys. He took fifteen football players to postseason games in Oregon and Washington in 1910. In 1911 and 1912, they went to Boston and won interscholastic championships by defeating St. John's and Everett high schools. The team was undefeated in thirty-nine games.

While Zuppke developed the art of high school football coaching, college football became a prominent performing art. Midwestern intercollegiate football competition began in the 1880s. Illinois played its first football game on October 2, 1890. As the game's popularity increased, alumni and faculty became active in the association. Illinois had successful seasons, but had difficulty attracting players to a location over a hundred miles from a metropolitan area. In 1901, it trailed Michigan, Chicago, Minnesota, Northwestern, and Wisconsin in student enrollment. By 1903, Chicago, Illinois, and Michigan were playing twelve, fourteen-, and thirteen-game schedules. In 1905, a national outcry resulting from publicity concerning football injuries and deaths caused Western Conference universities to adopt five-game schedules. From 1905 to 1910, rules revisions opened up the game by expanding the use of the forward pass and specifying legal formations. Limited schedules reduced concerns about injuries, and eligibility regulations controlled professionalization.

The effectiveness of professional sports administrators and coaches became evident in the dominance of Michigan with Coach Fielding Yost and Chicago with Coach Amos Stagg. From 1895 to 1912, Michigan won 89 percent of its Western Conference games, Chicago won 81 percent, Illinois won 49 percent. Illinois presidents, alumni, and trustees were impressed by the free publicity given to football and the 27,000 spectators who watched the 1905 Chicago-Michigan game. From 1904 to 1912, Illinois compiled a 1–7–1 record against Chicago.

Illinois's director of physical training, George Huff, played on the university's first football team and was active in the Alumni Association. When the university's football games replaced spring baseball in popularity, Huff sought a promising young coach. Oak Park alumni Robert F. and George C. Carr called his attention to Zuppke's record. On December 13, 1912, Zuppke signed a three-year contract for $2,750, beginning September 20, 1913. Holding the lowest academic rank as an associate, his salary was slightly less than the $3,000 paid full professors.

Illinois was an expanding university in the third most populous state. Land-grant universities supplied thousands with the education required for business, industry, and agriculture. Railroads, automobiles, hard roads, typewriters, and telephones bound the nation together, and industry and technology created demands for educated men and women. A proliferation of academic specialties accompanied rising enrollments and increasing employment opportunities. Specialized engineering and commercial education supplemented, and often displaced, traditional academic disciplines. College education included classroom lectures, laboratory work, tests, field trips, and physical education. Extracurricular education occurred in concerts, dances, campus shows, and intramural and intercollegiate athletics.

The publications and extensive newspaper coverage of Yale's football coach, Walter Camp, touted football as an attractive part of student life and culture at the university. The administration saw athletics as an activity that provided favorable publicity. Faculty members were alarmed by riotous student behavior in class contests, such as push ball, flag rushes, sack rushes, and periodic vandalism of local businesses. By 1916, all class contests were discontinued. Loyal alumni were spectators at football games. Football's popularity made it a commercial entertainment property, which yielded an annual "profit." The revenues supported minor and intramural sports. The commercial beneficiaries of college sports were railroads, hotels, restaurants, movie houses, newspapers, and stores selling sporting goods and college paraphernalia.

Zuppke and Fanny Erwin, whom he had married in 1908 in Muskegon, arrived in Urbana in 1913. They found a small town bordering a rapidly expanding state university with 4,369 students. The Illinois Central railroad, running from Chicago to New Orleans, passed through Champaign a mile west of the campus. William McKinley's traction line afforded rail connections from the campus to the Illinois Central, St. Louis, and Indianapolis. The surrounding great swamp was being drained and becoming the fertile "Grand Prairie" envisioned by early land promoters and bankers. Muddy streets were paved with bricks, but the football team still practiced in a "mudhole."

A large crowd watched the first practice on March 29, 1913. In April, Zuppke spoke to alumni in Peoria and Springfield about college sport and football psychology. He stated that the game developed physical and moral courage by overcoming pain and increasing self-possession. Football ability was determined by a vital brain, executing the dictates of an aggressive mind. Noting that inexperienced men were creatures of habit, he said the coach's advice must be pounded into these green men by constant repetition in practice. Conceding that football was not a trade or a profession, he said it was helpful, but of secondary importance, in college. The team captain hailed a new era due to Zuppke's persistence and dogged determination and "the willingness of the men to be driven."

The Illinois football schedule required fight and determination. The team's record placed it in the middle of the Western Conference. After Michigan's withdrawal in 1912, Stagg's Chicago Maroons were the dominant team. Wisconsin and Minnesota were next. Zuppke won his first three games against Kentucky, Missouri, and Northwestern, but closed the season with a tie with Purdue and losses to Chicago and Minnesota. Finding Stagg's Chicago teams to be feared, Zuppe worked "to push Stagg from that throne." On November 1, Illinois lost to Chicago 28–7 before 19,000 fans at Stagg Field. After the game, he took the team to a cornfield several miles from Champaign. His message was "Notice the weeping skies and that the corn is down, but it will be up next year—just like you!" Two weeks later, he said the game "still sticks in my crop." For the yearbook, he wrote that the team did well considering that they were slow afoot and made "costly spiritless relaxations." He predicted that if they maintained their scholastic standing, possessed determination, and underwent intelligent training and arduous preparation, that it would make them better men and contribute to future success.

With a forceful personality and inexhaustible energy, Zuppke coached his team to a conference championship in his second year. A versatile backfield included George ("Potsy") Clark at quarterback, 142-pound Harold Pogue at halfback, Oak Park's Bart Macomber as kicker, and Gene Schobinger at fullback. Pogue and Schobinger were track stars. Schobinger recalled the many facets of his coach's complicated mind. "There was rare intelligence, humor, sarcasm, irony, kindliness, ready wit, philosophy, but above all a dynamic energy radiating from him to spark his every action and his teams." Illinois used the "T" spread and deep punt formations in an open style and an array of forward and lateral passes that gave an advantage to faster and smaller players. After a 31–0 win over Ohio State, alumni reported that Zuppke's "machine . . . runs in the most thrilling ways." Two trainloads of fans went to Evanston to see a 33–0 win at Northwestern. On November 14, Illinois defeated Chicago 21–7. The fans threw so many straw hats on the field that "it looked like a wheat threshing." Zuppke later rated this as "the best college football team I ever saw." On December 16, Huff signed him to a five-year contract at $4,000 a year.

Before the 1915 season, Zuppke warned of overconfidence. Champions often tended to overlook football rules, training, and conditioning. Despite a "green" line, Illinois had a nucleus of men with proven ability. Led by Captain John W. Watson at center, the Illini compiled a 3–0–2 record for a shared conference championship. A player recalled that, "to put it mildly," he "was entirely out of sympathy with his football coach," but that in later years he came to "realize the value of discipline and hard work," which the coach "so ably expounded." "You worked the tail off of us but we did not lose any games in 1914 and 1915—which seems to indicate that you knew better than we did what was good for us."

After the undefeated seasons, Zuppke cautioned St. Louis alumni that "dark days" were bound to come. The 1916 season began with a 30–0 win over Kansas. The dark days began with losses to Colgate and Ohio State. Captain Macomber produced a 14–7 Illinois win at Purdue. On November 4, Illinois met an undefeated Minnesota team, which had tied them for the 1915 championship. Preparing his team for an expected defeat, Zuppke celebrated with a dinner and show the evening before the game. A spread formation and a pass interception gave Illinois a two-touchdown lead. Zuppke then directed a tenacious defense and stalling tactics by Macomber that earned a 14–9 victory. Thousands of fans at Illinois Field followed telegraphic reports of the game by watching a sliding gourd on a wire and responded with a "roar that crashed over the prairie" and a two-day celebration. From 1913 to 1929, Zuppke's teams won 70 percent of their games and claimed seven outright or shared Big Ten championships in 1914–15, 1918–19, 1923, and 1927–28.

World War I provided opportunities to arouse popular enthusiasm for football by exposing prospective students to the game, and it provided advocates with data on the necessity for physical education and fitness training. Zuppke did not recruit players, but was available on campus. He advised alumni and friends that prospective players should write him about admission and contact fraternities about campus visits. He never missed a practice. He was less interested in training rules if players performed well on the field. Ernie Lovejoy, quarterback in 1919, recalled that he was scared of Zuppke and doubted that "any of his players really loved the guy, but their respect and affection were tremendous, and their production prodigious."

In 1918 and 1919, Illinois again claimed Big Ten titles. In 1918, after losing two games to Navy teams in Chicago, they scored 83 points and shut out Iowa, Wisconsin, Ohio State, and Chicago. In 1919, led by Ralph Fletcher and Lawrence Walquist, they lost at Wisconsin, and then ended the season by using Zuppke's "queer formations" and "fancy emergency plays" to defeat Chicago, Minnesota, Michigan, and Ohio State. Zuppke was skeptical about claims for the invention of plays. For those who credited Notre Dame's Knute Rockne with the first forward pass in 1913, he observed that "there were 70,000 passes completed in the Midwest in 1906—when Rock was in knee pants." Because of his fondness for trick plays and surprises, sports writers credited Zuppke with inventing the spiral pass from center and the multiple passes of his "flea flicker" play. The only football innovation that he claimed was the regular use of the huddle for calling plays.

In 1917, Illinois won a 28–0 game with Camp Funston in Kansas before an estimated crowd of 50,000 soldiers. In 1918, 1,700 students participated in an intramural program. The Student Army Training Corps fielded sixteen football teams. In 1921, Zuppke's team scored a major upset. On November 19, Illinois was 0–4 in Big Ten games as they prepared to play Ohio State, which needed a win for the conference title. A spirited pass defense stymied the Ohio attack. Laurie Walquist caught a screen pass for

Coach Zuppke at a football practice, ca. 1930.

a 7–0 victory for the "Fighting Illini." Zuppke described the major upset of his coaching career with an assessment that "you should be able to get one lemonade out of a bunch of lemons." Returning to a celebration in Champaign, he told the team that they were creating "an imperishable, undying tradition."

Unfortunately, the players were soon involved in two other traditions: speculative investment and compensation for services rendered, or gambling and "professionalism." The city of Carlinville promoted a November 27 Sunday game with Taylorville. A Notre Dame player from Carlinville invited several teammates to join him for $200 each and expenses. Word of heavy betting spread among local and regional gamblers. An Illinois sophomore from Taylorville also invited several teammates to join him for the game. Illinois players entered the game to protect the Taylorville lead. Ten thousand spectators enjoyed a 16–0 Taylorville victory. On December 11, George Huff received an anonymous letter alleging that Illinois players received a percentage of the gambling "take." After the 1919 Chicago Black Sox scandal, Huff led the antigambling fight at Illinois and condemned gambling in alumni club speeches. The Illinois faculty banned nine athletes who played in Illinois's only win over Notre Dame.

Zuppke's skills were appreciated by the university's presidents. Arriving in 1904, University of Illinois President Edmund J. James was an aggressive builder of the university and adept in securing publicity for a growing institution. He attacked the problem of establishing a large university in a small prairie town by securing legislative support and hiring faculty for a research institution. David Kinley, who succeeded James in 1919, told alumni that football prospects were encouraging. "We have high hopes the Illinois eagle will scream in victory in the homecoming game with our old rivals of Chicago." He had graduated from Yale four years after Walter Camp, the "father of American football," and four years before Amos Stagg, the first full-time college coach. At his inauguration, a Yale professor noted that the campus was "encompassed by vast prairies, highly cultivated, studded with farmsteads and villages from which come the great majority of its 10,000 students" and characterized it as "an oasis of intellectuality in a desert of fertility."

Under Kinley, the university continued the construction of athletic facilities. A huge armory in 1914, a 60,000-seat stadium in 1923, a 7,000-seat gymnasium in 1925, and a women's gymnasium and ice rink in 1931 provided brick-and-mortar symbols of growth. Construction contracts and the crowds at athletic events benefited the local economy. When the stadium was completed in 1923, the president began distributing tickets to trustees, legislators, and "distinguished guests." In a 1919 open letter to Zuppke, Kinley wrote: "I have watched with pleasure and pride the splendid progress of the football team under your direction this fall and have rejoiced with all other Illini in its great success. I pictured you as a leader of men, fusing their individual wills, merging their characteristics, combining their activities into one complex unit of force for the accomplishment of your purposes. That is an educational achievement of no small moment. It is the training of character. You were teaching self-control, obedience to orders, respect for authority, surrender of self-seeking, cooperation, and unity of purpose. The development of these traits is a large part of the making of men."

Zuppke's close and harmonious relationship with George Huff was a major factor in his success. The striking physical differences between the six-foot, 240-pound Huff and the five-foot-seven, 160-pound Zuppke was accompanied by mutual confidence and a strong commitment to amateur athletics and good sportsmanship. Illinois was noted for "simon-pure" athletic programs and seldom incurred conference warnings or penalties. Zuppke was also on good terms with John L. Griffith, who was an Illinois coaching instructor before serving as Big Ten commissioner from 1922 to 1944. Strong line play was instrumental in Zuppke's offensive and defensive strategies. Justa M. Lindgren combined a career as a chemical engineer with service as line coach from 1904 to 1947. Trainer Matt Bullock handled conditioning, injuries, and menus from 1914 to 1941. Burt Ingwersen, Milt

Olander, Frank Rokusek, and Ray Eliot were outstanding members of his coaching staff. Ingwersen recalled that Zuppke was fiery and unpredictable, and that one never knew what he would say. He was sarcastic if a player didn't work hard. They couldn't get very close to him, but respected him as a great psychologist and strategist.

Zuppke kept detailed notes from his Wisconsin psychology courses. After 1920, psychology professor Coleman Griffith attended football practices and discussed applying psychological testing and measurement to football. A pioneer in sports psychology, he respected Zuppke's "extraordinary knowledge of human behavior and of the fundamental facts of psychology" and admired his ability to apply psychology to football and campaign strategy. He thanked the coach for the "instruction you have given me" and the privilege of seeing psychology as "a science of actual human beings." Zuppke appreciated the compliment and liked to see him on the field. "Red" Grange recalled that Griffith, "disguised as a common human being," talked with players during practice and prepared a "special psychological serum" for each freshman. Griffith published *The Psychology of Coaching* in 1926 and Zuppke published *Coaching Football* in 1930. In his book, Zuppke observed that coaching required "courage, tact, perseverance and dynamic inspirational qualities." He advised students to keep a respectful distance from players and praise sparingly, but not be unduly aloof. A coach should be a developer of men and encourage loyalty win or lose. By 1935, Zuppke and Griffith had compiled a manuscript on "The Psychology of Football," which called for the study of reaction time, memory, learning, attention, emotional balance, and perception. These topics formed the bases for many of Zuppke's aphorisms.

Aphorisms or witticisms, Zuppke's quips were well received by audiences. With a staccato delivery, he combined humor and criticism in pithy prose. Speaking at sports and civic dinners, he delivered his messages in an hour, and had the audience clamoring for more. A 1920 collection of published "Zuppkeisms" included: "We don't set out to win championships at Illinois, we just go out to prove that our team is as game as any other." Among later "Zuppkeisms" were: "The greatest athlete is one who can carry a nimble brain faster than anybody else to the place of action and execution," "Football is still a great kicking game—however, the kickers are in the stands," "Neutrality is being afraid of one side and ashamed of the other," and "All quitters are good losers." One of his witticisms was that it took a poet in the press box to make an All-American. Talent in the press box was also an asset for a football coach.

In 1922, Louis M. ("Mike") Tobin succeeded John Griffith as director of athletic publicity. He prepared statistics and press releases for the media, distributed complimentary tickets, composed tributes for ceremonies, edited publications on the athletic coaching and football programs, and collaborated with Zuppke on articles for *Liberty* and the *Saturday Evening Post*. One of his challenges was interpreting the coach for the media. Ted Ashby of the *Des Moines Register* described the coach as a "gymnastic conversationalist" who could be "extremely funny" and also employ sarcasm with "an edge on it like a new razor blade." The *New York Times* reporter John Kieran wrote that Zuppke would talk about football "or any other subject under the sun and pour out his ideas for hours, thirteen words to the dozen, with gestures." Red Grange recalled that Zuppke was never at a loss for words and that "he'd say anything" to inspire the team or create a good story for reporters.

Big Ten football championships between 1914 and 1923 brought personal financial security for Zuppke. By 1924, his $8,000 salary included $1,600 from the university, $1,500 from the coaching school, and $4,900 from the Athletic Association. In 1929, it was increased to $10,000. Summer coaching schools provided excellent contacts with high school and college coaches. Late in 1913, Big Ten faculty representatives condemned professional coaches. At the same time, Huff toured eastern universities and found a big demand for coaches. Illinois approved his plan to teach physical training and athletic coaching. In 1914, Zuppke began teaching a summer session football course for high school and college teachers. In the next decade, 1,200 coaches came for the summer course. In 1920, the College of Education approved a four-year course in athletic coaching and physical education. In 1922, Zuppke and Ernest Bearg published the summer lectures as *Football Techniques and Tactics*, in which they diagrammed plays and addressed the coach's moral obligation for good sportsmanship following the rules. At the December 20, 1924, meeting of the National Collegiate Athletic Association (NCAA), in New York, Zuppke was elected president of the American Football Coaches Association to succeed John Heisman. By 1925, six Big Ten universities and Notre Dame advertised summer schools. In 1929, the Carnegie Report noted that the Illinois Athletic Coaching program was an example of "professionalism." The university hired professional educators to prepare students for professional careers. The strong demand for physical education administrators, teachers, and coaches created a national market for students with a degree in athletic coaching. The four-year program produced athletic directors and coaches until 1932.

Football's popularity demonstrated the need for a stadium. Illinois Field with its wooden bleachers and youths in nearby trees was inadequate. Three thousand of the 23,000 spectators at an Ohio State game in Urbana were Ohio State rooters. Budgetary strategies led the university to seek private funds for a large stadium and war memorial. A highly visible structure for widely publicized events would be an impressive demonstration of public support for the university's building program. Zuppke's coaching success led to his role as a moving force behind the construction of the Memorial Stadium. On April 25, 1921, Zuppke and Huff spoke to 7,000 students at mass meetings. Zuppke's sentences "zig-zagged" across the halls "like lightning." His appeal produced $700,000 in student pledges, which was far beyond what was expected. Under Huff's guidance, the university had established eighty-one Illini Clubs in Illinois and fifty-one clubs in other states. Zuppke and Huff spoke at alumni meetings in the East and on a trip to California. In December at the Chicago Illini Club, Huff reported $1,642,000 in pledges. "Robert the Devil" talked about philosophy, psychology, architecture, religion, politics, literature, relativity, science, agriculture, law, music, and football. The "whirlwind orator" concluded "in a blaze of pyrotechnics." He served on the Stadium Drive Executive Committee and subscribed for $1,000 for the fund. The drive was the university's first major attempt to secure private funds.

In 1923, seventy candidates reported for the three-hour spring practices. The prospect of a stadium and an eight-game schedule created a demand for tickets. Although not listed on varsity list, sophomore Harold ("Red") Grange scored three touchdowns in an opening win over Nebraska. He added two more in a 21–7 win over Butler and one in a 9–6 win at Iowa. On October 27, when Illinois played Northwestern before 33,000 at Wrigley Field, Grange scored three touchdowns. On November 3, Illinois hosted the Chicago Maroons in the first game in the stadium; 60,632 spectators, including 7,500 Chicago rooters, sat in the rain. A few complained about plowing through a sea of mud between the trains and the stadium. Grange's touchdown supplied a 7–0 win. Chicago radio station KYW carried the game and hundreds of letters were received from owners of wireless crystal sets. Illinois defeated unbeaten Wisconsin 10–0 in the first Dad's Day game. The season ended at Ohio Stadium, where Grange ran for a thirty-two-yard touchdown. At the Chicago banquet, Zuppke kept alumni in an uproar with his "cyclonic sallies." The *Chicago Tribune*'s Walter Eckersall noted that five wins without giving up a point indicated that few of Zuppke's teams were weak defensively and praised the coach for building offenses around talented players.

The stadium was dedicated at the October 18, 1924 homecoming game, when Illinois hosted Michigan, which had not lost since 1921. Grange scored four touchdowns in the first twelve minutes to lead his team to a 39–14 victory. Eckersall credited Zuppke for designing plays for Grange and developing the blocking that led to the touchdown runs. The Athletic Association profit on the game was $74,127. Every fall, 1924 fullback Dwight Follett recalled the "sound of crashing lines" at old Illinois Field, the battle cry "Get in there, you bloke!," the "creak of tackling dummy," the "smell of leather, wintergreen oil, and wool jerseys, the burn of benzine on taped ankles, the warmth of a hot shower, and the memories of a vital little man in an enormous lambskin lined coat." He recalled Friday evenings at the country club before an open fire with Zuppke "trying to relight a half-inch cigar that had gone out" while telling stories about the "giants and boobs" of other days. "I can see you walking back and forth, head down, hands behind your back. I can almost hear you tell about the game tomorrow and feel the surge of excitement that sends a shiver down my back and leaves my legs weak."

In 1925, Grange gained national fame on October 31, by leading a team with three losses to a 24–2 win over Pennsylvania. The intersectional victory supported Zuppke's claims for the superiority of midwestern football. After a season-ending 14–9 win at Ohio State, Grange signed a contract with the Chicago Bears in the National Football League. On July 15, 1926, Zuppke held the Los Angeles Illini Club audience spellbound for forty-five minutes, chatted with Grange, and then joined a thousand Illini among the 62,000 who watched Grange and the Bears defeat the Los Angeles Tigers. "Red" made $50,000 in Los Angeles and critics cited the Bears' nationwide exhibition tour as a commercialization.

In 1926, the Illini again defeated Pennsylvania. Zuppke's defensive alignments stifled the Quakers' offense, and Frosty Peters drop-kicked a winning field goal. The year's football profit declined from the record $305,168 in 1925 to a respectable $220,000. Conference championships in 1927 and 1928 brought extensive publicity, which attracted football talent. Grange recalled that "every kid in Illinois wanted to play for Coach Zuppke if he thought he could make it." Hugh Fullerton in *Liberty* hailed Zuppke as "the keenest and most analytical type of coach" and added that "the talkative, merry, witty little Dutchman" was supreme in football. Zuppke attributed the game's popularity to automobile transportation. At a football convocation celebrating the 1927 undefeated season, Zuppke reminded students that they were a small nest compared with the world, even though they included plenty of "hard-boiled eggs." He advised them "to keep moving, thus to fight against time." He explained that the team's success was due to "harmony, exactness, speed, punctuality and enthusiasm." At the fall banquet, Kinley said that any evils in the sport were due to the public and the alumni, and added that he loved Zupp "in spite of his vagaries." Zuppke added remarks about Mike Tobin, Frosty Peters, Butch Nowack, President Kinley, Arthur Schopenhauer, and Friedrich Nietzsche. He ended with, "Our defense is our home. Cooperation, harmony, lack of envy, strong hearts—that is our combination." In Chicago, Knute Rockne got in some "good cracks" at Zuppke's expense, but praised him for playing difficult schedules, He mentioned "the little Dutchman's pocket editions of the psychology classics." Zuppke conceded that Rockne was a better storyteller, and said that he relied on coaching.

Amateurism was the underlying credo of college athletics. Administrators proclaimed it and critics responded with charges of involuntary servitude. High salaries paid to professional coaches and the hiring of assistant coaches contrasted with the enforced amateurism of the players. Gross inequalities in faculty compensation reflected demands made by appropriations and actions of the legislature and trustees. Profitable enterprises that captured public attention were especially favored. The problems of financial aid for student athletes arose from athletic competition in a society dominated by the ethos of market demand. Public demand for entertainment, corporate demand for accountants and engineers, government demand for lawyers and scientists, and popular demand for medical practitioners and performing artists shaped curricula in public universities. Colleges of Agriculture, Engineering, Commerce, and Physical Education developed along with intercollegiate sports.

As Grange toured with the Chicago Bears, academic criticism of intercollegiate football gathered momentum. In April 1926, the American Association of University Professors called for immediate reforms, and charged that football caused a "distortion of values" and that professional salaries would "unsettle ideas and ideals." University administrators denied that abuses were as bad as alleged. The New York Times editorialized that "the idea that young men may be made to hero-worship scholarship by blocking their tendency to hero-worship athletic prowess involved a non sequitur of the kind" that led to Prohibition. Under pressure to deemphasize football, Big Ten athletic directors called a meeting in 1927. When a four-game schedule was proposed, Zuppke asked who was going to pay their salaries and pay for intramural activities. He said that presidents didn't "expect us to schedule ourselves out of business." His effective speech forestalled a curtailment of schedules.

Since the 1890s, critics of "big-time" football called for its abolition or drastic deemphasis. The 1929 Carnegie Report on intercollegiate athletics was a direct challenge to athletic directors and coaches. Although Illinois was the only public Big Ten university listed as not using subsidies to recruit athletes, it couldn't evade the broad charge of commercialization and allegations that sports were an over-rated by-product of the educational process. Zuppke questioned the critics' understanding of football and claimed it was educational for both players and spectators. He held that the millions who attended games testified to its popularity as entertainment, and that football provided communication with a mass audience about sportsmanship and higher education. Professionalization of athletes also increased awareness of higher education. A Seattle report described Grange as "collegiate to the soles of his gold-bringing feet." Zuppke reflected public opinion in confessing that "we do not know when amateurism becomes professionalism." He and Huff obtained George Halas's support for a National Football League rule that collegians couldn't be signed as professionals until their classes graduated. The Carnegie Report attacked intersectional games as commercialization, but administrators sought them for the financial return and publicity. On April 11, 1928, Kinley, Huff, and Zuppke met with the Army coach and scheduled the military academy's first game in Champaign in 1929 and a 1930 return match in New York.

An opponent of recruiting, Zuppke refused to contact prospective football players. Illinois had no athletic scholarships or "free rides." Eighty percent of the athletes worked their way through school. When the president's office suggested a legislative scholarship, Zuppke objected, as Illinois would be known as a proselytizing school, and he claimed that political scholarships would be bad publicity. Winning football was popular with alumni clubs, which took a keen interest in the team's success and held football banquets. Alumni, coaches, and former players asked Zuppke to meet prospective athletes. The Carnegie Report listed fraternities as a means of recruiting football players, and cited fraternity rushing at high school athletic meets on campus. Nearly all Illinois varsity players were fraternity members. They were not concentrated in one or two fraternities, but distributed among fifty houses. Male students had two housing options—boarding houses or fraternities.

The Carnegie Report's criticisms were not isolated events. Academic historians have been nearly unanimous in condemning intercollegiate football. Their studies have often been lengthy recitations of abuses, crises, hypocrisy, hysteria, problems, professionalism, recruitment of unqualified students, reform failures, scams, scandals, unethical acts, and questions about the relevance of athletics to higher education. The critics often adopted a patronizing tone in discussing exercise and sports. Sports claimed a major presence in urban life, and the print and broadcast media met popular demands for increased sports coverage. Extensive coverage provided ample evidence for both the excessive glorification of sports and the failures to resolve its problems. In 1939, University of Chicago President Robert Hutchins persuaded Chicago's trustees to discontinue intercollegiate football. While he could ignore public opinion, administrators in public universities could not. Politicians delighted in public appearances at games. University officials knew the value of favors in relations with those who funded their operations, shaped public opinion and decided legal questions. By 1937, the President's Office was delivering 3,255 "free" tickets to guests of the president and the governor, state officers, supreme court justices, state department heads, ex-governors, legislators, heads of industrial and labor organizations, newspapermen, and other guests. Despite financial problems during the Depression, football grew in popularity. Alumni nostalgia, young athletic heroes, publicity in the sports pages, radio broadcasts, movies, building contracts for stadia, bands and cheerleaders, free tickets for politicians, and competition among universities contributed to make football an All-American sport.

By 1929, Illinois football was enjoying sunny days. The defending Big Ten champions finished in second place with a 3–1–1 record and set a home attendance record that would last until 1946. Most of the games were broadcasted by Chicago or university stations. The Illini closed the season with decisive wins over Army, Chicago, and Ohio State. At the Army game, Secretary of War James W. Good. Governor Louis L. Emmerson, assorted generals, Grantland Rice, Paul Gallico, and nearly 70,000 fans attended the first appearance of the West Point team and cadets in the Midwest. Gallico reported that "for thrill and color, the western bands and cheering sections are in a class by themselves." Commenting on Zuppke's style, the *Alumni News* reported that his charm is his disconnectedness. "Take a tip from Zupp and be abrupt, contradictory, fill your talk with spinners, fake punts, and what have you. Keep the audience guessing. Say the ideal education is three years in high school, three years in jail and three years in college." At the Chicago Illini Club dinner, the "Dutch Master" leaped from the English of the street to the "super compounds of the scientist and philosopher." His German accent, humorous stories, and nicknames held the attention of audiences. Speaking to the Chicago Executives Club, he regaled them with humorous stories, prohibition jokes, comments on stu-

Robert Zuppke as a performing artist, ca. 1934.

dent behavior, classical allusions, and the benefits of football. Coaches were obliged to win games, receive recognition by ratings and championships, inspire the team during practices and games, raise funds for the athletic program, deal with the media, attract crowds to home games, recruit talented players, and assist in placing graduates. These activities required a public image and ability to generate publicity. Zuppke excelled as an inspirational speaker.

The 1930s highlight was an appearance in New York. The team's train arrived for a Friday practice at Yankee Stadium and Zuppke's evening NBC radio talk. On Saturday morning the 160-piece Illinois band paraded from Grand Central Station down Fifth Avenue to their hotel playing the "March of the Illini." They were preceded by a Fox Movietone truck. Playing "Illinois Loyalty," they led 1,600 West Point cadets into the stadium. After the game, they played a half hour concert for NBC. The band's performances were hailed by the five New York daily newspapers, one of which noted that the football team "was also present." Playing before 70,000, Illinois was outweighed eleven pounds per man by an Army team that had a 6–0 record and included two former Illinois players. The defense took advantage of a muddy field and excellent punting to hold on for a scoreless first half. They made only one first down in the game, and lost 13–0. The Army game afforded excellent publicity.

The onset of the Depression brought lower appropriations and financial cutbacks. Sports successes were overshadowed by financial problems. In a disastrous 1931 season, Illinois lost all six Big Ten games. At the postseason banquet, Zupp ripped into his players' faults, but tempered criticisms with witticisms and occasional "downright sympathy and understanding." After a 5–4 season in 1932, he said that in 1907, he was the "only coach who could spell psychology" and quoted George Huff: "I believe everything you say, Zupp, but I wouldn't say it." In 1932, Zuppke's salary was cut to $8,500 before being restored to $10,000 in 1935. It exceeded that of the deans of Engineering and Liberal Arts and Sciences. Zuppke's salary was also supplemented by the "New Zuppke Line" of football equipment, which the Rawlings Company introduced in April 1925. From 1929 to 1940, he received additional income from the "Ned Brant" sports comic strip. In 1930, he contracted with the National Newspaper Service to provide feature articles for sports pages. His articles were distributed by the Christy Walsh sports syndicate to a national newspaper market. He received $250 for speaking "to the stuffed shirts at their banquets."

A Chicago reporter characterized Zuppke's demeanor as "shrewd and thoughtful and instinctive" and observed that he seldom stepped "out of character." His German accent was "retained long beyond the day he mastered precise enunciation." In 1941, Ryan recognized that "age may have blasted a gulf between Zuppke and the undergraduates," but the sincere warmth of the players' admiration for Zupp bridged the gap.

In 1935, the Illini traveled by train via Arizona to a Southern California game. The Trojans outweighed them by twenty-one pounds per man. Zuppke "uncovered his flea circus" and the backs passed for 109 yards and a 19–0 win. For its halftime show, the Southern California band formed an outline of Illinois and a silhouette of Zuppke. The team was gone for a week and a half. Its triumphal return was greeted by crowds along the railroad track. Six thousand welcomed them at the Illinois Central Station. A second welcome packed Wright Street on campus and the *Alumni News* editorialized that the "athletic depression" had ended. A week later, Iowa defeated Illinois 19–0 in Champaign. Zuppke acknowledged that injuries, fumbles, and poor kicking led to their 1–4 Big Ten record. At the Chicago dinner, Huff praised Zuppke as "one of the great coaches in America—a great coach, not a great recruiter." Commissioner John Griffith hailed Illinois as an "example for the world in the conduct of and its attitude toward athletics."

Bob and Fanny Zuppke enjoyed small town life in central Illinois, where football players would drop in for visits. At games, Mrs. Zuppke sat behind the Illinois bench. She joined the coach in postgame visits to the infirmary. She kept a scrapbook containing accounts of Illinois wins and explained that "I remember only the victories." In 1926, they moved from an Urbana apartment to a larger one in Champaign, where Zuppke had an art studio. Their home life was centered on reading, social events, theater, and dancing. He once declared that the leading contact games in college were football, wrestling, and dancing. At home, they played chess and bridge. He paid little attention to clothing and relied on her judgment. Her September 1936 death deprived Zuppke of "the only pal I ever had."

The 1935–38 average attendance in the huge stadium was 24,694. The "profit" dropped from $225,670 in 1930 to $106,109 in 1941. David Kinley referred to this time as "our period of football depression." He observed that in many universities this would have brought demands to fire the coach and attributed Illinois's "status of mental balance" and "sane viewpoint" to Huff's high standards. Meanwhile, the Athletic Association directors discussed the possibility that a new coach would silence the "wolves" who demanded victories and "hotel keepers, shopkeepers and commercial critics" who depended on business generated by winning football. Zuppke said that "no director of athletics as a rule holds office longer than two unsuccessful football coaches."

George Huff died on October 1, 1936. On February 27, 1937, the university trustees appointed Wendell S. Wilson as athletics director. On October 30, 1937, the association celebrated Zuppke's twenty-fifth anniversary season. Wilson arranged a colorful halftime tribute to the coach, who received hundreds of congratulatory letters from former players, alumni, coaches, and friends. Many players regarded football as the most important college influence in their careers. The public tributes and testimonials rekindled Zuppke's determination to stay and demonstrate his support among alumni and former players. The directors recognized that terminating Zuppke's twenty-five years at Illinois required careful planning.

In November 1938, depressed by losses to Notre Dame, Northwestern, and Michigan, an attack in the *St. Louis Globe-Democrat,* and questioning by Peoria alumni, Zuppke asked Wilson what he would get if he decided to retire before reaching the age of sixty-five in 1944. Wilson contacted President Arthur Willard, who approved any retirement plan accepted by Zuppke. Wilson had the legal counsel draw up a contract, which called for the coach's retirement in 1939 and becoming a consultant at $7,500 a year until 1944. Wilson obtained the directors' approval and secured Zuppke's signature on the evening before the November 29 trustees meeting in Chicago. News of the resignation had leaked to Chicago alumni and news services. Reporters packed the Blackstone Hotel lobby until 2:45 P.M., when the trustees announced that the resignation was rejected. The scene of jubilation then shifted to Zuppke's Champaign apartment, where he entertained the press until midnight. The master of deceptive plays had won the final game of the season.

Zuppke's victory did not silence his critics. They requested that the trustees investigate the athletic situation. Professor Fred Russell told a Pekin Rotary banquet that a new coach would need salesmanship and showmanship, and must speak up to seventy times a year. Zuppke responded with eleven speeches after the season, before leaving for a month in Phoenix. When he heard that the "wolves" were at work, he drove 1,968 miles to Champaign in three days to meet with supportive players. Local newspaper support wavered, but Zuppke believed that the trustees would let him coach as long as he wanted to. On November 4, with a record of three losses and a tie, the Illini hosted a powerful Michigan team led by All-American Tom Harmon. Zuppke won his last major upset, 16–7. The result brought national acclaim from sports writers and laudatory fan mail from former players, Michigan Illini, and an Ohio State coach. In 1940, he faced a tough schedule, which the directors had "egged" on him. The Illini lost to Southern California, Michigan, Notre Dame, Wisconsin, Northwestern, Ohio State, and Iowa. When two close losses brought compliments from an official on the Illini's spirit, Zuppke passed them on to the team.

The coaching controversy simmered until July 1941, when President Willard recommended that Wilson be given leave on September 1, 1941, and that Zuppke be reappointed for 1941–42 on condition that he retire between September 1942 and July 1944. The Athletic Board was deadlocked with three alumni who were former football players opposed and three faculty in favor. The Trustees' Committee on Athletics noted that Zuppke "continued to assert his well-known rugged personality and eccentricities." It recommended that Wilson retire and that Zuppke confer with the administration about his employment or retirement before March 1, 1942. Its report was adopted by the board on July 15. In 1941, the Illini lost the last five games to Notre Dame, Michigan, Iowa, Ohio State, and Northwestern. Zuppke said the team was conscientious and hard working, but not equipped to play Big Ten football. He wrote that "our boys had to fight like fiends to keep from being annihilated" in every game. On November 18, he notified the trustees of his resignation as coach after the November 22 Northwestern game. Illinois lost Zuppke's final game 27–0 as 35,000 fans watched "the last strong-hold of simon-pure university athletics" fall before the Northwestern offense. Zuppke had been head football coach for twenty-nine years. During this time, Wisconsin had nine coaches, Indiana, Northwestern and Purdue seven each, Iowa six, Michigan and Minnesota five each, and Ohio State four. Zuppke recalled that Huff always consulted him. "After his death, no one did." He summed up his retirement by stating "I began to think I was an Illinois man. Finally, I found out that I was only a hired man."

Zuppke's football career claimed continued public attention. In 1942, he coached the college All-Stars against the Chicago Bears. He assisted Halas in the Bears summer camps and was consulted by other coaches who were establishing and popularizing professional football. At a 1949 testimonial, football captains from 1913 to 1941 returned for four hours of continuous adulation during radio broadcasts and banquets. After a meal with "flea-flicker" appetizers and a "razzle dazzle" steak, the guests received Dutch Master cigars and listened to "the same old Zup, flashing from humor to seriousness, defending his sport, and making his points with words snatched from his fluid vocabulary." He recalled the "golden" stadia era and argued for the preservation of amateurism. In April 1957, he declared that there were both "honest" and "commercial" football squads. The honest program "tries to avoid under-the-table operations and can't." The commercial says what it's paying boys, and keeps football under the athletic association separate from the school. He didn't like either, but "took boys from Illinois and made something of them."

Throughout Zuppke's career, he painted hundreds of oil paintings and pastels for the love of it. His art was characterized by bold, free, and impressionist landscapes. He was "a lover of untampered nature" and more interested in color than form. In Arizona winters, he painted desert and mountain scenes. In Michigan, he painted lakes and dunes. With little formal training, he visited art galleries, filled sketch books, and exhibited in six states.

After seven years of health problems, Zuppke died on December 22, 1957. He was buried next to George Huff opposite the 50-yard line of the Memorial Stadium. In 1966, the stadium's playing field was named Zuppke Field. Red Grange drew on his memory for a tribute:

> I can see him now, still out in the cold at 7 P.M., and that big sheepskin coat—on such a little guy—almost dragging the ground. Yeh, and some of us would start loafing, figuring Zup wouldn't notice. But that little Dutchman could see in the dark—from the back of his head! . . . What a guy, ferocious and kind. Understood men; knew who to pat and who to kick in the pants. Many times, after I'd scored a touchdown or two, he'd take me out and raise the devil about some mistake I made. And I did lots of wind

sprints for mistakes in practice. I'll always remember those Friday nights at the Champaign country club, with ol' Zup reminiscing in front of the fire. He'd tell us about football's old days, and most always mention the Illinois upset of Minnesota in 1916. He'd intersperse remarks about the next day's game in his reminiscing. His voice was like syrup, and it was a wonderful way to relax us. You know Zup could fire up a scrub player to kill an All-American. I'll guarantee this: No matter how inadequate it was, no Zuppke team ever took the field thinking it was beaten! Zup was an idealist. To him, proselyting was a deadly sin. Zup was a salesman. He was months setting up that great afternoon we had against Michigan. All summer long he wrote every player, warning us of Michigan's greatness and Yost's trickery. So we were keyed up to beat anybody. What a guy, Zup. He'd have gone to the end of the world for one of his players.

A NOTE ON SOURCES

Correspondence and clippings in the Robert C. Zuppke Papers (RS 28/3/20, University Archives), Athletics Association records (RG 28, University Archives). Sources for Zuppke's youth came from Milwaukee Public Library, Milwaukee County Historical Society, and University of Wisconsin Archives. Published sources included alumni and student publications, John Watterson, *College Football: History, Spectacle, Controversy* (Baltimore: Johns Hopkins University Press, 2000); Robin Lester, *Stagg's University* (Urbana: University of Illinois Press, 1995); John Carroll, *Red Grange and the Rise of Modern Football* (Urbana: University of Illinois Press, 1999); and Harold Grange, *Zuppke of Illinois* (Chicago: A.L. Glaser, 1937).

PART III

THE POSTWAR
RISE TO
PROMINENCE

CHAPTER 12

Robert Emerson and Eugene Rabinowitch:

Understanding Photosynthesis

In the late 1940s and 1950s, the University of Illinois was home to the biologist Robert Emerson and the photochemist Eugene Rabinowitch, two brilliant scientists who played pioneering roles in explaining oxygenic photosynthesis. This fundamental process of converting light to chemical energy in plants, algae, and cyanobacteria turns carbon dioxide and water into the food and oxygen that sustains all life on earth.

The setting for this pathbreaking scientific work was the University of Illlinois, in particular, the Natural History Building (NHB) in Urbana, currently used by the geology department. The side entrance to this building, somewhat hidden by an old glasshouse on Mathews Avenue, leads to the building's basement and to a rather dingy corridor along which one walks south to a dark brown door labeled 157. The old door once led to the laboratory where Emerson and Rabinowitch worked.

In 1946, Emerson, then an assistant professor of biophysics at Caltech, accepted a joint position in the University of Illinois Department of Botany as director of the "Photosynthesis Project" (institutionally directly under the Graduate College) and as research professor of botany. An experimentalist par excellence, Emerson had shown in 1932, when he was at Caltech, that only one out of hundreds of chlorophyll molecules actually engages in chemistry.[1] The rest are handmaidens who collect and funnel light energy to this special molecule. He stated, "We need only suppose that for every 2,480 (chlorophyll) molecules there is present in the cell one unit capable of reducing one molecule of carbon dioxide each time it is suitably activated by light." We now know that two such special chlorophyll molecules must be activated by light, the so-called reaction centers. Twenty-five years later, Emerson would discover at the University of Illinois that photosynthesis is more efficient when algae are exposed simultaneously to two beams of light, one in the far-red region and the other of shorter wavelength (red or blue). This major breakthrough in the field of photosynthesis later became known as the Emerson enhancement effect. The result led to our current understanding that there are two—not one— primary photosynthetic light reactions.

Emerson had come to Illinois on the condition that the university would also hire a physicist or physical chemist. He had in mind the well-known photochemist, Eugene Rabinowitch, who was then at the University of Chicago studying uranium chemistry at the Manhattan Project's Metallurgical Laboratory. By then, Rabinowitch was already well known for several major contributions. They included his discovery of the "Franck-Rabinowitch" cage effect in photochemistry (published with the 1926 physics Nobel laureate James Franck), in which one photon of light leads to a chain reaction, producing a large number of photoproducts; the photooxidation of chlorophyll in solutions; and his finding at MIT of the photogalvanic effect, the storage of solar energy in chemical reactions. He was also known for his definitive three-volume treatise on photosynthesis, published in 1945, 1951, and 1956, respectively.[2]

In 1947, Rabinowitch joined Emerson as co-director of the Photosynthesis Project. In this work, in mutual friendship and cooperation with Emerson, until the latter's death in 1959, Rabinowitch built and maintained one of the most prestigious photosynthesis centers in the world and co-directed (with others at UIUC) the teaching and research program in biophysics that evolved into the present Center for Biophysics and Computational Biology in the school of molecular and cellular biology.[3]

Rabinowitch had been trained in Berlin, where he had attended lectures by Albert Einstein, Max Planck, Max von Laue, Erwin Schrödinger, and Walther Nernst. His doctoral thesis was written under Fritz Paneth; his postdoctoral work was guided by James Franck. As a Jew, Rabinowitch became a victim of anti-semiticism and was forced to leave Germany. In Copenhagen, where he went first, he built the first difference absorption spectrophotometer at the Niels Bohr Institute for Theoretical Physics (now the Niels Bohr Institute for Astronomy, Physics, and Geophysics). He also worked at University College in London in F. G. Donnan's laboratory.

Rabinowitch's research group in Urbana involved itself in studies of the storage of light energy in chemical systems and in the chemistry of chlorophylls. His 1945 book on photosynthesis had already discussed the possibility of two-light reactions in photosynthesis. He predicted in 1956 how the process might involve an intermediate called cytochrome, whose role in the two-light reactions was then discovered in 1961 by Louis N. M. Duysens of the Netherlands, long after his visit to Rabinowitch's lab. In 1960, after those working in Emerson's laboratory had discovered the enhancement effect, which ultimately led to the two-light reaction scheme, an English biochemist, Robin Hill, published a two-light reaction scheme based on theoretical grounds.

During these years in Urbana, Rabinowitch guided his graduate students to make some of the first biophysical measurements of the primary events in photosynthesis. Paul Latimer, Steve Brody, Tom Bannister, and others made the first biophysical measurements involving the quantum yield of chlorophyll *a* fluorescence (i.e., the number of photons given off by plants per photon absorbed by plants), the lifetime of this chlorophyll fluoresence (i.e., how long the excited chlorophyll molecules live), and other spectroscopic phenomena, including the sieve effect (the lowering of absorption of light when pigments are concentrated in specific areas) and selective scattering (scattering of light that depends on the absorption properties of the pigments).

Emerson's 1932 work had suggested that there are only a few chlorophyll molecules involved in chemistry. Bessel Kok in the Netherlands discovered one of them in 1956–57, about the same time Emerson discovered the enhancement effect in Urbana. Kok had called it "P700"—700 because it specifically absorbed 700 nm far-red light. At the same time, Rabinowitch's students discovered a spectral change at 680 nm (red light), and thought they had discovered the "other" chlorophyll molecule involved in photochemistry. Unfortunately, Daniel Rubinstein, another student of Rabinowitch, showed this observation to be an artifact of changes in light emission. Rabinowitch and I, however, knew that a P680 must exist. In 1965 we proposed the existence of this second special chlorophyll that engaged in chemistry.[4] It was not until 1969 that Horst T. Witt's group in Germany demonstrated its existence.

The basement corridor leading to Emerson's and Rabinowitch's laboratories is the same one that Otto Warburg, the 1931 Nobel laureate of physiology and medicine, had walked along when he visited Urbana in 1948 from Berlin, hoping to resolve a major controversy about photosynthesis that had arisen between him and Emerson, his 1927 doctoral student.[5] Originally trained in zoology at Harvard, Emerson had, under the influence of W.J.V. Osterhout, shifted his interests from animals to plants. He had gone to Munich to work for his Ph.D. under the Nobel laureate Richard Wilstätter on the subject of chlorophyll chemistry. But when Wilstätter ran into difficulties, because of the anti-semitic activities of certain students and faculty members, he advised Emerson to work instead with Warburg in Berlin.[6] It was in Warburg's laboratory that Emerson wrote his thirty-two-page thesis.

Warburg believed (and often stated) that "in a perfect world, photosynthesis must be perfect." He had published the result that a minimum of four light photons are needed to produce one molecule of oxygen. Using state-of-the art instruments, Emerson found however, consistently, that this minimum number is in fact eight.[7]

Rabinowitch later wrote of Warburg's stay at Urbana:[8]

> Like so many best-laid plans, it all went wrong. Warburg arrived in the midst of the heaviest thunderstorms I have experienced in my fifteen years in Urbana, and this proved to be an augury of his stormy stay in Urbana. Warburg had been accustomed to work with highly trained technical assistants and only rarely with colleagues or even graduate students with independent opinions. He was Warburg and he was right. Emerson, at first modest and helpful in his usual way, and full of respect for his famous teacher and guest, also was a stubborn man, particularly when it came to devising experiments, a matter in which he felt he also had great experience and sound judgement. After several months of fitful attempts at collaboration, and an unsuccessful attempt for a third person's arbitration, Warburg left in anger, without saying good-bye.

Emerson followed this bitter experience with his painstaking research aimed at resolving the controversy.

For his part, Warburg never forgave Emerson—or the rest of the group, which he would refer to as the "Midwest Gang." Andrew Benson, the co-discoverer of the path of carbon in photosynthesis, with 1961 Nobel laureate Melvin Calvin, recalled recently: "On a beautiful afternoon I drove Otto Warburg and Herman Kalckar to 'Hamlet's Castle' at Helsingör. . . . Warburg peered through an iron gate into the darkness below, 'Ach, that's a perfect place for that Midwest Gang.'"[9] Martin Kamen, the co-discoverer of radioactive carbon-14, has attributed Warburg's misconception about the minimum quantum requirement of four rather than eight per oxygen, to the "implementation of Liebling's Law," known in the field as "ILL"[10] Kamen paraphrased the famous reporter A. J. Liebling: "If you are smart enough and work hard enough, you can pick yourself up by the scruff of the neck and throw yourself on the street." Thus, according to Liebling's law, Warburg adopted a faulty premise that hardened into dogma and then into belief, despite its consequences. Warburg himself realized, and once told the late Birgit Vennesland: "Of course, I have made mistakes—many of them. The only way to avoid making any mistakes is never to do anything at all. My biggest mistake was to get much too much involved in controversy. Never get involved in controversy. It's a waste of time. It isn't that controversy itself is wrong. No, it can be even stimulating. But controversy takes too much time and energy. That's what's wrong about it. I have wasted my time and energy in controversy, when I should have been going on doing new experiments."[11]

By 1955, Emerson had uncovered the major causes of error in Warburg's measurements. In 1957 he published the discovery of the two-light effect in the *Proceedings of the National Academy of Sciences* (USA).[12] These experiments were conducted in a darkroom at the back of the labyrinth of rooms that one entered through the door to the Room 157. Ruth Chalmers, the technician, who was called "Shorty" (as she was short), grew the algae that Emerson used. Carl Cederstrand, a research assistant trained in physics, calibrated and checked all the instruments. Emerson's results were initially published in *Science* as abstracts (1956, 1956, 1957, and 1958); his major presentation was at the 1958 annual meeting of the Phycological Society of America, held in Bloomington, Indiana. Hardly any major photosynthesis researchers were present.

The discovery of the Emerson enhancement effect settled the controversy between Warburg and Emerson in favor of Emerson. The evolution of one oxygen molecule requires the transfer of four electrons in two steps, from two molecules of water to carbon dioxide. Since two primary light reactions are needed for oxygen evolution, it was easy to convince everyone that oxygen evolution needs a minimum of eight photons. Einstein had stated long ago that we need one photon to transfer one electron. Thus the transfer of four electrons twice requires eight photons, as Emerson asserted, not four, as Warburg had insisted, per oxygen. It is interesting that in spite of this, Warburg wrote in his notebook (now in the hands of Professor Dieter Oesterhelt in Munich, Germany): "Finally, Emerson has confirmed my results." (I have often wondered whether Warburg thought that

Portrait of Robert Emerson sitting at his desk in 157 Natural History Building, Matthews Avenue, Urbana, Illinois, in April 1957.

he, rather than Emerson, should have been the one to find the two-light effect and discover the Emerson enhancement effect!)

By 1963, Emerson's discovery was accepted by most workers in the field. Bessel Kok and André Jagendorf wrote: "Soon followed the observation by the late Emerson of the enhancement effect in which lights of two different wavelengths proved to exert a greater effect if given simultaneously than if given individually. This enhancement of the net rate was rationalized by the observation of a push-and-pull effect of two different colors upon intermediate catalysts of the process. . . . Every so often someone manages to remove another stone from the wall through which we all want to see, and the crowds tend to flock around the new peep-hole."[13] In this case, the stone was removed by Emerson, working in the inner rooms behind the door to Room 157 in the Natural History Building.

At the time this discovery was made, I was lucky enough to be in Urbana as one of Emerson's first-year graduate students. Although my desk was flush with the wall of the darkroom in which the discovery was made, I was totally unaware of the importance of this work—that is, until I finished my course work and started conducting experiments of my own. To my surprise, I learned that although Emerson's enhancement effect is real, his concept that one light reaction is run by chlorophyll *a* and the other by an auxiliary pigment had to be replaced by the concept, put forth in my doctoral thesis under Rabinowitch, that both light reactions are run by chlorophyll *a* of different spectral types.[14] We postulated there that certain short wavelength-absorbing chlorophyll molecules bring about a primary photochemical process different from the one caused preferentially by the long wave quanta absorbed by another spectral form of chlorophyll *a*. Later, Rajni Govindjee, my wife since 1957, proved, with Rabinowitch in 1961, and then with me in 1964–65, that the Emerson enhancement does indeed occur in photosynthesis, not in respiration, as Larry Blinks suggested in 1957.[15]

On a personal level, although Emerson and Rabinowitch were great friends, they were poles apart in their appearance, personalities, and habits.[16] Emerson was tall, muscular, slim, and upright. He always had a ready smile on his face and he walked with such long strides that I had to jog to keep pace with him. He was often tense, strong-willed, fussy, and demanding, although still very polite.

He was a perfectionist in his experiments, which he always conducted himself. As a student I felt that he had eyes in the back of his head. His desk faced east; mine faced west. By listening to the sounds I produced while manipulating my instruments, he could tell exactly when I was not following the correct protocol. He would gently walk up to me and ask politely, "May I show you how to do this?"

Wearing a red tie tucked in his shirt, he would stand at the lathe making parts for his apparatus, or sit at a lab bench blowing glass or fixing the bank of lights used in growing algae. He had the patience to sit all day in darkness peering through cathetometers at the dancing minisci of liquid in the Warburg manometers. He did not believe in speculating too much and often checked his work twenty times or more before presenting the results. He was also a great carpenter. He built a crib for his grandchildren and a bed for his family.

Emerson and his wife Claire, whom everyone called Tita, were New Englanders. He was a grand nephew of Ralph Waldo Emerson; she came from a distinguished Boston family. Both were steeped in New England tradition. They were generous, yet thrifty. He would not use a university three-cent stamp for a letter that was not strictly written for university business. He would argue at the University Senate that professors should not strive for higher salaries. He believed in the value of working with one's own hands. After a long day of hard work in the laboratory, he would walk home along Matthews Avenue to 806 Main Street, and go right to work in his garden, weeding, digging, and pruning until dark.

During the summer months, the Emersons lived almost entirely from the produce in their backyard, "despising store-bought fruit, chicken and vegetables," as had Emerson's professor, Otto Warburg.[17] Raising chickens in the backyard did, however, cause some problems for Emerson. On

August 12, 1950, the Emersons received a letter from the city regarding complaints from the neighbors about the "chickens being raised on the premises at 806 W. Main, Urbana. Is there anyway that you can get along without these chickens? If so, I believe your neighbors would appreciate your removing them."[18]

The Emersons were very kind to students, especially international ones. On my first birthday in Urbana, Emerson cooked breakfast for me in the laboratory on the pretext that he wanted me to learn to cook so I would not starve in the United States. Rajni and I were often invited to their home for dinner. Once, when they asked Rajni to cook an Indian dish, Emerson watched her work, as he so often did in the lab. As she began to tap the pan with the stirring spoon to remove the food stuck to it, he smiled gently and said, "May I show you how to do this?" He proceeded to remove the food from the spoon with another spoon, making the tapping unnecessary. This is an example of his deep concern with doing everything properly. He and Tita both admired perfection in human labor.

Politically, Emerson was a pacificist and a democratic socialist. In the period following Pearl Harbor, when many Japanese Americans were held in concentration camps, his heightened sense of social injustice brought him into a concentration camp and led to his efforts to develop the desert shrub guayule as a source of rubber that could be produced under U.S. conditions, without exploiting native labor in Southeast Asia.[19] More generally, Emerson asked in 1951 (on notecards): "Does Science have a responsibility toward man or only toward his personal comfort, pride, what Orientals call 'occidental self gratification'?" His answer: "Science ought to serve primarily the man rather than his comforts. Science can be one of the ways, like music, poetry, painting in which man discovers his spiritual limitations, learns to put down his vanity & selfishness, makes himself and his fellows into higher rather than lower form of life. Do not worry about technology, I don't advocate return to dark ages."[20]

Distrusting airplanes, Emerson almost always took trains. He flew grudgingly to New York when the train there from Indianapolis was discontinued. February 4, 1959, was the saddest day for Rajni and me when the ill-fated Electra crashed into the frozen East River near La Guardia airport because of a faulty altimeter. Emerson had lived for only fifty-six years.

Emerson was highly regarded by U.S. scientists. In 1949 he was the recipient of the Stephen Hales Prize of the American Society of Plant Physiologists (now called American Society of Plant Biology) and he was elected in 1953 to the National Academy of Sciences. His long-term Harvard friend,

Eugene Rabinowitch sizing up his height with Govindjee's bride, Rajni Govindjee, Emerson's last student and later Rabinowitch's student, on October 24, 1957, at the reception in Urbana after the wedding.

the late Kenneth Thimann, wrote of Emerson: "Bob is not a man whom you can ever forget. In some way Bob was the very symbol of uprightness; he loved the truth just as much he loved the underdog, and he scorned the untruthful and could not have anything to do either with it or with the man who promulgated it. . . . Everyone who has come into contact with Bob must have been inspired by him to some degree; it is impossible not to be, just as it is impossible not to remember with clarity his every gesture, his ready smile—often belying fierce disagreement—his enormous ability for friendship and real tenderness. This is a kind of immortality—at least survival for another lifetime—in the memories and even to some extent in the characters of other people, which it is given to very few men to achieve."

In contrast with Emerson, Rabinowitch was short and round, his belt buckle buoyed up by his paunch. Whereas Emerson typically wore a red tie to work, Rabinowitch often wore a bow-tie. He walked with joviality and some difficulty. And he was easygoing, gentle, even-tempered, and hilarious. He had fun with his height. A photo taken after my marriage to Rajni shows Rabinowitch checking whether he was taller than her. He was standing on his tippy toes.

Rabinowitch led his group in an unobtrusive and loose-reined manner, never intimidating those who worked under him. T. T. Bannister wrote: "In his lab, intellectual life was accompanied by frequent hilarity, to which Earl Jacobs' banjo playing and Stanley Holt's progress reports on brewing experiments beneath his children's cribs contributed, and the hilarity was often infectiously sustained by Eugene's chuckling laugh which geysers up in a body designed for mirth."

Rabinowitch and his wife Anya gave the most fantastic parties; full of fun and enjoyment. Anya made Vodka, starting with grain alcohol, with glycerine as lubricant, and zubrovka, a special polish herb, as a flavor enhancer. Often I was the bartender, liberally serving drinks to everyone, including myself. Anya's Russian hors d'oeuvres were out of this world, and she was great to Rajni and me.

I was struck by Rabinowitch's tolerance. When there was conflict within the group, he was always fair and kind to all involved. When one of his postdocs decided not to discuss his research with him verbally, instead placing written comments on his desk at night, Rabinowitch would painstakingly respond in writing. He would leave his written responses on the postdoc's desk day after day. Another postdoc would send his papers off to journals without including Rabinowitch's name or even showing the work to his mentor. Rabinowitch only learned of the work when it was rejected. At that point, he would sit down, correct it, and return it to the postdoc with a smile.

Unlike Emerson, who was in every way a master craftsman, Rabinowitch often had difficulty when he tried to perform experiments himself. Once, while trying to help a graduate student put rubber tubing over a glass tube, he cut two fingers and a thumb. On another occasion he created a monster when trying to blow a glass bulb for an experiment. He would sit for hours with paper and pencil at a small desk cramped into a corner of the old Room 156 that once existed in the Natural History Building. His mind was free-associating and wide-ranging, as well as extremely sharp and imaginative. He built his ideas from his vast knowledge of chemistry and physics.

Rabinowitch came to live in three parts of the world and to use three different languages—Russian, German, and English—for studying, speaking, and writing. In addition, he knew French. When I interviewed him on January 5, 1964, at his home in Champaign (1021 West Church Street), he told me, "When I was a boy and I was asked what I wanted to become in life, I used to say I want to be everything everywhere, and fate has arranged it for me." He was born and spent his first twenty-one years in what was then St. Petersburg, the capital of the Russian Empire. After the end of World War I, he found himself in Germany, where he studied at the University of Berlin, became a German scientist, and wrote books and articles in German. After Hitler came to power, his life shifted to the English-speaking world—first to England for five years and then from 1938 the United States.

He also shifted his field of activity. His Ph.D. thesis at the University of Berlin was in inorganic chemistry, on the volatile hydrides, particularly tin hydride. When he left Germany, he first went to the Niels Bohr Institute for Theoretical Physics. Then, in 1947, when he finally got his first regular academic appointment, at Illinois, it was as a research professor of botany. In due time, it became a joint appointment in botany and biophysics.

To his several languages and scientific fields, Rabinowitch added journalism, poetry, and architecture. He told me he thought it was an interesting way of life, adding:

> But unless one is really extraordinarily gifted so that one can combine great achievements in one field with considerable amateur achievements in other fields, as ideally it has been possible for people like Leonardo Da Vinci, or Goethe, one ends this kind of dissipation by having not achieved anything particularly important in any one of the fields. The enjoyment of certain creative work and familiarity with different fields of intellectual endeavor does not leave one with the feeling that one has really achieved anything really worthwhile in any one of them. Still, I wouldn't like to exchange this for a moderate achievement in any special field, say, being a representative in Congress, in politics; or being a member of a couple of academies in science; or having received some sort of prizes in exhibitions as an artist.

Rabinowitch was very much concerned with science policy and politics, as well as with the problem of achieving peace in the world. He was the coauthor of the famous Franck Report urging the U.S. government to refrain from using nuclear weapons against civilian populations. The report was submitted to Secretary of War Henry L. Stimson in June 1945, a month before the first test of the atomic bomb, in Alamagordo, New Mexico. He was also the cofounder of the Pugwash conferences (the first held in 1957), aimed at bringing peace between the Soviets and Americans. He was the cofounder and editor of the *Bulletin of Atomic Scientists*, which showed the famous "doomsday clock" on its cover. The recipient of the 1995 Nobel Peace Prize, Sir Joseph Rotblat, wrote in 1973, after the death of Rabinowitch: "Eugene Rabinowitch was a man of many facets: a scientist and a teacher; a classics scholar and a modern philosopher; a poet and a man of letters; a journalist and an editor; a sociologist and a politician. But his main characteristic was simply as a human being, with a warm heart, filled with love and tenderness, not only for his family and friends, but for the whole of mankind. This love for humanity, and his profound belief in the potential of science to ensure a happy life for all, were the guidelines throughout his whole life, the philosophy on which all his activities were based."[21]

Rabinowitch would be recognized with many honors, including honorary doctorates from Brandeis University (1960), Dartmouth College (1964), Columbia College, Chicago (1970), and Alma College, Michigan (1970). His Dartmouth citation read: "one of the few generalists remaining in our time."[22] In 1966, he received the Kalinga Prize, for the popularization of science from The United Nations Educational, Scientific and Cultural Organization. In 1960, the Immigrant League of Chicago recognized him as the "outstanding citizen of foreign birth." In 1965, the University of Illinois recognized him by giving him full membership in its most distinguished academic body, the Center for Advanced Study. Three years later, in 1968, he retired from the University of Illinois, and accepted a position as professor of biology and chemistry at the State University of New York at Albany. In 1972, he received the Woodrow Wilson International Center for Scholars Fellowship. He was a member of the American Academy of Arts and Sciences, but not of the National Academy of Sciences. According to Rotblat "There are reasons to believe that this omission was a snub by the establishment for his involvement in many social and political activities, including Pugwash."[23]

Rabinowitch also wrote poetry in Russian. This work includes a self-epitaph:

> The game is up, for much too long I tarried;
> My thoughts were scattered and my deeds were tame.
> No earthly trace behind, I bring the loads I have carried
> Back into night and nothing whence I came.[24]

ACKNOWLEDGMENT

I thank Lillian Hoddeson for editing this chapter and Rajni Govindjee for reading it closely.

NOTES

1. Emerson published this work with his undergraduate student William Arnold (now famous for many other discoveries in light emission by plants). Arnold's daughter, H. A. Herron, later wrote, "Emerson did not stand on ceremony—not everyone would put an undergraduate's name as coauthor of an important paper. But when the experiment involved using a Warburg apparatus, Emerson trusted no one but himself to fill the vessels. So he routinely arrived early and set up the experiment; then Bill came in to take the readings and do the calculations. Hans Gaffron visited and was shocked. 'Arnold is

supposed to be your assistant,' he said to Emerson, 'but you are doing the assisting.'"
Govindjee, R. S. Knox, and J. Amesz, eds., "William Arnold: A Tribute," *Photosynthesis Research* 48: 1–46.

2. E. Rabinowitch, *Photosynthesis and Related Processes*, vol. I, vol. II (part 1), and vol. II (part 2) (New York: Interscience Publishers, 1945, 1951, 1956).

3. The original office door of the Photosynthesis Project, which also included a chlorophyll chemist Stanley Holt, is now lost to history.

4. E. Rabinowitch and Govindjee, "The Role of Chlorophyll in Photosynthesis," *Scientific American* 213 (1965): 74–83.

5. On November 12, 1948, *Science* published Warburg's photograph on its cover, doing experiments in the Natural History Building laboratory.

6. Although Warburg was also a Jew, he was considered "safe" to work with because he had been declared only a 25 percent Jew (even though he was actually a 50 percent Jew, as his mother was Christian). Thus, Warburg was allowed to be the director of a research institute.

7. Govindjee, "On the Requirement of Minimum Number of Quanta of Light for the Evolution of One Molecule of Oxygen in Photosynthesis," *Photosynthesis Research* 59 (1999): 249–54. Govindjee, "Lighting the Path: A tribute to Robert Emerson (1903–1959)," S43-001 (six pages) available at ‹http://www.publish.csiro.au/ps2001›: PS2001 Proceedings of the 12th International Congress on Photosynthesis. On line and CD" ISBN 0643-067116.

8. E. Rabinowitch, "Robert Emerson (1903–1959)," *Biographical Memoirs of the National Academy of Sciences* 25 (1961): 112–31.

9. Andrew A. Benson, "Following the Path of Carbon in Photosynthesis: A Personal Story," *Photosynthesis Research* 73 (2002): 29–50.

10. M. D. Kamen, "Liebling's Law ('ILL')" *Proceedings of the American Philosophical Society* 139 (1995): 358–67.

11. Birgit Vennesland, "Recollections and Small Confessions," *Annual Review of Plant Physiology* 32 (1981): 1–20.

12. R. Emerson, R. V. Chalmers, and C. N. Cederstrand, "Some Factors Influencing the Long-wave Limit of Photosynthesis," Proceedings of the National Academy of Sciences, USA 43 (1957): 133–43.

13. Bessel Kok and Andre Jagendorf, "Photosynthetic Mechanisms of Green Plants," National Academy of Sciences and National Research Council, Washington, D.C., Publication 1145, 1963.

14. Govindjee and E. Rabinowitch, "Two Forms of Chlorophyll a with Distinct Photochemical Functions," *Science* 132 (1960): 355–56.

15. Rajni, whom I had known quite well in India, was a year junior to me when we were both M.Sc. students of Professor Shri Ranjan during 1955–56. Rajni joined Emerson as a fellow of botany in the fall of 1957, one year after I joined as a fellow of physico-chemical biology. When we were married on October 24, 1957, in the University YMCA chapel, both the Emersons and Rabinowitches attended our wedding. Govindjee, "Milestones in Photosynthesis Research," in *Probing Photosynthesis*, ed. M. Younis, U. Pathre, and P. Mohanty (London: Taylor & Francis, 2000), 9–39.

16. To illustrate, I have taken the liberty of freely using some words of T. T. Bannister, who took his Ph.D. under Rabinowitch. T. T. Bannister, "The Careers and Contributions of Eugene Rabinowitch," *Biophysical Journal* 12 (1972): 707–18.

17. H. Krebs, "Otto Heinrich Warburg 1883–1970," *Biographical Memoirs of the Fellows of the Royal Society* 18 (1972): 629–99.

18. City Attorney Gene D. Weisiger to Robert Emerson, August 12, 1950.

19. M. S. Nishimura, F. N. Hirosawa, and R. Emerson, "Rubber from Guayule," *Industrial and Engineering Chemistry* 39 (1947): 1477–85: I. Ashkenazy, "As the Guayule Ball Bounces": *Westways,* LXIX (September 1977): 56–60. A good part of this research was done at Manzanar Relocation Center of the War Relocation Authority. The U.S. Army is also thanked for administrative support.

20. Emerson, 1951; original in Emerson's handwriting, on note cards, with the author.

21. Sir Joseph Rotblat (2000) "Fifty Pugwash Conferences: A Tribute to Eugene Rabinow-itch," ‹http://www.pugwash.org/reports/pac/pac256/rotblat.htm›.

22. A biography of Eugene Rabinowitch can be found at ‹http://library.albany.edu/speccoll/findaids/gero75.htm#bio›.

23. Rotblat, "Fifty Pugwash Conferences."

24. Bannister, "The Careers and Contributions of Eugene Rabinowitch."

SUSAN M. RIGDON

CHAPTER 13

Oscar Lewis and

the Anthropology of Poverty

The anthropologist Oscar Lewis (1914–70) once described himself as someone "who has a double commitment—first to the search for general laws of society and human behavior, and second to presenting the lives of the poor as they are in the hope that increased knowledge will lead to some amelioration of their condition."[1] Focusing public attention on the everyday lives of the poor, Lewis believed, was a necessary first step in "attacking and eradicating poverty," the "new historic task" of anthropology.[2] To this end, Lewis focused much of his energy on applied research, whether as project evaluator and field worker for public and private agencies or through his choice of problem as an independent researcher. In pursuit of his objective he crossed disciplinary lines unapologetically, using the tools of science to conduct the research and the fora of art to present the results.

From the earliest days of his career Lewis dreaded being limited to "dull" academic writing, and hoped to find a broader audience for his work. In the last decade of his life, in collaboration with his wife, Ruth Maslow Lewis, he did find that audience. Blurring the line between social science reporting and literature, *The Children of Sánchez* and *La Vida* (winner of the 1967 National Book Award for nonfiction) became best-sellers and reached readers in many different languages.

It would be impossible in these few pages to detail Lewis's distinguished career in anthropology or to summarize the research he carried out between 1939 and 1970 on a Blackfoot reservation in Canada, in Tepoztlán and Mexico City; in Estremadura, Spain; India; Puerto Rico; Cuba; and the United States.[3] Instead I will try to describe the creative impulse behind his research, and how the places in which he chose to work fed his creativity.

After completing a Ph.D. at Columbia University in 1940, Lewis spent the war years working for federal agencies. In 1946, he accepted his first academic position at Washington University in St. Louis. Two years later he joined the University of Illinois Department of Sociology and Anthropology. As his professional reputation grew during the 1950s, Lewis received many job offers, but he chose to stay in Champaign-Urbana, where in 1960 he became a founding member of the Department of Anthropology when it split off from Sociology. He stayed not because he had become any less a New Yorker, or because he was drawn to the small town pace of life, but because he was a full-tilt workaholic. Yet for the son of Polish-Jewish immigrants, coming to a small town on a midwestern prairie in 1948 was not the culture shock that it might have been for another East Coast urbanite.

Lewis was the product of a mixed rural-urban background, as were his parents, a yeshiva graduate and a miller's daughter. Chaim Leb and Broche Biblowitz Lefkowitz came to the United States from rural Poland, just outside Grodno (an area now in Belarus), and once in America were for the rest of their lives to shuttle between New York City and an upstate farm. The youngest of their six children, Oscar Lefkowitz (he changed his surname to Lewis in 1940) was the family's first native-born American. Born in the city, Lewis spent much of his childhood on the farm, hunting, fishing, doing chores, and attending rural schools near Liberty. After his parents converted the farm to a summer hotel, the family spent the winters in the city, where Lewis worked his way through the City College of New York (CCNY).

In 1936, the year he graduated from CCNY with a degree in history, Lewis entered Columbia University, where he was almost immediately unhappy in the history department. At the suggestion of his future brother-in-law, the psychologist Abraham Maslow, Lewis went to see Ruth Benedict, whose culture and personality research group Maslow had joined. After one conversation with Benedict, Lewis decided to take his degree in anthropology, signing on as her advisee. Although he did much of his course work with Benedict, his research interests—the relationship between economics and culture, and issues of class stratification and mobility—were decidedly different from hers.

The common denominator in all of Lewis's work was poverty.

> My interest in poverty goes back to my student days. Remember that I began college in 1930 in the heart of the depression . . . and most anthropology students of my generation at Columbia University were sensitized to the importance of economic factors both in their own lives and in the history of human society. We were also exposed to a good dose of Socialist thinking. It is no accident that it was during the thirties that anthropologists began to turn from a study of folk-lore to a study of economic systems among primitive peoples. My identification with the underdog has been persistent and deep throughout my career. Indeed I am happiest when I am doing field work with peasants in the country and with slum dwellers in the city. I once began a study of 100 middle-class Mexican families in Mexico City but I couldn't see it through because I found it boring.[4]

Indeed, Lewis was happiest and felt most secure in the field, in situations where he was working something out on the spot and in his own way,[5] or interviewing an informant with whom he had especially good rapport. Throughout his career he was equally at home at fieldsites in the countryside or in the city and almost all his research designs had both urban and rural components. His early work is associated primarily with rural and village life: the impact of trade on Blackfoot culture; cropping practices in rural America; the village study of Tepoztlán that launched his career in anthropology (*Life in a Mexican Village*); and *Village Life in Northern India*. Yet by the 1960s, Lewis was better known for his work in urban areas: *The Children of Sánchez* (Mexico City) and *La Vida* (San Juan and New York City). His culture of poverty thesis, first presented in *Five Families* (1959), a collection of rural and urban household studies, was invariably associated with urban "slum life," but was meant to encompass both urban and rural subcultures.

Lewis came to be identified as a Mexicanist but he was fundamentally a comparativist: rural and urban, hoe and plow cultures, Mexico and India, Puerto Rico and mainland United States; revolutionary and nonrevolutionary societies, poor, poorer, and poorest. His early work focused primarily on the social structures and economies of small communities, but over time community moved to the background and family to the foreground. This shift was influenced by his marriage in 1937 to Ruth Maslow, a psychologist by training who also had an interest in film and art. Maslow had met Lewis while she was still in high school and he at the City College of New York. In 1939 she joined her husband on his first field trip, to a Blackfoot reservation in Canada, and she remained his major collaborator for the rest of his life.[6] The division of labor that evolved between them would have a profound impact on the direction of the research and the way it was presented to the public.

In 1943 the Lewises were hired as a team to join a cross-national study of Indian personality organized by University of Chicago anthropologist Laura Thompson and John Collier, commissioner of the U.S. Bureau of Indian Affairs. The Lewises were assigned to the Mexican side of the project, with Ruth responsible for the personality research and Oscar the ethnography. Oscar also served as U.S. representative to the Inter-American Indian Institute, which had its headquarters in Mexico City. To bolster her college training, which had largely been in social psychology under the direction of Solomon Asch, Ruth received special training in the administration of Rorshachs, Thematic Apperception Tests (TATs), and other projective methods.

In the beginning, personality study was simply a mandatory part of the field assignment, but the importance of individual psychology and family psychodynamics grew as Lewis began to focus on the family as a mirror of culture. Eventually this emphasis would carry his work to another kind of place—away from community and social organization and into the human psyche. His Tepoztlán village study revealed a complex society characterized as much by conflict and competition as by cooperation, challenging the findings of Robert Redfield's earlier depiction of the village (*Tepoztlán, A Mexican Village: A Study of Folk Life*, 1930) as a nonconflictive pastoral society. Their two village portraits, drawn more than fifteen years apart, came to be seen as textbook examples of how field objectives and methods, as well as the personalities of the investigators, can affect the outcome of research. But the personality research, Lewis's longer time in the village, his large field staff, his holistic approach, and his leave-no-stone-unturned method were bound to produce a broader, more detailed account of life in Tepoztlán. And it was perhaps not his personality as much as his experience—a childhood in the Catskills, where the hardscrabble life of family farming and small business competition dominated the local economy—that predisposed him to see the village as something other than a near-idyllic folk society.

Clifford Geertz once observed that if anthropologists were ranked by the quantity of data they collected, Oscar Lewis might be "king." The Tepoztlán study established the exhaustive approach to field investigations that Lewis retained throughout his career. Readers who know only the later popular family studies may think of Lewis working primarily from taped interviews and be unaware that he was, for all the art in presentation, an empiricist and a champion bean counter. He was a serious student of household economy and material culture, who paid exceptional attention to the informant's physical milieu. He inventoried, item by item for hundreds of informants, every household possession and piece of clothing, how each was obtained and at what price. He tracked all income and expenditures, and all gift-giving and receiving in the principal households he studied. He trained local fieldworkers who could mingle as peers with informants and enter their households unobtrusively to observe and record all activity during the course of a day or evening and transcribe all conversations, repeating this exercise multiple times for some families.

In describing her husband's field methods, Ruth Lewis has emphasized his need to map everything at each field site, to see the structure and how all the parts were related to one another. He wanted to know how a village was situated within its region, the nation, or the world; how a household was positioned in the extended family, the neighborhood, and larger society; and how the individual fit within her household, extended family, workplace, or community. As he interviewed, Lewis sketched genealogies, sociograms, site maps, and household layouts to help frame in his mind how the individual fit into a given physical, social or psychological setting. His field papers overflow with rough genealogies, maps and diagrams drawn in margins of field notes, covers of file folders, on the backs of envelopes and flyers, napkins, and restaurant place mats, all carefully saved to guide subsequent interviewing or for possible insertion in a life history.

The importance Lewis assigned to defining how informants and their communities were articulated into their immediate environments and an ever widening circle of contexts was influenced perhaps by his original training in history but more so, according to Maslow Lewis, by his reading of gestalt psychology. His ability to "see the whole gestalt," and the fact that he was "critical by nature," drove him to see things in a new way. This she believes was the source of his creativity.

The near-obsessive scope of inquiry and the intensity of conviction and commitment that lay behind Lewis's choice of research problem led Jules Henry to describe his approach to the work and the results it produced as "passionate ethnography." Part of this passion came from Lewis's visceral nature; he believed more in the greater communicative power of the tactile and the visual—in short, the sensate—over the abstract and intellectual message. There was always a strong visual component in his work and something inherently dramatic about the places or the people he studied:

the spectacular hills of Tepoztlán, the labile temperaments and general panache of the Sánchez, the extreme disorganization and dysfunction of some families. A few of the field sites—the green-roofed, oceanfront barrio of La Esmeralda in San Juan and the red-doored Casa Grande *vecindad* in Mexico City—became symbols of urban poverty.

Even before the Tepoztlán study was published, Lewis had been looking for a way to present his field data that was, in his words, "half way between a novel and an anthropological report." The family studies the Lewises elected to do in Tepoztlán, in combination with the personality research they were assigned to conduct, led them to look for a way to write up their findings that could encompass all this detail and still hold a reader's interest. The division of labor itself was instrumental in the resolution of this problem: Oscar planned and ran the field investigations and wrote up the ethnographic and archival data, while Ruth did some of the interviewing, organized the life histories, and wrote up the psychological research. Small portions of the first family histories were integrated into the larger community study, *Life in a Mexican Village*, but it turned out that Ruth had a gift for editing life history material into narratives that could stand alone. This complemented her husband's interviewing skills and led to a greater concentration of effort on construction of informant biographies than on the writeup and analysis of other field data that Oscar continued to collect at a pace beyond his capacity to analyze.

By the time they were writing *Five Families*, both Lewises were talking about the organization of manuscripts in terms of scenes and casts of characters, and combining narrative form with social science reporting. Lewis called it "ethnographic realism," to distinguish it from literary realism. *Five Families* was given a "Setting" and a "Cast of Characters," and illustrated by Alberto Beltrán, whose wonderfully evocative pen and ink drawings, made at the field site, had been used in *Life in a Mexican Village*. Lewis often spoke about "capturing" his informants, as if in a snapshot or series of photographs, and Beltrán's drawings caught the informants in tableau-style poses that perfectly complemented the Lewises' visually sensitive and scenic-inspired editing. The drawings help establish mood and a sense of place, just as a good stage set can.

Nowhere was this used to better effect than in *Pedro Martínez: A Mexican Peasant and His Family*, which contains the most exquisitely rendered sense of place and the most finely drawn portrait of an individual in his culture to be found in any of the Lewises' family studies. This was not just artful presentation, but a triumph of method. By the time *Pedro Martínez* was published, interviewing had been under way for twenty years and Lewis

Oscar and Ruth Maslow Lewis worked as a team from their first field project among the Blackfoot in 1939 to their last in Cuba in 1969–70. This 1948 photo was taken just as they moved to the University of Illinois.

had counted every bean in the village. There was no field site he knew better or felt more comfortable writing about than Tepoztlán. And both Lewises understood that the very reserved and personally reticent Martínez was a better informant about the village than about his own life. Whereas their urban Mexican, Puerto Rican, and Cuban informants had broader horizons and were more mobile, psychically if not physically, Tepoztlán was the beginning and ending of Martínez's world. He was more a product of a physical place than any other of the Lewises' published informants.

By the early 1960s Lewis was better known for the family studies and theorizing about poverty than for his ethnography. In his "culture of poverty" thesis he hypothesized the existence among the poorest people in capitalist societies of a shared subculture, one perpetuated in families over generations through cultural agencies and with "distinctive social and psychological consequences for its members." Early versions of the thesis stressed the social consequences, especially the way the urban poor were articulated into class-stratified societies, while the later versions—following a research trajectory toward the inner life of the individual—emphasized the psychological consequences of poverty, specifically the formation of a distinctive personality configuration and high levels of psychopathology.

The double shift in Lewis's work—the greater emphasis on biography and personality study and his growing reputation as an authority on the causes of poverty—had an impact on the central role that culture, and consequently place, played in his research. First, the culture of poverty was by definition a cross-national phenomenon, with capitalism as the common denominator. But capitalism can and does function in many different cultural contexts. Readers discovering Tepoztlán in *Pedro Martínez*, Mexico City *vecindad* life in *Sánchez*, and a San Juan shantytown in *La Vida*, encounter three strikingly different places. It is not easy to think of them sharing a common culture or subculture. For anyone who threw the emphasis on *culture* in "culture of poverty" this could be confusing. "Culture" without "place" is only an abstraction, but there was no single place to associate with the subculture except perhaps one drawn from an image of an urban slum or ghetto. In Lewis's inflection, the emphasis in "culture of poverty" fell on *poverty*, and on its implicit partner capitalism. But that point was often lost in the sound-bite ready phrase "culture of poverty."

Second, the increasing importance Lewis placed on publishing family, rather than community, studies deepened his research on personality and family dynamics, and consequently led to greater emphasis on projective test analyses in the writeup of field research. Moreover in stressing the role of psychopathology in perpetuating poverty it was difficult not to associate the subculture of poverty with mental illness. But again, Lewis was primarily interested in the consequences for mental health of being poor, and only secondarily in the impact of psychopathology on culture. With the Sánchez and Ríos (*La Vida*) family studies Lewis was at one more remove from attaching a culture group (i.e., people living in a culture of poverty) to a specific place. Publishing edited interviews while excluding most of the ethnographic data made it more difficult to situate informants within contexts wider than the extended family circle and gave greater weight to what was happening in informants' minds and their households than what was happening in their communities. The families became little worlds or subcultures of their own. Compared to *Pedro Martínez*, for example, where the village is always in the foreground, in *Sánchez*, Mexico City is in the background and the individual and the family in the foreground.

The culture of poverty concept was given its first broad exposure in the United States by the labor activist Michael Harrington, who picked up the phrase while reviewing *Children of Sánchez* and set it down in an American context (*The Other America*, 1962). Harrington's best-seller brought Lewis's work, which had been associated almost exclusively with Mexican poverty, to the attention of Washington policy makers. Lewis became a consultant to Head Start, participated in Daniel Patrick Moynihan's seminars on Race and Poverty, engaged in a public dialogue with Senator

Robert Kennedy about the causes of poverty in America, lectured around the country on the culture of poverty, and gravitated toward the status of public intellectual.[7]

Lewis was surrounded by political controversy throughout the last decade of his life, no doubt in part because he received his greatest public attention during the politically volatile 1960s. At home there was contention over how Lewis was imputing causation in his culture of poverty thesis; its elasticity allowed users to shape it to fit their own agendas. "Culture of poverty" became a catchphrase and a verbal football in the War on Poverty debate over whether government or individuals bear greater responsibility for ending poverty. Those throwing from the Left used the thesis to target the economic system and called for government programs to eradicate poverty. Those throwing from the Right used the thesis to hold the subculture responsible and called for individuals to pull themselves up out of poverty. Trying to clarify this position in the highly charged atmosphere of the 1960s proved impossible for Lewis.

While the culture of poverty thesis was under attack in the United States, in Mexico the Spanish-language edition of the *Children of Sánchez* (1964) led to a national "scandal." A small group of academics and bureaucrats orchestrated a campaign against the book and its author, a foreigner they resented for exposing Mexican poverty to the world. Obviously Mexican poverty was not a secret, but *Sánchez* was not just another statistical report; it was a book accessible to any literate Mexican and about real people living in the heart of the city who, not coincidentally, were quite critical of their government. In formal charges brought by the Mexican attorney general, Lewis was accused of being an FBI agent and slandering Mexico. His publisher, also a foreigner, had to resign as director of his government-funded publishing house. Hundreds of newspaper stories, dozens of public fora, and a year later the government cleared Lewis of all charges. With a new publisher the book remained in print and in Mexican bookstores, as it does today. And "*los hijos de Sánchez*" passed into Mexico's lexicon as a *modismo* for its working poor.

The publication of *La Vida* in 1966 spurred additional attacks on Lewis, although nothing like the media frenzy that sustained the Mexican campaign against *Sánchez*. But again there were assemblies on university campuses, roundtables—some televised—and numerous newspaper and magazine articles attacking and defending Lewis's depiction of life in one of San Juan's poorest, and most notorious, barrios. One Puerto Rican legislator even felt compelled to give testimony against Lewis in the U.S. Senate for slandering his culture.

Six years into his research on the culture of poverty in Puerto Rico and New York, Lewis suspended the work to begin a new project in Cuba, where the nature of the economic system was to be at the center of the research. He had been trying to study poverty in a socialist system since the early days of the Castro government but had received permission only for brief visits; the first time on a reporter's visa (for *Harper's*) just after the Bay of Pigs invasion in 1961. But in 1968 he was allowed to attend a conference in Havana and on that trip met Fidel Castro and got Castro's personal assurance of investigative freedom.

With an official invitation in hand, Lewis got the necessary dispensation from the U.S. State Department for a prolonged stay on the island. In this setting he was convinced he could test his hypothesis that it was only in capitalist systems that the necessary conditions existed for the emergence of a subculture that perpetuated poverty. In 1969, Lewis and an international field team began what was intended to be a three-year project divided between urban and rural phases. The first major undertaking was a community study in an urban subdivision built expressly for the relocation of residents of a Havana shantytown that Lewis had briefly studied in 1946. Eighteen months into the research, amid a national economic crisis, the project was shut down by intervention of Cuban State Security; field materials were confiscated, and one informant was arrested.[8] From its inception the project had had high-level opponents who were opposed to giving a foreigner government sanction to do open-ended interviewing and the right to remove unreviewed research materials from the country. The foreign minister of Cuba, Raúl Roa, personally read Lewis the formal charges, which accused him of being a CIA agent. Already in poor health at the onset of the project, Lewis had a seizure while in Roa's office. He died of heart failure in New York six months later, not yet fifty-six, still convinced he could set things right and return to the island to complete his research.

The frenetic pace of Lewis's professional life undoubtedly contributed to his death at such an early age. Doctors had warned him off the high elevations at his Mexican fieldsites and the hot, humid climates of Puerto Rico and Cuba, but he refused to change venues, stay home, or even to slow down. By 1970 he had been working at fever pitch for thirty-one years. In his professional life the only time Lewis ever seemed to be in one place was when he was in the field. Except for a brief stint on a desk job at the Justice Department, he spent his other three years with the federal government at field sites in rural United States and Mexico. Of his twenty-two years on the faculty at the University of Illinois in Urbana-Champaign, he

Oscar Lewis, chatting with a resident of La Perla in San Juan, Puerto Rico, the site of community and family studies Lewis began in 1963, and which were still in progress at the time of his death in 1970.

spent between eight and nine in the field, not counting summers, weekends, and vacation periods traveling to and from field sites to fill in missing holes in the data.

Urbana-Champaign, however, was more than a waystation between field sites. Illinois offered Lewis all the advantages of a large research institution and his college was generous in granting him leaves and providing supplementary funding for fieldwork. Moreover, he was not unhappy to be away from the added attention focused on Ivy League and East Coast campuses during the McCarthy years. He had not been politically active since his youth and college years and had no party or other formal political affiliations, but his political values were not absent from his work. However thin the analyses he offered in books written for a general audience, the implications for political change were evident, as in his introduction to *Children of Sánchez*: "even the Mexican capacity for suffering has its limits, and unless ways are found to achieve a more equitable distribution of the growing national wealth and a greater equality of sacrifice . . . we may expect social upheavals, sooner or later."

As the political climate became more radicalized in the 1960s, Lewis became more outspoken in public lectures about the underfunding and overall inadequacy of War on Poverty programs. He attributed this in part to spending on the Vietnam War, to which he was adamantly opposed. In addition he had always been a defender of the Cuban Revolution, believing it was far more interested in the welfare of the people than the Batista government it had overthrown. These public stances could have made him the subject of surveillance in the 1960s, but the FBI had already been keeping a file on him since his first trip to Mexico in 1943. By the end of his life that file ran to hundreds of pages.[9]

Lewis was never eager to be held up to public scrutiny or to be distracted by any kind of attention or diversion of energy that took time away from his work. He was certainly not adverse to publicity, but he chose to pick his spots and to have attention focused on the work, not his life. During the last third of his career, when he was well known outside his own discipline, Lewis was able to maintain a role as a public intellectual while based on a campus where the national media seldom came looking for him.

Lewis was someone whose early research made him a textbook exemplar of community study method; someone whose prodigious accumulation of field data was legend; someone whose skill at establishing rapport made him a renowned interviewer; someone who coined a phrase that was ubiquitous in 1960s writing on world poverty; someone whose books achieved best-seller status and were translated into dozens of languages and adapted for film and stage, and yet someone who occupies a niche off the main corridors of American anthropology's pantheon. This had to do with a combination of personal style, method, and collaborative arrangements that is not replicable. In any case, Lewis was always too busy to invest much time or interest in cultivating "disciples" among graduate students. Moreover, from the beginning and almost exclusively after his first decade in anthropology, Lewis did not write primarily for other anthropologists; the motivation for his work was not to build the discipline. Unlike his friend and colleague Julian Steward, whose life work culminated in significant contributions to the theory of culture change, Lewis was more deeply rooted in applied research, with an eye to its impact outside the discipline.[10] Anthropology was the vehicle not the destination.

That fundamental focus separates Lewis from many of today's cultural anthropologists who, while bemoaning their inability to reach the general public, continue to write mainly in academic journals and for other anthropologists in their subfields. Many also see themselves as advocates for, perhaps protectors of, their informants and their cultures. Even during his lifetime this protectionist stance distanced Lewis from some of his contemporaries. In the introduction to *Five Families*, for example, he suggested that for too long anthropologists had undertaken studies of poor and underdeveloped societies accepting their poverty "as a natural and integral part of the whole way of life," and at times defending their cultures "against the inroads of civilization." He took exception to George Foster's characterization of peasant society as "'a successful social device' simply because it has persisted. The success of a social form must also be evaluated in term of its human costs." What he had learned from his work, Lewis wrote, was that poverty should not be defended or idealized and that it was the responsibility of all anthropologists to find ways to ease the strains in peasant communities during the "period of transition to new social forms." "The romantic view of the peasantry still held by a few anthropologists is, at best, a form of escapism from the problems of urban life and, at worst, a kind of inverse snobbism. To stress the problems and suffering of the peasantry is to envisage the possibility of fundamental changes in technology, means of communication, and general fund of knowledge, which would alter the very meaning of peasant life."[11]

Lewis had no Luddite tendencies; he believed in progress and never looked backward, only to a better future. And he believed it was his personal obligation to help bring this about, in some part by raising the consciousness of the general public about the human costs of poverty. This view was echoed by Ruth Lewis in accepting an honorary degree from the University of Illinois in 1988:

> In the field of humanities it is often difficult to gauge the results of research, either in the short or the long term. It is different from the physical and natural sciences and from technological research in which the impact on society is more immediate and dramatic, as well as more obviously profitable—all reasons why these areas receive more recognition and support than the humanities. Yet, no one denies that human beings are infinitely more complex and valuable than any machine or technological process. We tend to forget this because of the casual way people are mishandled, neglected, and destroyed. This is especially true of the poor—and most of the world's population *is* poor—and it is important to understand them, not only to make their lives more productive but also to eliminate poverty and the problems associated with it.

Oscar Lewis did not die a happy man. He was carrying the burden of the Cuba project's demise and the heavy cost to some informants. He was under attack from people on the Left who should have been his natural allies, but who apparently believed he was blaming the poor for their poverty or that he had given in to fame, or who accepted the trumped-up charge of spying in Cuba. Yet throughout his life Lewis had stayed pretty much the same in terms of his identity and politics. He was a critic of the maldistribution of wealth and class stratification in advanced capitalist systems. He remained deeply involved in his extended family, despite having changed his surname to better assimilate. He was for the most part a nonobserver of his Jewish faith, yet its basic charge to do good work was the centering factor in his life. He was never fully comfortable living or working in any upper- or middle-class gentile milieu. His closest friends in academic life, Jules Henry and Irving Goldman, for example, were out of the same New York, Jewish, Depression-era background. Outside his extended family, the people who knew him best, and around whom he felt most comfortable, were long-time collaborators in his work, such as the psychologist Carolina Luján and translators Muna Muñoz Lee and Asa Zatz.

Lewis's professional life is basically of a piece; to read what he was trying to do in 1943 is to know what he was trying to do in 1970. On the most general level Lewis was interested in the "good society," and how to bring it about. He may not have been certain of all aspects of its definition, but he knew it required the eradication of poverty. The most significant change in his work was the shift away from social science reporting in his later published works. But Lewis had always been interested in literature and the performing arts, had studied operatic voice all his life, shared his wife's interest in film and the conviction that certain ideas could be best communicated through the passion and subjectivity of art and literature. Lewis would probably have preferred to make his contribution as a writer rather than as a social scientist, so the accusation that he was a novelist who had invented his informants was something he could easily have lived with if not for the fact that it was essential to him that readers know his informants were not fiction and that their suffering was real.

In the introduction to his published *Essays*, just months before his death, Lewis wrote "the precise recording of the social facts of poverty and inequality in peasant villages and . . . urban slums, and their destructive effects on human beings, is in itself a revolutionary act." Ruth Lewis has said it is perhaps better characterized as "a progressive act," one "that might inspire people at least to confront situations that they were pushing under the rug." In the end she said, their work "aroused social conscience, and that's all we ever hoped to do."

NOTES

1. Letter to writer-director Elia Kazan, who had purchased the screenrights to *La Vida*, March 1, 1967. Lewis was describing the characteristics that should be assigned to a fictionalized version of himself in the screenplay.
2. Letter from Oscar Lewis to Maurice Halperin, April 11, 1958.

3. For more comprehensive coverage of Lewis's career, the evolution of the culture of poverty concept, selected correspondence, and a complete bibliography, see Susan M. Rigdon, *Culture Facade: Art, Science and Politics in the Work of Oscar Lewis* (Urbana: University of Illinois Press, 1988). No full biography of Lewis has been written. The Oscar Lewis Papers in the archives of the graduate library at the University of Illinois contain most of Lewis's raw field data and more than half of his professional correspondence, but none of his personal letters. Lewis's doctoral thesis and most of his major articles were reprinted in *Anthropological Essays* (New York: Random House, 1970).

4. Letter to Elia Kazan, March 1, 1967.

5. This observation is from Ruth Maslow Lewis; personal conversation with author, October 2001. All quotes from Maslow Lewis cited in this chapter are from that conversation or from taped interviews I conducted in 1987–88.

6. This summer field trip to two Blackfoot reservations in Alberta, Canada, was under Ruth Benedict's direction and led to Lewis's first published article, "Manly-Hearted Women Among the Northern Piegan," *American Anthropologist* 3 (April–June 1941): 173–87. Lewis's later research on the Blackfoot became his Ph.D. thesis; its publication was arranged by Julian Steward, later to become Lewis's colleague, friend, and department head at Illinois. *The Effects of White Contact upon Blackfoot Culture, with Special Reference to the Role of the Fur Trade*, Monographs of the American Ethnological Society, no. 6 (Seattle: Washington University Press, 1942).

7. The conversation with Kennedy appeared in *Redbook*, September 1967. Papers from the Race and Poverty Seminar were published in Daniel P. Moynihan, ed., *On Understanding Poverty* (New York: Basic Books, 1968), and James L. Sundquist, ed., *On Fighting Poverty* (New York: Basic Books, 1969).

8. By the time of project closure, the Lewises had carried about 30,000 pages of notes and transcribed materials out of the country on trips to the States. This material was written up in four books published by the University of Illinois Press: Oscar Lewis, Ruth M. Lewis, Susan M. Rigdon, *Living the Revolution: An Oral History of Contemporary Cuba*, 3 vols. (Urbana: University of Illinois Press, 1977, 1978); Douglas Butterworth, *The People of Buena Ventura: Relocation of Slum Dwellers in Postrevolutionary Cuba* (Urbana: University of Illinois Press, 1980).

9. David Price, "The F.B.I. and Oscar Lewis," paper delivered at the annual meeting of the American Anthropological Association, Chicago, 1999. Price used FOIA to gain access to Lewis's FBI file; the released segment was about 300 pages, with an unspecified number of pages withheld. The paper will be a chapter in Price's forthcoming book on anthropology and the Cold War.

10. Julian Steward, creator of the theory and method of cultural ecology, was a major figure in American anthropology. His biography has been written by Virginia Kerns, *Scenes from the High Desert: Julian Steward's Life and Theory* (Urbana: University of Illinois Press, 2003).

11. All quotations in this paragraph are from Lewis's introduction to the section on "Peasantry" in *Anthropological Essays* (New York: Random House, 1970), 251–54.

CHAPTER 14

Charles Osgood:

The Psychology of Language

Charles Egerton Osgood had enormous impact on a range of disciplines—psychology, communications, linguistics, and peace studies. He also had a love affair with the University of Illinois, where he spent almost his entire professional career. His work shows how being based at a great university can facilitate the development of an individual scholar and what a huge influence a single extraordinary faculty member can have on a university.

EARLY YEARS

A native New Englander, Osgood was born on November 20, 1916, in Somerville, Massachusetts. His parents divorced when he was six and he described a relatively unhappy childhood. Already in high school he showed a clear interest in communication. He was a reporter for the school newspaper and tried his hand at writing science fiction, fantasy, and horror stories.

He planned to major in English at the time he entered Dartmouth College and dreamed of earning his living as a reporter while writing the Great American Novel. In his first year there, he said he rushed around the campus in a raccoon coat reporting on events for the *Daily Dartmouth*. Then during his sophomore year, Osgood changed his mind after taking an introductory psychology course from Theodore Karwoski (who was known on campus as the "Count"). Osgood said that he "found what I had been, unknowingly, looking for all the time—the right combination of demand for rigor and room for creativity."[1] He decided that psychology was what he wanted to do with his life and he never looked back.

After graduating in 1939, he married Cynthia Luella ("Patty") Thornton, a resident of Hanover, New Hampshire. He spent an extra year at Dartmouth doing research and holding all-night parties that apparently involved listening to jazz records and dancing on the lawn next to a graveyard.

For his Ph.D. Osgood went to Yale. Soon he found himself teaching many of the undergraduate courses because most of the faculty members were engaged in war work. Among his students were a number of officer candidates. Osgood reported that he grew his mustache in an effort to appear more mature while teaching these older students. In Osgood's graduate studies he clearly tried to master *all* of experimental psychology. He stated, "there is no better way to discover what you really *don't* understand than to try to teach it to someone else."[2] Later he drew on the knowledge he gained from this experience in writing his first book, *Method and Theory in Experimental Psychology* (1953).[3] This was the last graduate-level handbook covering all of experimental psychology and written by a single individual. One might argue that Osgood was the last person to attempt to master all of experimental psychology.

After graduating from Yale, Osgood spent part of 1945 working at the Smoky Hill Army Air Force Base in Salina, Kansas, and then an additional year at the New London Submarine Base. His academic career began in 1946 when he took a job as an assistant professor at the University of Connecticut. He was still a relatively unknown assistant professor three years later, when he received a "bolt out of the blue": an offer from the University of Illinois. It was the kind of offer every young academic dreams about: a tenured associate professorship with a half-time research position. Osgood knew little about Illinois, having spent almost his entire life in New England. In one of his autobiographical pieces he described the offer as coming "from far away Illinois—which is much further from Boston than Worcester, as you all know."[4]

By that time, the University of Illinois had begun to attract a number of outstanding scholars in areas related to Osgood's interests. Three of them had their eyes on Osgood: Ross Stagner and Hobart Mowrer in the psychology department, and Wilbur Schramm in the Institute of Communications Research, a new interdisciplinary unit. Stagner had worked with Osgood at Dartmouth; Mowrer had known Osgood at Yale. Schramm's background was in English literature, but having worked with the Office of War Information during World War II, he had become impressed with the importance of using the quantitative techniques of the social sciences to study the media. Schramm had left the University of Iowa to develop the University of Illinois's Institute of Communications Research and he wanted to hire someone who could study language from a social science perspective. Schramm offered Osgood a faculty position that involved research half-time in the institute and teaching half-time in the Department of Psychology.

It is not completely clear why Schramm decided that Osgood was someone who could study language quantitatively, given that Osgood, as he himself reported in his autobiographical accounts, only began to focus his research on language in 1951, after attending a conference at Cornell University on Psychology and Linguistics. Hiring Osgood nevertheless worked out well for both Osgood and the University of Illinois. In later years Schramm said that it was the best faculty appointment he ever made.[5]

INTELLECTUAL CONTRIBUTIONS

Osgood's work contributed to four broad areas: psycholinguistics, the psychology of meaning, cross-cultural studies, and peace studies.

PSYCHOLINGUISTICS. Osgood knew little about the field of linguistics—the scientific study of language—at the time he was studying experimental psychology at Yale. But in 1951, when he was still relatively unknown, he was invited to the Cornell Conference on Linguistics and Psychology, because someone else had declined. He accepted the invitation, as he would later say, mainly because he thought it would be enjoyable to spend a summer in the Lake District of New York. This fluke had a major influence on the rest of his academic career, for in his typical fashion Osgood made it his job to learn everything he could about linguistics and how knowledge from this field might impact psychology.

In his later writings, Osgood made fun of his initial ignorance of linguistics, reporting that he had thought linguists "were strange, bearded, bird-like creatures who inhabited the remoter regions of libraries, babbling away in many exotic languages and constructing dictionaries for them." At the Cornell conference he found that they were "robust, rigorous, and objective, maybe even a bit more so than the young [experimental psychologist]."[6]

Osgood's involvement with linguistics matured rapidly. A year after the Cornell conference he became chair of the Social Science Research Council's new Committee on Linguistics and Psychology. He helped plan a conference that in many ways proved the birthplace of a new field of study in which Osgood was to be deeply influential. At this conference, held in 1953 at Indiana University, the name *psycholinguistics* was introduced for this new field. During the next decade, Osgood helped organize a series of Summer Institutes that molded early thinking in such topics within psycholinguistics as comparative psycholinguistics, bilingualism, meaning, style, language universals, and language disorders. Many in the first generation of psycholinguists attended these conferences as faculty or students.

By the 1960s ideas first put forth by Noam Chomsky resulted in a dramatic revolution in the way linguists approached the study of language and caused reevaluation of the field of psycholinguistics. As Osgood was opposed to many of the new approaches, his impact on the area declined.

MEANING AND THE SEMANTIC DIFFERENTIAL. Early in his intellectual life, Osgood decided that he wanted to develop a theory of meaning—a psychological theory that would, for example, give an account of why "little" and "small" mean roughly the same thing and why neither of them means the same thing as "big." In his autobiographical accounts he traced his fascination with the issue of meaning to his childhood, when his grandfather played word games with him using rare words. His grandfather would give Osgood pennies that he could use to buy jelly beans if the boy later used these words appropriately in new sentences. To help young Osgood in these word games his favorite aunt gave him a thesaurus for his tenth birthday. Most boys at that age would not be exactly overjoyed at receiving a thesaurus for a birthday present, but Osgood truly loved this book. He did not think of it as a reference book, but as something that gave him aesthetic pleasure. He said that he spent hours and hours reading through it.

As a young associate professor at Illinois, Osgood set out to develop a tool for measuring the meaning of particular words. He would call it the semantic differential. To use it, Osgood asked individuals to rate a word whose meaning he wished to measure on a series of 7-point scales that were anchored at each end by adjectives of opposite meaning, for example: fast-slow, alive-dead, rich-poor, old-young. The rater would take a word such

Charles Osgood discussing a model representing a word in multidimensional space with students and staff in the Psychology Building in the early 1970s. *From left to right:* Charles Osgood, Oliver Tzeng, Kay Bock, Farideh Salili (partly obscured), Flora Rodriguez-Brown, Patrice French, Gordana Opacic, Charlene Miles, Rumjahn Hoosain, and Bill May.

as *egg* and decide where it fell along the various dimensions. Most people would rate the word *egg* as toward the young end of the old-young scale. By having hundreds of individuals rate hundreds of words on hundreds of different scales, Osgood generated enormous amounts of data. Reducing the data using a statistical procedure known as factor analysis, he discovered to his surprise that these analyses consistently yielded the same three basic factors: evaluation (good versus bad), potency (strong versus weak), and activity (active versus passive). Any word could be defined by its location in the three-dimensional space described by these three factors. Thus the word *coward* was found to be low on evaluation, low on potency, and slightly above the mid-range on activity.

At first Osgood thought his technique provided a way to measure meaning in general. This claim, presented in his first book on the semantic differential, *The Measurement of Meaning* (1957),[7] was severely attacked by linguists and psychologists. Over time Osgood came to understand that the semantic differential measures the affective, not the denotative, meaning of words. Osgood thought this occurred because the raters were often forced to interpret the scales metaphorically. One reviewer of *The Measurement of Meaning* made the playful comment that the book was high on evaluation, potency, and activity. In saying that the book was high on potency, the reviewer was not saying that the book was literally strong, as a weight lifter is, but that it was intellectually strong in a metaphorical sense. In one of his early autobiographical pieces Osgood stated that his major contribution to psychology would be his "demonstration of [the] simple fact, that shared affective meaning of concepts is the common coin of metaphor."[8]

The power of the semantic differential to measure people's affective responses to words and concepts was quickly evident. Soon it was being used across clinical psychology, political science, sociology, and many other fields. Within the first ten to fifteen years of its development the semantic differential was used in thousands of published studies. In discussing this enormous proliferation of his work, Osgood later said, "I must confess that sometimes I feel like the Geppetto of a wayward Pinocchio who has wandered off into the Big City, and Lord knows what mischief he's getting into."[9]

CROSS-CULTURAL RESEARCH. Having completed a minor in anthropology as an undergraduate at Dartmouth, Osgood was always sensitive to the problem of knowing whether research by American experimental psychologists really studied how the human mind worked or only reflected the characteristics of American college students. That led to his interest in the degree to which his work on the semantic differential actually revealed aspects of the mind or only aspects of American English and American culture. To resolve this issue he developed one of the largest and most sophisticated cross-cultural studies ever carried out. This project developed semantic differentials for almost thirty different cultures and languages (e.g., Finnish, Serbo-Croatian, Bengali, Japanese, Thai) and used these semantic differentials to examine 620 concepts. In describing the beginning of this cross-cultural project Osgood once again drew on the Pinocchio allegory. He wrote, "Geppetto and his Pinocchio set out across the world, looking—not for fame and fortune—but for friends in foreign lands who might catch some of the excitement and join in the exploration of semantic space."[10]

There were enormous practical problems in carrying out this type of research with very different languages in different cultural settings. Osgood had never been outside North America when he began the project. In his autobiographical writing he described a number of quite funny episodes that arose out of his initial lack of sophistication in dealing with new cultures. For example, on a visit that Osgood described to the Maharaja of Mysore, Osgood's companion took off his shoes at the door to the Maharaja's private quarters. Osgood realized that he had a serious problem: "after some two months of travel, I had a hole in my sock that exposed my right big toe completely. But the door opens, there stands His Highness, and off come my shoes. I hobble in, trying to keep my left foot in front of my right, and sit down, trying to keep my left foot on top of my right. Every so often, in the excitement of the discussion, I see the Maharaja's eyes drift downward and I quickly re-cap my big toe."[11]

In spite of such difficulties, Osgood found colleagues in each of the culture/language groups and carried out the extremely complex data collection and analysis needed to answer the question of the generality of the semantic differential. The cross-cultural project found fairly strong evidence for the universality of the underlying dimensions of evaluation, potency, and activity, often with interesting region-specific or culture-specific variations.

PEACE STUDIES. A final area in which Osgood made important contributions was the study of international relations. He stated that for the first thirty years of his life he was apolitical and did not even bother to vote. But while spending the year 1958–59 at the Center for Advanced Study in the Behavioral Sciences in Palo Alto, California, he had a conversion experience. His office was next to that of Jerome Frank, a psychiatrist who had been trying to bring findings from the behavioral sciences to bear on the problems of international relations during the Cold War. Osgood described the reasoning that led to his newfound concern with international affairs. He asked himself, "Why run more rats through the maze if there will be no more human behavior, or rat behavior, to have a theory of?" And also, "how many intellectuals have lifted their brilliantly plumaged heads up out the sand and looked fully into the face of a nuclear holocaust?"[12]

After thinking about the problems raised by the confrontation between the United States and the Soviet Union, Osgood proposed a strategy designed to decrease the hostility between competing powers. He called this strategy GRIT (Graduated and Reciprocated Initiatives in Tension-reduction) and described it in testimony before the U.S. Senate. In this approach, "nation A devises patterns of small steps, well within its limits of security, intended to reduce tensions and designed to induce reciprocating steps from nation B. If such unilateral initiatives are persistently applied, and reciprocation is obtained, then the margin for risk taking is widened and somewhat larger steps of the same sort can be taken. Both sides, in effect, begin backing down the escalation ladder."[13]

Osgood tried hard to bring his work on international relations to the attention of people in power. He had one book on the topic privately printed and distributed to people he thought were in positions that allowed them to do something about the Cold War. On occasion he would send telegrams to every U.S. senator and representative. On May 25, 1966, he testified before the Committee on Foreign Relations of the U.S. Senate (chaired by Senator Fulbright) and on June 26, 1973, before the Subcommittee on Europe of the Committee on Foreign Affairs of the U.S. House of Representatives (chaired by Congressman Rosenthal). In 1977 he was invited to one of the Pugwash conferences that were designed to help reduce Cold War tensions through discussion by scientists from both sides. But for the most part, Osgood thought that he had failed to get his ideas through to those with power. Toward the end of his career he became very pessimistic about the future of civilization. The book he was planning to write outlining his beliefs was going to be titled, *Mankind 2000?* As he became even more pessimistic he changed the title to *Mankind 2000??*

There is evidence that Osgood's views played a calming role during one of the most dangerous episodes of the Cold War, the Cuban missile crisis. Osgood had made contacts with a number of individuals in the Kennedy administration and received word that Kennedy had read his basic book on the GRIT strategy, *An Alternative to War or Surrender.*[14] Osgood felt that Kennedy's approach of setting up a naval blockade with the eventual removal of the missiles was an example of his GRIT strategy in operation. After the crisis was over, Osgood received a note from John McNaughton, assistant secretary of defense for International Security Affairs, saying, "What did you think of our use of GRIT in Cuba?"[15]

Osgood's cross-cultural project also brought him some political notoriety that he surely did not want. In 1977, when several reporters used the Freedom of Information Act to gain access to papers dealing with the CIA's secret project MKULTRA,[16] Osgood was horrified to find out that the Human Ecology Fund, which had provided the funding for the early phases of his cross-cultural semantic differential project, was a CIA front organization. The highly censored documents released by the CIA stated that, although the director of the project was "unwitting," a CIA agent had been infiltrated into the project. These revelations were particularly hard on someone who had devoted a significant portion of his professional energy to activities designed to reduce world tensions. The degree of betrayal he must have felt can been seen in one of his early discussions of cross-cultural research in which he stated that researchers "must recognize the political sensitivity and the possible misuse of such information."[17]

HONORS. On the basis of his exceptional contributions across a wide range of topics, Osgood was granted just about every professional honor that it is possible for a psychologist to receive. In 1960 he received the Award for Distinguished Scientific Contribution from the American Psychological Association. In 1963 he was elected president of the American Psychological Association. In 1971 he received the Kurt Lewin Memorial Award from the Society for the Psychological Study of Social Issues. And, in 1976, he was elected president of the Peace Science Society. He was elected to the National Academy of Sciences in 1972.

OSGOOD AND THE UNIVERSITY OF ILLINOIS

At Illinois, Osgood was able to take advantage of the resources that a great research university could offer. He stated that most of his early work on the semantic differential was funded by the Institute of Communications Research and by the University of Illinois Research Board, which he (correctly) characterized as a unit that "takes overhead funds from those who hath and delivers them to those who hath not."[18] He also noted that some of the early analyses involved in developing the semantic differential were possible only because the University of Illinois was at the forefront in the development of large computers. For his complex factor analyses, he was granted large amounts of time on the ILLIAC digital computer.

Osgood also had a strong relationship with the University of Illinois Press. When he was carrying out his initial work on the semantic differential he had too much material for easy journal publication, so he approached the press and asked if they would publish a research monograph. They agreed, and *The Measurement of Meaning* (1957) went on to become one of the best-selling titles at the press. Later, in 1962, the press published *An Alternative to War or Surrender*, the primary source for Osgood's GRIT strategy to reduce tension in international affairs. And in 1975, the press published *Cross-Cultural Universals of Affective Meaning*, which contained the core findings of his cross-cultural research with the semantic differential.

Osgood's research flourished in the rich research environment of the University of Illinois. He wrote, "it is a real pleasure to look back on those early days at Illinois when we literally lived and breathed our research from morning to night. I used to be my own first 'guinea pig' in every experiment . . . to try to get a feel for what might go on in the heads of real subjects. In the midst of doing one experiment, others were always aborning—over coffee, over sandwiches and beer, and even over cocktails and dinner."[19]

The physical location of this research moved around the campus over the years. The early work on the semantic differential started in the sub-basement of Gregory Hall. From there the operation moved to a house at 909 S. 6th St. (now the Division of Management Information). This was one of the more interesting locations—it also housed a Mayan who had been brought with his kiln from the Yucatan by the anthropology department to demonstrate traditional pottery skills. As Osgood's research shifted toward cross-cultural work, the research group came to be called the Center for Comparative Psycholinguistics. The center next moved to a house at 1207 W. Oregon Avenue (now the Social Work Building). When the new Psychology Building opened in 1970 the center took up residence on the sixth floor. The final move was to 505 E. Green Street (now the American Indian Studies and Cultural House). During this entire period the actual carrying out of the research was greatly facilitated by Bill May, who came up through the ranks, starting out as a keypuncher and gradually taking on more and more responsibility for the day-to-day work. By the 1970s he had become co-director of the center. Osgood described him, not as his "right hand" but as his "right arm."

The university was very tolerant about supporting Osgood's extraordinarily broad range of research interests. When he began his study of meaning, this topic was not in favor in either psychology or linguistics, yet the university backed him strongly. Osgood was willing to tackle almost any intellectual issue to which he thought he could make a contribution. For example, with Zella Luria, he carried out a semantic differential study of a patient with multiple personalities (the case later known as *The Three Faces of Eve*).

As his career developed Osgood continued to receive strong backing from the university. In 1965 he was appointed professor in the University of Illinois's Center for Advanced Study, a position that freed him from all teaching obligations (though he continued to teach his favorite course on psycholinguistics for his own pleasure). Osgood repaid the university by helping to shape certain areas of study and by helping to bring many excellent scholars into its community. In those days hiring faculty was a more informal procedure than it is today. At least three of those Osgood hired report that they were offered their positions without ever having visited the university for a job interview! Osgood's active role in the hiring process over the years is one of his major legacies at the University of Illinois.

In 1957, when Osgood took over from Wilbur Schramm as director of the Institute of Communications Research, he emphasized the study of language and made the institute a world center for the study of psycholinguistics.

Some members of the first generation of psycholinguists, such as Merrill Garrett, took their degrees from the institute, rather than from the Department of Psychology. Not only did Osgood build up the study of language at the institute, he continued to develop the institute's strongly interdisciplinary nature, which it retains to this day, by hiring faculty with backgrounds in sociology, journalism, philosophy, psychology, and anthropology. For example, Osgood was strongly involved in having Howard Maclay offered a job in the institute. Maclay had been a graduate student in anthropology at the University of New Mexico at the time Osgood met him. Later Maclay took over the directorship of the institute for many years.

Osgood believed strongly in evaluating scholars on their intellectual merits. In particular, he arranged appointments for a number of women who were having trouble finding positions due to the pervasive sex discrimination of the time. In keeping with these beliefs he was also instrumental in breaking down the nepotism rule, which did not allow couples to hold tenured positions at the same university. For example, he fought hard to arrange a tenured position at Illinois for Rita Simon (see chapter 17), who later became chair of the sociology department.

Osgood also played important roles in establishing at least two departments at Illinois. As chair of the search for someone to head the new independent Department of Anthropology, Osgood persuaded Joe Casagrande, whom he had met in the course of his dealings with the Social Science Research Council, to come to Illinois as head of the new anthropology department. In 1955, Osgood and Henry Kahane from Romance Languages began discussing ways to form a Department of Linguistics; by 1956 they had established a program in linguistics. In 1961 Osgood helped bring Robert Lees to Illinois, who, soon after, became chair of the new Department of Linguistics.

Osgood also set his stamp on various parts of the Department of Psychology. At the 1951 Cornell Conference on Psychology and Linguistics, Osgood met Don Dulany, then a young graduate student from the University of Michigan. Osgood was instrumental in having the psychology department offer a job to Dulany in 1956, and later to William Brewer in 1969. Dulany and Brewer played a major role in establishing the cognitive division within the psychology department, a division that remains strong, rated third in the nation in the most recent rankings. Osgood would be pleased to know that the cognitive division of the psychology department continues to have a world-class psycholinguistics group that includes one of his own Ph.D.s, Kay Bock.

Portrait of Charles Osgood in the early 1970s.

Osgood also helped develop other parts of the Department of Psychology. Harry Triandis, while still a graduate student at Cornell, wrote a letter to Osgood raising the issue of possibly gathering semantic differential data on a Greek population. Osgood not only thought this was a good idea, but helped Triandis secure a grant to carry out the work. Later he arranged to have the data analyzed on the ILLIAC. When Triandis completed his Ph.D. and went on the job market Osgood saw that he received an offer from Illinois. Triandis, who accepted the offer, brought a cross-cultural influence to the social and organizational programs in the Department of Psychology that persists to this day.

OSGOOD AS A PERSON

One of Osgood's strongest traits was his intellectual integrity. Confident in his own positions, he truly believed that academia should be the playing field of competing ideas. He held his own positions with bulldog-like tenacity, yet he respected the fact that others might hold quite different opinions. His book, *The Measurement of Meaning*, received some very critical reviews, focusing especially on the authors' claims to have a general theory of meaning. Yet, in 1969 when Osgood and Jim Snider edited a handbook on the semantic differential, they included a number of the most negative reviews. At one point during his time at Illinois Osgood felt that a younger faculty member was not receiving a fair salary raise, so he demanded that the administrators take part of his own raise and transfer it to the junior faculty member's salary (and he never informed the younger colleague about his actions).

Osgood was quite opposed to Noam Chomsky's positions in linguistics, yet he arranged for a number of his best students to study Chomskian linguistics at MIT. He also arranged for the philosopher Jerry Fodor, who was vehemently opposed to Osgood's theory of meaning, to spend a year at the University of Illinois as a visiting professor. Osgood invited Fodor to sit in on his psycholinguistics class. This must have been good theater. Osgood described Fodor sitting in on his psycholinguistics class with the following wry comment, "if you could imagine Jerry just 'sitting in' on anything; bouncing between floor and ceiling would be more like it!"[20] At the end of these vigorous discussions Osgood arranged for Fodor to be offered a job at Illinois.

Osgood had a fantastic ability to get work accomplished. He worked day and night throughout the year, often going for many years without a vacation. One of his students said that it was embarrassing to be his research assistant. They would divide up some major task, and the next day Osgood would have his part of the task finished before the student had even started. Osgood stated that in his early days at Illinois, from 1950 to 1955, he completed over seventy empirical studies.

In class Osgood was an active and well-prepared teacher. A number of people who took classes with him have vivid memories of him jumping up on a desk and doing a rat imitation by bending over with his hands to his face, twitching his "rat whiskers" while showing how a rat would perform in a particular type of psychological experiment.

Osgood was a serious sports fan. Several people report that he had a tendency to become "sick" on the day of crucial games in the World Series. He also had a lifelong interest in jazz. Together with faculty and graduate students from the psychology department he organized an informal jazz group (Osgood's Oscillators) that played together for some years. (The group's range was restricted a good bit because Osgood could only play piano in the key of F!) When Osgood traveled he would often take time off to search second-hand record stores for jazz classics. One colleague recalled with pleasure a visit to Osgood's house in which Osgood "was like a little child pulling out this record or that one and giving a complete discography from memory." For a number of years Osgood was the host for a jazz program on WILL radio, where he played records from his extensive collection with knowledgeable commentary about the artists and the music.

In the period when Osgood was involved in his cross-cultural project, he had research associates and graduate assistants from many different cultures. He would occasionally host elaborate international parties where each guest brought a cultural dish to share. For one of these "International Buffets" in 1972, Osgood produced a four-page annotated menu. It stated, "This Menue makes a gemütlich souvenir of our productive hours on the prairie, and may, if needed, be shown to a physician within the next 72 hours." He annotated the dishes with comments such as: Chevet Polou, "Iranians have been preparing this dish for more than 2500 years, though it is not yet definitively known how many of them actually eat it." Flan, "A semantically interesting dish, since the exotic name assures that it will taste better than ordinary cup custard."

In his later years Osgood and his wife owned two miniature French poodles, Pierre and later Pierre II. Several people describe being invited to the Osgood's for supper and initially wondering who the extra place setting was for. They found out when it was time to eat. Pierre would jump into his chair and sit down to the meal with the other guests.

The physical setting that most people remember for Osgood was his huge office in Gregory Hall, three or four times the size of the usual faculty office. (The room has now been subdivided to serve as the administrative offices of the journalism department.) The office had dark wood paneling and built-in shelves overflowing with books, reprints, and computer printouts. The walls had pictures of Osgood with various research groups as well as many humorous pictures that had been given to him over the years. One picture featured Osgood the Dinosaur—it was a picture of a dinosaur whose head had been removed and replaced with Osgood's. Another picture was a visual pun. Osgood used the technical term *assigns* to refer to words that are learned from other words. The picture showed a set of human buttocks mounted on a pole. On top of one of the filing cabinets was a three-dimensional model made of rubber balls and wooden dowels designed to represent the meaning of certain concepts. Over the years this model of semantic space gathered considerable dust and some of the concepts began to sag and fall apart. Osgood appreciated the irony of this representation of the work of his youth and chose to leave it the way it had become.

Osgood was a vivid writer. In his later life he realized that many young researchers considered his approach to psycholinguistics outdated, so for one autobiographical piece he wrote his life story as Osgood the Dinosaur: "The baby dinosaur was teethed on Meaning by a dentist grandfather." He described his early days of working on the semantic differential as "Ah, happy, eager dinosaur! Now reaching maturity." He stated that initially he was not concerned about Chomsky's theoretical ideas and that he "kept right on nuzzling among and munching away at his semantic daisies." But as Chomsky's approach began to have a wide-ranging impact on psychology, Osgood noted, "By the middle 1960's even the middle-aged dinosaur in his Illinois daisy patch was beginning to eye the ominous storm with some concern." Finally, as most of his own students joined the Chomsky revolution, Osgood said wistfully, "it was a rather lonesome dinosaur who kept offering his daisies at the shrine of a near-deserted . . . paradigm in the late 1960's."

As some of the focus of work in linguistics moved from the study of syntax to the study of meaning, Osgood felt that his own approach was making a comeback. He said, "even the casual observer could see the brightening gleam in his eye and the increasing vigor with which he flicked his tail." In the early 1970s Osgood led an informal research group (the Cog Group) that included several faculty members (William Brewer from Psychology and Jerry Morgan and Georgia Green from Linguistics) and a number of graduate students. Osgood described these meetings as "exciting for the old dinosaur, downright rejuvenating, in fact." He ended his paper with a discussion of the future of psycholinguistics and then in a poignant last sentence said, "But I see that our old dinosaur, wrapped in his daisy chains, has fallen sound asleep."[21]

NOTES

1. C. E. Osgood, "Exploration in Semantic Space: A Personal Diary," in *The Psychologists,* ed. T. S. Krawiec (New York: Oxford University Press, 1974), 2:345–401, 348.
2. Ibid., 350.
3. C. E. Osgood, *Method and Theory in Experimental Psychology,* (New York: Oxford University Press, 1953).
4. C. E. Osgood, "Exploration in Semantic Space: A Personal Diary," *Journal of Social Issues* 27 (1971): 5–6, 7.
5. E. Wartella, "A History of the Institute of Communications Research," in *The Institute of Communications Research: The 40th anniversary* (Urbana: Institute of Communications Research, University of Illinois, 1988), 20–26.
6. C. E. Osgood, "A Dinosaur Caper: Psycholinguistics Past, Present, and Future," *Annals of the New York Academy of Sciences* 263 (1975): 16–26, 16–17.
7. C. E. Osgood, G. J. Suci, and P. H. Tannenbaum, *The Measurement of Meaning* (Urbana: University of Illinois Press, 1957).
8. Osgood, "Exploration in Semantic Space," in *Journal of Social Issues,* 38.
9. C. E. Osgood, "Introduction," in *Semantic Differential Technique: A Sourcebook,* ed. J. G. Snider and C. E. Osgood (Chicago: Aldine, 1969), vii–ix, ix.
10. Osgood, "Exploration in Semantic Space," in *Journal of Social Issues,* 20.

11. Osgood, "Exploration in Semantic Space," in *The Psychologists*, 369.

12. C. E. Osgood, "The Psychologist in International Affairs," *American Psychologist* 19 (1964): 111–18, 111.

13. U. S. Congress "Psychological Aspects of International Relations," *Hearing before the Committee on Foreign Relations, United States Senate, 89th Congress, Second Session, May 25, 1966* (Washington, D.C.: U. S. Government Printing Office, 1966), 17.

14. C. E. Osgood, *An Alternative to War or Surrender* (Urbana: University of Illinois Press, 1962).

15. C. E. Osgood, "Charles E. Osgood," in *A History of Psychology in Autobiography*, ed. G. Lindzey (San Francisco: Freeman, 1980), 7:335–93, 374.

16. P. Greenfield, "CIA's Behavior Caper," *APA Monitor* 8, no. 12 (1977): 1, 10–11. J. Marks, "The Search for the 'Manchurian Candidate,'" (New York: W. W. Norton, 1979).

17. Osgood, "Exploration in Semantic Space," in *Journal of Social Issues*, 21.

18. Osgood, "Introduction," ix.

19. C. E. Osgood, W. E. May, and M. S. Miron, *Cross-Cultural Universals of Affective Meaning* (Urbana: University of Illinois Press, 1975), 18.

20. C. E. Osgood, "The Tale of an Eager Then Lonely Then Contented Dinosaur," *Studies in the Linguistic Sciences* 22, no. 2 (1992): 42–58, 50.

21. Osgood, "A Dinosaur Caper," 16, 18, 19, 21–24. I would like to thank Ellen Brewer, Don Dulany, Lillian Hoddeson, Howard Maclay, Bill May, and Harry Triandis for comments on an earlier draft of this chapter. Additional material about Osgood's scholarly contributions can be found in W. F. Brewer, "Charles Egerton Osgood: 1916–1991," *American Journal of Psychology* 107 (1994): 583–96; additional personal information can be found in E. Hall, "Interview with Charles Osgood," *Psychology Today* 7, no. 6 (1973): 54–60, 64–72. Osgood's most complete autobiographical account is Osgood, "Charles E. Osgood," and the most detailed account of his relationship with the University of Illinois is found in a paper he wrote in 1974, later published as Osgood, "The Tale of an Eager Then Lonely Then Contented Dinosaur."

SYLVIAN R. RAY

CHAPTER 15

The ILLIACs and the Rise to

Prominence in Computer Science

Digital computers and their accompanying science evolved rapidly out of the frenzied technological activity generated by World War II. The University of Illinois jumped into computer research early and became a major international force in computer research and development. While the principal actors behind this push were machines, particularly in the family of computers referred to as ILLIAC (members of the Illinois Automatic Computer family), many human players fueled the move, among them, Louis N. Ridenour, Ralph E. Meagher, Wolfgang Poppelbaum, Abraham H. Taub, Donald B. Gillies, James B. Robertson, Bruce H. McCormick, and Daniel Slotnick.

RIDENOUR: ACQUIRING ORDVAC AND ILLIAC

Ridenour had served as the associate director of the MIT Radiation Laboratory during World War II, when timing and counting circuitry were greatly refined for use in radar, and when the laboratory had a reputation for "forward-looking policies." Ridenour came to the University of Illinois largely because of his friendship with Wheeler Loomis, head of the physics department, who had also been involved in the administrative leadership of the MIT Radiation Laboratory. Loomis was the critical connection behind Ridenour becoming the dean of the Graduate College of the University of Illinois in 1946.

Ridenour's background was strongly connected with the University of Pennsylvania, where in 1946 early attempts at digital computer design resulted in the ENIAC (Electronic Numerical Integrator and Calculator). This machine undoubtedly sharpened Ridenour's vision of the digital computer's potential as a scientific instrument. Given his scientifically aggressive temperament, his technical interests, and his professional associations, it is not surprising that Ridenour set out to acquire a digital computer for the University of Illinois soon after settling into his deanship. An advisory committee of interested faculty was assembled; Nathan M. Newmark, the head of Civil Engineering, served as chairman.

Meanwhile, in 1946–47, a new, scientifically attractive conception of the digital computer was being shaped by a seminal proposal of John von Neumann. The team surrounding this brilliant and highly respected mathematician from Hungary produced the basic design, still in use today, of the "stored-program architecture," in which both instructions and data are stored in the computer's common random access memory, now called "RAM." This design, still called the "von Neumann architecture," was formalized in a famous paper by Burks, Goldstine, and von Neumann, published in 1946 by Princeton's Institute for Advanced Study, and titled, "Preliminary Consideration of the Logical Design of an Electronic Computing Instument."

In 1947–49, the design and construction of a computer based on von Neumann's new plan was proceeding at Princeton's Institute for Advanced Study at the same time that the University of Illinois was planning its new computer. At first Newmark's University of Illinois advisory committee proposed contracting with a commercial firm to construct a computer based on the von Neumann-Institute of Advanced Study design. But after a good deal of inquiry into companies having the appropriate technical expertise, the advisory committee concluded that there was no commercial firm willing and able to take on the uncertainties of such an unprecedented project. After exhaustive inquiry, the advisory committee was thus left with no alternative but to locally organize a project to design and construct the new University of Illinois computer. Von Neumann gave this conclusion his powerful stamp of approval. In a June 26, 1948 letter to Chairman Newmark, von Neumann stated that "my own inclination in this matter would be . . . to push development at home." This recommendation of the advisory committee for a "do-it-yourself" project proved to be a felicitous step in the University of Illinois's climb to worldwide recognition in the computer field.

The ever-urgent question of funding for the new computer was resolved through an agreement with the U.S. Department of the Army's Ordnance Corps. The university agreed that for a total grant of $250,000 it would construct a computer for army use, with the understanding that an identical computer would be constructed for the university. Mutual cooperation of this sort between the government and academic institutions in the area of basic research was (and is) an integral part of the official national science policy established by Vannevar Bush during and after World War II. The organization of the "Electronic Computer Project" flowed from this arrangement. Construction of the ORDVAC (Ordnance Variable Automatic Computer), the first member of a pair of identical computers, began on April 15, 1949, with the understanding that a copy of this machine would also be constructed and would be owned by the University of Illinois. This copy would become known as the ILLIAC. The "AC" in such early computer names stood for "automatic computer," which meant that the instruction code allowed the machine to execute its program without manual intervention, unlike a desk calculator.

MEAGHER: BUILDING ORDVAC AND ILLIAC

The direction of this novel computer project was the charge of a board consisting of Newmark, serving as chairman, Abraham H. Taub, serving as vice chairman, Ralph E. Meagher, and J. P. Nash. The board planned to follow the von Neumann design, but utilize, as much as possible, the good work that had already been done on the basic logic circuits and physical design of the Princeton-Institute for Advanced Study machine.

As with all large research projects, the story of the success and ultimate vigor of the ORDVAC depended largely upon the director, who, in this case, was Ralph Meagher, in the Department of Physics. The primary problem of computer design that had to be solved at that point was the "reliability problem." The von Neumann design was "general purpose," which is to say, it could "compute anything computable." But to what avail if the hardware broke down every half hour? All the mathematical science and potential uses of the digital computer would be just interesting theory without a reliable machine.

As a junior engineer at the MIT Radiation Laboratory during World War II, Meagher had experienced problems with unreliable hardware. He had learned how to counteract the often unstable characteristics of vacuum tubes, which were used in that pretransistor era to amplify signals. His "secret" was a grindingly tedious, totally honest ethic used in the design of hardware circuits, that of "derated worst-case design." This meant, in practice, that every logic circuit had to be carefully calculated to withstand the worst possible heating, voltage, and current that it could conceivably experience in its projected lifetime of perhaps ten years. It would then be assumed that conditions could be twice that bad. His management policy was realized through meticulous oversight. Meagher's personality was calm and patient, but he was very forceful. He was the kind of boss whose policy one would not attempt to evade or sidestep, because the embarrassment of being exposed would be unbearable.

On submitting a circuit design to Meagher, there were always incisive questions about the most minute details of the ideas and calculations to be answered, usually by the graduate student-designer. The ORDVAC was thus designed and constructed according to the most severe criteria that had ever been applied before in the history of circuit design. After the ORDVAC passed its tests at the University of Illinois in November 1951, it was dismantled and shipped to the Ballistics Research Laboratory (BRL) at Aberdeen, Maryland. There it was reassembled and passed its contracted acceptance tests by March 6, 1952. The BRL staff was justifiably impressed. They already had two computers there, the ENIAC and the EDVAC. Neither had approached such reliability. The word began to spread that Illinois knew how to design reliable computers. About a year later, the ILLIAC went into service on the Urbana campus and further demonstrated the superior reliability achieved through Meagher's design philosophy and executed by his dedicated staff.

As a note of interest, the construction procedures and equipment for these machines was not much more sophisticated than those of a glorified home garage. For example, using a hand file, a graduate student, Ted Shapin, rounded out hundreds of oval-shaped holes that had been punched out as rectangles. Neon indicator lights were viewed through these holes. The building that housed the machines during their construction was the old barnlike Electrical Engineering Research Lab (now demolished), which in the fall of 1952 became the site of John Bardeen's

ILLIAC I Central Processor (without RAM) minus covers. Ralph Meagher, project
director. The visible regularity of the circuitry is fundamental to digital devices.

original semiconductor laboratory (see chapter 16) after the ILLIAC was
moved to the first floor of the Engineering Research Laboratory.

After the ILLIAC (later called ILLIAC I) went into service in 1952, more
research focused on elementary programming.[1] All the staff personnel,
and some adventurous outsiders, took a try at the game of programming
simple algorithms. We say "game," because in pure machine language, programming was a cross between modern programming and crossword puzzling. The first assembler programs did not begin to come into use until
1957; compilers (Fortran I) appeared a year or two later. All ideas for sim-
plifying programming were limited by the execution speed and memory
capacity of first-generation computers. Nevertheless, many interesting
problems were solved within the limited conditions of a 1024 word RAM
(5K bytes) and an equivalent clock speed of perhaps 200KHz.[2]

Soon more and more faculty in different fields became interested in
learning to program and solve problems using the ILLIAC. Attempts to
solve nonlinear differential equations were a high priority for mathematical physicists eager to provide fundamental descriptions of everything
from astrophysics to biological pattern formation. Researchers in psychology used the computer to "factor analyze" their questionnaire data; electrical engineers extracted roots of characteristic equations and designed
circuits. An early work in the area of "artificial intelligence" extracted the

statistical characteristics of classical composers and used this to generate new musical works. The ILLIAC was even used to compose music, as discussed in chapter 19.

An interesting unplanned use of computing machines proved to be the first step toward computer graphics. The ILLIAC had a 3-inch cathode ray tube, which displayed a 32×32 dot raster representing one bit of all 1,024 words. By sufficient mental convolution, programs could be written that crudely displayed characters or sketched sequences on this cathode-ray tube, much as on a graphics display today.

Although the first-generation computers were laborious to program under the limitations imposed by the primitive capabilities of their hardware and software, they allowed the pioneering researchers to sense the future possibilities and whet their appetites for bigger, faster machines, a process that is still rolling along today.

POPPELBAUM: THE NEXT BIG STEP

The next limitation of the first-generation computers was obvious to everyone: execution speeds of only 50,000 instructions per second blocked the path to visionary applications. Another major impediment was the limited RAM capacity of only 5K to 10K bytes. The focal point of execution speed, the speed with which the elementary logic circuits in a computer switch depends on the active devices used in the computer. Originally these devices were vacuum tubes; later they were transistors.

In 1954, when the Swiss physicist Wolfgang J. ("Ted") Poppelbaum came to Illinois as a postdoctoral student in John Bardeen's semiconductor laboratory, the available practical active elements were vacuum tubes and transistors. But the first transistors invented in December 1947 (see chapter 16), and even those available in 1954, were as slow as vacuum tubes, only smaller in size. Although these solid-state devices were potentially more reliable than tubes, their actual reliability was then still very shaky. Nevertheless, confident in the future development of better transistors, the staff of the university's new Digital Computer Laboratory (DCL), into which the Electronic Computer Project had metamorphosed, leaned toward transistors as the active elements of the next-generation machine. After ILLIAC I was finished in 1952, DCL was located within the Graduate College. Later, DCL would become the Department of Computer Science.

Designing high-reliability logic circuits with the transistor, a totally new element, required a leader with the supreme self-confidence of an explorer and the open-mindedness to consider any idea, however wild it might initially appear. Ted Poppelbaum, who stepped into the role of heading the second-generation circuit design effort, was such a person. He was a fount of ideas, expressed in an inimitable hybrid accent. Ted liked to project a "bad boy" image. He was addicted to high-speed cars, high-speed logic circuits, science fiction, and a variety of cuisines. He was also fascinated by games and puzzles. He changed cars frequently, preferring full-size "muscle" models, like Ford's Crown Victoria, which accommodated his rather rotund frame better than a cramped Porsche. The maximum speed of each car he owned was carefully tested by him, and often described at lunches and parties.

A session between Ted and his graduate students generally resulted in a set of challenges, in the form of "next things to try out" in the search for understanding the inner details of various circuits, how to model them, and how to make them faster. Graduate students liked the exhilaration of the challenge in exploring the unknown, and there was plenty of unknown territory in transistor circuit design to explore.

In the exploratory phase of hardware design using transistors, a limited scale model computer, known as a "Trance," was used to test circuit ideas using the transistors available in 1956. This experience made clear that if transistors were no faster than the Texas Instruments transistors then available, the second-generation computers would be only negligibly faster than first-generation ones. Nevertheless, the DCL staff wrote an informal proposal to the Atomic Energy Commission (later ERDA, and now DOE, the Department of Energy) for the design and construction of a new computer based mainly on improvements in architecture, as opposed to basic circuit speed. The reputation of DCL, resulting from the success of the ORDVAC/ILLIAC I design, resulted in encouraging feedback. At about this point, in February 1957, von Neumann passed away unexpectedly at the age of fifty-three. But the power of his positive opinion of Illinois's competence was a lingering benefit in dealing with the AEC Research Board.

As fortune would have it, James Early at Bell Telephone Laboratories had just solved the key problem of transistor switching speed, upon which faster computer execution speed would depend. In 1955, Early invented and demonstrated the "mesa" design, a radically new processing technique for bipolar transistors resulting in an immediate 100-fold speed improvement with major yield and reliability improvement. DCL soon acquired ten of the new mesa transistors (of germanium, not silicon) and after two to three months of preliminary work, DCL demonstrated the fastest computer circuits then in existence to the AEC Research Board. Initially, the 100-fold speed improvement, achieved overnight, was met with some disbelief, if not suspicion. Shortly thereafter, the AEC authorized a grant for a one-year preliminary design phase of a second-generation computer.

Poppelbaum's design group recognized that a critical advancement in computer design had become possible with the advent of superspeed mesa transistors. Poppelbaum went into "red alert" mode to design the necessary circuits for a new and much faster computer, the ILLIAC II. New insights and a high order of creativity were needed to understand the characteristics of the mesa transistors, how to optimize the speed, and how to satisfy the demanding derating principles set down by Meagher. Novel methods and ideas were needed. First, there was a lack of commercial test equipment. None of the oscilloscopes on hand, the primary tool of the hardware circuit designer, were fast enough to display the circuit operation using the new mesa transistors. Just to see the signals representing the "1's" and "0's" produced by the logic circuits, oscilloscopes had to be cobbled from existing equipment, by adding in-house designed amplifiers. Second, with only ten transistors available at first, the graduate student designers had to pass the transistors around and be extremely careful not to destroy any of them. The first set of transistors was literally more precious than a set of large diamonds, so much so that Ted kept four of the transistors in reserve in his desk drawer.

Another interesting "first" was to use an existing computer to design the next-generation computer, a procedure that has been standard since that time. Once the transistor properties had been measured experimentally, the new machine's circuits were modeled and simulated on the ILLIAC I. Several graduate students were each assigned to design a logic circuit. Each wrote an ad hoc program for his own logic circuit because general purpose design programs were nonexistent. The resulting class of circuits, which came to be called "Emitter Coupled Logic" circuits, was commercialized and for several decades remained the highest-speed family of integrated logic circuits available commercially.

GILLIES AND ROBERTSON: A NEW ARCHITECTURE

ILLIAC II was a pioneering computer in many respects, in both hardware and architecture. The architecture of its control unit embodied the original version of "instruction look-ahead." The designer of this architecture was Donald B. Gillies, a former student of von Neumann's at Princeton, who joined the University of Illinois in 1956 as an assistant professor of mathematics. "Instruction look-ahead," or "streaming," accomplishes speed increase by simultaneous operations on several program instructions. Gillies was also a major contributor to the "parallelizing" of the arithmetic calculations, using one arithmetic unit for primary arithmetic and a second parallel unit to calculate exponents and addresses. This architecture, in which various operations were separated and parallelized in the interest of speed, was a first in ILLIAC II and became a trend that continued in all later computers.

Gillies, incidentally, was a superb mathematician as well as a wonderfully fruitful person to discuss technical ideas with. After the ILLIAC II was completed, he designed a stringent acceptance test that contributed to the area of mathematics known as number theory. This was a program that computed a special class of prime numbers known as Mersenne primes. It was used on the ILLIAC II to discover the two largest prime numbers then known. The program was quite complex because it required treating the computer as if it operated on numbers that were not 32 or 64 bits long, but 15,000 bits in length!

Another major computer design improvement introduced into the ILLIAC II was a multiplication algorithm designed by James E. Robertson. This was a base-4 multiplier that doubled the speed of multiplication over that of the existing base-2 technique. In spite of its logical beauty, the method was not widely used in later computers for reasons too technical to discuss here. Robertson was also chief engineer of the ILLIAC II, which means he made final decisions on sometimes sticky and contentious choices as to what exactly to include or exclude from the overall design. The final decision-making role that he performed suited his character perfectly. His cleverness with numerical algorithms was supplemented with a flare for diplomacy, which manifested itself in his meticulous weighing of all facts before rendering a decision. In practice, the problem at hand would be argued out by the contending parties while Robertson sat, feet propped up on a desk, puffing gently on his pipe. At the end of the arguments, a silence of typically thirty to sixty seconds passed before a decision was rendered. Since Robertson was partially of Cherokee ancestry, his graduate students found this methodical, painstaking style of decision-making rather humorous, vaguely analogous to the passing of the peace pipe ritual in American Indian deliberations. Nevertheless, the quality of the decisions made in this way were borne out by ILLIAC II's success.

The most unreliable unit of the first-generation machines was its principal memory (RAM), which for the ILLIAC I had been based on a poorly controlled complex phenomenon in cathode ray tubes. In fact, the principal memory was the one section of the ILLIAC I that could not be fully designed to meet Meagher's rigorous criteria. But about 1956 a much more

ILLIAC II CPU and control unit. This shows the scale clearly. Harold Lopeman on ladder.

reliable component, the magnetic core, was coming into widespread use—in time for the ILLIAC II. So a unique magnetic core memory, emphasizing speed and reliability, was designed and tested (by me), and it proved successful. An electrical engineering professor, Harry Brearley, designed a secondary memory, the equivalent of a very limited hard disk drive of today. It was used as a unit of the ILLIAC II.

Thus, all of the ILLIAC II's hardware was based on original custom designs. And all of the machine, except for a few secondary devices (e.g., the power supply), was constructed on site, in the basement shops of the DCL building. Visitors from Canada (University of Toronto), Japan, Australia, and Israel and from other U.S. universities spent periods of time working with the DCL design team, learning and preparing to duplicate the ILLIAC II in their home locations.

TAUB: PROGRAMMING AND SOFTWARE

In the early years of computers, the principal problem was to engineer hardware with high reliability and speed. Finding numerical algorithms that were simple, efficient, and accurate was also pressing. Some of the early problems in this area were the computation of square roots, the roots of polynomials, and, perhaps the most vital scientifically, the solution of differential equations. The last was especially interesting to the project's sponsor, the Atomic Energy Commission, and to John von Neumann.

Abraham Taub, one of the department's leaders in algorithms for the solution of differential equations, was a mathematician with a strong relativity background. Taub was typical of professors in the sense that his life was strongly defined by and wrapped around his profession. But he was atypical in the strength of his commitment to the highest standards of scholarship and technical accuracy. This penchant for perfection took the form of detailed and thorough questioning of the accuracy of any scientific presentation. His advisees hated reporting their current progress verbally to Taub in their weekly meetings. For often, before one got three sentences out, Taub would break in and start to question the most fundamental assumptions on which the student's ideas were based. The more the student stumbled with fundamental concepts, the more penetrating the questioning became, often setting off a descending spiral that continued until the student lost his composure and was reduced to a nervous, acerbic blob. The end result, however, was that the advisee, after corralling his emotions, left the meeting determined to work doubly hard to demonstrate proof of his idea.

During the 1950s and early 1960s, the computer science department had a weekly colloquium on Mondays at 4:00 P.M. Attendance was required; some speakers were local and others were visitors. Taub showed no favors even to the visiting academics when it came to criticism. On a good Monday, he would let the speaker ramble on for perhaps twenty minutes. Then he would issue a fundamental challenge that attempted to undercut the basic premises of the topic at hand. A ten-minute argument would then follow, at which time someone would propose that the questioning be held in abeyance to allow the speaker to proceed. That reprieve usually lasted five minutes or so until the next question with its ensuing wrangle. When time ran out, the speaker finally got to state his conclusion, having presented little more than the introduction and conclusion. It is doubtful that any visiting or local speaker whose topic was mathematical ever forgot the intensity of his colloquium experience at DCL.

Outside his office, Taub was an extremely pleasant and thoughtful person to interact with. In 1959, when Meagher decided to pursue other challenges, Taub became the second head of the Department of Computer Science. Taub eventually also moved on to become department head at UC Berkeley, after he had seen ILLIAC II through to a successful finish.

Other people who had a major impact on the development of computer programming methods at DCL were John P. ("Jack") Nash, who left in 1957–58 to become a vice president at Lockheed Corp., and David Williams, who as a visitor from Cambridge University in 1952–53 and again in 1958–59, was internationally tops for cleverness. Williams wrote the first square root subroutine for ILLIAC I and also contributed much to the initial programming for ILLIAC II (as did Gillies). Lloyd Fosdick and David Muller, both of whom were mathematics professors, and later William Gear, also made major contributions.

What was the result and impact of ILLIAC II? The ILLIAC II project resulted in a completely successful machine, as measured by its reliability and innovative architectural ideas. It incorporated a range of new design features, which propagated and diffused into the international computer design community. By demonstrating that a computer using 50,000 transistors could be successfully designed to run error-free for many weeks at a time—a feat rarely accomplished by the best of the first-generation machines, the success of ILLIAC II was a major step toward today's CPU chips containing five to ten million transistors.

ILLIAC II was used as the campus's general usage machine for two or three years, until this task was moved over to commercial machines in 1966. By then it was becoming clear that integrated circuits would soon take the place of discrete transistors and the cycle of rapid outdating of computers, with which we are all so familiar today, accelerated. In the early 1960s, initially using ILLIAC I and later ILLIAC II, faculty at the University of Illinois introduced the first computer-assisted program of instruction, PLATO. Conceived by Chalmers Sherwin, a professor of physics, and developed by a team under the direction of Donald Bitzer, a professor of electrical engineering, PLATO is believed to have been the first on-line computer community.

MCCORMICK AND SLOTNICK—
THE FINALE OF THE BIG IRON ERA

The swelling fame of DCL for hardware and architectural design did not end with the successful completion of the ILLIAC II in 1963. At this point, it was not yet obvious that huge speed and complexity gains would eventually be achieved through integrated circuit technology. The direction for maximum effectiveness in computer design was widely seen as increased parallelism. Highly parallel architecture, whose great expected gains have been only partially realized, became the banner around which everyone could rally as the next great step forward.

Two scientists with big design plans for parallel machines, who were attracted to the mecca of computer design, were Bruce H. McCormick, who joined the department in 1960, and Daniel Slotnick, who came in 1965. McCormick, a physicist from the University of California at Berkeley, was able to generate Atomic Energy Commission support for a parallel architecture machine that could perform an efficient analysis for the problem in experimental physics of recognizing elementary particles in bubble chamber images. His design, ILLIAC III, was a conceptually beautiful machine centered around a square arithmetic-logic unit of 32 × 32 elements. Two-dimensional organization at the hardware level aided in the efficient processing of picture-type data originating from cameras and microscopes.

The ILLIAC III was never finished because of a mismatch in scale between the enormous size of the machine and the size of the facilities that a university research project could manage. A fire in the ILLIAC III construction area merely sealed the fate of the project. In my opinion, McCormick was the sharpest innovator ever to occupy a computer science faculty position, one of those rare inspired people who rolled out a great new idea literally each week. For example, in the 1960s, he championed the idea of a DNA reading device, a technology that has just recently been matured and is now widely recognized for its usefulness in personal identification, paleontology, and the like.

Dan Slotnick came to the Computer Science faculty from Princeton by way of Westinghouse, where he had been pressing for several years, without success, for a large general-purpose parallel machine. The faculty of the Department of Computer Science agreed to support his proposal, which eventually was funded at an unprecedentedly high level (some $10 million). His machine design, the ILLIAC IV, called for sixty-four arithmetic units, each executing in parallel, a variant of the central program stream (called a single-instruction, multiple-data, or SIMD architecture). Everyone, especially Slotnick, understood from the outset that university-scale construction facilities would not suffice for such an enormous computer. Thus the ILLIAC IV's detailed construction (using integrated circuits, at last) was farmed out to a commercial manufacturer, the Burroughs Corporation. It was eventually completed in 1974 and by 1976 performed some useful work in fluid dynamics computations at NASA's Ames Research Lab. When the ILLIAC IV went into operation, the news headline was that the "world's computing power has been doubled overnight." This news story was widely circulated and commented upon. It was obviously a huge publicity coup for the University of Illinois at

Urbana-Champaign and for the Department of Computer Science in particular. But, beneath the publicity, the IV turned out to be a very difficult machine to utilize. It was successfully applied only to specific problems that mapped well onto its architecture. And speaking of publicity, the hoopla generated by Slotnick's project reflected his quick-witted, make-no-small-plans personality quite well. He had an actor's knack for drawing attention. Emphatically a master of the humorous quip, and, when warranted, of the "put-down," he could have been successful at writing scripts for sitcoms. As it was, he guided the ILLIAC IV project to a successful conclusion.

The University of Illinois's Department of Computer Science (in its various embodiments since 1948) played a major, internationally recognized role in the drama of elevating the digital computer into an everyday device in the lives of people worldwide. In the early days of the digital computer, in the 1940s and 1950s, insiders understood the potential of such computers in a general way, but no one foresaw the full extent of the computer's eventual impact on everyday life. Using one of the early mainframe computers was, to the average citizen, about as remote from direct personal experience as an orbital rocket launch is today.

What, we may ask, are the root factors that led to this extraordinarily successful blossoming of a research program in a university that is not so different from many other large national universities? Indeed, a number of other universities built first-generation computers, but very few continued beyond that. At least five factors were involved. First, the University of Illinois got off to a strong start. Ridenour was a person with marvelous connections to the current national research scene. Some other early digital computer projects, such as the high visibility programs at Pennsylvania and Harvard, made design choices that proved to be less successful in terms of reliability and ultimate usefulness. His vision of the importance of scientific computing was as nearly on-target as was possible in his day. Second, in 1948, in choosing Ralph Meagher, Ridenour's original advisory committee chose the right type of personality to achieve initial success. Third, the strong initial success of the ORDVAC/ILLIAC was coupled with the advancing solid-state technology of the 1950s to yield a high-visibility second project, which further amplified visibility. Fourth, each successful step attracted a group of the most eager, creative, and energetic minds for the next step. McCormick and Slotnick were cases in point, as were the many excellent graduate students who worked on the computers. Finally, by educating and training a large number of graduate students in a world of expanding needs starved for leaders, the University of Illinois seeded a great many industrial and academic programs with its graduates. We should also not overlook the numerous international visitors who returned to their home countries to become national leaders there.

The great era of building pioneering computers at the University of Illinois eventually came to an end when the commercial value of computers grew beyond a certain point. The physical construction of machines in university facilities became impractical and the nature of computer engineering and science at the university had to be restructured to emphasize applications, theoretical architectures, real-time programming, artificial intelligence, and so forth.

In the week of March 10–15, 1997, many of those who had been involved in the "Big Iron" design era of the Department of Computer Science gathered on campus for a "Cyberfest" to celebrate the great computer achievements made at the University of Illinois and the fictional birthday of the computer HAL, who was born in Urbana in Arthur C. Clarke's book, *2001: A Space Odyssesy* (the basis of the popular 1960s movie, *2001*, which was shown on this occasion). Among those who participated in the Big Iron reunion that was part of the Fest were Joe Weir, Joan Slotnick, Liesel Poppelbaum, Betsy Gillies, Toshiro Kunihiro, Ken Smith, Maseo Kato, and Tom Murrell. To all who worked daily on designing the early machines, pushing the limits of speed, or whatever intellectual or technical challenge they happened to be fighting on any particular day, the era of the ILLIAC family of computers is regarded as a memorable and satisfying life experience.

NOTES

1. The generation number I, appended to these computers, as is commonly done for software, indicates that the machine was vacuum tube based. Later generations roughly corresponded to increasing degrees of integration of the solid-state electronics.
2. Since the ILLIAC was an asynchronous machine having no central clock, the comparison to a modern CPU chip is necessarily a rough estimate. Current PCs are a thousand times faster.

LILLIAN HODDESON

CHAPTER 16

John Bardeen:

A Place to Win Two Nobel Prizes

and Make a Hole in One

"I have to leave Bell Labs," whispered John Bardeen to his old friend, Frederick Seitz, in October 1950. The two theoretical physicists were at a resort in the Pocono Mountains of Pennsylvania attending a conference on Crystal Imperfections and Grain Boundaries. Surrounded by the brilliant leaves of fall, they had taken time out for a heart-to-heart talk.

Bardeen was troubled. Three years earlier, he and the experimental physicist Walter Brattain had invented the transistor in William Shockley's semiconductor group at Bell Telephone Laboratories, in Murray Hill, New Jersey. The two collaborators had wanted to carry the work to its next stage, but Shockley intervened and closed the door. While the working environment at Bell Labs had been ideal for Bardeen before the transistor's invention, it was no longer favorable, and his productivity had begun to let up.

The transistor had by then replaced vacuum tubes in some parts of the telephone network, but it had not yet begun to have the vast influence it now wields in everyday life as the core technology of the information age.

That would come two decades later, following the invention of the microchip. Well before, Bardeen, Brattain, and Shockley would be awarded the 1956 Nobel Prize for Physics for the invention of the transistor.

"But are you doing any interesting physics?" Seitz asked Bardeen during their talk in the Poconos. "Well, yes," said Bardeen, "but I can't work well under the conditions at Bell Labs. Walter and I are looking at a few questions relating to point-contact transistors, but Shockley keeps all the interesting problems for himself." Bardeen eyed Seitz. "Do you know of any jobs in academia?" Seitz hesitated and replied, "Why no."

In actual fact, Seitz, who had recently joined the faculty of the University of Illinois, was extremely excited by the possiblity of bringing Bardeen to Illinois. He hoped to add him to the new solid-state physics group that he was just then building up there. Seitz didn't want to disappoint his friend. So he veered him off: "I don't know of any teaching jobs off-hand, but I'll let you know if I hear of any."

Bardeen and Seitz were among the handful of theorists in the first generation of American physicists who would refer to themselves as "solid-state physicists." They had been friends and colleagues since 1933, when they overlapped as graduate students at Princeton University. Both had been trained to apply quantum mechanics, the powerful mathematical formalism invented in 1925, to problems of solid materials, including metals and semiconductors. The mathematics was intricate because of the huge number of atoms involved.

Bardeen and Seitz had both worked on doctoral theses under Eugene Wigner, a Hungarian mathematician and physicist who had joined the Princeton faculty in 1930. Their work had broken new ground in extending the quantum theory to real solids. Prior theoretical work had been limited to ideal materials—generalized models of metals, semiconductors, and insulators. Seitz's thesis, nearing completion at the time Bardeen arrived at Princeton, became widely acclaimed as the pioneering work that opened the field of modern solid-state theory. Working with Wigner, Seitz had developed a simple approximation that made the mathematics of estimating energy bands in actual crystals manageable. Bardeen's calculation of the "work function" of metals (the energy needed to release an electron from a metal) helped the field advance in its ability to calculate the interactions between electrons, or between electrons and ions.

Bardeen would continue to work for almost sixty years in this area of solid-state physics, which became known as "many-body" physics. He went on to a prestigious Harvard junior fellowship in 1935–38, and then to an assistant professorship of physics at the University of Minnesota. While at

Minnesota in the late 1930s, he began to work on developing a theory for superconductivity, an exotic state of matter discovered experimentally in 1911. In this state, at low temperatures, certain metals and alloys lose *all* their electrical resistance and currents flow forever.

But just as Bardeen seemed to be making real progress, he was called off to Washington, D.C., for war work at the Naval Ordnance Laboratory. Afterward, in late 1945, he accepted a position as one of the two theorists in a small semiconductor group at Bell Telephone Laboratories, the research and development arm of the American Telephone and Telegraph company.

BELL LABORATORIES

Bardeen decided to join Bell Labs partly because Mervin J. Kelly, the new executive vice president, had offered him the freedom to follow his own research interests in physics. In the mid-1930s, in an attempt to attract creative scientists, Bell Labs had instituted its "enlightened" policy of research. Shockley, the other theorist in the semiconductor group, had also been promised research freedom when Kelly hired him in 1936. At that time, Bardeen and Shockley were both in Cambridge, Massachusetts, enjoying a useful collegial exchange. Shockley was in his last year of graduate school at MIT; Bardeen was in his first year at Harvard. Shockley's doctoral thesis problem, supervised by John Slater at MIT, was a direct outgrowth of Seitz's thesis work with Wigner.

At Bell Labs, Bardeen's closest colleague would be Walter Brattain, an experimentalist whom Bardeen had met during his Princeton days, when the two had occasionally played bridge together. Brattain and Bardeen became partners in research, often working together in Brattain's laboratory with Bardeen playing the role of the "head" and Brattain that of the "'hands." Their work was enriched by Bell's many resources not available in typical academic settings, for instance, its generous funding for equipment and materials, its technicians and other specialists, even patent attorneys. Bell Labs offered such support to Bardeen and Brattain because their research on semiconductors was thought to have future value to the telephone system.

The enormous growth of the telephone network during the 1920s and 1930s had been based largely on vacuum tubes, but they consumed much power and were fragile, bulky, and expensive. Worst of all, they routinely burned out. It was natural to think of building a better device, perhaps using semiconductors.

Semiconductors were an obvious possibility to consider because the interface between a semiconductor and a metal, or between two different semiconductors, is electrically equivalent to a vacuum tube diode in that current flows more easily in one direction than the other. This property, arising from an electronic barrier at the surface and from the different electronic structures of the materials, had been the basis of the "cat's whisker" detectors that had captured the interest of many radio buffs (including teen-aged Bardeen and Brattain) early in the century. In the case of vacuum tubes, turning a two-element diode into a three-element triode that could amplify signals requires adding an element known as the "grid" to control the electron flow. In the 1930s and 1940s, a crucial question was: could one somehow add a grid to a semiconductor diode and turn it into an amplifier? If so, what would play the role of the grid?

Bardeen loved to hear Brattain tell his story of how Shockley had once asked him to build an amplifier by inserting a piece of ordinary porch screen into a copper-oxide rectifier (a device then used by the telephone company to reduce clicks). The interplay between the two illustrates the productive interplay of researchers at Bell Labs in the late 1930s. "I laughed at him," Brattain would say. "I was quite sure it wouldn't work." Yet he told Shockley, "Bill, it's so damned important that if you'll tell me how you want it made, and if it's possible, we'll make it that way. We'll try it." As the seasoned experimentalist expected, "The result was nil. I mean, there was no evidence of anything."

During World War II, every aspect of crystal rectifiers was studied extensively, especially in British and American wartime labs, because rectifiers were an essential component of radar receivers. The result was a rich research literature that Bardeen and others now studied. Most of the papers dealt with silicon and germanium, the two simplest semiconductors. By then, almost everyone working at high frequencies had switched to silicon, for it was known that this simple semiconductor was the one that worked best at high frequencies. The problem was that the available silicon worked erratically, rectifying only when the whisker contacted "hot spots" on its surface.

The work leading to the transistor began late in 1945, shortly after Bardeen came to Bell Labs. About six months earlier, Shockley had designed a silicon "field-effect" amplifier involving an electric field applied perpendicularly to a slab of semiconductor. Although Shockley had calculated that its effect would be substantial, the device didn't work in practice. He asked Bardeen if he could figure out why not. Within four months,

Bardeen had a possible theory: electrons were getting trapped in surface states and thus were not able to participate in the conduction process.

With a concrete theory to explore, the group now studied the problem of the field effect amplifier from different angles, dividing tasks according to their expertise. "I cannot overemphasize the rapport of this group," Brattain later reminisced. "We would meet together to discuss important steps almost on the spur of the moment of an afternoon." A few weeks later, Gerald Pearson, the other experimental physicist in the group, demonstrated that at liquid nitrogen temperatures a field effect occurs. It appeared the electrons had been frozen in surface states. Unfortunately, little more of interest was uncovered in this research during the next year and a half.

Then an apparently innocent experimental problem began the "magic month" that culminated in the discovery of the transistor. It started in mid-November 1947, when Brattain was trying to avoid an annoying magnetic effect in one of his many experiments on the photovoltaic effect in silicon. Attempting a quick fix, he immersed the whole system in various liquids and was "flabbergasted" to find that the photovoltaic effect he was exploring *increased* whenever the liquids were electrolytes. When Bardeen suggested that perhaps the mobile ions of the electrolyte were creating an electric field strong enough to overcome the surface states, the chemist in the group, Robert Gibney, suggested varying the electrical potential. The fact that using any electrolyte they "could vary the photo EMF (electromotive force) from anywhere to a very large value to zero" suggested that they could build a room temperature field-effect amplifier after all!

At this point Shockley, curiously, began to insulate himself from the group. Only later did they learn that working in the privacy of his home, Shockley was trying to design a new kind of semiconductor amplifier based on the special properties of junctions of p-type and n-type silicon, in which the conduction is by positive (p-type) or negative (n-type) charge carriers.

Meanwhile Bardeen and Brattain continued to explore building an amplifier using the Brattain and Gibney design. On Friday morning, November 21, Bardeen suggested a geometry that used a point contact, like in the old cat's whisker detectors. This was an easy move because of the extensive wartime research on point contacts in the radar program. In Bardeen's proposed design, the point was insulated and pressed down on the surface of a silicon slab. It was surrounded by a drop of water making contact with another metal. In this way, he hoped to modulate the current from the point to the semiconductor using the electric field through the water electrolyte.

Bardeen also suggested that the slab of silicon be p-type, with an n-type "inversion layer" on its surface. In this thin surface layer, which he knew would form under certain circumstances, most of the charge carriers would be opposite in sign to those in the bulk. From a practical standpoint, it was far easier to create such an inversion layer than to deposit a thin layer of semiconductor on the surface of the silicon. And because the layer is thin, they expected changes to have higher mobility. "Come on, John," said Brattain. "Let's go out in the laboratory and make it." The design worked to about ten cycles! It amplified current and power, but not voltage.

Over the next four weeks, Bardeen and Brattain explored many variations of the geometry and materials. On Monday, December 8, Bardeen suggested they try a slab of the special "high-back-voltage germanium," developed during the war by Karl Lark-Horovitz's group at Purdue University. Brattain happened to have a piece of the material in his lab. When they tried the experiment that afternoon, they were startled to measure both a voltage amplification of 2 and a dazzling power amplification of 330! They also noticed a mysterious change in the direction of the current.

Gradually the partners realized that in this design the *holes*—unfilled electron states in the semiconductor that behave like positively charged particles—were playing the role of the grid! Bardeen had learned about these ghostlike holes in his studies at Princeton and Harvard. Power gain was achieved because they had managed to increase the population of holes at the surface by applying a negative voltage on the point to drive the electrons away. They saw a much larger power gain—a factor of 6,000!— when they repeated the experiment two days later using a specially prepared sample of the high-back-voltage germanium. But the frequency response was still too poor to amplify the range of the human voice.

They decided to replace their gooey electrolyte with a green oxide film that Brattain had noticed growing on the germanium when he applied a steady electric field. Their experiment of December 15 utilizing the film worked! Strangely, "I got an effect of the opposite sign," Brattain reported. The sign change confused them, until they realized that their oxide was soluble in water. "When we washed the gu off, we washed the oxide off too!" They had accidentally created an amplifier that worked on a different principle than the field effect. It worked because "holes were flowing into the germanium surface."

All that remained now was to improve the gain. They did so using a clever geometry, which Bardeen suggested and Brattain developed, one that caused the holes to flow closer to the input signal. The experiment worked the first time Brattain and Bardeen tried it, on December 16, 1947.

That evening, Bardeen told his wife Jane about the breakthrough. Encountering her in the kitchen, where she was peeling vegetables, Bardeen murmured almost inaudibly: "We discovered something today." Without looking up, she automatically responded, "That's great, or words to that effect." But she knew it had been a special day, because her husband was the quietest person she had ever met and typically said nothing to her about his work.

The transistor had been born of the cameraderie among Bardeen, Brattain, and other members of the Bell Labs semiconductor group in the supportive environment they experienced at Bell Labs—up to this point.

THE BREAK FROM BELL

After the invention of the transistor, Mervin Kelly commanded Bardeen and Brattain to drop all their research and work only on drafting patent applications for the transistor. This was a reasonable request at an industrial laboratory, but the order effectively tied up their time and offered Shockley an open field to work on his new junction idea, the one he had been studying secretly since mid-November.

Then Shockley took a further step that destroyed the possibility of any future productive collaboration with Bardeen or Brattain. He called them each, separately, into his office and told them "he could write a patent—starting with the field effect—on the whole damn thing." The two were stunned by Shockley's overt determination to preempt their credit—and all the more when he added, "sometimes the people who do the work don't get the credit for it." For a time Bardeen tried to endure his changed working environment.

Shockley's plans to take all the credit were ultimately foiled. When the patent attorneys discovered that in 1930 a Polish-American inventor, Julius E. Lilienfeld, had already been awarded a patent on the field-effect amplifier (it is unlikely that he built a working model), Bell Labs could not risk the rejection of a claim based on the field-effect design and reworked their application so their claim rested on Bardeen and Brattain's point-contact design. That move clinched Shockley's resolve to exclude Bardeen and Brattain from the work on the junction device, whose features were more promising commercially than those of Bardeen and Brattain's original point-contact design. Bardeen and Brattain gritted their teeth, for they saw the junction transistor as the logical continuation of *their* research. When the laboratory allowed Shockley to relegate Bardeen to problems he knew were dead ends, Bardeen deduced that "it was the desire of the administration to give Shockley a free hand." Bardeen's anger and despair stifled his creativity.

One day early in 1950, Bardeen simply stopped working on the second-rate problems that Shockley offered him. Bardeen turned back to the problem of superconductivity that he had been working on in Minnesota at the time he was called to Washington, D.C. Explaining superconductivity was still one of the major unsolved puzzles of physics. What soon riveted Bardeen to the problem of superconductivity was a phone call he received on May 15, 1950, from Bernard Serin, an experimental physicist working at Rutgers University. In looking at pure mercury isotopes with mass numbers between 198 and 202, Serin's group had observed an "isotope effect": the lighter the mass, the higher the transition temperature. Emanuel Maxwell at the National Bureau of Standards had found the same effect independently. Bardeen instantly understood the meaning of the clue. "Electron-lattice interactions are important in determining superconductivity," he scribbled in his notes. Although his first attempt to use the new insight to revive his Minnesota theory failed, Bardeen was sure he was on the right path to cracking the riddle. That was partly why he so desperately needed to leave Bell Labs. He wanted to pursue this crucial problem in a favorable context.

All this Bardeen carefully explained in October 1950 to his old friend Fred Seitz, in their heart-to-heart talk in the Pocono Mountains. Seitz was just the right person for Bardeen to speak with. Seitz and Shockley had been friends since the summer of 1932, when they had traveled together across the country from California to their East Coast graduate schools. Seitz understood the great significance of the problem of superconductivity. He was aware of the failed work on the problem by dozens of leading theoretical physicists. And he knew how destructive the wrong environment can be for a creative scientist. He himself had recently left his post as head of the physics department at the Carnegie Institute of Technology because of "political problems."

By this time, the Department of Physics at the University of Illinois was already an exceptional place. F. Wheeler Loomis, who served as head of the department from 1929 to 1940, and again from 1947 to 1957, understood how to cultivate a supportive environment for research and teaching. That had been his special project since 1929, when he was approached by the University of Illinois. Initially, the idea of moving from New York City to central Illinois had not appealed to Loomis, but the idea of transforming a backward department into a world-class research center had challenged him. Milo Ketchum, dean of the College of Engineering, had assured

Loomis of his unreserved enthusiasm and financial support for upgrading the physics program. Loomis learned that Roger Adams in Chemistry had, under similar circumstances, brought a backward Illinois department into international prominence.

Unfortunately, things immediately went wrong after Loomis accepted Ketchum's challenge. The stock market crashed and the university could not deliver the resources it had promised. Loomis found it extremely difficult to attract physics stars to Urbana. Isadore Rabi of Columbia University rebuffed him: "I love subways and I hate cows." Loomis retreated to a strategy that proved successful: hiring promising postdoctoral level scientists. He brought Gerald Almy, a young nuclear spectroscopist, then Gerald Kruger, a molecular spectroscopist, and Donald Kerst, who would later invent the betatron, one of the early high-energy particle accelerators.

World War II undid much of Loomis's building of the physics department. To help him reconstitute the department, he drew heavily on the wartime connections that he had made while serving as associate director of the MIT Radiation Laboratory. Among those that Loomis now attracted to the University of Illinois was Louis Ridenour, who was appointed dean of the Graduate College. Ridenour proceeded to upgrade both Physics and Engineering, working closely with Charles Everitt, whom Ridenour helped bring to Illinois and who became dean of the College of Engineering in 1949.

Loomis easily convinced Ridenour that solid-state physics was an important area to build up. Ridenour released seed funding for new positions and in 1949 the two persuaded Seitz to join the physics faculty. Seitz brought along Robert Maurer and James Koehler, who joined as associate professors. Four instructors also came with the Seitz package: David Lazarus, Dillon Mapother, James Schneider, and Charles Slichter. Thus by the time Bardeen and Seitz spoke at the Pocono meeting, the Illinois physics department was a very strong solid-state center. If Seitz could add Bardeen, Illinois would have one of the best academic solid-state departments in the United States.

When Seitz returned to Urbana after the Pocono meeting, Ridenour was away. Seitz went to speak with Loomis and Everitt about making an offer to Bardeen, who was already famous in physics circles for co-inventing the transistor. (He had not yet received his first Nobel Prize.) The two administrators immediately agreed that Bardeen should have an offer, but there was no money available for new hiring. Student enrollments had fallen because of low birth rates during the Depression, and the GI Bill had pretty much run its course. Nonetheless, Everitt assured Seitz that he would find a way to piece together an attractive package. And when Fred relayed that message back, John replied: "Well, Illinois would be perfect. It's the kind of place I'd like to be at."

Seitz felt that the salary "was not quite enough for a person of John's stature," when early in 1951, Everitt offered Bardeen a joint professorship in physics and electrical engineering. Fred told John, "If you hang on maybe you'll get more." But John said, "That's enough." Bardeen's decision became more complicated when Bell Labs improved Bardeen's situation, placing him in a different department separated from Shockley's control. "But I am still inclined toward Illinois," Bardeen wrote back to Illinois.

The decisive factor in Bardeen's decision was Dean Everitt's letter assuring Bardeen that it was understood that "you would lay out your own research program, and that in no case would you be asked to work on contracts which were not of your own choosing." As for teaching, "you would be pretty much your own boss." He specified that you "would give such formal courses as you felt fitted into your program." In this period, when physics faculty typically taught two courses per semester, Everitt wrote, "if you felt that only one course a semester was the best way for you to work, that would be quite all right." Seitz followed up with the assurance that "everyone I have spoken to is more than enthusiastic and will do everything within his power to make you enjoy life here." He described the collegial life that he had encountered in Urbana as one free of "rivalries of any significance." Bardeen accepted the Illinois offer on April 28, 1951.

In Bardeen's letter of resignation from Bell Labs, he explained to Kelly, who was now president of Bell Labs, "I would not leave if I were not dissatisfied with conditions here." He detailed how his work under Shockley had changed after the invention of the transistor. "Before that there was an excellent research atmosphere here." At the present time, he said he "felt somewhat isolated working on superconductivity here as there are very few people in the laboratories who are interested in the problem." Most important, when he "decided to give up work on semiconductors and work on superconductivity," the working conditions became "intolerable."

Kelly responded by offering Bardeen an increased salary and his own theoretical group, but "when Bardeen makes up his mind, there is no use doing anything about it. It is too late," reflected Brattain.

THE UNIVERSITY OF ILLINOIS

Bardeen felt at home and appreciated in the friendly and exciting environment he found in the physics department at Illinois. In an era in which discrimination against Jews and other minorities was common, and at a time when many departments at other universities were intimidated by the anticommunists, Loomis had attracted many gifted candidates that other departments would not consider. Edwin Goldwasser, whom Loomis hired in 1951, suspects that "Loomis made the decision [to hire me] on the grounds that I was refusing to sign a loyalty oath."

Morale was exceptionally high because financial support for research was abundant. Much of the funding for the solid-state group, from the Office of Naval Research (ONR) and the Atomic Energy Commission (AEC), grew out of the personal relationships that Loomis developed during World War II between scientists and government officials. Loomis also went out of his way to offer each member a role in the department's operation. The social interactions, including his "wonderful parties," fostered a sense of "family." Most members regularly wandered over to the departmental lounge around 10:00 A.M. to drink coffee while catching up on the work of their colleagues or discussing recent journal articles. The faculty typically ate lunch together in the Student Union across the street, and they often gathered to talk physics in one another's offices. Bardeen's office became a popular site for such interplay. David Lazarus reported, "He was the one I would go to when I was stuck."

Bardeen was just as happy in Electrical Engineering, his other home at the university. One goal was to establish a semiconductor experiment group. The initial members of the Electrical Engineering Research Laboratory were two graduate students, Nick Holonyak and Richard Sirrine, and two postdocs, Harry Letaw Jr. and S. Roy Morrison. Holonyak, who would later invent the first semiconducting light-emitting diode and win many prestigious awards, such as the government of Russia's Global Energy Prize and the U.S. National Medal of Science, recalled that Bardeen would come by their semiconductor lab (which earlier had housed the historic ILLIAC—see chapter 15) nearly every day to ask the students what they had done and whether they needed help. Bardeen himself never "picked up a pair of pliers," but encouraged students to find out for themselves how to do an experiment. After 1954 when Paul Handler arrived as Bardeen's postdoc, Bardeen gradually relinquished control of the semiconductor lab to Handler.

In his new academic home, Bardeen made rapid progress on the theory of superconductivity. But given the quantum field theoretical intricacies of the problem, he decided to supplement himself with a collaborator having expertise in treating the electron-electron interactions. The department supported Bardeen by authorizing him to offer a postdoctoral position to David Pines, then at Princeton. Bardeen hoped to learn from Pines about recently developed mathematical techniques, such as those Pines had developed with David Bohm for separating the long-range Coulomb interactions from the short-range single-particle excitations. When Pines arrived in July 1952, Bardeen asked him to examine the coupling between electrons and lattice vibrations in a simpler system than superconductivity, the "polaron," which featured an electron in a polar crystal. Tsung Dau Lee, a young theorist spending the summer as Bardeen's postdoc, and Francis Low, then on the Illinois physics faculty, worked with Pines. They arrived at a formulation that would prove useful in developing the theory of superconductivity.

Bardeen and Pines also carried out a calculation in which they treated the combined influence of all the electron interactions in the metal. Comparing the size of the attractive interaction induced by the electron-lattice interactions with the ordinary repulsive interaction between like charges, they discovered that for certain cases, the attractive interaction is stronger. In this way, Bardeen came to recognize that in superconductivity, the net interaction between electrons would be attractive for pairs of electrons located close to a certain surface in momentum space known as the Fermi surface. This was another powerful clue.

In the same period, Bardeen undertook an extensive literature study of superconductivity. In a review article on superconductivity for the 1956 *Handbuch der Physik*, he argued for Fritz London's notion of a superconductivity as an "ordered phase in which quantum effects extend over large distances in space." He ventured that superconductors are "probably characterized by some sort of order parameter" and he stressed the important role of the energy gap, which was caused by the fact that the wave function was "rigid" with respect to magnetic perturbation, that is, small perturbations had no effect but large ones changed the state radically.

When Bardeen learned that Pines would return to Princeton at the end of the 1954–55 academic year to accept a teaching post, Bardeen telephoned C. N. Yang at the Institute for Advanced Study at Princeton, which was then a stronghold for quantum field theory. Bardeen asked Yang whether he knew of someone "versed in field theory who might be willing to work on superconductivity." Yang recommended Leon Cooper, who arrived in Urbana as Bardeen's postdoc in September 1955. At first Coooper didn't like the geography of this "cornfield place," but he soon recognized it as "a fantastic environment" for doing physics. The community was unusually "friendly and collegial."

The third member of the superconductivity team was J. Robert Schrieffer, Bardeen's graduate student, who had recently decided to work on superconductivity for his thesis. Schrieffer worked in an attic area reserved for a group of graduate students, with a sign on the door that read: *Institute for Retarded Study*. When Schrieffer came to speak with Cooper or Bardeen in their shared faculty office, both would wheel around their chairs and join in the conversation.

Schrieffer later described his collaboration with Bardeen and Cooper as "family-style," with Bardeen acting as the father who set the problems, made the assignments, and planted theoretical seeds in his younger associates, and with Jane Bardeen serving as the nurturing mother in the background. Bardeen asked Schrieffer to look into "*t*-matrix methods," while Cooper studied the Bohm-Pines theory, including the Bardeen-Pines work on the electron-electron interaction. Meanwhile Bardeen looked for other leads. Schrieffer feels that he and Cooper absorbed Bardeen's tastes in physics, his experiment-based methodology, his habit of breaking down problems, and his frugal style of using as little theoretical machinery as possible, "the smallest weapon in your arsenal to kill a monster."

Bardeen offered his team guiding principles, such as the London idea that superconductivity is "a kind of solidification or condensation of the average momentum distribution," or that the rigidity of the wave function and the long-range ordering between electrons brings about "a quantum structure on a macroscopic scale." Bardeen also stressed that there is only one stable current distribution and that there is no persistent current in an isolated superconductor in thermal equilibrium, unless the system is in the presence of a magnetic field. In that case, they "differ for every variation of the strength or direction of the applied field." Schrieffer recalls Bardeen pressing them to clarify the notion of long-range order using a "phase coherence" parameter of the size of typical correlations between the electrons.

Bardeen also encouraged the team to strike out into the unknown with the help of a bridging principle connecting the unknown theory of the superconducting state with the known theory of the normal state. The superconducting energy states, he said, must correspond one-to-one with the normal states. Thus it should be possible to express the wave function of the superconducting state as a sum of the normal state functions. That way of thinking helped them to concretize their meditations and concentrate on the small energy difference between the normal and superconducting states.

Convinced "that the essence of the problem was an energy gap in the single particle excitation spectrum," Cooper soon came to a breakthrough. Examining the case of only two electrons and making certain assumptions, he showed that if the net force between the electrons is attractive they will form a bound state that lies below the continuum states and is separated from them by an energy gap. Then followed many frustrating months for Cooper, months of trying to convince Bardeen and other colleagues of the importance of his result, which Cooper finally published in September 1956.

The problem that plagued Bardeen and the others was how to go from a single "Cooper pair" to a many-electron theory. They did not know how to represent the fact that the pairs physically overlap, a picture that Schrieffer later portrayed using the analogy of couples dancing the Frug on a crowded floor. The point was that partners might dance apart for long periods of time, with other dancers from other pairs coming between, while each pair remained coupled. They needed mathematical language to describe this picture. The team also worried about the validity of their approximations. They were uncomfortably aware that the energy change in the transition from normal to superconducting was much smaller than the accuracy with which they could calculate the energy of either state. In working only with the part of the system responsible for pairing, were they ignoring a more important part?

That was where things stood when, just before breakfast on November 1, 1956, the news broke that Bardeen, Brattain, and Shockley had won the Nobel Prize for the invention of the transistor! John's daughter Betsy and son Bill rushed into the kitchen of the Bardeens' house in Champaign shouting the news. They had heard it announced on the CBS *World News Roundup*. John dropped a frying pan of scrambled eggs. That evening the front doorbell rang at the Bardeens' house. When John opened the door, he saw Loomis followed by a parade of his colleagues bearing candles. They were marching up the driveway and singing "For He's a Jolly Good Fellow." They also carried cases of iced champagne. Handler reported, "Everybody was elated, everybody was on a high."

An important part of Bardeen could not engage with the celebrations. They were a distraction from his work on superconductivity. He sensed that his team was nearing a breakthrough and was worried that other physicists might be as close. Richard Feynman had recently lectured on superfluidity and superconductivity. On a deeper level, Bardeen wasn't sure the invention merited a Nobel Prize. The transistor was a gadget, he thought, not a new scientific theory. "He knew how important this was technologically, but from the point of view of physics he didn't think it was so great," Lazarus explained. And at forty-eight, Bardeen felt there were older physicists whose more basic work had not yet been recognized with a Nobel. "I really don't deserve this," he told Lazarus. "Wigner doesn't have a Prize yet."

John Bardeen accepts the 1956 Nobel Prize in Physics for the invention, with Shockley and Brattain, of the transistor. Co-laureate Brattain waits behind him.

For Schrieffer, the timing was poor for another reason. Now a fourth-year student, he had recently won a prestigious National Science Foundation fellowship for study in France the following year. But a condition was that he be done with his doctorate. Believing the team was at an impasse, Schrieffer met with his mentor shortly before Bardeen left for Stockholm and asked whether Bardeen thought it might make sense for him to switch his thesis problem. "Give it another month, or a month and a half," Bardeen muttered. "Wait 'til I get back and keep working. Maybe something'll happen."

On the trip, Bardeen remained anxious about not working on superconductivity, although he did enjoy the recognition and the chance to spend some personal time with Brattain, something that had not been possible for years. On the day of the ceremony, the phone rang in the Brattains' suite at the Grand Hotel. It was "a last minute call from John for a spare tie because of some accident to his." Brattain was used to such requests, for Bardeen had already borrowed a vest from him, as his own had turned green in the laundry.

Back in Illinois, Cooper and Schrieffer continued their work on superconductivity. It was a tense time because the problem still would not break. Whenever possible, Bardeen would relieve his stress by playing golf, a sport in which he could focus his attention inward and indulge his urge to compete. He competition was mainly with himself, with his own best previous performance. In many ways, the game of golf became Bardeen's second passion, after physics.

One day, not long after returning from Sweden, Bardeen achieved another of his lifelong goals, a hole-in-one. It happened on the golf course near the Champaign airport. "He thought that was almost as good as the Nobel," quipped Schrieffer. Years later, Bardeen was asked which he considered the greater accomplishment, a Nobel Prize or a hole-in-one. He replied "Well, perhaps *two* Nobels are worth more than one hole-in-one."

As for superconductivity, the turn finally came in the last days of January. Schrieffer was on the East Coast attending physics meetings. Stimulated by the talks, he began to engage in a bit of theoretical tinkering with mathematical formulations. He thought constantly about how to write down the wave function for the superconducting ground state. Scribbling down one promising expression while riding on the subway, he was astonished to find that it was ordered in momentum space! And the energy of the state was exponentially lower than the normal state! He was very excited. By chance, Schrieffer and Cooper flew into Champaign at the same time. Schrieffer showed Cooper his expression right there in the airport. "Great, looks terrific," said Cooper. "Let's go and talk to John in the morning."

When Bardeen saw the wave function that Schrieffer had written down, he said "he thought that there was something really there." It took Bardeen a few days to use the wave function to compute the energy gap. Several days later he calculated the condensation energy in terms of the energy gap and the critical field. "Things looked like pay dirt!"

Now all three began to race to complete the theory. Cooper remembered the period as one "of the most concentrated, intense and incredibly fruitful work I have experienced. New results appeared almost every day." Bardeen assigned Schrieffer to work on thermodynamic properties and Cooper to electrodynamic properties, while he worked on the transport and nonequilibrium properties. Bardeen's colleagues knew something was up, for when they asked him a question they were told, politely, that he was just too busy to think about anything else.

Bumping into his colleague Charles Slichter in the hall, Bardeen announced the breakthough in a characteristic way. "Well, I think we've figured out superconductivity," he whispered. Slichter remembers that instant as "the most exciting moment of science that I've ever experienced." He and his student Chuck Hebel were among the first to confirm the new theory experimentally, using it to explain their measurement of the rate at which nuclear spins relax in aluminum as a function of temperature. It took the team until mid-February to be ready to publish a letter on their

John Bardeen was an avid golfer and a good one. Whenever possible, he sought out golf courses during research or consulting trips. According to the stories, he was almost as proud of hitting a "hole in one" as he was to win a second Nobel Prize.

work in the *Physical Review*. Finally, in July, six months after Schrieffer's productive subway ride, the team sent off their full-length article. It was a classic paper in the history of modern physics.

Bardeen knew the work deserved a Nobel Prize. He fretted that his younger colleagues might be deprived of their well-deserved recognition because he had already won a Nobel Prize. To Bardeen's immense relief and joy, the Swedish Academy of Sciences broke with precedent in 1972 and honored all three—Bardeen, Cooper, and Schrieffer—with a Nobel Prize for their development of the BCS theory. Bardeen was the first person ever to win two Nobel prizes in the same field.

Both of Bardeen's Nobel Prize winning efforts had been carried out in supportive institutional contexts. Administrators—such as Kelly at Bell Labs and Loomis at Illinois—created environments offering necessary resources and support to facilitate work in small groups, the configuration in which Bardeen was best able to carry out his creative work. Colleagues offered critical feedback and personal support. And the day-to-day work was largely driven by the content of the problems, as well as the interests of members of the team, rather than by direction from above (although in both cases the goals of the institution aligned with those of the research team). After the invention of the transistor, Bell Labs no longer offered such supportive features to Bardeen, for Shockley "ruined" the team, as

Brattain once put it, by manipulating its members to serve Shockley's ends. As is characteristic of highly creative people, when Bardeen's creativity suffered he sought a new place where he could pursue the problems of interest to him. He found such a place at the University of Illinois, where he worked happily and productively from the summer of 1951 until his death in January 1991.

A NOTE ON SOURCES

This essay was prepared drawing from sources discussed more competely in Lillian Hoddeson and Vicki Daitch, *True Genius: The Life and Science of John Bardeen* (Washington, D.C.: Joseph Henry Press, 2002); detailed references to quotations and other information can be found there. Some related material can be found in Michael Riordan and Lillian Hoddeson, *Crystal Fire: The Birth of the Information Age* (New York: W. W. Norton, 1997); Lillian Hoddeson, "The Discovery of the Point-Contact Transistor," *Historical Studies in the Physical Sciences* 12, no. 1 (1981): 41–76; Lillian Hoddeson, Gordon Baym, Steve Heims, and Helmut Schubert, "Collective Phenomena," chapter 8 in *Out of the Crystal Maze: A History of Solid State Physics, 1900–1960,* ed. L. Hoddeson, E. Braun, J. Teichmann and S. Weart (New York: Oxford University Press, 1992). I thank my collaborators for letting me draw freely on work prepared jointly with them.

CHAPTER 17

Julian Simon:

The Economics of Population

In the years that Julian Simon was at the University of Chicago as a graduate student in the school of business (1958–61), he would proclaim loudly and clearly that he had no interest or plans to be a professor. He was going to be an entrepreneur, make lots of money, look after his parents, and then spend most of his time writing fiction. (He had already published a couple of short stories.) But two years after obtaining his Ph.D., he changed his mind and decided that a university was the perfect place for him to do what he most wanted. What that was only became clear later, when we were on the faculty of the University of Illinois.

As an undergraduate at Harvard, Julian had majored in psychology. After taking his bachelor's degree in 1953, he had spent the next three years in the Navy completing his ROTC obligations. Expecting to study medicine, he returned to Cambridge in the spring of 1956 and spent the summer taking a course in organic chemistry that he needed to complete for entering Tufts Medical School in the fall.

During the course of that summer, however, he decided that becoming a doctor was not what he wanted. He went to New York City and worked for two years in a couple of advertising firms. One day while at New York University, where Julian was taking a course in accounting, he noticed a poster advertising fellowships for the graduate program in business at the University of Chicago. He decided to apply and was awarded a fellowship. Julian and I met at the University of Chicago, and in June 1961, when he received his Ph.D., we were married.

In the few months before that, Julian went back to Millburn, New Jersey, where he lived with his parents and started several small businesses, most of them mail order ventures. His parents, especially his mother, who was an excellent bookkeeper, worked with Julian. I had just been considered for tenure at the college at the University of Chicago, where I was teaching in the sociology department after taking my Ph.D. in December 1957. Foregoing my tenure, I left Chicago in 1961 to join Julian in New York.

During the two years that we lived in New York, I taught part-time at the Yale School of Nursing in New Haven, where I offered a seminar on research methods to the faculty. I also worked at Mobilization for Youth, a major research and social action program at the Columbia School of Social Work that focused on social change on the lower east side of Manhattan. Julian, having run several mail order businesses, decided that he knew enough about such ventures to write a book that would help other future entrepreneurs. While writing the first edition of *How to Start and Operate a Mail Order Business* (there were to be five editions, the last published in 1993) the idea of becoming a professor occurred to Julian. His reason: "I find writing so enjoyable, why not work in a context that would allow me, and pay me, to do a great deal of it?"

So in the winter of 1963, Julian and I started applying to universities in different parts of the country. Back then, for a husband and wife to be offered full-time positions at the same university was something of a coup. We were both offered positions at the State University of New York at Buffalo, the University of Maryland, and the University of Illinois. We opted to go to Illinois because we were impressed with the facilities in the departments in which we were offered positions and with the overall reputation of the university.

I confess that when Julian and I first came to visit and find housing, after we had accepted our positions, I was somewhat taken aback by the flatness of the landscape, the cornfields, and the absence of theater, ethnic restaurants, or good bookstores in the community. (Remember, this was Champaign-Urbana in 1962.) We did not yet have any children, and in New York we used to go out to dinner and to the theater quite a lot. So we were a bit apprehensive about what our life in Urbana would be like and how long we would stay. But we started our family a year later (David, the first of three, was born in November 1964). That, plus our work life, kept us quite busy. Also we found that many of the people we met were very much to our liking and we formed close friendships that have continued until today.

Julian was appointed as an assistant professor in the Department of Advertising in the College of Communications. My appointment was a little unusual. Thanks to the interest in my work shown by the psychologist Charles Osgood (see chapter 14), I was offered a position in the Institute of Communications Research in the College of Communication. I had met Osgood several times when I was a graduate student at the University of Chicago and working on the famous Jury Project, one of the early major law and social science research projects supported by the Ford Foundation in the 1950s.

But the title of my new position was *visiting* associate professor. Why? Because, like many universities in that era, the University of Illinois had a nepotism rule stating that a wife could not hold a tenure-line position at the same university as her husband. Fortunately, with Osgood's strong support, before the academic year was over, we had petitioned the university to reconsider my position and grant me a tenure-line position with the rank of associate professor. With that decision, the nepotism rule suffered a major defeat at the University of Illinois.

Later, in 1968, when I was appointed head of the sociology department, I believe I was the first woman to chair a social science department at any university in the country. I held the position until we left for Jerusalem in 1970 to teach for a second time at the Hebrew University. Julian was supportive of my assuming the headship of the sociology department, but he told me to be sure to tell my colleagues that I did not have a wife. That should be translated to mean, "Do not expect the chair to do a lot of departmental entertaining in her home."

Julian remained in the advertising department, where he worked on the economics of advertising until 1966, when he decided that he could not do the kind of work he wanted to do in that context. The advertising department did not support Julian's work because he and the department's chair, Charles Sandage, did not see eye to eye on the direction of Julian's future research. He was not appointed for the following year, or as Julian wrote in his autobiography, he was "tossed out." That act proved decisive in Julian's career, as I will now explain, quoting extensively from Julian's

Rita Simon while
at the University
of Illinois, ca. 1983.

autobiography—*A Life Against the Grain: The Autobiography of an Unconventional Economist.*[1]

In the same year, with the help and strong support of Jim Heins, an economist in the College of Commerce, Julian obtained a joint appointment in the Departments of Business Administration and Economics in the College of Commerce. Julian and Heins were very close friends all the years we lived in Champaign-Urbana, and it was his idea and major contribution to establish a chair in Julian's honor after his death in 1998. Except for intermittent trips to Israel in 1968, 1970, and 1974, where we both taught at Hebrew University, Julian remained in the College of Commerce from 1966 until we left to go to Washington, D.C., in 1983. It was in this period that Julian finally came to grips with doing population economics.

DEMOGRAPHIC ECONOMICS

Shortly after Julian joined the faculties of Business Administration and Economics, he began to look around, trying to decide what topics or issues he was interested in working on. As he wrote in his autobiography, "I began a mental survey of possibilities. For two years, I devoted the last hour of almost every evening to mulling the question: What topic should I study? For example, I seriously considered health economics, but I decided that the major questions had already been asked."

He settled after awhile into studying population and immigration, a theme that has in the last couple of decades become one of the major research topics of sociologists and economists. But in the mid-1960s the area was of relatively little interest, despite its major policy implications. As Julian explained, he came to the area with strong opinions:

> When I began the study of demographic economics in 1966, and continuing until about 1968, I believed that rapid population growth was the main obstacle to the world's economic development, and one of the two main threats to humankind (nuclear war being the other). I had recently come across an article on population growth in the *New York Times Magazine* that showed the usual scary graph of supposed exponential growth in world population size, and I had assumed that the accepted view, as presented in that article, was scientifically sound. It seemed obvious that the world's population was growing too fast, and I decided to use my skills in economics and marketing to help the world contain its 'exploding' population. So I enlisted in the great war to have fewer human beings.

The fact that when Julian started to work in the area of population economics he thought "population growth, along with all-out war, to be one of the two fearsome threats to mankind and civilization," proved later to be of considerable importance to his credibility.

His first article on this subject, "Marketing Correct Methods for Promoting Family Planning," published in 1968 in the journal of the Population Association of America, responded to a piece by the well-known sociologist-demographer, Donald Bogue, the editor of *Demography*. Bogue's piece, "Some Tentative Recommendations for a 'Sociologically Correct' Family Planning Communication and Motivation Program in India," was, Julian later wrote, "entirely innocent of advertising and marketing knowledge," and thus came to "unsound conclusions about how to market birth control." He decided to explain why he thought so in an article, which he asked Bogue to publish under a pen-name, because "I was afraid that an advertising-related article as my first entry in the field would typecast me incorrectly as a marketer rather than an economist." Unfortunately, the request did not reach Bogue in time and the piece ran under Julian's name. "And lo and behold, a quarter-century later those anti-population-growth and anti-immigration experts (such as Paul Ehrlich) and organizations (such as Federation for American Immigration Reform) attack me on just those grounds," labeling him "a professor of marketing, not a demographer or labor economist," or worse, "little more than an information packager, i.e., a 'spin control' expert." One pamphlet went so far as to suggest that "Julian Simon should be exiled from any serious discussion of the effects of immigration on the United States, past, present, or future."[2]

After this dramatic entry into the field of population demography, Julian proceeded to study the field of economics and immigration. He hoped to yield results "from the standpoints of both economics and marketing."

> And miracle of miracles! When for a brief time (and luckily I published almost no work on the subject before I learned better) I joined the population-control movement—it was and is a "movement" in the sociological sense. For the first time in my life I found myself part of a mutual support group. For example, Steven Enke, an economist who had written a famous article showing how to calculate the value of averted lives had made a fundamental technical error, I found. I analyzed the matter and found an ingenious and technically correct procedure (though one I would certainly not advocate today), and I sent the article to him privately. I quickly received a phone call, saying, "That's wonderful, you've discovered an important error." That sort of behavior in the academic profession is exceedingly rare. I basked in the warmth of the sense of community, as never before. I was so glad to be part of such a network of mutual support and encouragement.

Julian continued to believe for some time that rapid population growth was a serious obstacle to world economies. As late as 1967 he felt that "vigorous population-control action was called for." About 1968, when he ran into Frank Notestein in an elevator during a professional meeting, he "seized the opportunity" to convince him of the urgency "of starting money-incentive programs in India and elsewhere to induce couples to refrain from having more than (say) two children." Notestein had founded the Population Council, and also the preeminent Office of Population Research at Princeton. "Notestein responded to me with the calmness of age, not disagreeing with the point but suggesting that it was worth proceeding deliberately with such matters. Of course I silently criticized his caution in the face of what I considered to be a raging inferno of a social problem."

Julian proceeded to immerse himself in studying the existing literature on population growth and economics—especially in its relation to living standards. "The then-standard formal economic theory of population (which had hardly changed since Malthus and of which there was little except for the book by Ansley Coale and Edgar Hoover, which adds little to Malthusian diminishing returns) asserted that a higher population growth implies a lower standard of living due to capital dilution." Gradually Julian's readings about population growth led him "into confusion."

While Julian and I were in Israel, he began to set down his ideas in a long treatise about the economics of population, taking as his point of departure the Coale-Hoover simulation model based on studying the effects of population growth in India. Julian's treatise, which in time grew into his 1977 book (largely completed by 1973), arrived at conclusions that were very different (in fact, contrary) from those of Coale-Hoover.

> The first challenge to my beliefs came from the empirical correlations (or rather, non-correlations) between the observed simple relationship of population growth and the rate of economic growth. The then-recently-published cross-sectional and time-series studies of nations presented by Simon Kuznets and Richard Easterlin, together with the historical allusions of Alfred Sauvy and Colin Clark did not confirm the conventional theory. These data did not then persuade me that population growth is good; I thought that the data were too weak for that. But the data were strong enough to cause me to distrust the Malthusian theorizing which is the basis of almost all academic strictures about population growth's ill effects. Shaken by this contradiction between the bare theory and the bare facts, I sought a reconciliation. So I dropped my original, unthinking assumption about the evils of more people.

Julian continued on that divergent course and "by 1972 or 1973 I was satisfied that I had found a better theory." "The difference between me and most others was that I took the data seriously, whereas they assumed that the Kuznets-Easterlin conclusion must be some sort of an aberration, and paid them no attention. It is important that I reached the conclusions and beliefs that I now hold because of the facts and analyses contained in the writings of my predecessors and because of the results of my own work as summarized in my 1977 book."

As already mentioned, Julian's thesis did not grow out of any "ideological predisposition" toward the prevailing view of population growth as a world menace; in fact, it began with that popular view. Because he was unable to "square the statistical facts with the standard theory," he was brought "to question the prevailing view, and also to inspect my own values." He turned to "studies based on as many countries as possible, showing the lack of correlation between a country's population growth rate and the rate of its economic development." The importance of this evidence lay in "its generality and its analytical dominance over conclusions drawn only from hand-picked samples of countries." What he derived was that "within a century, or within even as short a time as a quarter of a century, the positive benefits of additional people at least balance the short-run costs. Much of the work that I did in the 1970s—both theoretical and empirical—was intended to illuminate this fundamental broad fact by studying the forces that offset the simplest Malthusian diminishing returns. These factors include longer hours of work, additional investment in private holdings and public infrastructure such as roads, and the creation and implementation of new technology."

Julian then set out to explore more evidence about the question of economic growth versus population growth and density. He studied data on pairs of countries having different political structures but "otherwise comparable cultures"—East and West Germany, North and South Korea, China and Taiwan. He found that "the rates of economic development since their splits after World War II were much higher for the 'free-enterprise' members of the pairs than for the 'central planning' members, though their fertility patterns were not different. This demonstrates both that population growth does *not* account for economic development, and also that political structure *does* influence it heavily."

In the course of Julian's extensive reading during the late 1960s, he had encountered a few works that differed from the standard view of population growth in relation to economics—for instance, "Ester Boserup's *The Conditions of Economic Growth*, which directly contradicts first-edition Malthusianism with respect to subsistence agriculture." He had not yet uncovered a now famous 1951 article by Theodore Schultz, with its "truly amazing and prescient conclusion" that despite higher population farmland is becoming over time, less scarce and less important. Another such work, which he considered "completely persuasive," was the 1963 book by Harold Barnett and Chandler Morse, *Scarcity and Growth*, "which showed that natural resources were becoming more available rather than more scarce."

One spring day about 1969, Julian suddenly recognized that his own paradigm about population had changed. He was visiting the U.S. Agency for International Development office, located in a suburb of Washington D.C., to discuss a plan for lowering fertility in certain less-developed countries.

> I arrived early for my appointment, so I strolled outside on the buildings plaza in the warm sunshine. As I leaned over the rail, below the plaza I noticed a road sign that said "Iwo Jima Memorial." There came to me the memory of reading a eulogy delivered by a Jewish chaplain over the dead on the battlefield at Iwo Jima, saying something like, "How many who would have been a Mozart or a Michelangelo or an Einstein have we buried here?" And then I thought, Have I gone crazy? What business do I have trying to help arrange it that fewer human beings will be born, each one of whom might be a Mozart or a Michelangelo or an Einstein—or simply a joy to his or her family and community, and a person who will enjoy life?

Even after I learned that the standard outlook was ass-backwards, I still held the view that the U.S. as a nation, and each of us as individuals, could with clear conscience, help foreign countries attain the population goals they set for themselves. Indeed, much of my 1977 book *The Economics of Population Growth* is concerned with devices—cost-benefit analysis and marketing plans—that could help other countries make decisions and plans to lower population, though between the time of submission of the typescript and its publication, my beliefs were still evolving. And of course I still believe it is one of the good works of all time to help families have families the size they wish, either by helping limit fertility or cure infertility by making knowledge and aids available. But this is very different than much of what emerges as a result of present national policies.

Now working with a new paradigm—that population growth might actually benefit economies—Julian engaged himself through the 1970s and into the 1980s in a series of careful studies of the time-honored Malthusian analysis of the effect of population growth. He looked at the underlying relationships concerning population growth, size, and density, and economic growth. These included the effect of population growth on the construction of irrigation systems, the proportion of the labor force in agriculture, the amount of education students receive, and the effect of density on the rate of economic growth. "An example of these studies: Because prices for copper, wheat, oil and other resources are much the same all over the world (aside from tax and transportation costs) there is no obvious way to examine, in a sample of independent locations, how population growth affects those prices." The Barnett and Morse book showed that "the historical course of all those prices is downward even as world population has been growing." Julian turned therefore to "the matter of the effect of population growth on agricultural productivity."

As might be expected, Julian's work was not well received in the field of population economics. "I experienced great difficulty in publishing my work. An example was a critique of the central study in the field, the book by Coale and Hoover. I made an argument—very strong, I think—that that book was fundamentally flawed in a variety of ways; most obviously, the book added up to not much more than that the same postulated total output would be divided by a larger number of persons, yielding a lower calculated per-person income; this 'conclusion' derived from the fact that the analysis is mostly confined to a sufficiently short period of time that additional births have an effect on consumption but no effect on production." This particular piece of Julian's was rejected by journal after journal, and it was not published until it came out in his 1977 book. "Of course one should not be surprised at the inability to publish such a criticism of the dominant (indeed the *only*) viewpoint. But the inevitability makes the outcome no more welcome," wrote Julian.

I well remember Julian's unrest in these years. Often he would wander around our home in the evenings, puzzling about questions of population, such as, "how to reconcile a) Malthus' view of innovation as a cause of increasing population growth, with b) Boserup's view of innovation as a result of population growth. Boserup's model of population-pushed adoption of techniques from an already existing reservoir of technology is not consistent with observed up's and down's in the standard of living throughout history—perhaps most notably in Ireland in the decades around the Famine, and in Europe in the centuries before and after the Black Death. Finally I realized that Malthus and Boserup had in mind different sorts of innovations."

He wrote a paper explaining that the pictures presented by both Malthus and Boserup are correct descriptions of certain types of innovations, but to convey the more general picture of demographic-economic growth they needed to be put together. As the empirical evidence for Boserup's theory—that population density increases cause shifting to more labor-intensive techniques of agriculture—was based entirely on case studies, and "one inevitably desires a more 'objective' and systematic test," Julian now embarked upon "a systematic, cross-country test of one measurable step in agricultural intensification, the extent of irrigation." He found that "population density has a strong positive relationship to the proportion of a country's cultivated land that is irrigated. In light of the fact that agriculture typically at that time accounted for half or more of the value of a poor country's output, and given that irrigation systems are a key element of capital used in agriculture, this finding suggests that additional people lead to an increase in agricultural saving. The paper goes on to compare this partial savings effect with estimates of the aggregate savings effect of population growth presented in the literature."

When Julian and Roy Gobin, a Ph.D. candidate, looked at the data in various countries relating population density to rates of economic growth, "we found a positive rather than negative relationship; higher population density conduces to faster growth." It was gratifying, therefore, when in the early 1990s Allen Kelley and Robert Schmidt confirmed this finding in a careful study with additional data and using a density variable as a check. With another Ph.D. candidate, Douglas Love, Julian studied relationships among "City Size, Prices, and Efficiency for Individual Goods and Services."

One by one, Julian and his students continued to explore population increase in relation to various specific cultural factors, including road building (with Donald Glover), education (with Adam Pilarski), and unemployment (also with Pilarski). Glover's astonishing results were that "at any level of income, higher population density is associated with a higher level of road density, which is important because the presence of roads is a crucial element in agricultural and economic development."

When Julian and Pilarski studied "whether population growth diminishes the amount of education children get, comparing nations with different amounts of population growth," they could find no negative effect. In other words, "countries with higher population growth somehow find the resources to provide as much education as other countries." Similarly, their study of the unemployment effect showed that population growth doesn't inevitably result in unemployment, as is widely believed, because the implicit assumption that there is a fixed number of workplaces isn't true. Both economists and laypeople who speak on the subject neglect job *creation*, "which is the central process in an advancing, growing economy. Additional workers not only take jobs, they make jobs. They spend their earnings, thereby increasing the demand for goods and for workers to produce them, which in turn produces more income and more new jobs. This process continues until the economy approaches a new equilibrium, with the same rate of unemployment as before. This is why unemployment is no higher in large countries than in small countries, and no higher (probably much lower) now than in past centuries, on broad average."

Julian and Pilarski also came to a startling conclusion: "The most important economic effect of a person in the long run is the new knowledge that the person creates. Of course not everyone supplies new knowledge, but a wide variety of people do improve the techniques with which they work, and pass on the improved technique to others; it is not just the exceptional 'geniuses' who advance technology."

Julian considered it obvious "that if two countries are at similar levels of economic development, the country with the larger population will produce (that is, 'supply') more new knowledge." But since many scholars have argued against this notion, citing, for example, the great contributions that came from the tiny populations in ancient Greece, or the highly creative group of scientists that emerged from Hungary between the two World Wars, Julian noted that in "those periods when Greece (also true for Rome) had a larger population, its discoveries were greater in number." Julian and Doug Love went on to study "The Effect of Population Size and

Concentration Upon Scientific Productivity," and found "that the number of scientists is proportional to population, holding income constant." So here again, a greater population yields more scientific activity, which "is roughly proportional to population size."

The *demand* for new knowledge as a function of population size forms another strand of the argument. Julian noted that every additional person "spurs the creation and adoption of new knowledge through the demand mechanism as well as through the supply side." He argued that "the demand effect should be especially operative in agriculture, particularly in earlier centuries when food accounted for the largest part of a person's consumption in value terms." Examining the population of Great Britain between the middle of the sixteenth century and the middle of the nineteenth century, Richard Sullivan and Julian decided to examine the relationship between population and the amount of new agricultural technology (indicated by the number of patents awarded and books published on farming techniques). They found that population growth speeds the advance of technology. "Though the data are crude, we detected an increase in technology production when population is larger and when food prices are higher. A larger stock of prior knowledge also increases the flow of new knowledge."

Throughout the 1970s, Julian continued to draw much negative response to his work. An article he sent in 1970 to *Science* magazine was turned down. (In it he said that the "population controllers" were wrong about their facts, and making misleading statements.) In 1977, his major work, *The Economics of Population Growth*, appeared, but "fell deadborn from the press," as David Hume had once put it in speaking of his own first book. As Julian put it, "Nothing happened with respect to the book; absolutely nothing."

But after 1981, after Julian published a popular book, *The Ultimate Resource*, the response suddenly changed. An article about the book published in *Science* resulted in "an explosive reaction, the sort of thing every author dreams about. My new telephone answering machine served yeoman duty. (That's a Navy pun; 'yeoman' is the label for administrative enlisted men.) By the time I'd go to the office in the afternoon for weeks, each day the machine had accumulated ten, twelve, fifteen messages. People were calling and writing, 'I knew this was true all along! I had nobody else to talk to about it.' It turned out that there were (and are) a lot of people spread around the country who shared my conclusions on these subjects on the grounds of personal experience or general intuition, and felt lonely and sometimes a bit nuts. They didn't know anybody else in town who shared these ideas. And they were very glad when they finally found a kindred spirit in my article."

The article produced lecture invitations and brought Julian in contact "with a lot of interesting and amusing people," as well as large number of cranks. The article was also reprinted in many magazines and newspapers, reaching many millions of people. "When I saw the actual printed copy of *Science* containing the article, I had a rare sense of triumph, and I said to myself, 'I beat the bastards.' I thought that the data would matter—that the exposure of the facts would be devastating, and the false assertions that I attacked would be laid to rest. Was I wrong! That was the worst forecast I ever made. The article had shock value, produced lots of letters and phone calls. It raised the blood pressure of people like Garret Hardin. But it made little difference, at least in the short run. Aside from immediate republication in newspapers and magazines, it was not reprinted—never in a single collection, I think."

Still, there were many who appreciated Julian's work. *The Ultimate Resource* was considered a "landmark book," by *The Washington Post Book World*. *Fortune* Magazine described the book as "Compelling and often brilliantly original. . . . His economic analysis will leave a lot of readers revising their thinking about the world around them." And the reviewer for *Population Studies* wrote, "I can think of no very recent book in demographic economics . . . that is so well documented and has so logical a core, and yet will begin to stir such passionate disagreement."

Julian particularly appreciated a letter that came "out of the blue," in March 1981, from Friedrich Hayek, "with whom I had had no contact but whom I had recently begun reading seriously." Julian referred to it as the "most valuable letter of my life."

Dear Professor Simon,

I have never before written a fan letter to a professional colleague, but to discover that you have in your *Economics of Population Growth* provided the empirical evidence for what with me is the result of a life-time of theoretical speculation, is too exciting an experience not to share it with you. The upshot of my theoretical work has been the conclusion that those traditional rules of conduct (esp. of several property) which led to the greatest increases of the numbers of the groups practicing them leads to their displacing the others—not on "Darwinian" principles but because based on the transmission of learned rules—a concept of evolution which is much older than Darwin. I doubt whether welfare economics has really much helped you to the right conclusions. I claim as little as you do that population growth as such is good—only that it is the cause of the selection of the

Julian Simon,
ca. 1996

morals which guide our individual action. It follows, of course, that our fear of a population explosion is unjustified so long as the local increases are the result of groups being able to feed larger numbers, but may become a severe embarrassment if we start subsidizing the growth of groups unable to feed themselves.

Sincerely,
F. A. Hayek

What effect has Julian's population work had? Joseph Spengler, the ex-president of the Population Association of America, wrote in the introduction to Julian's 1977 book, *The Economics of Population Growth*: "Simon advances what may be treated as a new paradigm in the Kuhnian sense." But only a handful of economists or demographers agreed with the general conclusions that emerge from the work. Julian wrote, a decade later:

There undoubtedly has been considerable change since then. The settled wisdom concerning population growth has been increasingly questioned in the 1980's, especially with respect to less-developed countries. But it is not at all clear just how great that change has been. As of 1988, I read most writers on population economics as ranging somewhere between considering population growth *something* of a problem, to considering it *totally unrelated*, to economic development.

The shift in the mainstream viewpoint is evident in the great difference between the 1971 and the 1986 reports on the subject of the National Academy of Sciences. It is also evident in other recent representative reviews of the field, most of which remark on the changes in thinking that have occurred, though they themselves differ in their assessments of the extent of change as they also differ in their substantive conclusions . . . I despair sometimes because I see no sign of it in citations in technical economic work. But a few economists have been kind enough to suggest that my work has had large influence. . . .

Since Malthus and his frightening analysis, economics has been known as "the dismal science." It was only after working in the field for some time that I realized that the data point away from dismal conclusions, by showing that population growth can contribute to a better future. So my work in economics is cheerful rather than dismal. My traverse from simple Malthusianism to the conclusions I have held since then shifted my world view from pessimism to optimism. Now I believe that we need only forestall war to achieve a bright future for mankind.

I also believe that helping people fulfill their desires for the number of children they want—whether it be to increase or decrease fertility—is a wonderful human service. But to persuade them or coerce couples to have fewer children than they would individually like to have—that is something entirely different.

In 1742 (first edition), David Hume wrote: "Multitudes of people, necessity, and liberty, have begotten commerce in Holland." That says a lot.

FINAL COMMENT

In 1983, Julian and I left Urbana and the University of Illinois, with a good deal of ambivalence—Julian for a professorship in the business school at the University of Maryland and I for a deanship in the school of justice at American University. We had very much enjoyed working at the University of Illinois and we knew that we would miss the many close friends we had very much.

Why did we leave? Both Julian and I were doing a lot of work on issues that had a good deal of public policy implications. Julian's research and writing on immigration and the economics of population are controversial issues often debated in the Congress and the media. Living in the Washington area, it was easier to appear on national television and testify at congressional hearings.

The twenty years we spent in Urbana working at the University of Illinois were happy and productive ones. Our children describe their life in Urbana in very positive terms. They enjoyed the schools they attended and they had good friends. In the years we have lived in the Washington, D.C.

area, both Julian and I stayed in close touch with our friends in Champaign-Urbana. Some of my closest friends are still in Urbana and I visit them quite regularly.

NOTES

1. Julian Simon, *A Life Against the Grain: The Autobiography of an Unconventional Economist* (New Brunswick, N.J.: Transaction, 2002).
2. FAIR, 1996, 30, 1.

ALBERT V. CAROZZI

CHAPTER 18

Ralph Early Grim:

The Search for Industrial Minerals

in the Ivory Coast

The sophisticated modern laboratory of Ralph Early Grim (1902–89), the renowned clay mineralogist, who was on the Geology faculty of the University of Illinois from 1948 to 1967, functioned in many ways like a control room. From his work space at the university, Grim could monitor and direct research and engineering in far-away places, greatly expanding the range and influence of his university research. The saga of Grim's geological consulting work in the Ivory Coast during the 1960s and 1970s is but one example. It was Grim's greatest achievement and grandest adventure in his mineralogical consulting.

As Grim's colleague in the Department of Geology, I shared this adventure with him. It began on January 5, 1961, on an airplane flight from New York to Abidjan, the capital of the Ivory Coast. The flight attendant could not really grasp how two passengers could have depleted their supply of gin over the course of the ten-hour nonstop flight. We were celebrating the start of a venture that would last fifteen years and contribute to the welfare of some twelve million Africans. The team was ideal. Grim was an expert on clay mineralogy and industrial minerals; I was a structural geologist and a petrologist experienced in the techniques of exploration sedimentary rocks. Politically, as well as technically, our mission was a shot in the dark, for the Ivory Coast had only just become an independent republic in August 1960.

Before telling this "saga," I should offer some background about Grim.

IN SEARCH OF THE IDEAL CAREER

Grim began his professional career in 1926, as an assistant professor at the University of Mississippi and as Mississippi's assistant state geologist. He had come to Mississippi with a Ph.B. (bachelor of philosophy) from Yale, taken in 1924. During his four years in Mississippi, he published three papers that established the basis for his future leading position in the field of clay materials research. He then returned to school for his Ph.D., taking it in 1931 at the State University of Iowa.

That year he was asked to join the staff of the Illinois State Geological Survey as a petrographer. By 1945 he had been promoted to principal geologist of the geological group and he also became geologist and head of the newly formed Clay Resources and Clay Mineral Technology Section. But in 1948 he resigned from the Illinois State Geological Society and accepted an appointment as research professor of geology at the University of Illinois at Urbana-Champaign. He was to remain at the University of Illinois until his retirement in 1967.

Grim thrived in the academic environment at Illinois. Although his activities at the Illinois State Geological Survey had helped him to develop the techniques of his research, the university context offered him two additional opportunities: a base for the international expansion of his studies and the association of graduate teaching with his research and consulting. While writing books and articles for countless specialized periodicals, he also taught theoretical and applied clay mineralogy, directed the thesis research of more than forty graduate students, and hosted numerous postdoctoral students from all over the world in his laboratory.

Grim also consulted extensively with private clay-producing and clay-using industries as well as with technical agencies of foreign governments. Many of his students and co-workers moved into influential academic and industrial positions abroad, thus expanding the international reach and reputation of the University of Illinois as a world center for the study of clay minerals.

Grim's accounts of his travels to foreign lands, often under adventurous conditions, and his related technical experience became an intrinsic part of his lectures at the university. They kept his students spellbound. Cartoons would appear in the student newspaper showing Grim emerging from his laboratory bound for yet another consulting trip, with a heavy suitcase labeled "clay minerals" and bearing hotel stickers from countries such as, Iran, India, Brazil, South Africa, China, and Japan, to name only a few. This worldwide activity brought him scores of honors and medals. Yet Grim remained completely modest. He often stated that one day he would repay the University of Illinois for the opportunities it gave him. In due time, he did just that by establishing an endowed chair in the Department of Geology.

Grim's venture to the Ivory Coast was his last consulting assignment in distant lands. It was of fundamental importance to him because he wanted not only to help industrialize developing countries but to have an influence on the academic and administrative branches of their educational systems. He was fully aware that he might not be able to witness the completion of so lengthy a project in the Ivory Coast, but the country's unusual political stability (at present, unfortunately, no longer the case) was a major factor in his decision to move ahead. He persuaded the authorities in the Ivory Coast to select the country's brightest students and send them with government fellowships to the University of Illinois and other prestigious American institutions to undertake graduate studies in geology and geophysics.

THE IVORY COAST ASSIGNMENT

Located in West Africa between latitudes 5° N and 10° N, the Ivory Coast is bounded to the north by Mali and Burkina Faso, to the south by the Atlantic Ocean, to the east by Ghana, and to the west by Guinea and Liberia. Its terrain is relatively flat with only a few moderate reliefs in the west. The climate is hot all year long, with temperatures ranging from 70°F to 100°F and alternating dry and wet seasons. The annual rainfall ranges from 3.5 to 8.5 feet, and this staggering amount of precipitation has a profound effect on all natural processes and all human activities. The southern half of the country is an equatorial jungle fringed with spectacular open beaches; the northern half is a dry savanna with scattered trees grading northward into the Sahara Desert.

The entire country is an almost flat plain covered by a ubiquitous blanket of ferruginous and argillaceous red soils, 5 to 10 feet thick, called laterites. They represent the insoluble residue of the intense weathering that occurs in a hot climate with heavy rainfalls that have almost completely leached most of the minerals of all the underlying rocks, regardless of their original composition. The topographic surface cuts across complex series of Precambrian rocks (2.5 to 3 billion years old), standing on edge and belonging to numerous juxtaposed ancient mountain ranges, trending SW to NE, almost totally leveled by erosion and intruded by huge masses of granite. The surface of the land rises slowly in a S to N direction from sea level to 900 feet elevation over a distance of 1,500 miles, with only a few slightly higher sugarloaf granitic mountains in the western part of the country.

The view from the air is dismal, either green for the equatorial forest or tan for the savanna, and through the numerous gaps of vegetation the soil is blood-red with a pattern of huge chocolate-brown rivers. It was enough to discourage the most enthusiastic geologist, but in the long run it was a real challenge to pierce this red blanket and attempt to see the rocky substratum underneath with its promise of mineral deposits.

Until its independence in 1960, the Ivory Coast was a prosperous French colony. France had developed the region within the framework of its colonial empire. Emphasizing a diversified agriculture, this colony produced cocoa, coconut, coffee, palm oil, bananas, pineapples, rubber, precious woods (mahogany and ebony), and a limited amount of cotton, tobacco, cola nuts, and wild rice. As for natural resources, only small mines of iron, manganese, and gold, together with diamond placers, were active, but they presented a minor interest compared with other parts of the French colonial empire. Oil and gas production from offshore wells was also being developed.

The inhabitants—a population of about 12.5 million spread over about 130,000 square miles, with 40 percent concentrated in major cities—belonged to more than sixty tribes, differing in their origin, history, culture, dialect, and religion, but coexisting under remarkably peaceful conditions. French is the official language; the literacy rate was estimated at 70 percent.

In spite of the emphasis on agriculture, the French administration did not neglect other aspects of infrastructure in the Ivory Coast, such as a network of 3,000 miles of paved highways and 38,000 miles of secondary roads and trails. Electrification was widespread. International hotels in Abidjan, hospitals, airports, harbor facilities, and telecommunications were modern. These features, combined with a democratic government, represented important advantages for attracting foreign investments and promoting the development of the country.

The assignment that Grim accepted came from the U.S. Agency for International Development (AID). It was to generate, during the first five-year plan, an initial critical mass of field and laboratory data to promote or create any aspect of industrialization that would render the newly born republic self-sufficient. In 1960, a small geological survey (a state corporation for mining development) was created, with a well-equipped laboratory for chemical, physical, mineralogical, and technical investigations and testing. Staffed by Africans and Europeans, this corporation provided a base of operation, the logistical support for field operations, and the indispensable contacts throughout the country for successful exploration. The technical task proved a wild adventure that lasted through three five-year plans. At the end of the project, the geological survey grew to eighteen geologists, many with degrees from Europe and the United States, supporting personnel of 200 technicians in the field and in the laboratory, and an annual budget of $8 million, certainly a measure of success.

Time was of the essence because the country had to start operating in a modern way as soon as possible, in order to secure the necessary foreign investments. The geological research was directed toward two major targets: (1) systematic long-range geological mapping of the country (typical of all geological survey activities) focused on specific regions having the greatest potential for applied interest, followed by airborne geophysical surveys; and (2) short-range projects leading to immediate economic development.

The withdrawal of the French civil servants was rather abrupt, although some of them remained, by choice or by order. The native Africans, as yet inexperienced and in need of coaching, felt uneasy. For American scientists it was no small task to become leading members of the technical committee that was overseeing the geological survey and simultaneously shaking up the traditional and ponderous French colonial administration.

Grim stood firm in the long technical discussions that ensued. Although he did not speak French, he understood the language well enough to catch the critical points. He would remain silent during the entire exchange of arguments, relying on my temporary role as an interpreter (French is my native tongue). At the end he would clearly summarize the situation and offer the required advice, to the amazement of the group.

It was a common belief among French administrators, and even members of the technical committee, that Americans have hidden political if not hegemonic ambitions. Grim was asked hundreds of times, "What are your politics?" He would answer, "We have none." They could not believe that purely technical advising was our only assignment. So much for dying colonialism. The disbelief gradually changed to confidence, and the project began in earnest.

To establish the preliminary geological map of a country requires at least natural outcrops of rocks and some understanding of the structures in which they are involved. These geological projects remained a slow process of exploration, regardless of the fact that they were focused on regional areas. The only technique available for geological mapping under the adverse conditions of thick laterite cover is to dig painstakingly, by hand, pits as deep as needed to find rocks that have not been totally altered, and hence show identifiable mineralogical and structural properties. The trend of the rocks is then determined by combining the patches of data from pits with whatever subtle recognizable landforms are available and with small cliffs visible along river banks. Conditions are naturally worse in the jungle than in the savanna, but in both situations finding a loose rock that has escaped weathering is always a rare event. Calculations indicate that in the jungle the ratio of a natural outcrop, or even a single loose rock, versus the area of the land is 1 to 1,000,000 square miles. No wonder that the best solution is airborne surveying, using remote sensing techniques. Canadian pilots who fly specially equipped planes mapping the wide expanses of northern Canada, where rocks are similar to those of the Ivory Coast but are fully exposed by glacial abrasion, could not believe their eyes on facing the uniformity of African lateritic soils.

New technical problems arose every day, for as soon as administrators of various divisions of the government, or local and foreign entrepreneurs and investors, realized that the systematic development of the country was beginning, all kinds of projects were submitted. The projects were carefully reviewed and given priorities based on our general planning, financial, and technical means. The testing of our wits began!

One question that arose was: Should we drink water or beer? This appears a frivolous beginning for industrial development. Yet travelers visiting developing countries are commonly advised not to drink the water under any circumstances. If necessary, you are to brush your teeth with beer. Bottled water must be carefully examined to ascertain that the container, even if it is carrying the label of a famous French mineral spring, has not been refilled with tap water and recapped by unscrupulous merchants. This is a common practice even in the best restaurants and hotels. And even assuming that the bottled water is genuine, the fact remained that its price was as exorbitant as that of beer. Both were imported by the shiploads from Europe, their bottles discarded and eventually collected by the poor in search of containers.

Our concern was not the presumably safe (but not recommended for drinking) city water in Abidjan, which was obtained from natural springs or from wells drilled in groundwater aquifers around the city. It was the creation of a commercial production of bottles and other glass containers in the Ivory Coast, a prelude to the finding of natural springs from which a safe native table water could be obtained at an affordable price.

On the way from Abidjan to the beautiful beaches of the Atlantic, the highway crosses a swampy lagoon of variable width, then a series of low parallel ridges of white sand extending for many miles immediately behind the present-day higher beach ridge. The blinding whiteness of these lagoonal sands, contrasting with adjacent seaward beach sands and with the greenery of coconut trees and the ever present red laterite farther inland, had been observed previously by several geologists. Grim immediately grasped the possible use of these sands for manufacturing glass and insisted on taking a closer look at them.

Something was strange, for typical lagoonal sands are gray in color, impure, and argillaceous. They are not expected, as these were, to be white and to consist of almost pure quartz grains. Subsequent studies demonstrated that they had acquired their high degree of purity after their deposition, through an unusual process of leaching from the repeated vertical oscillations of the groundwater table, which destroyed all the other original mineral constituents.

Any hope for a deposit of commercial interest would be where the highest ridges of white sands were closest to the lagoon, because under these conditions the thickness of the leached material submitted to the variations of the water table would be greatest. This prediction turned out to be correct. This unusual leaching process was another unexpected product of the alternating of heavy rainfalls and dry seasons in the equatorial climate of the Ivory Coast. More surprises would be in store along these lines, part of the adventure of doing geology in a new country.

These white sands were tested for mineral composition and other physical and chemical properties required for potential use in glass making. Melted and poured into miniature molds in Grim's laboratory in Urbana, they were found to be an appropriate raw material for a diversified glass industry.

FINDING GOOD WATER INLAND: A TRIBAL PROBLEM

Many villagers in the jungle, and even more in the savanna near the headwaters of streams with smaller flow, were compelled to fetch water on a daily basis from the closest slough. This chore has been traditionally performed exclusively by chanting women and children in colorful attire, walking in long columns for four to six hours a day from their village to a putrid water hole and back carrying all kinds of water containers in equilibrium on their heads. This makes an attractive folklore picture, but the waste of human energy and the exposure to parasites appears intolerable today. Parasite infestation was a perennial cycle, debilitating thousands of Africans who drank polluted water and in turn recontaminated the water by their lack of hygiene. The government of the Ivory Coast was well aware that the rivers of the country were often contaminated by human waste or harbored parasites that penetrated the human skin with lethal consequences, even during a fast wade across a stream or a walk through a swampy area.

To solve this problem a pilot project was begun under the supervision of a governmental agency. Drilling a shallow well within a contamination-protected perimeter at a certain distance from a village, it was no major technical undertaking to reach an aquifer. A pump encased in a concrete cylinder was operated by an appropriate iron handle on the side.

A new problem began when clean water became readily available to the village. The social fabric was disrupted because women and children, although marveling at the pump and playing with the water, lost a fundamental role they had performed for generations. They were wandering aimlessly in the village. The elders were worried; the village chief was angry. Most of the men were grinning in silence.

This was the ideal time for mass education and showing our skills teaching about the health benefits of well water. Grim with his white hair, at times red from lateritic dust, was quickly taken for a wise man (he actually was one). My role was to translate his words into French, while an African geologist was translating my words into the local dialect. This was an unusual open air classroom that drew a tremendously enthusiastic and captive audience. We left rewarded and confident that we had succeeded in breaking up a harmful tradition and spreading the untold benefits of modern sanitation.

When we returned about two weeks later, to our great surprise, the pump was no longer operational. The iron handle had disappeared and women and children were back on the trail hauling containers full of water as before. No one would come forward with an explanation for the mysterious disappearance of the pump's handle. We replaced the lost handle with a new one made of steel. It also vanished within several weeks. We replaced it with another handle in chromium-plated steel, the hardest steel ever made. This one finally survived untouched.

Meanwhile the word came through the village grapevine that the culprit was the blacksmith, who was fond of showing his power at overcoming any

Explorations for nickel ores in equatorial forest using primitive
manual technique of pits dug by pick and shovel.

external technical intrusions in his field of expertise. The villagers however, continued to use water from the nearby slough in the traditional way. The government agency applied drastic measures by spreading lubricating oil over the slough to prevent its use. The reaction of the villagers was to send the women to another water hole at an even greater distance. Finally, many women tired of the long-distance hauling of water and began to use the well water. After many months, the villagers finally realized that the families using well water had less dysentery and other parasites than the others. Eventually nearly all the villagers used well water, and women and children found new social roles in their community.

Fifteen years later when our assignment came to an end, the initial fiasco had changed into a flourishing project consisting of more than 150 wells providing a widespread community with much-needed clean water.

THE TRAUMATIC SEARCH FOR PEBBLES

In temperate countries the concrete that is used for constructing highways is a slurry of cement, water, and rounded pebbles. It is common to hear the rattling slurries inside the huge rotating drums of passing trucks of concrete producers on their way to construction sites.. The pebbles are either dredged from the bottom of river beds or exploited from older sandy gravels forming terraces at different levels along both banks. They are washed and sorted according to size to meet the various needs of concrete producers. It is important that the source of the pebbles is close to the place where the concrete is produced, because the long-distance transport of huge quantities of heavy material having little value (like pebbles) would make the price of concrete prohibitive.

It can be safely assumed that the great axes of drainage corresponding to the major streams of the Ivory Coast flowing toward the Atlantic have remained the same during the recent geological past. At the low water stage, and all along their course, these huge rivers, which seem to transport only red muds during their flood periods, reveal extensive deposits of gravels, which also extend laterally as alluvial terraces of variable width. However, for the time being most of these gravels have remained a resource for the future except for those located in the vicinity of Abidjan, where the need for gravel was of the order of 200,000 cubic yards per year and rapidly growing.

Producers of concrete in the vicinity of Abidjan, hard pressed to meet the growing needs of expanding construction, had solved their major problem in a way that made the price of their product very high in the absence of competition. They located the closest masses of nonweathered fresh and hard granite, opened huge quarries, and began major and expensive crushing operations to reduce the granite to small angular fragments of the size required as a replacement for the traditional rounded river pebbles.

Alarmed by this monopoly, which was slowing the development of the infrastructure from highways to harbors and cities, the government asked Grim for advice on a major geological problem. Grim presided in his usual practical and quiet manner over many heated debates among members of the technical committee. The conclusion was to investigate in detail, over a width of thirty miles, the zone of Tertiary alluvial detrital rocks, including extensive pebbly formations that were partially exposed between the inland flat laterites and the area's coastal beaches. This zone, on which Abidjan, the capital, is built, is known to have been downfaulted toward the south into a succession of compartments disappearing beneath the Atlantic. Some of these compartments are the present targets for offshore oil exploration.

Indeed, extensive sheets of old fluvial gravels were found less than thirty miles from Abidjan. Surprisingly, these gravels had undergone the same kind of leaching as the above-mentioned lagoonal sands; they were clean and consisted mainly of white quartz pebbles. The discovery of a few more deposits of this kind, combined with dredging the alluvials of present streams, eventually brought the production of gravels close to competing commercially with the process of granite crushing.

Grim's finest hour would soon come with a breakthrough in his major field of expertise, the industrial application of clay mineralogy. The population of Abidjan was reaching 2,300,000 inhabitants, and its suburbs were growing steadily. They consisted of a maze of one-storied family houses and a few multistoried apartment buildings. The most affluent dwellings were made of cement blocks and concrete, but the majority were built with adobe whitewashed or plastered in different colors on the outside. The roofs, gently sloping or flat, consisted of different materials, such as straw, twisted palm fronds, or banana leaves. These picturesque dwellings, originating from the much drier northern areas of the Ivory Coast, are not suited for the rest of the country, where they crumble and melt under the huge monsoon rains. They have to be repaired, if not rebuilt, after each rainy season. Yet they were the only possible answer to the materials available locally for building cheap dwellings. Construction of more permanent houses was a major social concern of the government because poor living conditions breed political unrest and crime, two evils that the developing country certainly did not need.

To the amazement of the government, Grim suggested the creation from scratch of a brick-manufacturing industry. This was an obvious answer, but the perspective of an outsider was needed to find it. One should also remember that bricks are the favorite construction material of many college campuses in the United States, including the University of Illinois at Urbana-Champaign. At any rate, clays suitable for making bricks and tiles were bound to exist in the zone of Tertiary alluvial detrital rocks located between the inland laterites and the coastal beaches, as mentioned above, as well as in other places throughout the blanket of laterites with which the reader is by now familiar.

At first a systematic sampling was undertaken in the immediate vicinity of Abidjan, a sampling that would later be expanded to other cities of the country where similar construction problems were brewing. In a short time, samples of potential interest were flown to Grim's laboratory in Urbana, where small-scale bricks were molded and fired in appropriate kilns. A few were found to be perfectly suitable for industrial production.

Two well-known French and Italian brick manufacturers stated their interest in making large investments in the most modern equipment for this large-scale operation near Abidjan. This included excavators to dig the clays in assigned perimeters; equipment for mixing, molding, and extruding the soft bricks; transportation of the soft bricks to the kilns for firing by narrow gauge railroad cars; and adequate storage facilities.

Within six months large-scale production had begun. A few days later a telegram arrived at Grim's laboratory: "bricks disintegrate upon exiting kiln STOP major disaster STOP production stopped STOP your presence requested immediately STOP." Grim went livid and took the first available plane to Abidjan. No gin-and-tonics this time. The matter was very serious indeed. The manufacturers claimed to have used the same time-proven techniques that had been successful in Europe and that the only possible culprit was the improper nature of the clays. This of course was a major challenge to Grim's reputation.

Upon arrival, Grim examined the production line with great care and came across a strange situation that appeared very much like a railroad traffic jam. Many cars loaded with soft bricks were waiting up to twelve hours in the open, on a siding, to take their turn entering the kiln for firing. When Grim asked the irate managers for an explanation for this lack of smooth continuous flow of the loaded railroad cars into the kiln, the answer was that this was common practice in Europe because production was during the daytime and the kilns were operating for twenty-four hours a day. Therefore a high number of loaded cars had to be stored in advance on the siding.

Grim's answer was devastating. "Gentlemen, it is precisely because you have transplanted European techniques to the Ivory Coast without thinking that instead of relatively dry air you have here 100 percent humidity. During their stay in the open, some of the clay minerals of the soft bricks hydrated and expanded, destroying the internal cohesion of the material, which disintegrated upon firing. Good-bye and have a nice day."

The narrow gauge railroad traffic was reorganized so that the bricks no longer waited in the open air for long periods of time. Production resumed and resulted in adequate bricks. This was science at its best.

The story was not finished however. About a year later, another telegram arrived at Grim's laboratory: "bricks appear sliced in several way after exiting kiln STOP cause unexplainable STOP production stopped STOP your presence requested immediately STOP." "Here we go again," said Grim, and he very reluctantly took the next plane to Abidjan. On arrival he carefully examined the entire operation and noticed that the soft bricks coming out of the extruding machine already showed an irregular network of brown curved lines along which the fired brick would later break. Closer examination showed that the lines were in fact cellulose fibers of vegetal origin. The managers appeared uneasy when Grim asked to visit the clay pits,

Exploration for nickel ores in equatorial forest by airborne techniques using high-wing jet-prop planes.

which originally had been outlined very clearly by the exploration teams as being the best areas. Outside them no extraction of clay was permitted.

There were good reasons for specifying these locations precisely because they were located between abandoned coconut plantations. To avoid the additional costs of digging deeper for the clay they needed, and without requesting permission, the managers had extended their operations laterally and consequently had dug clay containing the tough fibrous roots of dead coconut trees. Upon extrusion of the soft bricks, the highly resistant fibers separated the bricks into irregular pieces. Upon firing, the fibers disappeared by burning, causing irregularly fractured bricks.

Of course there are no coconut plantations in Europe, but this was mismanagement at its best motivated by greed. Some firing took place this time at the executive level and the original clay pits were deepened. The production of adequate bricks resumed. Honesty in business should match scientific dedication, Grim said.

LIMESTONES, WHERE AND WHY?

A pathetic sight that one cannot forget is the cultivation of soils. Lateritic soils are replete with iron crusts, which are traditionally broken with primitive wooden plows pulled by men, while women and children spread out whatever meager fertilizer besides human waste is available. This was the daily plight of family farmers all over the Ivory Coast cultivating their main staples of corn, manioc, plantain, and yams. In the southern half of the country a partially industrialized production of coffee, cocoa, bananas, cotton, and tobacco was more successful.

The entire spectrum of agricultural activities would benefit by adding calcium carbonate in powder form, essentially pulverized limestone known in the Western world as lime. Lime is used to condition the soils and indirectly promote plant growth by improving such qualities as porosity, moisture retention, and chemical balance. The government was deeply concerned by the plight of family farming and requested advice for creating an industry based on the use of calcium carbonate to be made available not only to farmers but to chemical plants, which would use it as a carrier for insecticides, for the manufacture of Portland cement, for paints, for the filtration of water, and so on. This meant searching for limestone all over the Ivory Coast.

Unfortunately, except for a few beds of marble, which were part of the old and completely eroded mountains beneath the lateritic cover, no limestone existed in the country. Just as Grim had been struck by using the white quartz sands as material for the future glass industry, I was interested by the fact that the shores of the adjacent lagoon showed shell banks in numerous places. These banks, about three feet thick, had been formed by unconsolidated accumulations of mostly unbroken shells of brackish water mollusks several thousands of years old. Their chemical composition was 88 to 98 percent calcium carbonate. Here was the source of pure calcium carbonate we had been looking for! This was a good illustration of teamwork between a clay mineralogist and a sedimentary petrologist.

A pilot project was started. Many such banks of shells were discovered all over the lagoon, usually close to the shores as well as along them. Eventually, a small industry provided farmers inland with their bags of lime, a much appreciated contribution to their agricultural efforts and one that made their life more bearable.

TIRE TREADS ALSO PEELED OFF IN THOSE DAYS!

Calcium carbonate has many industrial uses that are little known to the general public. One is the mixture of a certain amount of it with rubber during the manufacture of tires. A famous producer of tires felt that the Ivory Coast could sustain a factory that took advantage of the appreciable local rubber production and the calcium carbonate that came from the lagoonal shell banks. Because of the corporation's extensive experience, it did not request technical advice and production began. The tires soon showed a variety of defects. The major one was that their treads peeled off after a short time in use. Production was discontinued and Grim was belatedly asked for advice.

In Europe and elsewhere, the company used calcium carbonate powder produced by crushing geologically older limestone. In the Ivory Coast the calcium carbonate material came from the recent lagoonal shell bank. It had never been tried before. Grim reminded the corporation manager that calcium carbonate exists in two different crystal forms: a stable form called calcite having rhombus-shaped crystals and an unstable form called aragonite with needle-shaped crystals. With the passing of time, aragonite becomes stable by reverting to calcite. Therefore, older limestone consists of calcite whereas aragonite is deposited today in warm equatorial to tropical seas and is used by numerous species of marine to lagoonal mollusks to build their shells. Given these conditions, it is easy to realize that when the pulverized lagoonal shells were incorporated in the rubber during the manufacturing of tires, aragonite reverted to calcite with a change of crystal shape sufficient to introduce a fatal weakness in the tires. This mineralogical incompatibility terminated the project of replacing imported tires by locally produced ones.

The major lesson to be drawn from many of the industrial problems discussed above is that techniques involving regional geology, basic mineralogy, atmospheric factors, and agricultural practices cannot be transplanted from one climate to another without careful consideration of all the new factors involved.

Grim did not live to see the final results of his efforts, but I had the great pleasure to do so in supervising the doctoral thesis of a student who became the Republic of the Ivory Coast's general director of petroleum exploration in the Ministry of Mines and Energy.

SELECTED REFERENCES

Carozzi, Albert V. "Field Notes on the Ivory Coast (1961–1980)." Unpublished manuscript.
Grim, Ralph. E., "Memoirs." Unpublished manuscript, chapter XII, 356–89. University of Illinois at Urbana-Champaign, Geology Library, closed stacks.

PART IV

FINE ARTS

JAMES BOHN

CHAPTER 19

Lejaren Hiller:

Early Experiments in Computer

and Electronic Music

On August 9, 1956, a crowd of some 200 people gathered in the Wedgewood
Lounge of the Illini Union of the University of Illinois for what proved to
be a unique and historic concert. Part of the Illini Composers series, this
concert featured the first piece of music to be composed with the aid of a
computer. The computer that was used was the historic ILLIAC (see chapter 15). The piece, *The ILLIAC Suite for String Quartet*, was the brainstorm
of chemistry professor Lejaren Arthur Hiller Jr., who was assisted in this
novel endeavor by Leonard M. Isaacson, a research associate in chemistry.

BACKGROUND

Lejaren Hiller was born on February 23, 1924, in New York City. His father,
who changed his name from John to Lejaren when he moved from Milwaukee to New York, had studied painting and illustration at the Chicago
Art Institute and spent time in Paris working in various studios. After
the turn of the century, he turned his attention to photography and was

considered by some "the creator of American photographic illustration."[1] Sarah Plummer, who married John Hiller, had left home at seventeen because of strife with her parents. Moving to New York, she worked for a time as a model for Charles Dana Gibson, the originator of the Gibson girl, and later became a member of the chorus line for the Ziegfield follies.

The family in which Hiller was brought up was somewhat unconventional. "Sometimes my parents gave wild parties, with nude women and models running around the house. The police would raid our place occasionally because there was so much noise."[2] The other members of Hiller's household, besides himself and his parents, were thirty-five cats and a pet monkey. As a boy, Hiller traveled extensively with his family, receiving a lot of attention. He was most likely a little spoiled from the experience. Among other childhood luxuries, he enjoyed an elaborate multiple-room model railroad. More important perhaps, "My parents owned a Duo-art player piano. I often fooled around at the keyboard and even tried to jot down my own tunes. I found however, that I could obtain highly satisfying effects by cutting designs and punching holes into the piano rolls."[3]

From grammar school through high school Hiller attended the Friends Seminary, a private school run by Quakers. In his later years at this school, he became increasingly active in music, singing in choirs, playing in a percussion ensemble, and composing his class's graduation march. He earned his first money in music in this period, singing a pet-food jingle for a radio station. From 1938 to 1941, Hiller's parents attempted to formalize his music education with piano lessons. He also learned to play the clarinet and saxophone. But his primary interest was composition, not performance. To this end, he studied harmony under Harvey Officer from 1939 to 1941. By the time Hiller was eighteen, he had written orchestral music and a choral piece.

At Princeton, Hiller majored in chemistry but he also studied music, taking courses in counterpoint, ear training, and composition from Milton Babbitt from 1941 to 1942, and studying composition, analysis, and fugue with Roger Sessions from 1942 to 1945. After taking his B.A. and M.A. in chemistry, Hiller also took his Ph.D. in chemistry there at Princeton, in 1947, at the age of twenty-three.

He then moved to Waynesboro, Virginia, to work as a research chemist for DuPont. When he became dissatisfied with industrial chemistry, Frederick Wall, who had been a consultant for DuPont and was dean of the Graduate College at the University of Illinois at Urbana-Champaign, encouraged Hiller to enter academia. The relative independence offered in an academic atmosphere sounded attractive to Hiller, who in 1952 became a research associate and assistant professor of chemistry at the University of Illinois.

"THE ILLIAC SUITE FOR STRING QUARTET"

Hiller's research, directed by Wall, involved the statistical computation of the dimensions of idealized polymer molecules in solutions, a project that drew on the university's ILLIAC I computer. Hiller coordinated the interaction between Dean Wall and the programmers. Although Hiller had had some experience with analog computers in his work at DuPont, this was his first exposure to a digital computer. He followed up with a course in programming from John P. ("Jack") Nash. This work also offered him an introduction to Markovian processes and other approaches to simulating probabilistic environments.

By 1955, Hiller was teaching a variety of chemistry courses, including chemistry of the metallic elements, inorganic chemistry, quantitative analysis, general chemistry, and research in inorganic chemistry. At the same time, he studied composition with Dr. Hubert Kessler, focusing much of his studies on Schenkerian analysis. While working on his chemistry research project, Hiller realized that the code he was using "could be adapted to writing some counterpoint exercises." He formalized this idea as his master's thesis in music composition, "On the Use of a High-speed Electronic Digital Computer for Musical Composition." This study was conducted under Kessler's guidance, with assistance from J. Robert Kelly, another professor of composition in the music department. The thesis was later revised and published as *Experimental Music: Composition with an Electronic Computer* (McGraw-Hill, 1959), the book for which Hiller is best known.

The format of Hiller's thesis was in some ways similar to certain chemistry articles that he had written. "The Reaction of Cellulose Acetate with Acetic Acid and Water," which appeared in the *Journal of Polymer Science*, is the clearest example of this similarity. The four section titles of this article ("Experimental Methods," "Experimental Procedures," "Experimental Results," and "Interpretation of Experimental Results") also appeared in *Experimental Music: Composition with an Electronic Computer.*

Like Hiller's chemistry study, *The ILLIAC Suite for String Quartet* was a series of four movements that Hiller called "experiments," each created through a different process. The first experiment was a study in one-, two-, and ultimately four-voice first species counterpoint (the process of writing one line of music against another). The second experiment was a

Lejaren A. Hiller Jr. next to the ILLIAC I computer.

progression from randomly generated diatonic pitches to strict four-voice first species counterpoint. This was accomplished by adding the rules of counterpoint one at a time. Focusing on modern composition techniques, the third experiment features computer-generated rhythms, orchestration, and serially composed pitch material. The final experiment, which was added later, in November 1956, was a study in using stochastic procedures to generate musical materials.

The ILLIAC Suite had a huge impact in the music world and in the larger society. There was great general interest in Hiller's unique experiment. Hiller recalled, "Well, the thing hit the headlines. It was really a very strange summer, because I went from total obscurity as a composer to really being on the front page of newspapers all over the country. One week I was nobody, and the next week I was notorious."[4]

The notoriety that heralded Hiller's official entrance into the musical world derived partly from the fervent opposition that was expressed to his use of a computer to create art. "There were even calls in from *Time* and *Newsweek*. This all happened within a period of weeks . . . I enjoyed all the attention, [the] phone ringing all the time, and so on. And then the concert itself had a very electric atmosphere, because there were a lot of people who were very resentful on general grounds. I can remember one person from a humanities department coming up to me on the street and saying that I was doing a terrible thing, that I was the worst person to turn up since Cesare Borgia, that I was an anti-humanist and I was destroying human uniqueness. I was burned in effigy at some point. All of which is fun for a composer, really."[5] Despite the negative general reaction to his work, Hiller was often invited to give talks on computer music across the country, including a lecture at the American Association for the Advancement of Science in Washington, and a talk arranged by Hiller's programming instructor, Jack Nash, at the Association for Computing Machinery convention in Los Angeles.

THE EXPERIMENTAL MUSIC STUDIO

After completing his master's degree in music composition, and following the notoriety surrounding *The ILLIAC Suite*, Hiller was transferred from chemistry to the school of music to start up an electronic music studio. To avoid controversy, this change was made during the summer of 1958. In the fall, the university's Experimental Music Studio became operational. This facility was the second electronic music studio developed in the United States. The first, at Columbia University, had been established in 1952.[6] In the Experimental Music Studio Hiller taught one of the first courses on electronic music in the country. The avant-garde nature of the course was disguised by its title, the "Seminar in Musical Acoustics."

The funds used to supply equipment for the Experimental Music Studio in its first five years came to only $8,000, which was, even for the 1960s, a rather small amount.[7] Hiller managed to proceed because of his pragmatic resourcefulness. Much of the equipment for the original studio came from miscellaneous sources within the university or local outside sources. For instance, an old broadcasting studio control panel, which had belonged to WILL, the local public radio station, made do as the station's central control console and some of the equipment was constructed from kits.

Hiller's first composition in the Experimental Music Studio was written at the request of Jack Leckel, a graduate student in theater. Leckel had asked Hiller if he would compose a tape score for the production of the one-act play he had written, *Blue is the Antecedent of it*. Hiller had previously composed incidental music for several theatrical productions, including Strindberg's *A Dream Play* and Aristophanes's *The Birds*. Hiller's wife Elizabeth, an actress, played the role of the "Middle-Aged Virgin" in the premiere production of *Blue is the Antecedent of it*, presented on March 18, 1959, in Urbana's Sixth Street Theater.

The next work that Hiller created in the Experimental Music Studio was also incidental music for a theatrical production of Christopher Newton's *Cuthbert Bound*, a short piece of abstract theater. Newton, who was then a doctoral student in theater, went on to become the artistic director of the Shaw Festival at Niagara on the Lake in Ontario, Canada. In the original production, Elizabeth Hiller played the part of Cressida Bound. Originally premiered on January 14, 1960, in Urbana's Sixth Street Theater, the work was later revived in 1964 in Urbana's "Round House" series.

THE HARMONIC TONE GENERATOR

One of the most flexible sound sources used in the Experimental Music Studio was the Harmonic Tone Generator, a novel unit designed and built by James Beauchamp, who at the time had a fellowship, funded by Magnavox, in electrical engineering and music.[8] This fellowship provided "for basic research into the generation and creation of new musical sounds." The research, directed by Hiller, resulted in the creation of the Harmonic Tone Generator. This device produced a set of sine waves tuned to create an overtone series. It was possible to control the amplitudes and phases of each harmonic. A foot pedal-controlled amplifier was provided as a step toward proposed live performances. Initially providing only three harmonics at the time the Harmonic Tone Generator first became available, in 1963, a year later it offered six harmonics.

One of the performances that utilized the Harmonic Tone Generator was the premiere of Hiller's *Computer Cantata*. This unit was used in conjunction with a Theremin. Hiller also used this machine in the tape parts of *Machine Music*, *A Triptych for Hieronymous* and *Suite for Two Pianos and Tape*. Other compositions that utilized the Harmonic Tone Generator in the 1960s include Herbert Brün's *Futility 1964*, Burt Levy's *Gnomes*, and Salvatore Martirano's *Underworld* for tape, percussion, string basses, tenor sax, and four actors.[9]

THE MUSICWRITER

Another project of Hiller's using the ILLIAC I was the Musicwriter. Proposed in 1959, this machine was originally a Remington-Rand "Synchrotape" electric typewriter equipped with a paper tape unit. It was rebuilt, changing the typeface to musical symbols and disengaging the automatic forward spacing. The backspace and shift functions were added into the control circuitry and a printing pointer indicator was added. The platen was reduced in size. The mechanism controlling the vertical motion of the platen was altered to provide five functions: vertical up step, vertical down-step, vertical return to control point, clutch lock, and clutch release.

With these modifications the Musicwriter functioned as an electric music typewriter that could also punch and receive five-hole paper tape. This aspect allowed it to be coupled to ILLIAC I. After a page of score had been created with the Musicwriter, the paper tape corresponding to the keystrokes and platen motion could be loaded into the computer. ILLIAC I would be able to perform three functions: horizontal spacing errors, margin changes, and part extraction. Guitarist Thomas Binkley, for whom Hiller wrote his composition *Five Appalachian Ballads* (1958), did much of the original programming; Robert A. Baker, a graduate student in composition, completed the essential aspects of the program. Hiller considered Baker a "talented composer" and "a very bright programmer."[10]

As the first research assistant for the Musicwriter, Jan Bach, then a graduate student, had the job of preparing scores for publication on the Musicwriter. He did this with help from Baker, for Hiller was on sabbatical in Europe. Hiller had selected his *Quartet No. 2 for Strings* for entry into the Musicwriter, so that transposition would not be an issue. It was projected that the Musicwriter would be able to compile a score from performance parts, translate older notation into modern notation, transpose parts, create piano reductions, and synthesize a score into sound. None of these proposals were accomplished. When ILLIAC I was taken out of service, Hiller planned to have the Musicwriter program rewritten for a new computer, but that rewriting never occurred.

HPSCHD

By the early 1906s, Hiller was well aware of John Cage's major contributions to the field of composition. He regarded Cage as one of the most important figures in avant-garde music, expressing this opinion in a review of Cage's book *Silence*. Hiller articulated in this review what he felt were Cage's most important contributions to avant-garde music. "Underlying the sometimes circusy and bizarre aspects of his works, there exist substantial and valuable musical ideas and innovations. Perhaps the most significant of these are the following. First, an intense interest in new sounds, with emphasis on percussion and noise . . . Second, an interest in novel musical forms . . . Third an interest in new technical means such as electronic music. Fourth, an interest in the dramatic use of music . . . Finally, he is one of the few composers around today with a sense of humor. Some of his music is simply funny."[11] It should be noted that the attributes that Hiller highlights here are also aspects of his own music.

In 1967 Hiller approached Cage with the possibility of generating a composition at the University of Illinois, utilizing some of the university's computers. Cage accepted, proposing two pieces. One work would become *HPSCHD*. The other, *Atlas Borealis with the Ten Thunderclaps*, was eventually abandoned. Conducted under the auspices of the university's Center for Advanced Studies, both compositions were intended for the hundredth anniversary of the University of Illinois. The computer used for most of the programming was ILLIAC II. *HPSCHD* also served as a commission from Swiss harpsichordist Antoinette Vischer. Up to that point, Cage had avoided writing for the harpsichord, because he felt that the instrument sounded like a "sewing machine," with little dynamic variability.

Early in the work, Cage suggested to Hiller that they collaborate on this project. Gary Grossman was to have been the programmer, but as Grossman was too busy to help, Hiller became Cage's assistant. The two composers were well paired, as they had a mutual interest in computer music, aeleatoric processes, and theater.

Cage wanted to make using the computer necessary by designing "an enormous project" that encompassed "so many details in it that, were one to sit down with pen, ink, and paper, it would be a project exceeding the time one could spend at a desk." The initial conception of *HPSCHD* was based on Cage's comparison of Johann Sebastian Bach's and Wolfgang Amadeus Mozart's melodic writing. As Cage wrote: "In the case of Bach, if one looked at a few measures and at the different voices, they would all be observing more or less the same scalar movement; that is, each voice would be using the same scale. Whereas, in the case of Mozart, if one looked at just a small amount of his music, one would see the chromatic scale, the diatonic scale,, and a use of chords, melodically, like a scale, but made up of larger steps. I thought to extend this 'moving-away-from-unity' and 'moving-toward-multiplicity' and, taking advantage of the computer facility, to multiply the details of the tones per octave to fifty-six tones per octave."[12] This concept was expanded to encompass the simultaneous presentation of fifty-one pitch collections, each one equally tempered, encompassing a range of five through fifty-six tones per octave.

Because Mozart was offered as a musical model for the composition, Hiller suggested basing the harpsichord parts on Mozart's *Musikalisches Würfelspiel*, a chart that allows one to compose a minuet by rolling dice. Cage agreed enthusiastically. Five of the seven harpsichord parts were

John Cage and Lejaren A. Hiller Jr. with the ILLIAC II computer.

based on this piece of music. One final precompositional determinant was that the duration of each of the fifty-one tape parts and each of the harpsichord parts should be twenty minutes to allow it to fit on one side of an album. This established the shortest possible performance at twenty minutes, while longer performances could be achieved by overlapping the material or repeating it.

In keeping with the theme of "moving-toward-multiplicity," visual elements were considered an integral part of the piece, making it an inherently multimedia piece. All in all 8,400 slides were used, a hundred for each of the eighty-four projectors. Each slide was used only once during the performance of *HPSCHD*. Most were projected on a 340-foot circular sheet of semi-transparent plastic suspended from the rigging of the University of Illinois Assembly Hall. The remaining slides were projected onto the bay windows in the lobby.

Cage called *HPSCHD* "the ILLIAC II's swan song." ILLIAC II had been scheduled to be decommissioned on September 1, 1968, but the production tapes used in *HPSCHD* demanded so much computer time that this machine had to be kept in operation for two weeks beyond the first of the month. The computer was dismantled when the project was completed.[13]

HPSCHD was premiered at the Assembly Hall at the University of Illinois on May 16, 1969. The diversity of the work was met by the audience with several approaches to experiencing it. "Most of the audience milled about the floor while hundreds took seats in the bleachers. All over the place were people, some of them supine, their eyes closed, grooving in the multiple stereophony. A few people at times broke into dance, creating a show within a show that simply added more to the mix. Some painted their faces with Dayglo colors, while, off to the side, several students had a process for implanting on white shirts a red picture of Beethoven wearing a sweatshirt emblazoned with John Cage's smiling face."[14]

The performance was a resounding success, with almost 7,000 in attendance. The work remains to this day one of the largest, most notorious happenings of all time. "As the evening wore on, formally dressed couples from fraternity dances began to mingle with the mini-skirts and bell-bottoms. In the area beneath the screens a play group formed. Paper wads were tossed back and forth."[15]

The premieres of the *ILLIAC Suite* and *HPSCHD* span a crucial formative decade for computer-assisted composition pioneered in large part at the University of Illinois under the leadership of Lejaren Hiller. These efforts occurred at the same time, and the same place as the university's groundbreaking work in the field of computer science and cybernetics, in an artistic environment where collaboration and cross-discipline germination was common and where contemporary music flourished.

NOTES

1. Lejaren A. Hiller Sr., *Surgery Through the Ages: A Pictorial Chronicle* (New York: Hastings House, 1944), ix.
2. Vincent Plush, "American Music Series: Interview with Lejaren A. Hiller, Jr.," manuscript, November 12, 1983, 3.
3. David Ewen, *American Composers: A Biographical Dictionary* (New York: G. P. Putnam's Sons, 1982), 328.
4. Plush, "American Music Series," 33.
5. Ibid., 34.
6. Lejaren A. Hiller Jr., "Electronic Music at the University of Illinois," *Journal of Music Theory* 7 (1963): 99.
7. Ibid., 101.
8. James W. Beauchamp, *A Statement on the Research Investigation*, "Generation and Creation of New Electronic Sounds," Technical Report 7 (Urbana: University of Illinois School of Music Experimental Music Studio, 1963), 1.
9. James W. Beauchamp, *A Statement on the Research Investigation*, "Generation and Creation of New Electronic Sounds," Technical Report 10 (Urbana: University of Illinois School of Music Experimental Music Studio, 1964), 1–2.
10. Plush, "Ameican Music Series," 61.

11. Lejaren A. Hiller Jr., rev. of *Silence*, by John Cage, *Quarterly Journal of Speech* 48 (1962): 316.

12. Larry Austin, "John Cage and Lejaren Hiller: *HPSCHD*," *Source* 2, no. 2 (July 1968): 11.

13. Thomas Willis, "A Giant Happening at the U. of I. Assembly Hall," *Chicago Tribune*, May 11, 1969.

14. Richard Kostelanetz, *John Cage* (New York: Praeger, 1970), 173–74.

15. Thomas Willis, "Urbana Happening in Solar Setting," *Chicago Tribune,* May 18, 1969, 8.

MURIEL SCHEINMAN

CHAPTER 20

Celebrating Art:

From Plaster Casts to Contemporary

American Art Festivals

American colleges and universities seem not to have had the acquisitive instincts associated with great church, governmental, corporate, and private collectors of art. Portraits of distinguished teachers and patrons served a commemorative function and early hung in their halls, but recognition of art for its own sake developed unhurriedly and without special plan.

At Urbana, John Milton Gregory, the university's first regent, wisely did not raise the possibility of asking for state appropriations to acquire art or, for that matter, to include painting or sculpture in the curriculum. Proposals of that sort would surely have generated controversy among pragmatic legislators and trustees geared to the harsh realities of prairie life. Their chief interest lay in training Illinois youth in the most modern, efficacious methods of farming and what were known as the mechanic arts. The art department was confined to teaching basic freehand drawing and clay modeling courses to architecture and engineering students and remained a service facility until well into the twentieth century.

How was it, then, that a fine arts gallery opened to the public less than a decade after the start in 1867 of the Illinois Industrial University, which became the University of Illinois? With a profound commitment to the idea that appreciation of classical beauty enhanced life, Gregory assured trustees that the arts had played too important a part in civilization's history to necessitate "any new defense of their utility and power," and that the university would derive from the presence of an art collection "advantages and renown of no small extent." Attentive local audiences heard him tell of the incredible spread of art in New York and Boston and of how, if supporting funds could be raised, an Illinois museum would give Champaign and Urbana a "character abroad for art, genius and refinement, and in that respect [they] would stand ahead of the cities of the west." The student newspaper, the *Illini*, put it more bluntly: "The age no doubt is rapidly approaching when foreigners will no longer cry out against the supremely disgusting taste of Americans."[1]

By soliciting from area residents contributions that ultimately amounted to $3,000, and by traveling to Europe at his own expense, Gregory obtained 260 plaster casts of statues and busts, 286 photographs of famous paintings and Italian and Swiss scenes, 388 lithographed historical portraits, and an assortment of other art items. Displayed in a large room in the west wing of the university's main building, the assemblage attracted press attention. The *Chicago Tribune*, for instance, reported that "the grand collection is now the largest west of New York," containing replicas of the best pieces in existence, while the *Illini* asserted that the gallery "will undoubtedly, in its ultimate and beneficial results, be found to be one of the most valuable" of all university facilities.[2]

What happened to these treasures? The fact is that by the late nineteenth century, indifference and neglect led to the eventual loss of almost the entire collection; the gradually diminishing, sadly deteriorating remainder migrated to various campus locations. Surviving in what is now the Spurlock Museum are a small number of busts, some photographs, photoengravings, lithographs, miscellaneous items, and ten casts, among them the *Laocoön*, *Apollo Belvedere*, and *Venus de Milo*. There are busts also in the library attic, the armory, and the modern languages and classics libraries.

Over time, the atmosphere on campus changed. Starting in 1908, the four-member art faculty organized increasingly popular periodic loan exhibitions, often accompanied by lectures and sales, in the lobby of the newly built auditorium. These stemmed directly from an administrative recommendation that "we might well try to do for our art interests somewhat the same kind of service which is being done for the musical interests," and the recognition that knowledge of art history and aesthetics related "to the general development of human culture."[3] In 1924, in what surely foretold increasing academic status and professionalism, the art department held its first annual faculty art exhibition. Until the nineteenth exhibition, in 1943, all members of the faculty could show their works; after that, only the College of Fine and Applied Arts members participated.

A phenomenal nationwide awakening in art came with 1920s prosperity. Galleries and museums grew in scope and number, American artists and regional themes gained greater recognition, and the search for an authentic modern American artistic style intensified. On campus, the impetus to collect came from a realignment of the university's aesthetic interests that culminated in a unified College of Fine and Applied Arts, the erection of a special building for "architecture and kindred subjects," and liberal appropriations (until the Depression hit) to purchase works for its own "small but high-class art gallery."[4] Architectural historian Rexford Newcomb, the college's first dean, did everything he could to strengthen the position of art at the university and to enrich further the still modest collection. His commitment remained constant during the twenty-three years of his service.

With the art market developing and art collecting becoming more serious, attention everywhere turned not only to the original but to the rare, the novel, the unique, the irreplaceable. The university's committee on art objects accepted nearly everything that came its way, even if a home for the works could not immediately be provided. Early important acquisitions included thirty-nine Old Master and modern paintings that had been purchased during the Depression by alumni Emily N. and Merle J. Trees with a future gift to the university expressly in mind; photographs, paintings, graphics, and miscellaneous objects originally underwritten by the New Deal's Works Progress Administration Federal Art Project (WPA/FAP); 200 items of Far Eastern art donated by Mr. and Mrs. Spenser Ewing of Bloomington, Illinois; and the contents of Lorado Taft's Chicago studio purchased after the sculptor's death in 1936.

After World War II, when funds again became available for university collecting, the university's own art department launched an exciting series of pioneering exhibitions of contemporary American art. With greater possibilities for expansion of the art program and a general, nationwide movement toward collecting and showing professional art at universities and colleges, the art faculty of thirty members in 1947 urged resumption of its annual purchases of art. The distance from Chicago deterred students from seeing original current art except at infrequent intervals, department head Frank Roos pointed out to Newcomb. Proposing that the university run competitive annual or biennial exhibitions, on a grand scale, with sizable purchase awards, Roos noted that since no other university was mounting such a show, it would bring national attention in the art press and in the news columns as well. "We could, through such an exhibition," he asserted, "let the country know not only that we are here, but that we have a contribution to make in the development and knowledge of American culture. The mid-west State University has too long let the eastern endowed schools lead the way in such matters."[5]

Roos recommended that representative work from all phases of recent art should be shown, and the jury should be composed of "three top-notch men in the art field." An illustrated catalogue would list painters and prize winners and would include a historical essay on the relationship of art to higher education. "It would be desirable that the catalogue be regarded by the public at large, by those interested in art and by librarians, as a book" Roos wrote. Outstanding scholars and artists might be brought to campus to participate in roundtable or workshop discussions on American art. If they disagreed with one another about abstract art, so much the better. "The resultant publicity," according to Roos, "would again tell the country we are here."[6]

Funds would be obtained by putting to different use monies already requested for the 1947–48 budget: with the consent of the Carnegie Corporation, transferral of $4,000 given by it for a visiting artist; curtailment of programs and cutting of operating costs for the gallery by $2,800; and reduction of the $10,000 previously asked for the restitution of annual purchases in order to have $7,500 for purchase awards. "If we knew, sometime in May, that we could have the green light for the show," Roos added, "it could be held in November, next. If not, it would have to be postponed [until 1948). Several members of the staff are so enthusiastic about the project that they have offered to curtail their vacation time to work on it, should it be approved."[7]

As might be expected, Newcomb found the proposals constructive, and good for students, staff, and the community in general. The new university president, George D. Stoddard (who in his former capacity as dean of the Graduate School at Iowa had closely supported the innovative programs of showing American and European art there), also gave the enterprise his full cooperation. Thus a nationally significant university-sponsored series of month-long "Festivals of Contemporary Arts" was initiated, for presentations (as it developed) in the fields of music, dance, theater, film, architecture, landscape architecture, and urban planning as well as in the fine arts. The first "University of Illinois Competitive Exhibition of Contemporary American Painting" was held February 29 through March 28, 1948.

Two thousand notices were sent out announcing the nationwide competition and calling for oil, egg tempera, or encaustic paintings executed within the past three years; no watercolors, gouache, or pastels would be considered. All works were to be framed and only one painting could be submitted by each artist. A three-man faculty jury visited New York City galleries and invited seventy-one works by recognized artists. Because of the large purchase prizes, dealers had their best paintings out for examination. Another seventy-three acceptances came after winnowing by the faculty from an astonishing 953 entries.

As space was limited and the Krannert Art Museum did not materialize until 1961, the 144 works were hung in the Hall of Casts, in Room 120, and in the East Gallery of the Architecture Building. Thirty art professors and fifteen student volunteers became carpenters and clerks and attended to jobs of correspondence, storage, hanging, and publicity. Newcomb later recalled the difficult logistics, telling Stoddard that "the first year we had 953 entries which nearly killed us off as each had to be uncrated, judged, recrated and shipped. We can accommodate only about 150 canvases at most."[8] From then on, all shows were invitationals.

Subjects extended to laborers and minorities; landscapes, seascapes, and urban scenes; portraits, nudes, and still lifes; the devastation of war and its aftermath; social, mythical, and religious images; and the inexplicable. Styles reflected tendencies then current or just beginning to emerge, from the naturalistic to the abstract, and the cubist, surrealistic, nonobjective, and expressionistic. Among better-known artists whose works appeared were Max Ernst, Phillip Evergood, Adolph Gottlieb, Hans Hofmann, Edward Hopper, Alexander Brook, Walt Kuhn, Yasuo Kuniyoshi, Jack Levine, John Marin, Lazlo Moholy-Nagy, I.Rice Pereira, Philip Guston, Abraham Rattner, Karl Knaths, Eugene Speicher, Andrew Wyeth, and Max Weber.

The costs for the entire venture amounted to $14,137.49. Purchase awards totaling $7,500 made it possible for the university to acquire ten paintings constituting a cross-section of prevailing major trends. An outside jury selected the winners, a practice that changed in 1950, when the art faculty determined the outcome. Hans Hofmann's *The Third Hand*, an early manifestation of the abstract expressionistic style and probably the most con-

Sorting crates submitted for first contemporary exposition, 1948.

troversial object in the first show, was not chosen. The university acquired one of his important and valued paintings, *Apparition*, in the third show.

A slightly defensive note, perhaps anticipating public misunderstanding or rejection of the more extreme works, can be discerned in statements written for the first exhibition catalogue. President Stoddard maintained that "a work of art, however unique, possesses qualities related to the time and place in which it was produced. [Artworks] are the product of the artists and the times—and either (or both) may be out of joint. They carry psychological and sociological meaning. They may well arouse visitors to a degree of self-analysis, or even revolt. In this way the spectator becomes, in a measure, creative in his own right. In short, we trust that the paintings in their total impact will enlarge the insight and experience of all concerned."[9]

Dean Newcomb spoke of the sampling process necessary to put together a varied and thought-provoking exhibition, and noted how appropriate it was that the university should recognize not only "established reputations, but that it should also encourage and acquire for its permanent collection the work of new and vigorous talents."[10]

Frank Roos and Allen Weller (who prominently figured in all the shows and served as dean after Newcomb retired) placed the selections in context, reminding the reader of the university's emergence as a special kind of art collector, one that could illuminate technical and humanistic teaching and display for a larger audience the vital and experimental directions of current art. "Progress can only be achieved through change and evolution," they proclaimed. "Controversy is inherent in the idea of change. This exhibition should give rise to much healthy controversy."[11]

How times had changed since Regent Gregory assembled—for a not very enduring public—his carefully chosen collection of authenticated ancient masterpieces in plaster casts, which he believed would suffice in every way to educate in as good stead as the originals. Organizers of the 1948 show, by contrast, put up works they knew might seem "disjointed and lacking in clarity," reflecting chaotic conditions and unresolved "conflicts of existence." Whether one regarded the paintings as conservative or radical, the exhibition guaranteed that a range of styles and art movements would reach a diverse audience.

Journalists, professionals in the art field, and the public came to study what was acknowledged to be a highly stimulating university and midwestern event. Due to its large purchase funds, the exhibit was the second most lucrative show (after Pittsburgh's Carnegie) in the nation. Peyton Boswell of the *Art Digest* said the exhibition "attained in its initial presentation the status of national importance," adding that "within the State's borders, it gives the Chicago Art Institute its first serious competition." By the time of the 1952 festival, the *Chicago Herald American* critic, Copeland Berg, noted that Urbana "now not only leads all universities surpassing even Iowa and Nebraska, which formerly held top honors, but is rated above the exhibitions of all museums in the country." He also wondered why the Illinois president and trustees willingly spent "thousands and thousands of dollars on art, while the University of Chicago and Northwestern University, both richer than rich, spend practically nothing and neither has had any exhibitions of any consequence compared with the Illinois show."[12]

The jury of the initial exhibition thought the pictures would prove a good financial investment and that students would find the exhibition of tremendous cultural value. Roos told reporters that "if any part of the exhibit gives anyone 'aesthetic indigestion,' it is the same reflection of life as that which will give anyone indigestion over a third or fourth political party." Fran Myers of the *News-Gazette* observed that some paintings belonged to the old school, others were the latest in abstraction. Still other works left the layman asking, "What is it?" Myers wondered if another visit would make the art more comprehensible. "The show is the 'new look' in art," she concluded. The art critic of the *New York Times*, Howard Devree, who came to campus to lecture, labeled as "utterly absurd" the condem-

Opening day in the gallery in Hall of Casts, February 29, 1948.

nation of a work not understood, and said that the show was a good example of experimental "and therefore the healthy" aspects of contemporary art. But a student, Bob Wilbert, writing in the *Daily Illini*, disagreed: "Representative to the point of being wishy-washy, the show should make enemies of no one. By the same token, the exhibit cannot be heralded as the champion of the art 'isms' and will make no real friend in the art world."[13]

Attendance was recorded as high: nearly 10,000 persons viewed the first show during its month of display; thirty-five groups of from twenty to 120 people came from all over the state and the region. Faculty members and prominent visiting artists and critics gave lively gallery talks and illustrated lectures. The public voted for their favorite paintings (it made no difference; all choices for purchase had been made before opening day). Speicher's stalwart *Farmer* proved most popular. Trailing closely behind was Wyeth's standing figure of a woman in the painting *Afternoon*. Art students preferred two of the more avant-garde works, Hazel Janicki Teyral's dreamy *Fragment: Three Heads* and John O'Neil's swirling biomorphic fantasy, *Labyrinth*. Of these four, only the Teyral was among the ten bought for the permanent collection.

In all, the university held fifteen Contemporary American Arts Festivals over a period of twenty-six years, the first six annually. Starting in 1953 (when sculpture began to be shown too), shows were held biennially because of the extraordinary amount of time required to organize them and because of financial inadequacies. Prohibitive insurance costs in the early 1970s and the realization that it no longer seemed imperative to mount special shows of vanguard art—such exhibitions were held routinely by then—brought the series to a close in 1974.[14]

What had been accomplished? Comprehensive illustrated exhibition catalogues containing artists' statements, biographical information, and insightful introductory essays by Dean Weller reached an even wider audience than those actually attending the shows through dissemination by galleries, collectors, and later the Krannert Art Museum. Even the Department of State, on several occasions, distributed them overseas. Over the years, a curious, receptive public had enjoyed not only a series of provocative art exhibits and lectures, but a variety of entertaining modern dance recitals, new music concerts, film screenings and theatrical presentations, and special events in literature, radio, and television.

Over a thousand different artists exhibited a total of 2,036 works. From the first nine shows, the $7,500 allotted for each was sufficient to obtain a total of seventy-six paintings and sculptures for the collection. After that, supplementary nonrecurring funds frequently became necessary to balance the budget. A record high of $20,280 in 1963, for example, could buy only four now price-inflated art objects. The last exhibition yielded just two: James Prestini's nickel-plated steel *Construction #216* and William Wiley's large-scale abstract acrylic and watercolor canvas, *Spirit Line*.

In all, ninety-eight notable works of art swelled the university holdings. Eminent artists, many of whose works accrued many times in value since being acquired, include Kurt Seligmann, Hans Hofmann, Yves Tanguy, Ben Shahn, Max Beckmann, Abraham Rattner, William Baziotes, Adolph Gottlieb, Rufino Tamayo, Morris Graves, Leonard Baskin, Charles Burchfield, Loren MacIver, Phillip Guston, David Park, Matta Echaurren, Stuart Davis, James Brooks, Robert Indiana, Peter Saul, and Sol LeWitt.

Controversial art given public exposure by a prestigious educational institution engendered a serious interest in a rich panoply of new art forms. Substantial purchase awards lent credibility to the worth of American artistic production. Greater numbers of prospective art students nationwide applied for admission to the art department's graduate programs. The idea of universities as legitimate, active patrons of art gained momentum.

In his last report as dean (1970–71), Weller summed up the benefits of the university's support of the arts. He noted that it had been his great good

fortune to serve "during a period of expansion, when new ideas and programs were welcomed by the sympathetic attention of the central administration, when new facilities were provided for parts of the College, and
when funding was granted for some of the many requests and programs
which originated within the departments. At times it seemed as if all we
could do was to simply keep up with the burdens imposed by increased
enrollments, but important educational developments and innovations
were also accomplished."[15]

NOTES

1. Board of Trustees of Illinois Industrial University, *7th Annual Report* (Springfield, 1875),
   91–92; *Champaign County Gazette*, March 4, 1874; "Editorial," *Illini*, May 1876, 226–27.
2. *Chicago Tribune*, January 2, 1875; "Editorial," *Illini*, May 1876, 227. Actually, the University of Michigan had the only comparable collection west of New York, and Gregory must
   have known of it from his years of educational work in the state. Professor Andrew D.
   White, a collaborator in assembling Michigan's group of plaster casts and engraved and
   photographed views of antiquity, visited Gregory in Urbana in 1871.
3. College of Literature and Arts, "Annual Report for 1906–07," March 1, 1907.
4. *President's Report 1927–1928* (Urbana, 1929), 31. The cornerstone for the Architecture
   Building was laid November 16, 1926. Classes began to be held there in February 1928.
5. Frank Roos to Rexford Newcomb, "A Proposal for a Revised Use of Funds Requested by
   the College of Fine and Applied Arts, for the 1947–48 Budget," May 5, 1947.
6. Ibid.
7. Ibid.
8. Rexford Newcomb to Nelson Rice, May 18, 1950.
9. George D. Stoddard, "Foreword," in *University of Illinois Competitive Exhibition of Contemporary American Painting* (University of Illinois, 1948).
10. Ibid.
11. Ibid.
12. Peyton Boswell, "Progress in Illinois," *Art Digest*, March 1, 1948, 7; Copeland Berg, "Illini
    Art Show Opens on March 2," *Chicago Herald American*, February 23, 1952.
13. Fran Myers, "Broadway Tatler," *News-Gazette*, February 26, 1948; "Times Critic Lauds U.I.
    Show," *News-Gazette,* February 29, 1948; Bob Wilbert, "Realism, Surrealism, Abstract,
    Non-Objective Art to be Seen at Exhibition of American Painting," *Daily Illini*, February
    28, 1948.
14. The usual biennial exhibition was canceled in 1971. In its stead, all works purchased
    from earlier shows for the permanent collection were brought together for the first time.
15. Allen S. Weller, College of Fine and Applied Arts "Annual Report 1970–71," 17.

CHAPTER 21

William Warfield: Creating Home
for Students at Illinois

Lord I'm bearing heavy burdens tryin' to get home.
Lord I'm climbing high mountains tryin' to get home.
Lord I'm standing hard trials tryin' to get home.
Lord I'm standing, climbing, bearing, tryin' to get home.

NEGRO SPIRITUAL

The highest compliment one can bestow on a community is to call it home—a place for family, a people linked in time, purpose, and place who enjoy meaningful relationships with one another. Home is where we can feel loved, gain our sense of ourselves, and learn what we can aspire to. Our experiences at home determine how our lives will play out on the world stage. William Ceasar Warfield knew this.

I first came face to face with Warfield on an October afternoon in 1979, when he walked unannounced into one of my rehearsals. I was preparing for a recital to take place at the West Virginia Cultural Center in Charleston, West Virginia. I was completely surprised. The encounter had been arranged by a mutual friend (Dr. Charlotte Giles), but I had not been informed.

I was of course familiar with many of the famous singer's songs. I had a couple of his recordings—Mozart's *Requiem* and Handel's *Messiah*.

I had even attended a couple of his concerts. And once, as a little girl from Mount Hope, I had mustered up the courage to stand in line for Warfield's autograph.

So on that memorable October afternoon, in walks Porgy himself. (Imagine that!) In walks the man famous for singing "Ol' Man River"—the man with whom composer Aaron Copland recorded sets of the *Old American Songs*. I didn't quite know what to do. So I did what was easiest for me and what came natural. I kept on singing.

I happened to be singing Serena's aria, "My Man's Gone Now," from *Porgy and Bess*. To my amazement Warfield began to sing with me! After that I thought I should stop and talk to him. But he insisted that I keep rehearsing. I sang a German Lied, "Mondnacht," by Robert Schumann. Again, he sang with me. I was totally blown away, in awe, inspired all at the same time. I can't remember what else I sang.

At the end of the rehearsal, Warfield complimented me and encouraged me to come to Illinois. "You'll do well there," he said. "It is a good place. It will be good for you." He gave me the name of the graduate admissions director and encouraged me to apply. I don't believe I really heard him at the time. I was still trying to come to grips with the fact that William Warfield had listened to *me* rehearse!

Family and home had been significant themes throughout the life of William Warfield, who was born on January 22, 1920, the eldest of six children of Robert E. and Bertha McCamery Warfield. When telling of his years growing up in Rochester, New York, Warfield often spoke of the nurturing environment he had enjoyed in the Warfield household and in other communities.

From his maturing years, Warfield created supportive communities everywhere he went. During his military service in the Army, he enjoyed a "charmed" environment (his words) at Camp Ritchie, Maryland, with a special home at Shiloh Baptist Church on weekends in Washington, D.C. It was a place where he felt "fussed over and cared for." His subsequent theater experiences (including *Call Me Mister*, *Set My People Free*, *Regina*, and *Showboat*) would offer a sense of family for him. He likened his friends to "a clan of relatives" who got along like "close kin."

Warfield's artistic life spanned virtually every area open to musicians. Before coming to Illinois, he had already enjoyed over a quarter of a century of worldwide successful performances. His first big break came in 1950, with his professional recital debut at New York City's Town Hall. This successful debut thrust him instantly to the forefront of concert artists. Another important opportunity came while he was on an Australian tour.

The Australian Broadcasting Commission had invited him, on the heels of his Town Hall success, on a thirty-five-concert tour of the Australian continent. The tour included performances with their five leading symphony orchestras.

During this Australian tour, Warfield learned that the role of Joe in the Metro-Goldwyn-Mayer film *Showboat* had not been filled. He submitted a recording and was offered the part. Generations remember him for his powerful singing of "Ol' Man River" and for his vivid portrayal of the dock hand in this film. The beautiful, moving rendition of "Ol' Man River" that the world enjoys on the 1951 recording was intended as the "trial run-through." It is now referred to as the legendary "flawless, one-take" that brought tears to the eyes of cinema magnate Louis B. Mayer. In an interview with Howard Reich, Warfield reflected on the experience, "When I finished that performance, I really didn't know what all the screaming on the set was all about. I had always been taught that you're supposed to get it right the first time . . . When we finished the take, everyone on the set was so excited they called (studio head) Louis Mayer from his office to come listen to the recording. Afterward he began weeping and said, 'I can't believe it, I can't believe it.' But I've always liked to joke that when he burst into tears, it wasn't so much because of how well I had sung the song, but because of how much money I had saved him." "Ol' Man River" became a staple of Warfield's repertoire, and a selection that he said he never tired of singing.

Another turning point in Warfield's career was the 1952 revival of George Gershwin's *Porgy and Bess*. This revival, which lasted for four years with performances in the United States, Western Europe, and Russia, is considered Warfield's greatest contribution to the world of music performance. It brought him international fame. He starred in the title role, along with Cab Calloway and opera soprano Leontyne Price, who played Bess. In 1952, Warfield and Price married. But the demands of two professional careers were very difficult on their marriage. After many years of separation, they divorced in 1972. The two remained friends, however, and when Price performed at Illinois, Warfield would personally host her receptions.

The years following his New York debut and his appointment to the Illinois faculty saw Warfield's career expand without interruption. He even made his mark as an actor with performances as "De Lawd" in the Marc Connnelly version of *Green Pastures*. Warfield was chosen by composer Pablo Casals to sing his oratorio "El Pesebre" at the Casals Festival in Puerto Rico. Warfield was the first American solo artist to penetrate and traverse the African continent, paving the way for additional State Department ventures in Africa. In addition to his countless musical performances he added stirring performances as a nonsinging narrator.

In 1976 Warfield embarked on a Bicentennial tour as narrator for Aaron Copland's *Lincoln Portrait* with the New York Philharmonic Orchestra, and with Leonard Bernstein conducting. The tour began and concluded with performances in New York, with intervening performances in Chicago, Miami, London, Munster, Frankfurt, Vienna, Linz, and Paris. A unique feature of the tour was Warfield's speaking Lincoln's words in English, German, and French for best communication with each particular audience.

Later in 1984, Warfield would receive his first Grammy in the Spoken Word category for his narration of Copland's *Lincoln Portrait* with the Philharmonia Orchestra of the Eastman School of Music, with David Effron conducting. Other highlights of his career in the years before coming to Illinois include his work with Bruno Walter and Otto Klemperer and countless concerts, recitals, and solo appearances with this country's major orchestras. He received many impressive honors and awards. And he made six separate tours for the U.S. State Department, more than any other American solo artist.

The University of Illinois's voice faculty search of 1974, which brought Warfield to Illinois, was an unusual variation on the standard process of filling a faculty opening at the research university, which initiates a flurry of activity in which officers and individuals spring into action. The procedures generally follow a prescribed format: the dean approves the search, a committee is issued a charge, and a position notice is drafted citing relevant details (e.g., starting date, duties, rank and salary, etc.). The search committee, often the entire faculty, consider questions such as: Who is the best person? Who will best complement the existing faculty? This is serious business, and many hours are spent poring over the responses of applicants.

But in the voice faculty's search of 1974, opportunity meshed easily with the desires of all involved, and the process was shortened. For just when Illinois needed a voice professor, Warfield was thinking about devoting himself to teaching. He sensed it was the right time for him to pass his art on to those who were coming along after.

Thomas Frederickson, who was then serving as the director of the school of music, recalled hearing about Warfield's availability from John Wustman, a professor of accompanying and a longtime friend of Warfield: "Wustman called and told me that William Warfield might be ready to settle down and that he might be interested in coming to Illinois." Frederickson explained that after the decision "to go after him," the search was not done in the traditional manner. Given Warfield's stature, there was no need for an audition. "John Wustman conveyed the initial offer. There was some coordination of resources from the Afro Studies Department and the School of Music to satisfy the salary requirement. Once that was settled, we did it."

In his autobiography, *My Music & My Life*, Warfield reflected, "From the outset, the University of Illinois meant more to me than the sum of its educational parts. In a very real sense, I'd come full circle to the bosom of an extended family." Wustman may not have used the words *family* or *home* in describing Illinois to Warfield, but the idea that Illinois was working for Wustman, and should work out nicely for Warfield as well, must have been clearly communicated.

Robert Ray, the coach and accompanist for the string division, was ecstatic about hiring Warfield. He was eager to have the opera *Porgy and Bess* performed. No one but Warfield could pull that off. Warfield managed to get the rights from the Heyward and Gershwin estates and to garner the support of the entire University of Illinois. With Warfield's help, *Porgy and Bess* was launched in 1976, with performances in Champaign and Lake George. Warfield of course played the leading role, the last time he performed it in costume on his knees.

Many others were excited about Warfield coming to Illinois. Roger Cooper of WILL-FM remembered, "From the day it was officially announced that William Warfield would be joining the faculty, he generated a great deal of excitement and curiosity among the voice students as well as a great deal of pride to the black students. I remember the buzz when he gave his first presentation. It was at a music conference and he talked about spirituals and sang a few. I thought it the most beautiful and expressive singing I had ever heard from a male singer. The community agreed and there were requests from many churches for him to sing on their Christmas 'Messiah' programs and to speak here, to adjudicate somewhere else, and 'couldn't you just listen to my little Timmy?'"

One of those requests came from the Village Chorale of Mahomet. Emeritus Professor Daniel Perrino told the following story to illustrate his point that Warfield was "a people person." "When scheduled to sing with the Chorale, Bill arrived early for his rehearsal at the Lake of the Woods. He encouraged them to continue to rehearse and sat in a corner of the room and listened. After he had rehearsed, he stayed on an hour or so to listen to the Chorale rehearse. He could have remained in the upper echelon of society, but he didn't. He interacted with people."

Professor Emeritus Austin McDowell recalled, "When I first met with William Warfield as he joined the faculty, I knew, of course, of his international reputation. However, I had no knowledge of his gifts as a teacher, his willingness to be available to students, to act as a mentor or father figure, always within his commitment to excellence in performance. His warmth and disarming manner endeared him to both faculty and students."

According to Cooper, "You could see the pride on the faces of the African-American community whenever you were out with Bill. They would recognize him and come to wish him well or whatever, and he'd be so gracious." Even his barber expressed his pride, telling everybody (or whoever would listen), "When Mr. Warfield accepted that Grammy, he was sporting one of my special haircuts."

It is not known how Warfield came to be called "Uncle Bill" at Illinois. This persona is thought to have been transferred from Vienna to Champaign via publicity written at the time Warfield started at the university. However it happened, Warfield performed the part extremely well, offering a space to those in his community where one felt relaxed, accepted, and supported. Something within him caused him to create this nurturing sense of community. He was motivated to "perform" the role of professor and colleague. He inspired many with his humanity and humility. He was always willing to serve in any way that he could. There are endless stories recounting his good deeds—from welcoming new faculty to leaving congratulation notes following a colleague's performance.

Warfield's understanding with the university was that he would maintain an active performing schedule while balancing the demands of his teaching schedule. This arrangement allowed him to focus on his creative output in the studio and on the stage. Warfield needed this support and flexibility, yet his relationship to the university was also crucial. Professor James Keene, the director of bands, summed up the relationship: "Bill Warfield gave us a package, of which talent was a major part. But why he was able to flourish and how we were able to gain was because of three components that are often forgotten—availability, sincerity, and humility. These three components Bill combined with talent. Talent, alone, doesn't ensure good mentoring, but he combined these three components."

Many people in Champaign-Urbana benefited from Warfield's presence, and most have their own stories to tell. There's the story of Warfield's visits to the "cultural capital" of Champaign-Urbana, a doughnut shop on the corner of First and Green, where a cross-section of people gathered, mostly blue-collar workers. Mr. Perrino recalled Warfield's interactions there. "He kidded, talked, was open, and never changed his personality. They thought he was the 'cat's pajamas.' After his book (*My Music & My Life*) was published, I took a copy to the shop. About half of the regulars read it. Bill seemed to penetrate the outer walls that people build around themselves to get to the core of the individual."

There are the stories about his expert cooking, particularly, his sweet potato pie—"the best thing ever tasted," "just the greatest." And there are the stories about his stories. Ronald Hedlund, chairman of the voice division, remembered that Warfield always had a story or joke to share. "Some you couldn't repeat, and he never repeated himself." On more serious note, Hedlund spoke of Uncle Bill's temperament. "I never saw him in a bad mood. He was always up, at meetings, in the hall, at recitals and auditions." Aus McDowell also remembered "Bill, an accomplished singer, with a million stories to tell—yet always with the intent of teaching, making a point, enlightening. I would say he was a natural teacher, rare among highly talented beings."

Warfield brought a way of thinking to the university that deviated from the norm. Balking at the tradition of being unapproachable in student-professor relationships, he viewed the world of the performing arts in the university context as an open, socially fluid environment. As an artist with twenty-five years of successful performance experience, he understood the importance of a learning environment whose mood is generally relaxed and informal. Having moved from an active performing life to an equally active life of teaching, he was in current touch with the needs and interests of the protégés entrusted to him. Above all, I believe he remembered what it was like to be poor, hungry, and trying to study music.

As one of the first black professors in the school of music, Warfield had a special role. Many of the first black students who earned their doctorates in voice were his students. Roger Cooper explained that black students "were privy to special treatment from Uncle Bill." Cooper related a story about the informal network that Warfield offered black students. "There was a time when he first came that we were all expected (about five to six as a core group) at his house for dinner every night—seven nights a week. You were asked about if you missed." For the black students who may have been away from their families for the first time, Warfield provided a home away from home. He was willing to come to the rescue as an uncle might. Whereas the initial community consisted mainly of of the black students studying music, the group quickly developed to include a racial mixture from all across campus and extending out to those not associated with the school of music.

William Warfield in his studio in Smith Memorial Hall demonstrating at one of his master classes, ca. 1977.

Having received numerous honorary doctorates (Arkansas, Boston, Rochester, LaFayette, Milliken, and others), as well as several cities' and state's highest honors (New Orleans citation, Order of Lincoln, Special Regents Medal of Excellence from University of the State of New York, and others), and many other accolades, Warfield could have chosen to teach only selected students, or perhaps to offer only master classes. Instead, he committed himself to teaching undergraduate and graduate students at Illinois. He once said, "I believe our most priceless possession is our mind; to be in a profession that gives one the power to mold and shape a young mind is to me a sacred trust. It demands that I pass on the best of what I have learned and experienced from life with unstinting energy and dedication." He did just that. Teaching, for him, was the act of passing on what he had learned, the perpetuation of the art form through students. It was a lasting commitment. From 1983 until his retirement in 1990 he served as the chairman of the voice division, leading by example. He took his work at Illinois very seriously. While most of his teaching, advising, and counseling involved undergraduate applied music and music education students, his influence was campus-wide. Students from many disciplines benefited professionally and personally from him. His commitment and effectiveness as a professor was recognized with a Campus Award for Excellence in Undergraduate Teaching.

I would like to use these final pages to share what William Warfield has meant to me. He meant more to me than all of his accomplishments. Uncle

Bill, as I knew him and called him, was a mentor, not just a role model who would be showing or telling me how to do something, but a model who touched my life and allowed me to touch his. He was part of my family.

Shortly after that afternoon twenty-three years ago when Warfield walked into my rehearsal and sang with me, he extended the invitation for me to come to Illinois as a graduate student. "What a nice man," I thought. "He probably tells everyone what he told me." It took much prodding from Dr. Giles before I would apply, audition, and then wait to hear. I was admitted during the spring of 1980.

Illinois offered me the opportunity to form relationships that have empowered me, enabled me, and equipped me in my quest for sufficiency and security as a professional. What was intended to be a two-year visit turned into a rather extended stay. Uncle Bill was right. Illinois has been good for me. A daughter (Kirstie), a master's degree, a son (Jonathan), another daughter (Ashley), a doctorate in musical arts, an appointment to the faculty, and a third daughter (Charity) later, I can still say it's very good to be in Urbana-Champaign. The hand of the school of music attracted me; its heart has sustained me. Warfield represented that hand and that heart for me. He was glad that I came to Illinois, and he was committed to helping me finish well.

Uncle Bill was on sabbatical on that cold January afternoon when I auditioned, and also when I arrived on campus in the fall of 1980. I didn't study voice with him until my fourth year. But I always knew that if I needed anything, he was available. Knowing someone who was further along in the profession and in life experience willing to share his wisdom, his time, and his talent has meant a great deal to me.

I have a reservoir of Uncle Bill stories. There were the voice lessons, two in particular that I must mention. One afternoon I was singing Schubert's "Nacht und Träume." Everything lined up perfectly, the accompaniment, the intonation, the legato line, the breath. It was a magical musical moment for me, truly spiritual. Tears began to stream down my cheeks as I sang the last phrase. I wasn't out of control, but I couldn't control the tears. I decided to go with it and stay in the moment. When the final chord died away, the three of us, my accompanist, Uncle Bill, and I just sat in silence. After a few moments, I started to offer an apology, which he quickly interrupted, saying, "No apology is needed, this is what we're after every time." And then there was the time when he played the middle section to Schumann's "Mondnact" in the style of a Baptist hymn to show me how to achieve an effective rallentando and sing the correct rhythm.

Coaching with Uncle Bill was always informative. He asked lots of questions, always probing, pulling, making me commit to an idea or thought. Perhaps those interactions caused him later to write in my open letter of recommendation from him that our lessons were "more like artistic collaborations than mere teaching on my part." For me, it was enough to have him for a teacher and quite an honor to be becoming like my teacher. He would later offer me one of the highest compliments I've ever received. He signed my copy of his book, "For Ollie, with deep affection and pride in the wonderful work she is doing. William Warfield, 'Uncle Bill,' 1/4/94."

I could go on and on about my time with Uncle Bill. There was the joy of performing alongside him and learning from a legend. And of course, there were the times I enjoyed being in his home. On several occasions, Uncle Bill hosted receptions following my recitals. For the first reception, he asked me how many people I wanted to invite. I think I said, "Ten, is that too many?" With his characteristic laugh, he answered, "Is that all?" I think I changed the number to fifteen, and when I got to his house after the recital, there was a houseful. I also enjoyed meeting his distinguished guests. I remember his receptions for Leontyne Price and Jessye Norman. He seated me next to them. Whenever an artist came to Krannert, he'd call and ask if I had a ticket. He wanted me to have every good experience. I hope he knew that I was enjoying a choice relationship with him.

Uncle Bill embraced my family. He always asked about my husband, Harold (he called him "Buddy"), and the children. He was always supportive of my performances, in recital, concert, and with the Black Chorus. On two occasions, I was privileged to conduct Uncle Bill in concert. He narrated James Weldon Johnson's "God's Trombones" with the Black Chorus, and Jonathan Bruce Brown's "Legacy of Vision" with the Chorus and Champaign-Urbana Symphony. These were special performances and characteristically "Uncle Bill" did something unconventional. He kissed my hand—a tribute that the conductor usually pays to the artist.

The last time I saw Uncle Bill he was narrating Copland's *Lincoln Portrait* with the Illinois Symphonic Band at the Krannert Center. It was a beautiful, inspiring performance. At the end of the concert, I went backstage to spend a few minutes with him. He asked about the family. He wanted to know all about the children and what we all were doing. After I filled him in, he looked me in the eye and said, "Ollie, if I've never done anything right in life, I did right by bringing you to Illinois." It was a precious moment for me, because many times I had thought that very same thing. I agreed, and added, "Uncle Bill, you've done a lot of things right."

William Warfield,
1990.

In his autobiography, Uncle Bill told how his Town Hall debut came to be. He wrote that a man named Walter Carr had told him that at a crucial point in his life somebody stepped forward and did the things that made him successful. Carr figured that before he died he had to pass that on to someone. He decided it was going to be William Warfield. For me, Warfield was the one who at a crucial point in my life stepped forward and did what he could for me. I am eternally grateful and have inherited a tremendous responsibility to do what I can for those who follow after.

A NOTE ON SOURCES

The Warfield quote from H. Reich's interview can be found in Howard Reich, "Still Show-boating: William Warfield—He Just Keeps Rollin' Along," *Chicago Tribune*, January 22, 1989. The other quoted material in this chapter comes from interviews by the author with Austin Mc Dowell, January 21, 2003; Daniel Perrino, January 22, 2003; Roger Cooper, January 22, 2003; Ronald Hedland, January 22, 2003; Thomas Frederickson, January 24, 2003; and James Keene, January 24, 2003. For additional information consult, William Warfield, *My Music & My Life* (Champaign, Ill.: Sagamore, 1991).

NATALIE ALPERT served as instructor and assistant department head from 1971 to 1991 in the Department of Landscape Architecture at the University of Illinois. She taught courses in history and planting design and authored many papers on the contributions of women to the profession. She received a Special Award of Recognition from the Council of Educators in Landscape Architecture for her "dedication to counseling and supporting generations of women students and faculty." She passed away January 20, 1997.

JAMES BOHN had his music and video works presented at "Most Significant Bytes 2000" at the "MAXIS festival," at "MEDiA CIRCU[it]S," at the "Florida Electro-Acoustic Music" Festival, and on "The New Composers 27 Minute Companion." He has also given papers at conferences for the American Musical Instrument Society, the Association for Technology in Music Instruction, Technological Directions in Music Learning, and the American Chemical Society.

WILLIAM F. BREWER is a professor in the Department of Psychology in the Institute for Communications Research and the Beckman Institute for Advanced Science and Technology. He carries out research in the areas of knowledge representation, knowledge acquisition, human memory, structure of discourse, and the psychology of science. He was a junior colleague of Charles Osgood during Osgood's later years at the University of Illinois.

MAYNARD BRICHFORD is emeritus university archivist and professor at the University of Illinois. His published articles relate to archival appraisal and history, sports history, and the Olympic movement.

RICHARD W. BURKHARDT JR. is a professor of history at the University of Illinois. His teaching and research focus on the history of science, with special interests in evolutionary theory, the study of animal behavior, and zoos as scientific and cultural sites. He is the author of *The Spirit of System: Lamarck and Evolutionary Biology* and *Patterns of Behavior: Konrad Lorenz, Niko Tinbergen, and the Founding of Biology* (in press). He is currently writing a book on the early history of the Paris zoo.

ALBERT V. CAROZZI is an emeritus professor of geology at the University of Illinois. His expertise is in the petrographic study of limestone as a reservoir for petroleum and host for metallic mineral deposits that he investigated in Europe, West Africa, Latin America and the Philippines. In addition to numerous technical textbooks and articles, he is the author of several books on the history of geological concepts, in particular *Theories of the Earth of the XVIIIth Century in Europe*.

OLLIE WATTS DAVIS is an associate professor of music on the voice faculty at the University of Illinois and conductor of the UI Black Chorus. She made her New York debut at Carnegie Hall, and has appeared throughout North and South America and in Europe with major orchestras and opera companies. Her other creative projects include "Talks My Mother Never Had With Me," a mentoring curriculum for adolescent females, and two musical recordings, *Have Thine Own Way, Lord,* with the UI Black Chorus, and *Here's One,* a CD of spiritual arrangements for solo voice and piano.

RONALD E. DOEL is an associate professor at Oregon State University in Corvallis, Oregon. He is writing books on the integration of scientists into foreign policy after World War II, and on the rise of the environmental sciences in America during the twentieth century; he is also co-editor (with Thomas Söderqvist) of *Writing Recent Science* (London: Routledge, forthcoming). With Pamela M. Henson he is writing a book-length essay on photographs as evidence in writing the history of recent science. His most recent contributions are forthcoming in *History of Science, Social Studies of Science,* and *Osiris.*

GOVINDJEE is a professor emeritus of biochemistry, biophysics, and plant biology at the University of Illinois. He is author of many research papers, reviews, and chapters in the area of the primary reactions of photosynthesis. He is a co-author of a 1969 book, *Photosynthetis*. His edited books include *Bioenergetics of Photosynthesis* (1975), *Photosynthesis* (2 vols., 1982), and *Light Emission by Plants and Bacteria* (1986). He is the series editor of *Advances in Photosynthesis and Respiration*; currently, he is editing "Chlorophyll a Fluorescence" and "History of Photosynthesis Research."

WILLIAM J. HALL, professor emeritus of civil engineering, University of Illinois, and consultant, served on the faculty from 1954 to 1993, and was head of the department from 1984 to 1991. As an instructor in structures and structural dynamics, his research centered on steel materials, blast and shock, earthquake engineering, and defense protective structures. Among many endeavors, he was a member of the Trans-Alaska Pipeline System design team and is a member of the National Academy of Engineering.

LILLIAN HODDESON is a professor of history at the University of Illinois. Her books, all with collaborators, on subjects in the recent history of science and technology, include *Critical Assembly: A History of Los Alamos during the Manhattan Project* (1993); *Out of the Crystal Maze: A History of Solid-State Physics* (1992); *Crystal Fire: The Birth of the Information Age* (1997); and *True Genius: The Life and Science of John Bardeen* (2002). She is completing a history of "megascience" based on Fermilab during the eras of Robert Wilson and Leon Lederman.

ROBERT W. JOHANNSEN is the James G. Randall Distinguished Professor of History Emeritus at the University of Illinois. His books include *Frontier Politics on the Eve of the Civil War* (1955, 1966); *The Letters of Stephen A. Douglas* (1961); *Stephen A. Douglas* (1973, 1997); *To the Halls of the Montezumas: The Mexican War in the American Imagination* (1985); *The Frontier, the Union, and Stephen A. Douglas* (1989); and *Lincoln, the South, and Slavery: The Political Dimension* (1991).

GARY KESLER is associate head of the Department of Landscape Architecture at the University of Illinois. His work focuses on the management of significant historical and cultural landscapes and the history of landscape architecture in the United States. He is currently collaborating on a landscape management plan for a cultural sanctuary at Champaner-Pavagadh, Gujarat, India, and will begin work on a history of the first one hundred years of the Department of Landscape Architecture at Illinois. He is a fellow of the American Society of Landscape Architecture and a recipient of a Distinguished Educator award from the Council of Educators in Landscape Architecture.

DONALD KRUMMEL is a professor emeritus of library science and of music. His work in historical and music bibliography includes the National Endowment for the Humanities guide, *Resources of American Music History*; *Bibliographies: Their Aims and Methods*; the Grove-Norton handbook on *Music Printing and Publishing*; and several essays on the University of Illinois Library and its librarians. He is completing a monograph entitled *Bibliography and the Care of Written Memory*.

PAUL KRUTY is a professor of architectural history at the University of Illinois. His research focuses on European and American architecture and art at the turn of the nineteenth century, especially the midwestern milieu of the architects of the prairie school. His books include *Frank Lloyd Wright and Midway Gardens* and *Walter Burley Griffin in America*. He organized "The Griffins in Context," an international symposium hosted in 1997 by the University of Illinois, and served as content consultant for the PBS documentary on Griffin, *In His Own Right*.

BRUCE MICHELSON is a professor of American literature at the University of Illinois and director of the Campus Honors Program. His most recent book is *Literary Wit*; others include *Mark Twain on the Loose, Wilbur's Poetry*, and the forthcoming *Mark Twain and the Information Age*. He also authors the Web site for *The Norton Anthology of American Literature*.

SYLVIAN R. RAY is a professor emeritus of computer science at the University of Illinois. He designed and implemented the core memory (RAM) of the ILLIAC II and specialized memory systems of the ILLIAC III. His current research deals with brain-model driven robotic heads using neural network techniques.

SUSAN M. RIGDON is a former research associate in the University of Illinois's Center for International Comparative Studies and anthropology department. She taught political science at four other universities and co-authored an American government textbook. Her research interests are culture and politics and poverty and development. She has written a book on culture of poverty and, with Oscar and Ruth Maslow Lewis, a three-volume study of the Cuban Revolution. Forthcoming is the co-authored *Surviving in Prosperity*, a sixty-year overview of a Chinese township.

MURIEL SCHEINMAN is a University of Illinois adjunct assistant professor of art, with a focus on American and twentieth-century European art. She is author of *A Guide to Art at the University of Illinois: Urbana-Champaign, Robert Allerton Park, and Chicago*, published by the University of Illinois Press in 1995.

DANIEL W. SCHNEIDER is an associate professor in the urban and regional planning department and an aquatic ecologist at the Illinois Natural History Survey. In addition to his work on freshwater ecology he has written on the envrionmental history of the Illinois River. He is currently working on a history of sewage treatment as ecosystem management.

RITA J. SIMON is a sociologist who earned her doctorate at the University of Chicago in 1957. Before coming to American University in 1983 to serve as dean of the school of justice, she was a member of the faculty at the University of Illinois, at the Hebrew University on Jerusalem, and the University of Chicago. She is currently a university professor in the School of Public Affairs and the Washington College of Law at American University. She has authored twenty-nine books and edited seventeen. Her most recent books are: *In Their Own Voices* with Rhonda Roorda (2000); *Adoption Across Borders* with Howard Altstein (2000); and *In the Golden Land: A Century of Russian and Soviet Jewish Immigration* (1997).

WINTON U. SOLBERG is professor emeritus of history at the University of Illinois. His special interest is American intellectual and cultural history, which he has taught in universities in the United States, Italy, the USSR, Japan, and India. In addition to many articles, he has published *The Constitutional Convention and the Formation of the Union* (1958: 2nd ed., 1990), *Redeem the Time: The Puritan Sabbath in Early America* (1977), *A History of American Thought and Culture* (1983), *The University of Illinois, 1867–1894; An Intellectual and Cultural History* (1968), and *The University of Illinois, 1894–1904: The Shaping of the University* (2000).

PAULA A. TREICHLER teaches in the Institute of Communications Research, the College of Medicine, and the Women's Studies Program at the University of Illinois, Urbana-Champaign. Her most recent book is *How to Have Theory in an Epidemic: Cultural Chronicles of AIDS*, published by Duke University Press in 1999. Her co-authored or co-edited books include *A Feminist Dictionary* (with Cheris Kramarae, 1985), *Language, Gender, and Professional Writing: Theoretical Approaches and Guidelines for*

Nonsexist Language (with Francine Wattman Frank, 1989), *Cultural Studies* (with Lawrence Grossberg and Cary Nelson, 1992), and *The Visible Woman: Imaging Technologies, Gender, and Science* (with Lisa Cartwright and Constance Penley, 1998). Treichler is currently writing a cultural history of condoms in the United States since 1873.

PHOTO CREDITS

331

Charles Osgood discussing a model (214) and portrait of Charles Osgood (221), photos courtesy of William Brewer.

ILLIAC I Central Processor (230) and ILLIAC II CPU and Control Unit (235) courtesy of the University of Illinois Department of Computer Science Archives.

John Bardeen accepts the Nobel Prize (255) courtesy of William Bardeen.

John Bardeen golfing (257) by and courtesy of Thomas J. Greytak.

Rita Simon (262) and Julian Simon (272) courtesy of Rita Simon.

Explorations for nickel ores by pick and shovel (283) and exploration for nickel ores using high-wing jet-prop planes (287) courtesy of Albert Carozzi.

Lejaren A. Hiller, Jr. and ILLIAC I (296) and John Cage and Lejaren A. Hiller, Jr. with the ILLIAC II (301) courtesy of Elizabeth Hiller.

William Warfield, 1990 (324) by and courtesy of Carlton Bruett.

Details on part and chapter openers courtesy of the University of Illinois at Urbana-Champaign Archives and University of Illinois Photographic Services.

INDEX

The University of Illinois Press
is a founding member of the
Association of American University Presses.

Composed in 10.5/13.5 Adobe Minion
with Meta display by BookComp, Inc.
Designed by Copenhaver Cumpston
Manufactured by Thomson-Shore, Inc.

UNIVERSITY OF ILLINOIS PRESS
1325 South Oak Street   Champaign, IL 61820-6903
WWW.PRESS.UILLINOIS.EDU